Good fishing!
Jim C. Chapralis

PanAngling's WORLD GUIDE TO FLY FISHING

BY
JIM C. CHAPRALIS

PanAngling Publishing Company
180 North Michigan Avenue
Chicago, IL 60601

Library of Congress Cataloging-in-Publication Data

Chapralis, Jim C.
PanAngling's world guide to fly fishing.

Includes index.
1. Fly fishing. I. Title. II. Title: World guide to fly fishing.
SH456.C47 1987 799.1'2 86-62705
ISBN 0-9618193-0-8
First Edition
10 9 8 7 6 5 4 3 2 1

In Memory of

Don Dobbins

Bob Feldtman

Joe Godfrey

They were more than fishing companions. Each at a different stage of my life, and in a unique way, became an invaluable mentor. They were my guideposts. We fished some. We laughed a lot. I will never forget them.

Acknowledgements

Thanks to the fishermen and friends—too many to list here—who have contributed unselfishly to this book.

Thanks to the many camp owners who gambled small fortunes on fishing lodges so that we could comfortably enjoy our favorite sport.

Thanks to associates Tim Clark, Bill Cullerton, Cam Dobbins, Ken Gould, Paul Melchior and Al Schaefer for their encouragement, patience and counsel.

Thanks to Leon Danilovics for graphic design; to John Tianis for cover design; to Lou Bolchazy and Dave Rohe of Composition One for their typographical wizardry; and, to Kurt Scharrer of Bookcrafters for his helpful advice.

And thanks to the women who helped in this project: my wife Sally, who encouraged me to write this book and for reading the manuscript; to Debbie Donberg, who edited the book; and, to Ursula Grzesik, a former employee, but an always-friend, who suggested this guide book and helped me launch it.

Introduction

In 1933 George Bonbright landed a 136-pound tarpon on a fly rod. Consider his tackle: a 12-ounce split bamboo fly rod, a large, multiplying-salmon reel so heavy that it had to be taped unto the rod; a five-foot cable leader; and, a crudely-tied fly on a heavy hook. A. J. McClane accurately describes this outfit as a "toupee lifter in a vagrant breeze." George probably was the first angler to land a tarpon of over 100 pounds on a fly rod. Today's fly fishing tackle and tactics have vastly improved.

At one time, the fly fisherman's world was confined to trout and salmon; then it was extended to include bass and other freshwater species. Later a number of adventurous anglers fly fished for bonefish and eventually tarpon. As each challenge was met, a new one popped up or was even "invented." Fly rodders looking for new worlds to conquer turned to billfish—first to sails and later to marlin—and succeeded! Of all the major gamefish, only the broadbill swordfish hasn't been landed on a fly rod. Anglers have already tried it, and surely, one day, they will succeed!

The evolution of fly fishing, particularly for the larger marine species, would not have been possible were it not for the recent refinement and improvement of fishing tackle. It gained momentum in the 1950s with the development of glassfiber fly rods. Manufacturers then experimented with space-age materials, and, today, graphite, boron and composite rods have virtually taken over the market.

Reel makers have constantly improved their products, as did the manufacturers of fly lines, leader materials, hooks and other tackle.

Just as important, it was the shared knowledge among the pioneering fly rodders that popularized fly fishing. Certainly, men like Dr. Webster Robinson, Stu Apte, Billy Pate, Homer Rhode and many others unselfishly divulged the valuable information that they gathered the hard way—through many years of research. They shared willingly so that others could enjoy, and anglers, such as Winston Moore, spent hours on the phone or writing letters to help anglers whom they have never met.

Writers including Joe Brooks, Lee Wulff, Al McClane, Lefty Kreh, Tom McNally and Keith Gardner carefully explained technique, tackle and theory and often divulged new, exciting secret places. Another generation of energetic writers—Bob Stearns, Mark Sosin, Bob McNally and others—continue to disseminate new techniques and methods so that you and I can participate in the exciting sport of fly fishing.

Today, because it has all come together—the tackle, the information—fly fishing is attracting anglers like never before.

With the increased number of fly fishermen, will we run out of waters to fish? Certainly, in some corners of this earth there is tremendous fishing pressure, but there are thousands of lakes, rivers, and great parcels of oceans that have hardly been touched.

PanAngling's World Guide to Fly Fishing doesn't cover the United States...the most obvious reason is that there's a plethora of fine where-to-fish books and numerous excellent fishing journals that do that job nicely. Where possible, it provides current fishing rates, but, alas, they change continually.

Enough! Bring your favorite fly rods, hop on a seat next to me and let's go fishing. Fly fishing in some of the world's best places.

Jim C. Chapralis
Chicago, IL
June 1987

Contents

MICHAEL'S
RIVER
LODGE

BYRON BAY, LABRADOR

ONTARIO/CANADA
WILDERNESS FISHING
Reserve-A-Resort
1986

MAZATLAN
MEXICO

PLUMMER'S
GREAT BEAR LAKE LODGE LT
TREE RIVER CHAR CAM

alaska

TURNEFFE
ISLAND
LODG

CASA
MAR
TARPON AND SNOOK PARADISE IN JUNGLE
RIVERS ON COSTA RICA'S NORTHEAST COAST

El Pescador
Punta Arena Bay
Ambergris Caye, Belize

The Trip Planner

Successful trips aren't pure chance; they're planned!

There are dozens of mischievous gremlins ready to ambush your fishing trip. Here are step-by-step instructions on how to combat them effectively: Camp deposits and balances. Air reservations. How to pack. What to take with you. How to handle guides and camp managers. And everything else you need to know to plan a successful trip.

There are thousands of fishing camps around the world. First step: Outline the type of fishing you want.

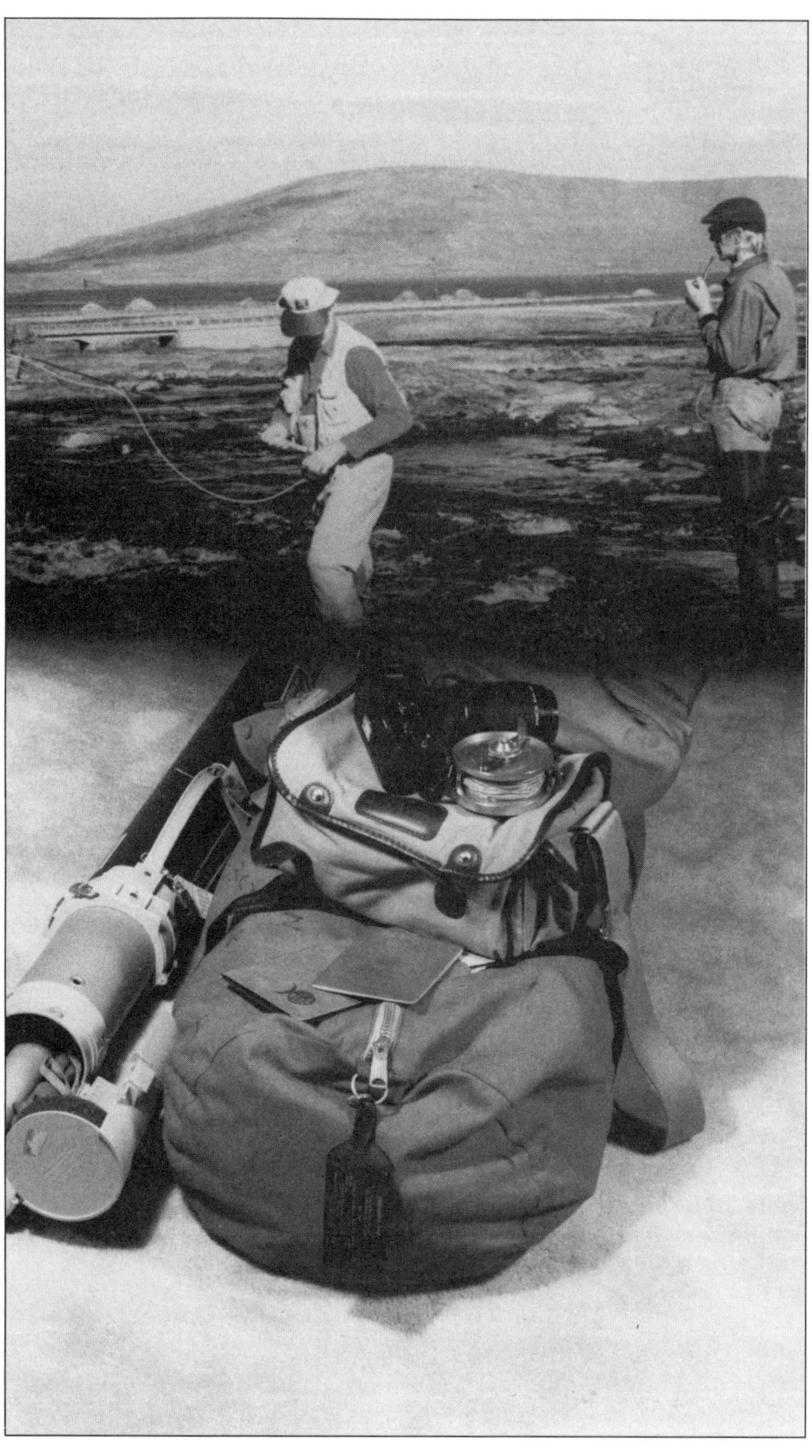

Chapter 1

TRIP PLANNER

WITH THE HIGH COST of fishing these days, it's vitally important to carefully preplan every segment of your trip as there are dozens of gremlins ready to ambush it. It's not simply a matter of selecting the right waters, or having the proper tackle, or acquiring detailed knowledge of various species—as crucial as these factors are.

A number of years ago, a fishing companion was on his way to fish the Alta River in Norway, famous for its huge Atlantic salmon. The Alta is among the world's most expensive rivers to fish; furthermore, there is a long waiting list. He flew to New York, loaded with anticipation, only to discover that he had forgotten his passport. He knew that the airline personnel would not allow him to board the plane without it. Miraculously, he was able to have his passport delivered through a courier service, and since the outbound flight was delayed for other reasons, he didn't miss out on a single cast. But it could have been disastrous. There are many other examples that could be cited in which trips were ruined because details were overlooked.

Here are dozens of tips that will make your next fishing trip more productive and pleasurable. I would like to "walk you" through the planning and thinking stages of a trip—from start to finish.

SELECTING A CAMP

First, outline your requirements. Are you interested in saltwater or freshwater fly fishing? Lakes or streams? Offshore or thin-water fishing?

Proper packing of your gear and clothes is essential to a successful international fishing trip.

When can you go? Are you flexible or do you have a specific time frame? How many anglers are in your party? How many days do you have available for fishing and travel? Are good accommodations necessary? Are you on a budget?

Once these general questions are set in your mind, you can proceed to contact a camp or travel agency. Your letter or call could be stated as follows:

"Our party of four men in their mid-fifties is interested in a week's fishing for bonefish. We are flexible, so we would appreciate your suggestions as to the best time. Two members of our party are experienced fly fishermen, the other two prefer spinning gear. We would be interested in other species if available, but primarily we wish to concentrate on bonefish. We fish hard and have no dietary problems. We've all caught bonefish before during our two trips to the Bahamas, and consider ourselves skilled anglers..."

From this one paragraph the camp owner or travel agent has an accurate thumbnail sketch of your party and is in an excellent position to offer his recommendations.

On the other hand, a letter that states, "We're interested in bonefishing. Send me your brochure," will get a response, but a number of letters will have to be exchanged before one can zero in.

Is it better to book a camp directly or through an outdoor travel agency? Unless you have been going to a lodge for a number of years, a reputable travel agency that specializes in fishing trips is your best bet. It usually costs nothing additional to book through an agent (he makes his livelihood from camp commissions, airline tickets, hotels, etc.), and there are several advantages: If he is a good agent, he continually takes the pulse of many fishing camps; he does the legwork; you benefit from the experiences of his past customers; and, he can save you money on airline tickets. Also, you have a better chance of getting a good trip for one distinct reason: If your agent books a fair number of customers to a particular camp, the resort manager will do his utmost to please you, as he doesn't want any bad reports filtering back to an agent who funnels considerable business to his lodge. On a direct booking (no agent involved), a few camp managers may take the easy way out if problems develop. They reason: "We can replace these two characters next year. To heck with them."

There are some disadvantages with outdoor travel agents. First, each season there are a number of persons attracted to this "glamorous" business who are totally inexperienced. I know one agent who books a few fishing trips—but mostly hunting safaris—who doesn't know the difference between a barracuda and a muskie. Second, a few agents suddenly appear on the horizon only to disappear just as quickly a few months later with thousands of dollars of deposits and balances that were never transmitted to the lodge.

How can you tell a good one from a bad one? If an agent has been in business for a number of years, he is probably competent. If his agency has ARC or IATA airline appointments (which allow him to issue tickets), he is probably financially responsible, because airlines withdraw their appointments if any financial discrepancies occur. If there is any doubt, ask the travel agent for a bank credit (and more importantly, check it). Don't be bashful; it's your money. If you don't have an outdoor travel agent, you can contact the agency that I work for: PanAngling Travel Service, 180 North Michigan Avenue, Chicago, Il. 60601. Phone: (312) 263-0328. (Frontiers, Wexford, Pa., Fishing International, Santa Rosa, Ca., World Wide Sportsman, Islamorada, Fl. and Sportsmen's Travel Service, Palatine, Il. have all been in business for more than ten years.)

If you have any questions concerning a prospective fishing lodge, request a couple of references from past customers. Most anglers don't mind answering a few questions about a particular camp that they have fished. If you phone them, outline your questions first to save time, and, of course, if it is a long-distance call and you can't reach them, have them call you collect. If you write, enclose a self-addressed stamped envelope. One caution about references: Camps and agents are only going to provide names of satisfied customers; however, you can obtain a recommendation of a guide or two, a special fishing area or several fly patterns that have been successful.

With the great popularity of video recorders, many fishing lodges have video cassettes that they will send to interested prospects. It is a good way to get the feel of a place: the type of accommodations offered, types of waters fished, quality of boat equipment, type of gear, clothing and even fishing methods used. Common courtesy dictates the return of these cassettes as soon as possible. Video cassettes may never replace the standard four-color brochure, but they certainly help market a fishing camp.

DEPOSITS, BALANCES, ETC.

You've selected your camp and you are satisfied that this is the place for your party. Upon confirmation, you will be asked for a deposit (usually 25 to 30 percent of the camp's fees). Today, many camps also insist on the balance prior to arrival.

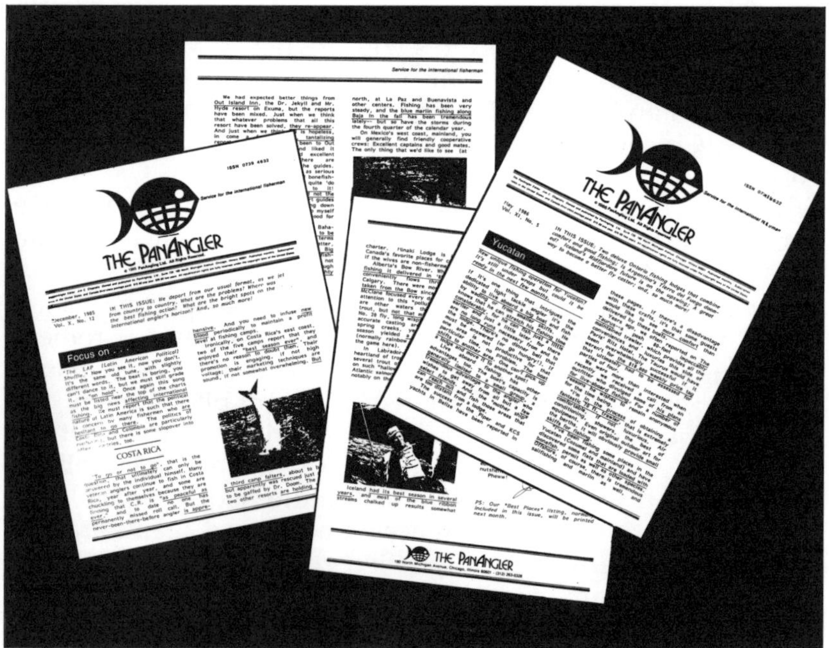

Best way of keeping tabs on international fishing? Subscribe to *The PanAngler* monthly newsletter ($20 per year).

Deposits: They are totally misunderstood by some anglers (perhaps, conveniently so). A deposit is the camp's guarantee that your reservation will be held for you. It is also your guarantee that you will show up for that specific period. Many things can happen, of course, so most camps have a grace period. Depending on the camp, your deposit is usually refundable if you provide a cancellation notice well in advance of your booking. In some cases this may be 30, 60 or 90 days in advance. In other words, if you cancel within a specific time, your deposit will be refunded. Some camps charge a small cancellation fee; others do not return deposits no matter how much advance notice is given (Icelandic camps are one example). Check this out before you submit your deposit.

What happens if the cancellation notice is less than the prescribed time? Usually you lose the deposit. And don't blame the camp owner. If there were no policy concerning deposits, or penalties, there would be utter chaos. Many camps, however, will credit your deposit for another period, usually during that same calendar year. (There is a ploy tried by some anglers that usually doesn't work. Let's say a guest is booked in March, and he discovers that he can't make it. He purposefully postpones his trip to November, and in the summer, he cancels. In this case, he wouldn't be entitled to a refund of his deposit.)

Balances: More and more, camps are insisting on prepayment of the trip. Whereas *The PanAngler* (the newsletter that covers international fishing) has vigorously campaigned against this practice, it has lost the battle. The camps point out that prepayment is practiced in the general travel and tour field. "You buy an American Express trip to Europe, and you prepay it," they argue. "Why shouldn't this apply to a fishing tour?"

Probably 90 percent of the camps will refund the balance in case of cancellation (even if the deposit is forfeited). Example: You sign up for a $1,000 trip. You send a deposit of $250 and later the balance of $750. A week prior to the trip, you find it necessary to cancel. With most camps, you would lose the $250 deposit, but your $750 would be refunded.

Be sure to check the camp's policy carefully before submitting your payment. If it is not clearly stated in the camp literature or in a letter, ask for it in writing. It could save you hundreds of dollars!

AIRLINE AND HOTEL RESERVATIONS

Even if you book your fishing trip directly with a camp, by all means use a reliable travel agency to obtain your airline tickets and any hotel reservations needed. The airline business has become so complicated since deregulation—with hundreds of special fares—that the traveler will be totally confused. Provide the agent with all the information, such as, full names of the people in your party, dates at camp, destination city, type of hotel accommodations required (superior, moderate or budget), and he'll take care of the details. If you prefer flying first class, tell him so at the outset. If there is a choice of carriers, state your preference. Ask about required documentation (tourist card, passports, visa photos) and whether any inoculations or vaccinations are required. Be sure to provide your agent with your home phone number as well as your office number. (If there is a delay in your original flight, the airline will inform you.)

Here are a few hints in planning your itinerary: If you are flying from your home town to an international gateway airport (such as Miami, New York, Los Angeles), ask your agent to allow sufficient time between flights. If you are flying from Detroit to Miami to Panama City, Panama, it is required that there is at least one hour's connecting time in Miami. I suggest two hours. If your plane into Miami is late, or if you have to obtain a tourist card, you could miss your outbound flight. On the return trip, the minimum connecting time in Miami is 1 1/2 hours because one has to go through customs. At times, customs inspection is a very slow procedure. I recommend a minimum of 2 1/2 hours. This is especially true if you have supersaver or promotional fares for the domestic portion.

Your agent will provide you with an itinerary and tickets well in advance of your trip. While agents, for the most part, are very conscientious, I advise that you call the first carrier listed on your itinerary and check your reservations. If they are not in

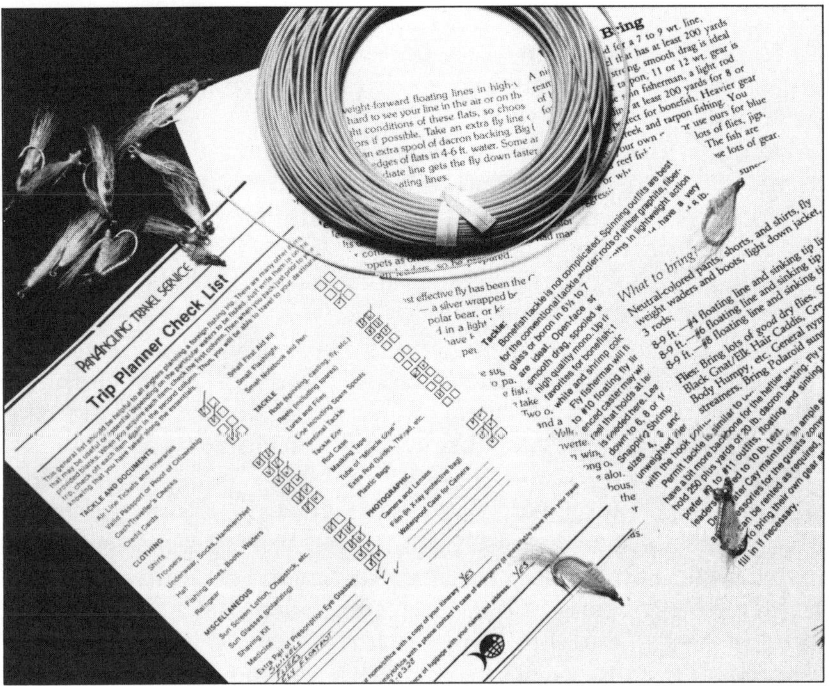

Obtain tackle recommendations and gear well in advance. Then make a list and check off the items.

order, call your agent. While modern electronic reservation systems employed by most airlines are very efficient, they are only as good as the input. If the airline reservations personnel punches in the wrong date or flight number (we all have those kind of days), you have problems. Ask for confirmation of date, flight number and departing times.

ADVANCE PLANNING

Find out from the camp or travel agent what type of gear is recommended. Most camps print a tackle suggestion list. Ask if backup tackle is available at the camp, including flies, lines, terminal gear as well as rods and reels. Many camps stock an extensive supply of flies, but I still recommend prepurchase of an essential assortment of fly patterns. Sometimes, when fishing is "red-hot," guests can go through dozens of popular fly patterns.

Weeks before you depart, I suggest that you make a list of all items you plan to take, and as you acquire them, check them off your list. As you pack them, check them off again. Your list should not only include fishing gear, but also clothing, photographic equipment, medicines, shaving kit, tickets, passport, itinerary and other items.

When it comes to clothing, think flexibility. If you are going to the northern climes, bring along plenty of warm clothing, including thermal underwear. Remember, you can always take off clothing, but you can't put it on if you don't have it.

The mistake that some anglers make when going to a tropical climate is that they take mostly shorts and short-sleeved shirts. Many trips have been totally ruined because of sunburns. The tropical sun can be very intense, and even on cloudy days the ultraviolet rays can produce a severe burn. Take lightweight, long trousers and lightweight long-sleeved shirts! Short-sleeved shirts and shorts can be worn around camp in the evening. Most camps offer some laundry service, but, of course, check in advance. Sufficient changes of underwear and socks should be included even if there is frequent laundry service (washing machines break down).

Let's discuss some other items that could make your trip more comfortable.

Wide-brimmed Hat: I prefer these to "baseball" caps. If it is raining, the brim will prevent water from running down your neck. If the sun is intense, your ears won't burn. The Florida Keys type of hat is very popular. Many anglers like to blacken the inside of the front brim to cut down on reflection. This can be done with a black felt tip pen, or by using a few strips of matte-finish black tape.

Eyeglasses: By all means use polarizing sunglasses to reduce the glare. If you wear prescription glasses, you can obtain flip-on polaroid sunglasses that fit over them for about $5.00. I definitely recommend wearing glasses during fishing for protection of your eyes: A fish can throw a fly back to your face, or the wind can alter a false cast.

I suggest that you attach a loop of monofilament or other line around your glasses (you can tape about 24 inches of line to the end of your glasses). If you lean over, they won't slip and fall overboard. Or, you can purchase Snuggers (eyeglass lanyard) made by Burke Flexo Products Co. If you have a second, older pair of glasses, use those for fishing. Insect repellents and sunscreen lotions can ruin frames or plastic lenses.

Anti-Fog, a chemical compound that can be applied to your lenses, reduces fogging and condensation; it's especially useful in the hot, steamy tropics. World Optical Co., Arlington, Texas, makes the product.

Sunscreens: You're inviting trouble, and lost fishing time, if you head for the tropics without a good sunscreen lotion. Several tropical camp folders erroneously recommend "suntan lotion." *You want a sunscreen.* Most of these products contain "Paba," which blocks out ultraviolet and other harmful rays. Remember to apply thin coats periodically (every few hours). Be sure to apply another coat if you go in the water. Use a sunscreen even in cloudy weather. There are a number of good preparations available, such as Pre-Sun and Sol-Bar. Lately, I've used Eclipse 15 and found it exceptionally effective. Some anglers who have trouble with the sun also take along zinc oxide ointment and apply it to their lips. Another good product—especially in windy conditions—is a lip balm that contains a sunscreen.

Wristwatches: If you normally wear an expensive wristwatch, by all means leave it at home, and buy an inexpensive watch. There are several reasons for this: Insect repellents and sunscreen lotions ruin crystals. Twice I've observed expensive watches go overboard while anglers were casting. Furthermore, valuable watches are subject to thievery. Leave all costly jewelry at home!

Plastic Bags: Plastic bags come in very handy. Take a few in several sizes. Some uses? Laundry bag. Great for protecting cameras from rain or salt spray. If you are fly fishing from a skiff, tape a large plastic bag to the bottom of the boat or deck so that you can strip your fly line on it. You can even fashion a rain jacket (albeit sleeveless) from a large plastic bag by cutting holes for your head and arms.

Lightstick: I carry a couple of Cyalumes in my tackle bag. They're plastic tubes (7" x 3/4") that contain two chemical compounds. By bending the tube sharply, a small tube inside breaks and the two compounds produce a light source that is visible from a fair distance for about 12 hours. It is an excellent night-signaling device in case of a boat problem. It can also be used to mark an access spot or tent camp if you are fishing at night. Cyalume has already saved one life that I know of. It's made by American Cyanamid Co.

Rain Gear: If you are going north, you should have a heavy two-piece rain suit (parkas are cumbersome and don't do the job). For the tropics, K-Mart, Sears and other major department stores offer a light plastic, translucent two-piece raingear for about $10.00. The jacket, incidentally, makes a good windbreaker (it can be cool in the tropics too, especially when boating back to the camp in the evening). Remember: When packing, be sure to put your raingear right on top of your duffle.

Insect Repellents: Even if the camp brochure claims that insects are nonexistent in the area, be sure to take along a small bottle or can of insect repellent. I use Muskol which is expensive but powerful. The effective compound is known as "deet," and the higher the percentage the more effective the product. If the insect problem is not severe, I prefer a spray product such as "Off".

Salt Tablets: In the tropics, where you can expect great water and salt loss through perspiration, some anglers periodically take salt tablets. Others simply use a lot of salt with their meals. In recent years, some doctors have cautioned against the use salt tablets. Gatorade has become the substitute for salt loss on the athletic fields, but obviously you're not going to find this product at camps. A good alternative, according to several doctors, is to eat a banana and drink a carbonated beverage.

Medicines: If you are under medication, be sure and take your prescription with you—as well as your medicine. Don't put your medicine in any bag that will be checked (and, therefore, could be lost). If the medicine is extremely important, bring two bottles: Put one in the carry-on bag and the other elsewhere.

Tackle: I won't cover tackle here because it is covered thoroughly throughout this book.

Boots and Shoes: For tropical fishing, I like to take along sneakers or boat shoes. Make sure that the sole has good gripping qualities (fish slime, oil or water on the bottom of the boat or deck can send you tumbling overboard). For northern climes, I prefer boots that cover the ankle. For stream fishing with rocky bottoms, felt-soled waders are a must. A word about waders: They simply "don't make them like they used to." They puncture or tear easily. So bring along a tube of "Goop" or "Shoe Mend," both of which do a fairly good job of sealing a hole quickly. If I am traveling to a remote area where waders are totally unavailable, I also take along an inexpensive pair of plastic waders (about $10.00). They do the job, but obviously rip easily. You can wear your wading shoes over them or wear the plastic waders inside your regular waders that may have been punctured. Above all, if you purchase new waders, boots or shoes, break them in prior to an extensive fishing trip. If your waders are too tight at the foot, there is a good chance that your big toe will blister. If this occurs, wrap a piece of tape around your toe; it will bring instant relief.

PACKING FOR YOUR TRIP

Leave your good suitcases at home. They don't belong on a fishing trip. They will be scuffed and scratched, and just as importantly, if you are using a small charter plane to get into the camp, hard suitcases are inconvenient. A duffle bag is ideal for fishing trips. The zipper bags provide easier access than the army or navy duffle bags that open at one end. Duffle bags are not completely waterproof, but here is an excellent tip from Hal Lyman of *Salt Water Sportsman* magazine: Put all your clothes in a large plastic garbage bag and then insert the bag in the duffle.

It will keep your clothes dry during heavy rains. In addition to clothes, I also put some of my reels packed in hard boxes and few other essential fishing items in the duffle in case my tackle box or bag is lost. A pack rod, in a hard case, fits nicely in a duffle bag and is added insurance.

Most tackle boxes have accommodations for small locks. (Don't lose the keys!) Additionally, I like to run some strong color tape around a tackle box to discourage "sticky fingers." Don't expect to check your rods with an airline unless they are in a strong rod case. The airlines will refuse them. There are a number of good aluminum and plastic cases on the market, such as those made by Plano, but if you like to make things, look up Norm Strung's article in *Mechanix Illustrated* (May, 1980, issue). For about $25 and a little work you can make an excellent case with PVC plumbing pipe.

Run strips of bright color tape around your duffle, tackle box and rod case. You will be able to spot them easily at baggage terminals. The rod case should be spiral-wound with bright

Today there are a great number of reels available in various price ranges. Buy the best you can afford.

tape. Aluminum rod cases (as well as others) can roll around the plane's luggage compartment and be overlooked by baggage handlers.

Make sure that your name and address are clearly printed on all luggage. I prefer to have my office address rather than a home address on my bag for security reasons. (Burglars have been known to note passengers' home addresses at airports and rob their homes in their absence.)

Liquor: It's best to obtain it at duty-free shops located at international airports such as Miami, New Orleans, Los Angeles, etc. It's less expensive, and the shops will package it in easy-to-carry cartons. The liquor purchase is presented to you as you board your international outbound flight. No hassle. If you bring your own from home, here's a suggestion: Pour the liquor into empty soft drink plastic bottles. You can pack them in your duffle and need not worry about broken glass. Incidentally, you can also purchase cigarettes, cigars and other items from the duty-free shops.

Film And Photographic Items: If you are taking a lot of film and plan on packing it in your duffle, purchase a "Film-Shield" or other lead-lined pouch from your photo supply store. The pouch provides protection against airport X-ray inspections that may fog the film. However even these "Shields" aren't the total answer, since X-rays are cumulative. The best way to transport film is in hand-luggage that can be visually inspected. Extreme heat can damage film so many photographers like to keep their film refrigerated in tropical climes until needed.

The surest, safest way to transport cameras is in a carry-on camera case. Don't check it! Take it with you in the plane cabin.

Important: If you are taking expensive, relatively-new cameras and accessories out of the country, make a list of all major items, including serial numbers of camera bodies, lenses, motor drive units, etc. Have a customs official stamp your list at the U.S. international airport before you board your outbound flight. With this documentation, you will have definite proof that you purchased the equipment in the United States, and are, therefore not subject to any duties for foreign purchases. A bill of sale will also suffice. Another method is to notarize the list of serial numbers before you leave for your trip. This applies not only to distant fishing trips but even close-to-home places like the Bahamas and Canada. Keep this list for future trips. Staple it to a page in your passport.

CASH VS. TRAVELER'S CHECKS

There is one tremendous advantage with prepayment of camp fees: You don't have to carry a lot of cash with you. But you will need some money for meals en route, personal purchases, tips, emergencies, etc. Most hotels and many restaurants accept credit cards (although some only accept bank credit cards such as MasterCard or Visa). If you are taking a fair amount of money, it is best that you obtain traveler's checks. Be sure to keep a list of their serial numbers *separate* from the checks, in case they are lost. Additionally, you will need some cash. I suggest that you take mostly U.S. currency, but depending on the country, it might be wise to take some foreign money as well. In Costa Rica or Panama, as an example, there is no problem with American dollars, but in the "outback" area of Colombia there is. It depends on your destination. The more "exotic" the area, the greater the need for foreign currency (obtainable at major banks and at international airports). Sometimes one can obtain a better rate of exchange by dealing "in the streets," but the black-market exchange can lead to major problems. Avoid it.

Suggestion: Take 20 to 30 one-dollar bills with you. They come in handy for tips at the airport, hotel porters, etc., until you obtain local currency. (In foreign countries, U.S. coins have no value.)

BEFORE YOU DEPART

Be sure to leave phone contacts and a copy of your itinerary with your family and office in case of an emergency. If you are using a travel agency, make sure it has your home number, too. The night before you depart, check your list again, keeping your tickets, passport, or proof of U.S. citizenship handy.

GETTING THERE

You should arrive at the airport well ahead of the scheduled flight time. Different carriers have different baggage allowances. It is very hard—if not impossible—for an angler to travel anywhere (with tackle, cameras, clothing, etc.) under the free-baggage allowance. If your home airport has porter "curb" service, use it. Porters seldom have baggage weighed. Give the porter a good tip, and ask him if he will personally make sure that the luggage is delivered quickly to the airline.

If a domestic flight is required prior to your international flight, you must decide whether to check your baggage all the way through to the foreign country or pick it up and transfer it from point to point. It is by far more convenient to check it to your destination city, but if luggage is lost, and if several airlines are involved, invariably each carrier will blame the other. If, however, it is checked point to point and it is lost, you know exactly which airline is responsible. It appears that 70 to 80 percent of the anglers check their baggage all the way. I don't. I don't like surprises.

There are several insurance company booths at major airports that offer trip baggage and travel insurance. Mutual of Omaha even has an annual traveler's policy. Most anglers have accident and life insurance policies, but I do recommend baggage insurance. There is a high incidence of lost baggage, particularly tackle boxes and rod cases.

Upon arrival at the destination airport, you'll go through customs. It's my experience that 99 percent of the customs officials are courteous and understanding. Occasionally you'll come across a baggage inspector who may have had a bad day (or more accurately a bad night!). Respond to him courteously and avoid arguments at all costs. Honey is by far more effective than vinegar.

Many camps, especially in Latin America, have representatives stationed at destination cities who meet guests at the airports and assist them with the transfers to the lodges. Usually they will also reconfirm return flights for the guests. International carriers insist that passengers reconfirm their return flights at least 72 hours in advance of departure. If they don't, passengers can be "bumped off."

Your guide can determine the success of your trip. Treat him fairly, but don't spoil him. Lefty Kreh caught this great salmon from the Alta.

If there is no camp representative available for this purpose, here's what I suggest: While at the airport, take your ticket to the counter of the outbound carrier, and explain that you will be at a fishing camp and, therefore, you would like immediate reconfirmation. *Have the clerk initial your ticket next to the outbound flight*. This is the best way of reconfirming a flight on your own.

If you are overnighting at a hotel, you can ask the bell captain to do this for you. *Write out* the reconfirmation instructions, give him a $5.00 tip, and ask him to obtain the name of the person at the airline who reconfirmed the flight. While much of this may sound petty, it can save you hundreds of dollars, especially if you are traveling on a promotional or excursion fare.

AT CAMP

The most important person in determining your fishing success is your guide or boat captain. You definitely want him on your side. Establish a team effort. Here are some tips: Listen to his suggestions, at least at the beginning of the trip (what patterns, where to fish, type of retrieve, etc.). If his methods fail, you might try out some of your own. Remember: He lives in the area and his advice should not be ignored. If he speaks English, ask him about his family. Establish a rapport. If you catch an outstanding fish, thank him for his assistance. If you are upbeat, even when fishing is slow, he will try harder. Show some compassion; don't expect him to paddle all day against the wind.

On the other hand, some fishermen spoil their guides. Many guides like to fish, and overlook the fact that they are there to satisfy the customer. Treat them well, but at the same time be firm. Guiding is a full-time job. Sometimes, especially when fishing is slow, I ask the guide to fish while I take a short break. I observe his technique carefully and have learned a lot this way.

If your guide is inattentive or lazy, mention it to the camp manager. Perhaps he can make a change or talk to the guide. Some guides will take advantage of an angler's good nature. By establishing a friendly but no-nonsense attitude at the outset, numerous problems are avoided.

Check with the camp manager concerning beer drinking policies established for guides. Some managers permit an angler to give his guide one beer on the way back to the lodge after fishing. Others frown on the practice. Above all, you never, never want to give your guide a supply of liquor at the completion of your trip. The manager will not appreciate it, and more importantly, the incoming party may not have a guide in "working condition."

The camp manager is also very important to a successful fishing trip. He can instruct your guide to take you to a special fishing place, provide you with a better boat or faster motor, or offers a couple of fishing tips or fly patterns that are exceptionally effective. If you return to his camp during another season, you may have a better guide, or a better room; in effect, he can tip the scales in your favor. His job is certainly not without numerous problems. Some tips: Don't discuss with other guests how great fishing was at a competing camp or area; let the manager know how much you appreciate his efforts and acknowledge that his job is difficult; avoid abusive language; and, remember, no one appreciates serving or handling a drunk, so confine any serious drinking to your room! You want the manager on your side!

Tipping: There is no standard on tipping procedures; it varies from camp to camp. Ask the camp manager (who is usually not tipped) for advice. He will suggest a range of tips (low, moderate or high) for the guide, dock man, kitchen staff and others. If your guide has done an outstanding job, you may decide to tip on the high side. But don't overdo it. You may also wish to give him some tackle, a pair of pliers, a fishing knife or some other items in addition to money.

Conversely, if the guide does a poor job, he should be rewarded accordingly!

Other Suggestions: Each morning, prior to departing from camp, I like to mentally check items to make sure everything is on board. Is there a landing net? A gaff? Lunch box? There have been countless big fish lost because a gaff or net was forgotten at camp.

If you are at a tropical camp where there is fresh fruit available, don't overindulge. Some anglers become ill and blame the drinking water, but often it is because they consume a great quantity of fruit. In a few fishing areas, where there is a problem with drinking water, stick to beer or soft drinks, and be sure to avoid the ice.

On many Canadian fishing trips, where the shorelunch is a ritual, always make sure that the guide has doused the campfire thoroughly. The land is too valuable to lose to an unnecessary forest fire. Don't throw cans, bottles or paper overboard. With today's concern for ecology, it's important that anglers and guides protect the wilderness.

*AND FINALLY...*Assuming that your flights are reconfirmed, you should have no difficulties flying back home.

If you have promised to send your guide photos of that outstanding snook or bonefish, be sure to do so. Guides look forward to receiving photos and letters of appreciation.

Drop the camp manager a note. If you were well satisfied with the trip, tell him so. If you were displeased, you might offer some constructive criticisms that may help improve the camp and its services in the future.

Rods and reels that have been used in saltwater should be thoroughly cleaned and rinsed in running freshwater. If there are any tackle repairs needed, this is the time to make them.

These guidelines should make your next fishing trip smoother, worry-free and rewarding.

Alaska

The Fly Fisherman's Dream Place

Five exciting species of salmon, trophy trout measured in pounds (not inches), grayling that consistently slash at dry flies, Arctic char and Dolly Varden for "fill-in" fish. Add a breath-taking, scenic backdrop, and that's why fishermen return again and again to the 49th state.

What could possibly cause Mr. Winston Moore to smile (and strain) so much? Turn page for answer.

Chapter 2

ALASKA

I FIRST BECAME intimately acquainted with the silver salmon on a beautiful, pristine river that meandered gently through most of its course, though at places where the stream narrowed and where boulders interrupted its smooth flow, the current seemed impatient, if not angry. You always vividly remember that first fish. Where you caught it, its first long run and the way it jumped, so majestically, splashing thousands of water droplets in every direction. You see it all again. As you bring it near the bar, your hands seem to tremble. And then, when you finally ease it safely on the gravel, you pause momentarily, absorbing the intrinsic beauty of the fish; you admire that package of energy, silver-coated, with a touch of iridescence. The salmon flops impatiently now, for it inexplicably knows that you are going to remove that hook and place it back in the water to continue its journey upstream for a very important appointment—the mating ritual. And you do just that. You release it. You hold the salmon gently in a soft current until it has a chance to recover, and suddenly, with a swish of its tail, the fish propels itself out of sight, leaving you with a memory that won't easily be erased.

On that particular trip, I took only five fish in the two days that were allotted to silver salmon fishing, which was a satisfying number; never mind that other fishermen cussed and complained that it had been the worst run of silvers in many years.

On another trip, to Kodiak Island, I became re-acquainted with the silver salmon, and it was an entirely different experi-

Ahhh! A freshrun king salmon from the Unalakleet River. Winston's fine catch weighed 47 pounds!

ence. The river was loaded with thousands and thousands of silvers from the mouth of the Karluk, where it hastens to pour into the ocean up to the weir where biologists intently count every single salmon. That's a distance of four to five miles. Someone estimated that in that short piece of river, there might be as many as 20,000 salmon!

There were 10 of us casting flies that first week of September, and every evening Rob Sikes, the youthful manager of Karluk Lodge, kept a daily count of our results. By the end of the week it totaled an amazing 1,500 salmon—give or take a few fish. I know that I exaggerated the number of fish I caught one afternoon at the beginning of the trip (when I didn't have the hang of things), and maybe several others did that too. But then again another member of our group always reported a lesser number of fish than what he actually caught and what he fastidiously recorded in his personal notebook. Anyway, we caught and released a lot of salmon, and no one could have possibly felt shortchanged. Not on that trip. It would be good, I thought, if every fisherman in the world who has endured the countless hours of angling frustration could experience this type of action at least once in his lifetime.

These two experiences realistically illustrate the divergent results that can occur on an Alaskan fishing trip. In the case of the first trip, where hundreds of casts were required per salmon, the bottom line is not impressive, although personally I enjoyed the experience immensely.

You save and scrimp, and wait all winter long (and spring), and when you finally arrive at your destination, it could be that the run is poor, or that it hasn't started, or maybe it's over. This can be frustrating. True, most anglers rightly philosophize that the beauty of the area, the joy of fishing in totally pure waters and the possibility of catching a glimpse of wildlife are certainly worth the admission price, albeit it's expensive to fish anywhere in Alaska these days.

In the case of the Karluk trip, fishing was so good that, at times, it was almost "boring" because the edge of the challenge was slightly dulled. After all, if you missed one salmon, why worry? There was another fish ready to grab your streamer. Maybe on the very next cast!

The fly fisherman who plans an Alaskan trip is likely to find his results fall somewhere in the middle of the above incidents: much faster than my first silver salmon encounter but not as good as the Karluk episode. As Bill Cullerton rightfully states: "All Alaskan fishing trips are good. There's no such thing as a bad trip. However, some are better than others. If there's a disappointment, it generally occurs to a first-timer, who expects to have a fish on practically every other cast. That happens occasionally, yes, but not often."

The main reason for the difference in fishing results is that the five species of salmon are anadromous by nature's design, and while most knowledgeable anglers, camp owners and guides can predict fairly accurately when these migrating fish will enter and ascend a river, weather conditions and other factors can delay or hasten the process. It's not sufficient to know, as an example, that the king salmon have entered a particular river as they could be near the mouth, they could be 20 miles upstream or they could be anywhere.

It is for this reason that a strictly freshwater fisherman on his first Alaskan trip is somewhat perplexed when he discovers that only a few camps provide fishing in front of their doorsteps during much of the season. He finds out that he must use float planes, boats or rafts to transfer him to the areas where fishing is good for that specific time.

The other aspect of Alaskan fishing that is critically important is that one must first choose the species of highest priority and then arrange his trip accordingly. There is overlap of some of the salmon species, of course, but basically it's king salmon, then the sockeyes, followed by the chum, the humpbacks and, finally, the silvers. (Bob Stearns, fishing with Ron Hyde's Alaska Fishing Safaris, was able to obtain all five salmon species during his late July 1986 trip, but this is an extremely rare experience.) The migration of the salmon also affects rainbow trout fishing. For the best chance at a trophy rainbow, knowledgeable guests fish most Alaskan areas during the month of June and again in late September, or, if they are capable of withstanding severe weather, October. In many watersheds, the rainbows are there during the entire season. But during the heavy salmon run, anglers have a relatively poor chance of

The rainbow trout is one of Alaska's most precious resources. It's important to handle and release them carefully.

catching big rainbows because the trout feed voraciously on salmon eggs. Why should they bother to chase a fly when they can gorge on salmon eggs right in front of their noses?

Following is a description of the most popular Alaskan species' approximate seasons, sizes and other information (there may be some variances from area to area).

RAINBOW TROUT

This restless traveler can be totally reckless, whacking just about any fly that swings by its nose, or it can be as selective as a brown trout. A rainbow can thrill any angler with its sky-high leaps, its spectacular dashes for freedom or its unpredictable change of directions. The rainbow is a showman, sometimes gaudy or glitzy, but always, this trout is highly listed on any angler's "top 10."

The rainbow trout grow larger in Alaska than anywhere else, including New Zealand, Argentina and Chile. The main reason for growth is that all summer long they gorge on the salmon's spawn (although in some waters, they may drift back to the lakes to feed heavily on forage fish).

While 30-inch rainbows are taken each season at just about all camps that offer trophy rainbow trout fishing, the fly rodder should not consider landing this size fish as a common occurrence; to do so would surely lead to disappointment. The run-of-the-mill rainbow is probably from 16 to 20 inches—a very respectable specimen anywhere. The bigger the fish, of course, the larger the odds against catching it. If a fly fisherman insists on landing a 25- to 30-inch rainbow, he would do well to book September (the later in the month the better), but he ought to be aware that the weather becomes even more unpredictable than it is during the summer. It may be mitten-and-ear-muff time, and L. L. Bean's best outerwear should be readily available.

The reason for the effectiveness of the mid- to late-September period is that, by that time, most of the salmon have completed their spawning rituals and have gasped their last breath. Thus, the angler's flies aren't competing with the salmon's spawn for the rainbows' attention. Furthermore, during the early heavy salmon runs, salmon often attack a streamer before a rainbow has a chance to even see it. (Some knowledgeable guides, primarily in the Iliamna area, insist that trophy rainbows summer in the lakes and come into the streams in September, and thus aren't available earlier in the season.)

If a September trip is impossible, the next best time is June. Again, it appears that the lack of competition between the fly and spawn (since the salmon haven't spawned) accounts for the better rainbow fishing. Of the two months, September is definitely the better for the biggies.

What about July and August? Should these months be avoided for Alaskan rainbow fishing? Absolutely not. Ken Owsichek's Fishing Unlimited, fly-out camps in the Iliamna district, maintains fastidious records. Here are the 1985 monthly results for rainbow trout (Fishing Unlimited's capacity is 16 anglers):

June (last two weeks only)	129
July	173
August	335
September	869

June produced the largest rainbow of the season (12 pounds). During July the emphasis was on king salmon, but in August there was an increased concentration on rainbow trout fishing, which is reflected in the above numbers. The most ardent rainbow trout fishermen book September, but the above illustrates that rainbow trout fishing is indeed available during the entire season.

If there is some disappointment that taints Alaskan rainbow fly fishing, it centers on the fact that sinking lines are mostly used, possibly 80 percent of the time; sinking or sink-tip lines are more effective than floating lines. The reason is that the rainbows hug the bottom of the river much of the time, especially when they are gorging on salmon eggs. They insist that the fly tumbles close to the stream bed right to them. Simply, the trout aren't going to move far for the fly.

A second objection, again during spawning time, concerns the type of flies used. They are generally imitations of salmon spawn, often weighted, and some anglers feel that the sport loses a touch of glamour with the absence of the traditional trout fly patterns.

There is a third objection, though admittedly personal, in that many guides adhere to the practice of recommending very short leaders of two to three feet. They rightfully contend that the short leader, when used on a sinking line, causes the fly to swim close to the bottom. There's no argument here. Lefty Kreh proved that Alaskan fish aren't leader shy by taking a number of rainbows with only a few inches of leader material attached to his line. There is something iconoclastic, to my mind, in using less than seven-foot leaders, but again, this objection is strictly personal.

The dry fly guy is not totally out of his game in Alaska, for there have been many outstanding catches made right on top. Bob Stearns, outdoor writer, reported that he had fantastic trout fishing on dry flies while fishing out of Bristol Bay Lodge.

As a matter of fact, he even experimented with hair mouse patterns and caught many huge rainbows on them. One's chance of success with the dry fly depends on weather (you want a warming trend, not too cold) and water temperatures (in the 50- to 60-degree range). A hatch is very helpful, although hatches aren't very prolific in Alaska.

Nearly all major Alaskan fishing camps have instilled a catch and-release policy for rainbow trout. Although Alaska is one of the world's great rainbow trout fisheries, it takes this species a long time to grow and the ecology is very delicate. The rainbow's primary food source is the salmon's spawn, and this is limited basically to a three-month summer season. It's a different matter with the salmon because they feed continuously in the ocean where food is very abundant, and thus they grow very quickly. An occasional rainbow is kept for mounting, or if one is fatally hooked, it may be saved for lunch. Beyond these exceptions, the camp owners insist that rainbows are released, and they are commended for their adherence to this policy, although unquestionably, they lose some customers.

At Ken Owsichek's camp, only 13 rainbows were killed out of 1,506 that were caught. In other words, 99.91 percent of the landed rainbows were released by camp guests.

KING SALMON

This salmon isn't called the king for nothing. It's the mightiest of all Pacific salmon in terms of sheer strength, stamina and explosive leaps. The king (also known as chinook), grows to over 90 pounds (this is very rare), but the fly fisherman concerns himself mostly with the 18- to 30-pound kings. While some kings are subdued in less than 30 minutes, others can take well over an hour to land on a fly rod. This depends on the individual fish, type of waters fished, agility of the fisherman (he may have to run downstream), weight of the fly rod used and the angler's fish-fighting technique.

Some fly rodders enjoy the challenge presented by the king salmon; others don't. Under ideal conditions, the persistent fly fisherman on prime waters will hook far less kings in a week than he would in a day's fishing for silvers under similar conditions.

The king is usually the first salmon species to ascend the fresh water spawning grounds, so it's a late June, early July proposition on most rivers. They are strongest when they first enter a river, but as they remain in freshwater and travel upstream, they lose some of their steam.

Winston Moore, who fished the Unalakleet River in 1980, landed 16 kings on a fly during "horrible" water conditions, as the water was practically the color of chocolate. But his perseverance paid off, and his best Pacific salmon was a 47-pounder—a superb accomplishment on a fly rod.

He returned the following year for two weeks, and under more favorable conditions, connected on 48 kings, with the best being a 39-pounder. A dozen fly-caught kings, regardless of size, during a week of of concentrated fishing is considered well above average.

King salmon addicts agree that the fly must bounce on the bottom, and this dictates the use of fast-sinking lines on most rivers, and short leaders (15-pound tippets) to keep the fly deep. However, many do not hesitate to lengthen their leaders

They are strong, powerful. That's why they are called kings. W. Moore about to release a 39-pounder, caught with Dave Duncan & Sons.

considerably in relatively shallow waters (such as the Karluk River) on bright, blue-sky days. If they are sure that their fly patterns are ignored after several changes (including sizes), they lengthen their leader to 12 or more feet and decrease their tippets to an alarming eight pounds. Can they land a powerful king on a light tippet?

"Most of the big ones break off fairly quickly," one king salmon addict explains, "but since I use barbless hooks, they get rid of the flies easily. It depends on the waters, but if one takes his time he can land the smaller kings. It's go light, or fishless at times, and I get tired of casting without an occasional pullback!"

SOCKEYE SALMON

The most colorful of all salmon, the sockeye eventually turns crimson red in rivers, and I've seen some streams so loaded with them that the water takes on a red cast. Tens of thousands of sockeyes ascending a small river give an observer the impression that there's more fish than water in a stream. It's one of Alaska's most alluring sights.

Not everyone considers the sockeye an ideal fly rod species, and it's hard to understand why. It's packaged right—six to nine pounds—an ideal size for the fly rodder. (Bob Stearns landed a 14-pound sockeye in 1986; that's the largest we know of). It can be taken on a variety of flies after it has spent some time in a river. And the sockeye, in shallow, slow water, can make some of the most spectacular leaps of all salmon. What else can a fly fisherman demand from a fish?

While fishing one of the famous sockeye streams near Bristol Bay Lodge, I caught the sockeye under ideal conditions. Armed with a No. 7 weight rod, sink-tip, I enjoyed fast action from these colorful fish. They took the fly in deeper water, but then would rush for a shallow part of the river and unleash two to four outstanding jumps very close to the alders. In the case of one sockeye, it actually landed on the branches! They reminded me of small tarpon, the way they jumped.

All the fly fishermen were having good sockeye action, but I noticed during the evening that the other guests spoke somewhat disparagingly of the sockeye ("Yeah, I ran into a lot of sockeyes today—darn it!"). I know some of this rubbed off on me. The first night I was so excited over my sockeye fishing that I expressed my enthusiasm to anyone who would hear it. (This was my first sockeye fishing experience.) By the third day, my outward enthusiasm was reduced to something above a whisper, and there weren't any exclamation marks after each sentence.

Some of the negative remarks made about the sockeye are due to the species' aggressiveness. "I don't like them because they hit a fly before the rainbow trout has a chance to grab it, so they ruin the fishing," one angler said. "There's no finesse required. You cast, roll a fly on the bottom, they hit. That's it." Sometimes we have a tendency to be so selective in our angling pursuits that we lose out on some some great fishing.

While sockeyes are a "sunken fly" fish, I was amazed to see one rise to the surface and sip in a hairwing dry fly intended for a grayling. I was so startled that I never set hook. The camp manager acknowledged that occasionally sockeye will come to the top for a dry, but that "this is a once-or-twice-a-year occurrence."

On some rivers, the sockeye come with or right after the kings. One can enjoy good sport for sockeye in July and in August; however, there are differences in time schedules on various streams.

CHUM SALMON

I haven't caught many chum salmon, but the few I've taken on a fly have been totally delightful experiences. They are powerful fighters, take out plenty of line and are frantic jumpers.

Chum salmon average eight to 10 pounds, and if a beauty contest were held, the chum would probably finish a dead last. Even the humpback salmon is considered a more attractive fish. That's why, some claim, the chum is also called "dog" salmon, though the truth is that the chum salmon acquired that name because it was caught and fed to the sled dogs.

Its somewhat tarnished reputation as a gamefish is quickly changing, and if the angler were truly unbiased, he would rate it high among Alaska's premier species.

The chum is a tough critter on a fly rod. Pound for pound, it might be as strong as any of the Pacific species: at the minimum, just a notch behind the king and silver salmon. It's an important species because the chum, along with the sockeye and humpy, bridges a seasonal gap between the highly-touted king and the silver salmon. If an angler can only fish Alaska in late July or early August, he may be a little too late for the kings and too early for the silvers. So Alaska camp owners would do well to promote the chum, and they can do this without feeling that they are shortchanging their customers.

I've caught them on sinking lines, but I've also hooked them on floating lines from slower stretches by casting a weighted fly up and across and feeding out some line through the guides to allow the fly to sink closer to the bottom.

The chum enjoys a good distribution, and I suspect that in future years, he'll develop a substantial following, as more fly fishermen become intimately acquainted with this species.

HUMPBACK SALMON

Also known as humpy or pink salmon, this species is the smallest of the anadromous Pacific salmon and consists basically of three- to five-pound fish, with a seven-pounder considered a "trophy." Because they are lightweights, lighter fly tackle is used. The humpy can be taken consistently on a variety of streamers and wet flies, including salmon egg imitations. On most Alaskan streams, their heaviest runs are from mid-July to mid-August.

The humpy is a good fighter, but lacks charisma. He is not a leaper like the other salmon species but splashes on the surface, and most sportsmen would rate him as a "fair to good" species.

Personally, I've never been overly fascinated by the species; I enjoy taking a few humpbacks when available, each day, but fishing for them on a concentrated basis is not high on my priority list. The humpy is basically a "fill-in" fish. If the other, more desirable species, are unavailable or not hitting, landing a half-dozen pink salmon can take the edge off ruffled nerves and tends to improve one's disposition. It's a "Valium fish."

I've known a few anglers who go to an area, mostly, *if not specifically,* for pink salmon, but I'll admit, they aren't many. It's a good species, usually cooperative, fights fairly hard, but lacks mystique and excitement. This salmon is, in fact, the good kid on the block who does what it should but is much too predictable in comparison with the other salmon species, and is therefore somewhat dull.

SILVER SALMON

Sleek, fast, certainly powerful, often a good leaper, the silver salmon is unquestionably the best fly rod salmon of Alaska. It is sized right for fly fishing; most of them will weigh eight to 12 pounds, but certainly, on prime waters, the angler has the opportunity at 15- to 18-pound silvers.

With the unfortunate shrinking world of the Atlantic salmon, there's no better substitute than the silver salmon. In fact, these species so closely resemble each other that it would be difficult for the casual fisherman to tell them apart. They are also simi-

Fly out trips are an effective way to fish Alaska. The author admires a sleek silver caught from the Togiak.

lar in the type of waters they prefer and in general fighting ability. In addition, basically the same fishing techniques are employed for both species. There are dissimilarities: The Atlantics can be taken on dry flies (it's seldom that a silver can be coaxed to take one); silvers are generally easier to fool; and, of course, the Atlantic salmon has been soaking up tradition and prestige for centuries. It's also true that the traditional fly patterns used for Atlantic salmon are probably the most beautiful of all of man's fly creations, and they come with such fascinating names as Jock Scott, Durham Ranger, Dusty Miller and Night Hawk. Silver salmon patterns? "The purple one," or "the silver and blue one."

The Atlantic salmon addict may never venture to Alaskan waters and it's a shame too, because he is missing out on a wonderful opportunity. An Icelandic Atlantic salmon river that yields 2,000 salmon for the entire 90-day season is considered a fantastic river, commanding a steep rate and boasting a long waiting list. Furthermore, there are only a half-dozen Icelandic rivers that produce that many Atlantic salmon these days!

At Kodiak Island's Karluk Lodge, on the other hand, our group probably landed 1,500 silver salmon during *one week of fishing!* The silvers run larger than Icelandic salmon and the cost of the trip was considerably less.

I point this out specifically because there is a crop of new anglers interested in Atlantic salmon, but the demand for good waters greatly exceeds the supply. The silver is a good substitute.

It's a mid-August to late-September species on most of the Alaskan waters. In the Bristol Bay and Iliamna regions, the best time historically is the second half of August and the first week or two of September. On Kodiak Island, the heavy run is a little later (the last week of August and the first three weeks of September).

ARCTIC GRAYLING

If an angler prefers to use dry flies, he will find the Arctic grayling a willing customer most of the time. It is a splendid dry fly species, provided that very light fly gear is used. Unfortunately, many anglers who fish Alaska tend to ignore this species and spend all their time and energies pursuing the larger salmon or rainbow trout. True, the average grayling weigh somewhere between 1 1/2 to 2 1/2 pounds on most Alaskan streams, but if a light 7 1/2-foot fly rod that takes a No. 5 (or lighter) is used, optimum sport is achieved. The grayling cuts a pretty picture on the take, when its outsized dorsal fin slices across the surface, and for a small fish, it is a good fighter since it also uses the current to advantage.

If one finds a good grayling hole, and weather conditions remain stable, he can enjoy an unending series of takes, slashes and runs. I recall fishing one of Bristol Bay Lodge's fine grayling streams with a No. 4 outfit and enjoying fantastic dry fly fishing. I didn't move more than a dozen feet and probably hooked 70 to 80 grayling using the Disco Trout dry fly (see "Mid-Canada" chapter for dressing). These grayling ranged from 12 to almost 20 inches. I've spent hours and hours working over smaller brown trout on Wisconsin streams for a few rises, so this activity was invigorating and certainly welcome.

"I like to tussle with the big salmon," says Al Schaefer, "but I also enjoy fishing for Arctic grayling. Recently when I fished at Tikchik Lodge, I devoted some time to grayling fishing. Maybe the other guests didn't quite understand it, but then that's why they make chocolate as well as vanilla ice cream."

I'm not suggesting that one books a $3,000 trip at an Alaskan camp and devotes the entire week to fishing for grayling. But I'm recommending that the fisherman packs his lightest fly rod in his case and invests a few hours fishing for grayling with dries. If fishing is very fast for the salmon and/or trout, the angler (and his arms!) might find it refreshing to switch from heavy gear and big fish to light tackle and grayling. In contrast, if the fishing is slow (or downright lousy), I'm sure that the frustrated angler would welcome some fast action from this highly-spirited lightweight. The grayling is a season-long species, so there's no particular time that's best.

DOLLY VARDEN AND ARCTIC CHAR

These two species are quite similar in many respects. First, they are found during the entire season on most Alaskan waters. Second, they range mostly in the 2 1/2- to five-pound class, although occasionally a biggie of eight or more pounds is taken. Third, both species are exceptionally tasty (smoked Arctic char is a delicacy).

When one observes Dolly Varden flashing and slashing near the surface, this is the time that the angler should pull out a No. 5 fly rod and cast small white streamers. Often one finds the Dollies intermingled with silver salmon, so it's possible to hook a silver on light gear.

The Arctic char has a tremendous following with anglers who fish Canada's Northwest Territories, where rivers like the Tree and Coppermine are magical places to char addicts. Ironically, a similar fervor hasn't developed for the Alaskan Arctic char. The main reason is that the Alaskan char don't grow as big as their Northwest Territories' cousins (which sometimes exceed 20 pounds). But on the positive side, the Alaskan char can be readily hooked on flies, in gentle streams or in soft currents. In the Territories, most of the char are caught on hardware and heavy tackle, because some of the rivers have very heavy currents that minimize fly fishing potential.

Both species—Dolly Varden and Arctic char—can be caught during the entire fishing season.

SALMON TECHNIQUE

Ron McWilliams (Bristol Bay Lodge) showed me a tip on the Togiak (a prime silver salmon river) that could be useful to Alaskan first-timers. I had spent much of that summer, prior to the trip, fishing brown trout, which requires a fast strike, especially when using dry flies. Being very anxious (and no doubt stupid), I tried to strike the first couple of silvers the same way. Fast. I missed them.

Ron demonstrated the right way to set the hook. First he would strip in the fly very slowly, sometimes a few inches at a time. Whenever the fly stopped, indicating a fish or a snag, he would continue to strip in line with his left hand until he was convinced that there was something solid at the other end. With the line tight now, he would bring the rod up and set the hook several times.

"Often silver salmon mouth the fly, release it, and mouth it again. If you strike fast, the fly swooshes away from the salmon, and the fish is alarmed or loses total interest. By not setting hook with the rod tip immediately, but by merely stripping in the line, even if the salmon spits out the fly, or if it comes out of the fish's mouth, it often remains interested and whacks it again." Ron's explanation was plausible, and upon adopting his system, I proceeded to solidly hook nearly all the salmon that came my way that day. In some cases, I did feel the fly being released, only to have it taken by the same or possibly another fish. Incidentally, this system worked very well for large rainbows, too.

It's important when casting down and across a stream with a sinking line to (1) allow the fly to sink close to the bottom, (2) allow it to drift without dragging if you are using salmon egg patterns and (3) stripping in some line periodically to remove most of the slack. On some occasions, you may have to cast upstream and mend your cast (by throwing loops of line upstream like a partial roll cast) in order to give the fly an opportunity to sink.

Continued Ron: "It's very hard to explain, and more difficult to know what to do on each occasion. Different salmon holes or stretches require different techniques. My advice is to experiment when fishing is slow. Also, if you're not getting fish, but another angler in the area is, take the time to watch him carefully. How far does he cast? Where does he cast? What is the angle of his cast? Speed of his retrieve? Length of leader and tippet size? What weight line is he using? Observing the successful angler, and precisely imitating his technique, certainly makes more sense than beating your brains doing what has already failed for you. Basically, I like the tight line and slow strip drift, with the fly traveling, close to the bottom, as naturally as possible. In tricky currents, you have to mend that cast to allow the fly to sink and to drift naturally. All of this applies when fishing is slow. On other occasions, when the salmon are in thick and on a feeding spree, you can do everything wrong and still hook some fish!"

On the Karluk River (Kodiak Island) where there were undoubtedly thousands and thousands of fresh run salmon, I

To select the proper week. First pick the species, then the time. This supercharged salmon awaits you.

made numerous mistakes, such as striking too quickly or not worrying about the retrieve. Yes, I got strikes, but not anywhere as many, as when I applied Ron's good advice given to me on that previous trip.

SELECTING A WEEK

For the first-timer, the decision as to when to go proves to be a frustrating experience, mostly because you want to catch as many different species as possible. By trying to do too much in a week, you will probably be disappointed. Here are some tips that hopefully will help you and eliminate some frustration:

1. Select one or two of the most important species, and consider them your main targets. We've already described most of the important Alaskan species and, of course, there are others, such as northern pike and lake trout, but for these two species there are much better places (and less expensive) than

Alaska. Naturally, you can't fish for king salmon (an early runner) and silver salmon (a late bloomer) at the same time. Of the two, silver salmon would be the more compatible species for the first-timer (strikes are usually more plentiful and the silvers are easier to land). If rainbow trout is your primary interest, and you want the trophy fish, consider late September. If you prefer more variety, and would like better weather conditions, late July and early August will give you a shot at sockeyes, chum and humpies, as well as char, grayling and some trout. Remember this chapter merely provides an overview of the species and the best time to fish for them, and there are variations from region to region. Most of the camp brochures present approximate running times for the anadromous species.

2. Weather is the most important criteria for a successful trip. I'm not only referring to weather conditions for that particular day or week, but for the overall season. Sometimes, spring and summer come quickly, so the salmon runs tend to be earlier. Or vice versa. You can hedge your bets somewhat by selecting the middle period of an expected run. Let's say that the silver salmon run at a particular camp is from August 7 to September 18. If you selected the week that starts August 21 or better yet August 28, you would protect yourself in case of a late run, but at the same time, would no doubt have good silver fishing if the main run were early.

3. While quality of fishing may be the most important criterion, there are other considerations. If an angler is allergic to insect bites, the last half of the season should be considered. If cold, blustery weather is intolerable, avoid the early and late parts of the fishing season. Settle for a mid-summer season (and there's no guarantee on weather at this time either). I've fished the north at the end of the season when it was so cold that some anglers stayed in camp just about the entire trip, and at an Alaskan lodge, that's a very expensive motel rate! Obviously, if you insist on your evening comforts, and bad weather bothers you tremendously, a float trip may be a poor choice, especially if the selected week turns out to be cold and rainy. A deluxe camp, instead, would be recommended.

4. If you plan to fish Alaska with friends, it's important to establish *in advance* your group's priorities: What are the preferred species? What type of camp is desired? What price range? What week? While this appears basic, some camp owners have described violent disagreements that have occurred among friends. By advance planning, discussion and *prior agreement,* many problems can be eliminated. You want to fight fish—not each other.

ALASKAN CAMPS

Twenty-five years ago, there were virtually no fishing camps in Alaska. Northern Consolidated Airlines operated its Brooks River resort, and several hunting guides offered some fishing from their hunting lodges. If there were any other fishing camps at that time, I was totally unaware of them.

Today, however, there is a plethora of fishing camps and outfitters to choose from. My guess is that there are at least 250 fishing resorts or outfitters, with several new lodges sprouting up each season. There are four different outfitting arrangements that a visiting angler can choose from, and each has its advantages and disadvantages. We will outline them plus include a few representative camps that can be considered, but by no means should this list be construed as the only outfitters I recommend:

CAMPS THAT OFFER DAILY FLY-OUT TRIPS

Usually this is the most productive type of trip offered. Basically, anglers stay at a main lodge, and each day fly out to various rivers or lakes. The camp manager consults with every party, learns its preference and then attempts to match its desires with available waters.

Advantages: (1) You can fish those waters where the action is reportedly good. (2) You can fish waters that are considerably off the beaten path, and therefore fishing tends to be a few notches above the norm. (3) You can see a greater variety of topography, and much of Alaska's appeal is its fantastic scenery. (4) Each night you come back to a very comfortable resort. (5) Some of the resorts, on the other hand, have small outpost camps so you can even overnight on other waters if you desire.

Disadvantages: (1) It's expensive. Planes, pilots and fuel are costly. (2) Weather conditions dictate what areas you can fly to, and sometimes, if visibility is poor, you may not be able to fly at all. (3) Although there are very few accidents reported by camps, they occasionally occur. (4) You must take whatever you need for the day each morning and must break down your tackle. (5) You don't have the great time flexibility, as planes generally are used to transport several parties during the day. FIFO (First In, First Out) is generally practiced. (6) You are limited to those waters where a float plane can land.

RAINBOW KING LODGE: Ray Loesche, one-time hunting guide, switched to fishing long ago and through the years developed an outstanding resort in the Iliamna region. In fact, his camp could be considered among the most elegant fishing lodges in terms of service, quality of meals and supportive equipment. Ray is always on the lookout for new fishing places or new ideas. As an example, in 1982 he purchased several Hovercraft because he thought these air-cushion vehicles would enable his guests to fish waters heretofore considered impossible to reach. They didn't work, but he tried!

This camp accommodates 32 anglers in grand style and comfort and nothing is spared in producing the best possible meals. He is a no nonsense operator, and he may aggravate an occasional client (who probably asked for the impossible), as Ray insists on running a tight ship.

This camp operates on a Monday-to-Monday week and the $3,700 weekly tab will buy you a 50-yard seat in one of Alaska's great fishing areas.

BRISTOL BAY LODGE: This popular fishing spa, operated by Maggie and Ron McWilliams, is strategically located on Aleknagik Lake in the Wood River-TikChik region. Up to 18 anglers are comfortably accommodated in modern, heated rooms in individual cabins or in the main lodge. There is an air of congeniality and warmth that originates with Maggie and prevails throughout the entire staff. Ron, soft-spoken, unassuming, but knowledgeable and most helpful, supervises the guiding staff and fishing arrangements. The lodge features all the conveniences one could expect from a fishing resort,

The sockeye is an excellent target for the fly rodder once it ascends the rivers.—Photo by Silvertip Lodges.

including an angling library, fly-tying table, a very complete tackle shop and even a sauna. A half-dozen or more highly productive waters, considered among the best in the area, are easily reached by the camp's float planes. If weather is inclement, the camp's outboard powered skiffs can whiz their guests to nearby "Wak" river. Bristol Bay Lodge operates a Saturday-to-Saturday week, and the $3,250 fee includes the charter plane service from Dillingham.

TIKCHIK NARROWS CAMP: Bob Curtis is one of the pioneers in Alaskan fishing camps. Years ago, he correctly envisioned a curtailment of hunting activities in Alaska and forecast a thriving sportfishing industry. His camp, which accommodates up to 20 guests in comfortable, modern cabins, is located in the TikChik-Wood River region, which is approximately 350 miles southwest of Alaska. Superb meals have always been featured at Curtis' camps.

Tikchik offers all the important Alaskan species, plus this camp is one of the few resorts that arranges sheefishing trips. The sheefish is a rare anadromous species, often called the "tarpon of the north" because of the similarity in appearance and its aerial acrobatics. According to Bob, it can be taken via fly fishing. Tikchik was sold prior to the 1986 season to Bud Hodson who has had tremendous experience in operating fishing camps including nearby Golden Horn. Bud is committed to the same high standards established by Bob Curtis. Tikchik is operates on a Saturday-to-Saturday basis, and the weekly tab is approximately $3,200.

FISHING UNLIMITED: Ken Owsichek's two camps on Lake Clark (Iliamna region) are unique in that the capacity of each is limited to eight guests. The camp has Cessna 206 float planes, and among the advantages of the limited capacity is that Ken and his assistant each take out four fishermen and the plane stays with the party for the entire day. Thus, if fishing is poor or uneventful at one area, the party can be transferred to another place. In large-capacity camps, guests are not accorded this luxury, since a plane may be used to transfer other parties each day.

A "homey" atmosphere prevails at these lodges: All meals are served family style (the staff and Ken's family eat and socialize with the guests), so there's a congeniality that is not easily duplicated at other camps. The weekly rate is $3,450.

VAN VALIN'S ISLAND LODGE: Glen and Sharon Van Valin have operated this camp for more than a dozen years and have earned a solid reputation. It's located 150 miles southwest of Anchorage in scenic Lake Clark National Park.

Van Valin's consists of a main lodge overlooking Lake Clark, plus five guest cabins that are fully modern and feature private bathrooms, electricity, heat and all the comforts one could logically expect.

The weekly package, which includes six days of fly-outs, costs $2,950 per person (plus the round-trip transportation from Anchorage). The lodge at times offers a wilderness float trip on the Chilikadrotna and Mulchatna rivers for approximately $2,000 per person.

ALEKNAGIK MISSION LODGE: It's one of Alaska's most elegant and comfortable camps, but at the same time it blends personal service, and, of course, excellent fishing.

AML is relatively new and is located in the Bristol Bay region, 30 miles from Dillingham, the gateway to many great angling adventures.

"We've sunk a ton of money in the lodge," says owner Jerry Hermanson, "but we wanted to start off with a very comfortable base.

"Then we wanted to insure a homey, efficient atmosphere, with a personal touch, so we've limited our capacity to 12 anglers. Maybe, sometime down the road, we might increase capacity slightly, but we want to keep it small. It's the only way we can be in total contact with our guests. We want them to feel like they are houseguests, rather than computer numbers at a huge franchise chain."

Fishing? The Bristol Bay area is one of the most prolific regions of Alaska, offering all species of salmon, rainbow trout, grayling, char and Dolly Varden.

A full week (Sat. to Sat.) is $3,150. Four- and three-night packages are also available. The rate includes transportation from Dillingham, all accommodations, meals, guides and daily fly-out fishing. If you don't have the proper tackle, the lodge will supply it.

TUWALAQUAH LAKE LODGE: Dean and Suzi Carrell's resort may not be Alaska's most luxurious fishing facility, but few if any camps can match its spectacular setting on Tuwala-Quah Lake, with a snow-capped mountain range serving as a backdrop. It's a comfortable lodge, with all the creature comforts, but it main attraction—beyond great fishing—is the total dedication to personal service. In 1986, the camp operated with a capacity of 12, but in 1987 it will reduce reservations to ten. "We're acquiring a third plane, so we will have a float plane with each party during the entire day," Dean explains. If flying weather is poor, the camp's jet boats will whisk guests to secluded rivers located fairly close to the lodge for a shot at salmon. TuwalaQuah offers all five species of salmon, plus rainbows (on fly-outs), Dolly Varden, grayling, lake trout and even halibut fishing for those who want to try something different. The weekly rate is $2,895.

OUTFITTERS THAT OFFER FLOAT TRIPS

Anglers are transported to a predetermined location, and they are guided down a river by boat or rubber raft. Each night a tent camp is erected at strategic locations, and at the completion of the trip, anglers are picked up (usually by float plane). The guides do most of the work, but a helping hand by the guests is always appreciated.

Advantages: (1) Scenic value of a wilderness float trip cannot be overestimated. (2) Fishing hours during the day are extended. (3) Often one can fish stretches of rivers, or even

Rubber rafts are used on Alaskan float trips to transport anglers from place to place.

entire streams, inaccessible to float planes. (4) It's less expensive than the classic fly-out camps. (5) You are not concerned with weather visibility as in the case of fly-out trips.

Disadvantages: (1) There is a lack of comfort in tent camps. (2) Meals aren't of the same quality as those prepared in a lodge. (3) If weather (such as heavy rain) is against you, obviously some discomfort will be experienced. (4) If the particular river you are floating is poor, you have almost no options. (5) In case of an accident or emergency, severe problems can develop.

B & B FISHING ADVENTURES: This small organization is operated by Bus Bergmann, who despite his youth—38 years old—has already achieved a tremendous following and has all the credentials. He started fly fishing at 10 and has taken a 30-pound steelhead, tarpon, sails, huge kings and other species on a fly rod. Above all, he is an excellent teacher, so many customers who arrive with only a modest amount of fly fishing experience increase their skills many fold by the end of the trip.

Jim Branch reports: "The fishing was absolutely fabulous. Rainbows were up to six or seven pounds. There were plenty of kings, sockeye, humpies and Dolly Varden. It was nothing to catch 50 to 60 fish per day, if someone wanted to work that hard. In fact, Jim Collingsworth landed over 100 fish on a fly one day. Bus and Pat (Bus' assistant) worked 14 to 15 hours each day and there was always a smile on their faces."

Bus and his partner handle a maximum of four anglers at a time (two anglers and one guide per raft). These trips emanate from Dillingham on a "secret" river and the weekly rate is $2,250 per person, which includes the charter plane service from Dillingham to the selected fishing river.

ALASKA RIVER SAFARIS: Ron Hyde operates float trips in the Togiak Wildlife Refuge. Each night a camp is set up at a strategic location, and while living under canvas is not anywhere as comfortable as staying in a lodge, Ron provides the best possible camping equipment and excellent meals. His guides are competent and thoroughly understand that the guests who choose a float trip are dedicated anglers. They do everything possible to satisfy their clients and to produce the type of fishing that fishermen expect from Alaskan waters. When favorable weather conditions exist, the guides generally deliver exceptional fishing.

"It was a fantastic experience and in five days of fishing, I landed over 125 silver salmon and probably hooked another 80," reports Josh Polan. "Most of the silvers were 10 to 14 pounds and were superb fighters. We also caught rainbows up to six pounds and many Dolly Varden and char. It was a great experience."

The weekly rate is $1,950 with an additional $200+ charge for the round trip charter plane service from Dillingham to the selected fishing grounds.

DAVE DUNCAN & SONS, LTD: This family-operated business is famous for its float trips operated down the "Chosen" River. All five species of salmon, plus rainbows, char, grayling and Dollies are offered. Avon Pro 16-foot inflatable rafts, specially designed free-standing "community area" tent, comfortable sleeping tents and superb meals make the Duncan float trip a memorable experience. Two trips are generally offered: Eight-day (six days' floating/fishing) for $2,500; or, ten-day (eight days' floating/fishing) for $2,880. These are 1986 rates and include the air transportation from Seattle, WA.

HEADWATER EXPEDITIONS: Wayne Dawson pesonally guides each float trip in the Aniak region (350 miles west of Anchorage). Fishing is for rainbows, grayling, char, king and silvers. While his outfitting service may not be as well known as several others, Headwater Expeditions is quickly developing a fine reputation for the personal service rendered and superb fishing available on the Aniak River. The weekly rate is $1,750 per person. His season starts in late June and terminates in early September.

CAMPS THAT OFFER FISHING "AT THEIR DOORSTEP"

Basically, these camps provide outboard-powered boats for transporting their guests to the fishing areas.

Advantages: (1) The rates are generally less costly. (2) Some camps that utilize jet boats can reach quality waters that are inaccessible to float planes.(3) You don't have to break down and set up your tackle several times each day, which is a nuisance but a requirement on fly-out trips. (4) You aren't dependent on weather visibility as you are with fly-out camps. (5) In some cases, anglers can fish practically right in front of the camp via wading or from boats.

Disadvantages: (1) If the particular river system you are fishing is having a poor season, there aren't many options. (2) You are basically confined to waters that can be reached by boat during a day. (3) During certain periods, salmon runs may be absent from the "home" waters. (4) At some camps, you fish primarily the same waters each day, which can be somewhat monotonous.

KARLUK LODGE: By now, every reader comes to the conclusion that it is mighty expensive to fish in Alaska. Good news. There are a number of camps that offer reasonably good fishing, fine accommodations and above-average meals. One such bargain is offered by Rob Sikes, owner of Karluk Lodge, on Kodiak Island. The waters are superb. It would be hard to find better silver salmon fishing than at Karluk in prime time. It's also a great river for king salmon, which becomes obvious because one notes that some of the deluxe camps fly their clients great distance to fish the Karluk River. In between these two species there are big runs of sockeyes, humpies (even years) and some chum salmon as well. Also the Karluk offers huge Dolly Varden trout, and even steelhead at times (late fall but sometimes early in the season). The camp is not luxurious but offers indoor plumbing, comfortable beds, fine meals and skiffs and motors suitable for these waters. The 1987 weekly rates: $1,500 for the king salmon season (June and first week of July); and, $1,850 for the silver salmon season (early August to early October). But the real bargain is the five days of fishing for sockeyes, Dolly Varden, humpies and chum for $795. Guests are provided a skiff and outboard but guides aren't necessary as the fishing is within a couple of miles from the lodge. There is also wading available at the river's mouth within sight of the lodge.

UNALAKLEET LODGE: This spacious modern lodge is located only 10 miles from the mouth of the Unalakleet River, so the anadromous species that ascend it are fully energized. The Unalakleet is about 400 miles northeast of Anchorage and empties into the Bering Sea. Much of this river's reputation centers on the splendid king salmon runs that begin in late June and continue until mid-July, but there's more to Unalakleet than the big fly-caught king salmon. There's an excellent run of silver salmon (late August, early September) and chum salmon (July), as well as grayling, Dolly Varden and a million humpies (pink salmon) that reputedly migrate up this river in late July and most of August. The weekly tab is $2,650 per person per week. The lodge accommodates up to 20 anglers, and guests fly from Anchorage to the sleepy village of Unalakleet where they are then transferred to camp.

ALASKA RIVER SAFARIS: In addition to operating his popular float trips, Roy Hyde also has a "river camp" that is unique in that it is moved up and down the river periodically, depending on the salmon runs, conditions of the river, and the season. Naturally, it would be impossible to relocate a lodge, so this setup is a deluxe tent camp that consists of a huge (25 x 40-foot) unit, which in addition to the dining area, also serves as a

Outdoor writer Bob Stearns spends several weeks in Alaska every summer—often on float trips.

central gathering place for anglers. The camp setup provides toilets and even hot showers. Individual tents (8 x 15 feet) provide comfortable accommodations for every two anglers. These are equipped with two cots, foam mattresses, sleeping bags and heaters. With fishing literally right in front of the camp, the lack of a permanent lodge, and its comforts, becomes unimportant to Hyde's clients, many of whom dislike getting into light planes each day. Jet outboard-powered boats swiftly transport guests to choice waters. This "moveable feast" is not inexpensive at $2,750 per week, since it rivals the cost of deluxe fly-out camps.

KEN STOCKHOLM'S TOGIAK CAMP: Those of us who have fished the Bristol Bay/TikChik region are probably familiar with the Togiak River. It's a superb salmon river especially for silver salmon. It also offers good rainbow trout, char and Dolly Varden fishing.

The deluxe fly-out camps often fish the Togiak during the silver salmon season because of its reliability. It is also among the most beautiful rivers I've fished in Alaska.

Ken Stockholm owner/operator of the Wood River Lodge, Bristol Bay region, will operate a new river camp on the Togiak in 1987. The Sunday-to-Sunday package costs $1,495 per person. This includes: six days of fishing, seven nights' accommodations, all meals, one guide, boat and motor for each two anglers, and the round-trip charter plane service from Dillingham.

Ken will limit his capacity to six anglers for 1987. It's ideal for parties of six, because they would have the total camp to themselves.

CAMPS THAT OFFER SEVERAL OPTIONS

Some Alaskan fishing resorts offer several options from their base camps. You can fly out on some days, arrange for a mini-float trip or use a jet boat. Most deluxe fly-out resorts offer several options.

Advantages: (1) Flexibility. E.g. If flying is impossible because of the weather, one can take a boat trip. (2) Flying out on a daily basis becomes monotonous to some anglers; thus, you can mix several of the options offered.

Disadvantages: (1) Usually camps that provide a combination of options are more expensive (someone has to pay for the planes, jet boats, rafts and outposts). (2) Services are offered on a first-come, first-served basis. There may not be sufficient equipment to handle every guest if they all choose the same option.

Fishing Unlimited, Bristol Bay Lodge, Rainbow King Lodge and Golden Horn Lodge are just some of the fishing camps that offer optional trips.

FISHING TACKLE & MISCELLANY

Just about any size fly rod, from ultralights to the heavyweights, has some use in Alaska. I recommend taking at least three different types of outfits.

HEAVYWEIGHT: A heavy fly rod is essential for king salmon, but is also recommended for silvers (No. 10 rod) under certain applications including very windy conditions. If you are fishing an area that doesn't feature these species or are not booked during their specific runs, this outfit may be omitted.

Fly Rod: No. 10, 11 or 12 (you need plenty of power to subdue a king, especially in "heavy waters" or fast currents).

Fly Reel: Don't skimp on quality here. A smooth-running, high-quality reel is essential. Spool it with at least 200 yards of 30-pound Dacron or Micron backing.

Fly Lines: On some waters (i.e. Karluk), slow-sinking lines work well, but in many cases, fast-sinking lines such as Scientific Anglers' Deep Water Express or Cortland's Kerboom or Super Hi-D heads are essential. Also take along floating, intermediate, and sink-tip lines.

Leaders: In deep-water situations, most anglers prefer shorties of four or five feet with tippets of 12 or 15 pounds. On Kodiak Island, some anglers use 12-foot leaders tapered to 10 pounds on clear days for kings.

Flies: Most king salmon flies are tied "steelhead style" on extra stout hooks, often with Mylar tubing bodies. Best predominant colors include orange, white and black. Add a few Mylar strips for flash. Flies should be weighted, and some anglers report good results by using fluorescent materials. For silver salmon, purple and silver flies are very deadly. Most resorts carry a supply of effective patterns.

MEDIUM: This outfit can be used for all salmon (except kings), big rainbows, char and Dolly Varden.

Fly Rod: No. 7, 8 or 9 (for most salmon fishing the No. 9 rod is preferable).

Fly Reel: For the salmon and large trout, it should have a capacity of 150 yards. For the other species, 50 yards of backing is sufficient.

Fly Lines: Floating, intermediate, sinking and sink-tips.

Leaders: Shorter leaders of a few feet for fast-sinking lines. 7 1/2- to 9-feet for floating lines. Leaders should taper down to six, eight or 10 pounds depending on circumstances.

Flies: Mostly subsurface patterns that imitate baitfish (large Muddler Minnows, Sculpin and Olive Matukas in sizes 2 to 2/0) or salmon drifting eggs (such as the Babine Specials, Two-Egg flies). Dry flies that have been productive include Royal Wulff, Grey Wulff, Elk Hair Caddis, and Irresistibles.

LIGHT: Be sure to pack a light fly rod in your case; you won't regret it. It's ideal for grayling, smaller trout, Dolly Varden and char.

Fly Rod: No. 4, 5 or 6.

Fly Line: Floating and sink tips.

Fly Reel: Very light—to match the rod.

Leaders: 7 1/2-footers or longer. Tapered to four-pound test or appropriate.

Flies: Disco Trout for grayling and small trout if surface feeding. Standard trout dry flies, such as the Wulff series, streamers and nymphs.

CLOTHING: Alaska's climate changes quickly. Pack underwear, wool socks, wool shirts, heavy jacket, a good two-piece rainsuit, a hat and other clothes that can keep you toasty warm. Felt-soled waders, preferably insulated, are essential.

TEMPERATURE: The *average* temperatures, as reported by Ken Owsichek (Fishing Unlimited) for his area in 1985, are as follows: June—54 degrees; July—60 degrees; August—61 degrees and September—53 degrees. However, there is also a wind chill factor involved (and the wind blows often).

ALASKAN DANGERS

The brown bear (or grizzly or Kodiak) represents this continent's most formidable animal. Man is absolutely no match for this magnificent mammal that possesses awesome power, tremendous speed and surprising agility. I recall a conversation among experienced big-game hunters as to the outcome if the

Dangers? Addiction to Alaska is one of them. Hank Looyer spends three months every year fishing Alaska.

African lion were pitted against the brown bear. After some discussion, it was concluded that the bear would win the battle. Only man's more powerful firearms become an equalizer in a face-to-face confrontation.

It's very seldom that the brown bear will attack without provocation. But it does happen. During the heavy salmon runs, they will select their vantage spots and efficiently catch all the salmon their hungry bellies demand (and they don't give a hoot about limits or possessing a fishing license). If the angler wishes to challenge them by encroaching on their territory (and especially if there are any cubs present), the bear quickly interprets this as an act of provocation, and his/her decision as the omnipotent judge is final.

It's for this reason that camp owners sensibly use all caution, and in areas where brown bear are often spotted, guides carry firearms and clients are not allowed to wander off on their own. The macho angler who ignores this advice and continuously wanders in brown bear country is very likely to miss his next birthday celebration.

The advice is short and sweet: Listen carefully to what the camp owner or your guide says and follow it. Fishing is darn important, but *not that important.*

When walking along banks, or anywhere for that matter, look ahead, sidewise and everywhere. This is not the time to daydream over that 28-inch rainbow that gobbled a Royal Wulff. It is always a good idea to make as much noise as possible; sing (any key will do), yell, clap your hands, recite Shakespeare or take along a whistle and blow it periodically. Unprovoked attacks are often a result of startling a bear.

Thankfully, there are very few bear attacks. After a number of fishing trips to various areas of Alaska, I've never seen a brown (but plenty of sign).

ABOUT ALASKA

The 49th state, which is more than twice the size of Texas, is laced with numerous crystal-clear rivers, deep lakes, mountainous ranges, glaciers, fiords and some of the most beautiful natural sights in the world. There is a unique sense of energy and vitality that is characteristic of Alaskans, and there are constant reminders that the state is still a frontier—and will be so for a number of decades. This is evident not only in the sparsely-populated areas, where there are more animals than people, but also in Juneau, Fairbanks, Anchorage and other cities.

The first-time visitor is immediately shocked when he discovers the tremendously high cost of living that prevails in Alaska; he eventually understands that shipping costs must indeed be taken into consideration. But he must also wonder, as I did while dining at a restaurant in Kodiak, why seafood is so expensive? Just a few hundred yards away, the wharf harbored hundreds of huge, efficient commercial fishing boats!

He is also made aware that in Alaska the most popular mode of transportation may not be the car, but, in fact, the float plane. It seems that everyone has one.

Alaska is so dissimilar from the "lower 48" that, if it were not for the common language, visitors might suspect that they are indeed in a foreign country. Above all, one is impressed with the vigor that permeates most of the state and with the fact that its citizens have a certain sense of optimism that is often absent elsewhere.

Anchorage: This is the largest and fastest growing city in Alaska (population of about 210,000 out of a total of 500,000 for the entire state) and serves as the gateway city to dozens of fishing camps and areas that hold special appeal to the fly fisherman. The frontier spirit still prevails here, despite a number of classy hotels and elegant Anchorage restaurants that feature continental cuisine.

The best hotel is the Captain Cook. Other recommendations include: the Anchorage Westward Hilton, the Sheraton Anchorage Hotel, the Holiday Inn, and numerous motels near the airport. Deluxe hotels charge $70 to $100 per night for a double.

My favorite restaurant is Elevation 92, but other excellent choices are Cattle Company, Bobby McGee's, Simon and Seafort. Additional favorites among fishermen are restaurants located in hotels, such as Whale's Tail and Crow's Nest (Captain Cook), King's Dining Room (Holiday Inn) and Top of the World (Anchorage Westward Hotel).

AND FINALLY... Most of the fishing information presented in this chapter centers around specific areas that were selected because they are most conducive to the fly fisherman's needs. There is the "pan handle" section of Alaska, for example, but most of the fishing resorts there seem to cater to trolling and not to the fly fishermen. Also there are species that have been omitted simply because of the lack of camps in areas that specifically feature these species. The foremost is the steelhead, and there are a number of rivers that feature a spring run out of Petersburg, Alaska, but unfortunately there are no fishing camps that I'm aware of (some hotels can arrange trips). The best place for steelhead in the areas covered in this chapter appears to be on Kodiak Island, but it is a late September and October proposition (with October being the best month). The weather elements can be so poor at this time ("I had to keep my rod constantly immersed in the water as the line was freezing to the rod") that it takes a very dedicated, hardy, if not irrational, angler to try it. There are still many areas that need exploring, developing and publicizing. I hope this is done slowly, however, so that future generations can enjoy and appreciate the same sense of adventure that we do today.

Northwest Territories

Home of Trophy Lake Trout, Arctic Char and Grayling

N.W.T. is over over 1.3 million square miles. It's desolate (its largest town has a population of 12,000). There are thousands of lakes, rivers, and islands, and many waters have not been fished. Trophy lake trout, char and grayling and, at places, fast northern pike fishing are offered. Obviously the Territories represent a potent frontier to the fly fisherman.

The author admires a small lake trout. When taken on a fly rod, they are exciting and often challenging.

Chapter 3

NORTHWEST TERRITORIES

OF COURSE I was flattered. It was the first and only time that I was asked to be in a commercial fishing film. Jeanne Branson, who at the time owned Branson's Lodge on mammoth Great Bear Lake, was approached by a Canadian movie crew who wanted to shoot a film demonstrating all angling methods: trolling, plug casting, spinning and fly fishing.

Jeanne, having impeccable taste and being an excellent judge of superb, though latent, talent, asked me to do the fly fishing portion. (Okay, so all the other guys she asked first were busy.)

"I have no filming sessions for *that* week, and since I was planning on being in the neighborhood anyway, I could devote a little time to catching a few fish for the cameras." That's what I told her.

Now whenever a film is to be shot, Murphy's Law quickly goes into effect: The weather is miserable. The fish do a Houdini disappearing act, never to reappear until the cameras are safely packed away. The best guide gets sick. Outboards break down. The fisherman misses strikes or develops backlashes (even in fly reels). Any number of assorted disasters and catastrophes occur.

Not on this one, baby. I was determined. True, the lake was still half-frozen, even on this second week of July, and the outgoing guests complained that fish were hard to locate. But no matter. How often does one have the opportunity to be featured in front of cameras? No way was I going to let little things like that interfere.

The crew collected scenery and background shots while I warmed up on a few trout, honing down my casts to poetic per-

"For big pike on a fly rod use big flies..."says outdoor writer and TV personality Mark Sosin.

fection and trying to decide which was my best side ("none" was the consensus of the other guests, who obviously were outraged with jealousy).

On the third day, the fly fishing sequence was to be shot. Upon Jeanne's suggestion, we flew to her outpost camp on the Katseyedie River because here the water was shallow and filming lake trout on a fly rod would be better. While the cinematographer (class!) was putting together his equipment, I landed several lake trout that weighed in the mid-teens. We decided to try the mouth of a small river because, according to the cinematographer, this provided better lighting and background. Who was I to argue? When we finally made our way to the selected spot, I noticed that the water was slightly murky, very shallow and not at all what I would call classic lake trout water. But since we were already there, the camera guys said that they would take a few feet of fly casting action. I had a strike on the

Jack Parry, popular outdoor writer, displays a big Arctic grayling caught from the Kazan river.

second cast and I was amazed that it was a lake trout. The camera grinded away as fish after fish, up to perhaps 14 pounds, hit the blue and white streamer.

Then one of the most spectacular things that I've ever encountered in lake trout fishing occurred. From my vantage point on a knoll I observed the largest lake trout I have ever seen following the streamer nonchalantly. This tremendous trout—40 pounds, maybe even 50, maybe larger—came from out of nowhere and appeared interested, when suddenly a smaller trout (about four pounds) greedily swiped the fly. The big trout was so infuriated that it chased the smaller fish, intending to grab it for lunch. The small fish, realizing the danger, dropped the streamer and wisely took off for the hinterlands with the monster hot on its tail. First I gawked and then cussed the snotnose trout in English and Greek and probably French, too.

"Did you see that!" I yelled at the photographer. "Did you get that on film?" No, he was reloading his camera.

We rested the area, I switched to a large streamer and got the big fish interested again in the fly. I tried various retrieves. The fish continually followed it but would suddenly lose interest. I decided to tie on a much larger streamer, when one of the other guests who had been fishing nearby from a boat motored up to us. He had heard my yelling and wanted to see the huge trout. I frantically tried to wave him off. His outboard silted the bottom so much that fishing the area was now hopeless. We left to investigate the upstream waters and planned to return later, but the pest homesteaded the area and never stopped casting his six-inch spoon. He didn't see the monster fish again. ("Good!" I thought. It served the slob well.)

We couldn't find that laker in the afternoon, but I believe that I would have had a reasonable chance of hooking it on a huge streamer. Later on that season, another guest, using hardware, landed a tremendous laker, just beyond the mouth of the river that I was fishing. It weighed over 60 pounds, and in its gullet was a half-digested trout of about five pounds. I would like to fantasize that it was the same fish that toyed with me. Apparently, big trout are attracted to this area because they can catch the smaller trout easily in the shallows. Toward the end of the season another giant, a 65-pound lake trout, was also landed from the same area and was officially accepted as the new world record.

We found some grayling upstream and took some footage. I had switched to a lighter fly rod (No. 6) and attached a small Irresistible dry fly to my light leader.

As we quietly walked the bank, I noticed a very big fish finning right next to me. Just a few feet away. I didn't dare move, for fear of scaring it. It was a big northern pike! There are some pike in Great Bear, but they are mostly long and skinny; this one was long and fat—I'd estimate it at 20 pounds. Undoubtedly the pike was feasting on the small grayling in the river.

I explained to the photographer that this was a very large pike and that while I didn't think it would be interested in the dry fly I had on, I would try it. "Pike have sharp teeth, so it will cut the leader quickly. Maybe you can get some footage of its reaction."

Carefully, without much arm movement, I flicked the fly in the pike's direction; it landed right in front of the fish's head. You could almost sense its bulging alligator-like eyes moving upward in their sockets. Food! And with a flip of its tail, the pike surged to the surface and engulfed the tiny dry fly. I set hook, and the fish made a half-hearted jump upon feeling the sting of the barb. But, of course, the pike's teeth quickly cut the fine leader.

"Did you get that? Did you get that action?" I was darn excited. Not often can one induce a big northern pike to take a small dry fly.

"No. The camera jammed!" the photographer said. "Can you do that again?" Gulp.

So much for my movie career. It would have been great to have hooked that huge lake trout and to have captured the northern pike hitting a dry fly on film, but, nonetheless, a good fly fishing segment resulted. I waited next to the phone for weeks after the film was released, but amazingly not one Hollywood producer called. I was sure that I would get the call for Sophia Loren's next film, but I never made it as a leading man.

On the positive side, this experience vividly points out that the fly rod can be a very effective tool in the Northwest Territories (N.W.T.). By the time the week ended, I had landed well over 100 lake trout (on the fly rod), mostly in the eight- to 15-pound bracket, with the largest weighing 18 pounds. These results compared favorably to those turned in by most of the other guests who were using spinning, plug casting or trolling gear. Fly fishing—on most waters in the Northwest Territories—has a place along with the other fishing methods.

While the fly rodder can often compete with the hardware fisherman in terms of numbers of fish landed, the spoon-and-spinner man consistently delivers the bigger lake trout and northern pike. There are two reasons for this: (1) The trophy trout and pike are attracted to the larger lures used by the hardware anglers (underlining the "big lures attract big fish" theory), and (2) in the Northwest Territories, there are hundreds of hardware casters for every fly rod man, so it stands to reason that they take the larger share of big fish.

Occasionally the fly rodder may have the advantage. I've heard hardware fishermen express their frustrations fishing at Great Bear or Great Slave Lakes because trout, big trout, were observed sipping in dark flies off the surface while totally ignoring most of the "meat and potatoes" spoons and spinners tossed their way. This is, however, a short-term phenomenon, so don't expect to commonly experience it.

Bill Cullerton, Jr., tells me that on one of his trips to Kasba Lake (N.W.T.), there was a tremendous caddis hatch and thousands of these flies were funnelled into a drift line formed by the wind and water current. Lake trout gathered at these concentrations and gulped the delicacies unceasingly. While he didn't have any caddis patterns with him, he took many lakers on other flies, and for the most part, the trout ignored hardware.

Bill offers: "On other trips, when we weren't as fortunate to experience a heavy caddis hatch, we caught many lake trout by casting the shoreline, allowing the streamer to sink first and then retrieving it slowly but with some pizzazz. The lakers were four to seven feet deep, and in this clear water, you could see the strike develop. We even interested lake trout to take surface poppers. Spoons are generally more productive, so an angler must decide whether he wants the most action possible—in which case he sticks to hardware—or whether he appreciates the challenge and quality derived from fly fishing."

The angler who decides on the Northwest Territories will be attracted to lake trout, Arctic char, grayling and northern pike as the primary species. Let's take a closer look at these species.

LAKE TROUT

The lake trout is the most common species in the Northwest Territories. While some camp brochures describe trout of over 50 pounds, bear in mind that these giants are exceptionally rare. Realistically, most of the lakers average five to 15 pounds, and a 20-pound plus trout today is considered in the trophy class. Lake trout are a slow-growing species and some biologists claim that a 20- or 25-pound fish may be 20 years old or more. Furthermore, the waters near or above the Arctic Circle are relatively infertile, so the big trout must rely heavily on cannibalism and longevity.

When sportsmen first began to pioneer Great Bear and several other waters in the Territories, their catches often consisted of lake trout of over 15 pounds.

"In those days," a very articulate guide explained, "I would have bet that more trout would weigh over 15 pounds than under seven pounds, and I know that I would have won most of the time. My parties would often land a half-dozen big lakers, 20 to 30 pounds, in a single day. The reason was that the small trout feared for their lives and mostly hid among the rocks. The big trout are cannibalistic, but as they were removed one by one, the small fish became more brazen, so they began to hit lures. It's too bad that we didn't have the foresight to return the big fish and to keep the smaller ones for fillets or shorelunch. I suspect that fishing would be almost as good today had we practiced conservation at the outset, but we all thought that the supply of trophy lake trout was endless. We were wrong."

Today, many camp owners, realizing their mistake, have finally instituted stringent conservation measures that allow an angler to kill one trophy fish while releasing all others except the badly hooked fish. Many resorts have implemented the use of barbless hooks so that the fish can be returned unharmed.

A camp owner laments: "We were caught in a bind. The resort business was highly competitive. We had invested heavily in our camps, and because our trips were very expensive, we had to do everything possible to attract guests. At sport shows, we promised big fish and we delivered them. Many camps had big boxes constructed for trophy fish, which were labeled, 'Another Trophy Fish from ABC Lodge'."

Thankfully, today's conservation policies have helped tremendously, and most of the lakes that were heavily abused have made good strides toward recovery. Furthermore, many owners of new camps on "untouched" waters, realizing the folly of their colleagues, have established release fishing from the outset. Kasba Lake Lodge is an excellent example.

"The investment of constructing, maintaining and operating a lodge today is enormous. A camp owner has to look at it as a long-term investment—not a four- or five-year deal," claims Doug Hill, owner of Kasba Lake Lodge. "At first, there was some hesitance by some fishermen to book our camp when they heard of our self-imposed trophy regulations, but eventually they understood their importance. Our guests prefer to have quality fishing rather than the ability to take home lots of fillets."

While the hardware caster may not be satisfied with "smaller trout," the fly fisherman has his hands full with trout in the eight- to 15-pound bracket. Landing a half-dozen trout in the low teens is certainly a most satisfying fly fishing accomplishment, especially if the fish are found in the shallows; the trout can only streak away from the fisherman, as opposed to deep-water trout fishing, which presents an uninspiring up-and-down epic often termed "yo-yo" fishing. Lakers from shallow, crystal clear waters taken on a fly rod provide superb sport. Incidentally, since it has a forked tail, the lake trout can be landed by hand-tailing the fish, much like in Atlantic salmon fishing.

Doug Hill claims that there are an increasing number of fly fishermen coming to his camp each season. "Fly fishing can be spectacular during most of our season. We had two fly rodders land as many as 60 lakers in a single day of fishing. Of course, this represents super fishing and not the norm. The largest in

1982 was an 18-pounder, but I'm sure as fly fishing for trout becomes more popular, our camp will produce much larger fly-caught fish."

What are some of the outstanding lake trout waters of N.W.T.? Great Bear and Great Slave are perhaps the two most famous lakes. Kasba Lake must also be listed among Canada's top waters. Huge Victoria Island, known for its fine Arctic char fishing, is also an excellent lake trout fly fishing destination. Other good lakes are Dubawnt, Snowbird, Nueltin Narrows and Chantrey, and, of course, there are many other waters that have not yet been explored.

ARCTIC CHAR

The Arctic char—one of North America's most exotic species—was virtually unfamiliar to most fishermen until the early 1960s when articles penned by George Laycock, Tom McNally, A.J. McClane and others appeared in the outdoor magazines. The colorful photos of crimson red char with white trimmed fins dramatized this mysterious nomadic species of the northlands and helped to create a sudden burst of popularity for this fish. Anglers who could afford it rushed to the Tree River, Baffin Island and other soon-to-become-famous places in search of this fish. In effect, the Arctic char was the darling of the "60s as far as the freshwater angling set was concerned.

The Northwest Territories produces the world's largest Arctic char, and the Tree River is undoubtedly the most famous place for trophy fish. The largest Tree River Arctic char caught on hardware was 32 pounds, 9 ounces while the fly rod record char is 21 pounds, 6 ounces. Fly rodders who have fished the Tree, however, are quick to point out that there are strong, swirling tricky currents and plenty of white water here, so it isn't an easy place to fish (albeit one doesn't have to worry about hanging a backcast on a branch in this treeless region).

Before the advent of high-density and fast-sinking lines, dedicated fly rodders in search of big char used heavily weighed streamers to get the fly below the fast surface currents. Some anglers, including the late Art Mercier, used a spinner in front of the fly, not only to help sink it but also because char like bright lures.

Today the problem is mostly solved due to the ingenuity of fly line manufacturers, who have created products that sink fast and deep. Furthermore, with fly tying materials such as sparkle yarn, prismatic tape, Flashabou and Mylar, the innovative fly tier can compose on his vise a bright, if not gaudy, deadly fly. The key adjectives describing productive char flies are shiny, glitzy, colorful and flashy. "If you have to wear sunglasses when you tie char flies on, they are probably bright enough," quips Cecil K. Lewis.

The trouble with fishing the Tree River is that a fisherman is limited to a 24-hour session. Plummer's Great Bear Lake Lodge, which has exclusive access and rights to the Tree, offers a side trip to its outpost camp, but because of the great demand for the exotic char, the camp has no recourse but to limit its guests to 24-hour gigs on a first-come, first-served basis.

The Arctic char was the darling of the 1960s. Numerous places in the N.W.T. offer fast char fishing.

If one wishes to fish for char on a more concentrated basis, there are a number of destinations that can be considered. Among the best is Victoria Island. High Arctic Lodge provides two-day fly-out trips to its outpost camps for char or lake trout in addition to fishing the home waters near the main camp. Dr. Elmer Rusten set two IGFA fly rod records for char at Victoria Island: (1) an 18-pound, 2 ounce char on an eight-pound tippet, and (2) a 15-pounder on a 12-pound tippet. The best fly fishing for char and lakers appears to be during second and third weeks of July.

Baffin Island is another very productive place for Arctic char, and while a 15-pounder is considered a trophy fish here, there is good reason to believe that char of over 20 pounds can be found at Clearwater Fiord, one of the best char places at Baffin Island.

Another N.W.T. char destination is Chantrey Inlet, although its fame was derived mostly because of its giant lake trout. There is usually a period of about two weeks during the beginning of its short six-week season when big char are readily taken.

There are a number of other rivers that flow into Coronation Gulf (particularly near the village of Coppermine) that are excellent char waters. Some of these rivers are not named, while in other cases, camps that use these rivers as optional fly-out places are not interested in divulging exact location or river names.

But for the fly rodder looking for char, the Tree and Victoria Island are recommended in the N.W.T.—all things considered.

ARCTIC GRAYLING

Under the right conditions, the grayling is an exceptionally fine target for the fly fisherman who enjoys using light tackle and who can appreciate the fighting antics of two- to three-pound fish. The key words are "right conditions", and some of the criteria are: (1) the potential of the occasional large fish (three pounds or larger); (2) stream fishing as opposed to lake grayling; (3) rising fish.

Super-fast grayling fishing can ultimately lead to boredom. A small party who had never fished for Arctic grayling was especially interested in this species. They had the right ultralight spinning gear and they were well stocked with No. 0 or 1 Mepps spinners, which are "deadly" grayling lures. They arranged to take a special charter fly-out to a river known for its fast grayling fishing. They had waited a long time for their N.W.T. trip to materialize, relishing the thought of unending grayling action. They had an extremely good day for grayling fishing but after a couple of hours, boredom began to set in. Just about every cast yielded a grayling, and they were all about the same size. There was no challenge. If they missed a strike, there was no cause for alarm; other grayling were ready on the firing line.

There are times when a fly fisherman may experience fishing almost that fast, but I believe that watching a grayling slice at a dry fly is infinitely more exciting than the underwater spinning lure strike, and the fly fisherman can build in a variety of challenges by using very light rods, leaders and the tiniest dry flies.

While the Arctic grayling is synonymous with stream fishing, which is definitely more exciting than lake fly fishing, at times I enjoy "still water" fishing for this species. One year, fishing with Al Junquera at Branson's Lodge, we decided to try Great Bear Lake for grayling and passed up the optional stream fishing trip. Our guide confided in us that he knew of several places near camp that produced very big grayling. So Al and I concentrated on lake trout fishing, and just before quitting time, when all the other boats were in, our guide took us to several of his secret grayling spots. We both caught several huge grayling that I'm sure weighed four pounds, if not slightly more. Al had a particularly large grayling on, and while he was fighting it close to the boat, the grayling shot underneath so quickly that Al was unable to swing the rod around the stern or bow. Snap! There went a very expensive and light split bamboo. He grieved for only a few seconds, picked up another rod, and a smile returned to his face.

We released all these fish, and the guide appreciated this. "I save this place for special people who enjoy big grayling but release them. That way the area isn't spoiled," the guide told us. We didn't know if this were true, but Al and I tipped him considerably higher than we normally would have.

I have sometimes found the Arctic grayling so cooperative that, frankly, the challenge evaporates, while on other occasions, it can be a very stubborn fish. Sometimes it won't budge more than a few inches to the left or right, rising only to flies that drift down its exact feeding lane. But most of the time the quality of grayling fishing lies somewhere between the two extremes, and it becomes a most pleasurable experience. Obviously, there are many other species that draw a fisherman to a particular area, but I rarely pass up an opportunity for a few grayling sessions.

There are many excellent places in the Northwest Territories to fish for grayling. The Great Bear River is one of the best, but there are a number of streams that flow into Great Bear and Great Slave that offer grayling in the two- to 3 1/2-pound class. Chantrey Inlet is an excellent grayling place, but the best fly fishing grayling stream is the Kazan River (fished from Kasba Lake Lodge). Lately, it's produced more grayling of over 3 1/2 pounds than any other place.

NORTHERN PIKE

Northerns of over 30 pounds have been taken from the Northwest Territories, and there are a number of good pike waters. However, except for the mouth of the Mackenzie River (where it empties into Great Slave Lake), the northern pike isn't a particularly big draw here. It's the lake trout and the Arctic char that jointly rule the Territories' kingdom.

The best place to fish for northerns in N.W.T. is Brabant's Lodge at the Mackenzie River. While the majority of the anglers fish for pike with spoons, the fly rodder can score big here, with pike of over 20 pounds, by casting large streamers. The best streamers are five to six inches in length, tied with long white hackles or FisHair with a touch of red and a number of silver Mylar strips. At times, large popping bugs, such as those designed for saltwater fishing, are not only productive but very exciting to use. The strike can be sensational. Sometimes it's a smashing, surface "explosion" that can shock you. At other times, you may notice a roll of water or wake developing behind the popper, moving faster and faster, that finally hones in on the target just like a guided missile.

To pump these air-resistant flies into the wind one needs a substantial fly rod such as a No. 10 graphite. Intermediate or floating lines can be used. It's double-haul casting; it can be tiresome but the results are usually rewarding.

In addition to the Mackenzie, good pike action can be found at Kasba, Great Bear, Great Slave and Nueltin lakes. At Kasba, an angler took a tremendous 33-pound pike on regulation gear.

THE WATERS, THE CAMPS

Let's briefly look at some of the N.W.T.'s major fishing waters and representative camps:

GREAT SLAVE LAKE: This huge body of water (just south of Yellow knife) is considered one of the best lake trout waters in the N.W.T. Each season, Great Slave yields many 20- to 35-

The Arctic grayling is a small species, but there's something about the way they slash at a dry fly!

pound lakers. Nearby Great Bear Lake has produced the largest trout (over 60 pounds), but Great Slave, in the opinion of a number of knowledgeable anglers, is more dependable for the 10- to 30-pound lake trout. There are numerous bays, islands, inlets, reefs and sharp dropoffs—an ideal lake trout environment. Arctic graying and northern pike can also be caught. Two excellent camps should be considered: Jerry Bricker's Frontier Fishing Lodge and Plummer's Great Slave Lake Lodge ($1,795 per week from Winnipeg).

GREAT BEAR LAKE: Located northwest of Great Slave, Great Bear has produced more giant lake trout than any other place in the world. The Arctic Circle bisects the top third of this lake. Some fly rodders believe that the early season (first two weeks of July) is the best time for lakers in the five- to 15-pound class, since they generally congregate at the mouths of inlets and are therefore easy to find.

For trophies, 1985 was certainly a vintage year; in fact, it probably was the all-time best at Plummer's Great Bear Lake Lodge. Eight lakers weighing over 50 pounds were landed that year!

Big Arctic grayling can be found in some sections of Great Bear, and occasionally one finds a big northern pike, but generally the pike are smallish in these oligotrophic waters.

Plummer's Great Bear Lake Lodge has a distinct advantage in that it holds an exclusive arrangement for fishing the fabulous Tree River for Arctic char. Guests who wish to fish for char are flown to the Tree River Camp where they can fish to their hearts' content for the next 24 hours (or as long as their casting arms hold out). This optional trip costs $275 per person, which includes the charter flight in the camp's own DC3. August is the time for Tree River char.

The weekly rate at Plummer's main lodge on Great Bear is $2,195, which includes the flight from Winnipeg.

Other excellent camps on Great Bear include Branson's Lodge, Arctic Circle Lodge and Great Bear Lodge. I believe all these camps offer fly-out trips to various Arctic char rivers, most of them near the village of Coppermine. The names of rivers are closely guarded among camp owners as good char waters are a premium.

KASBA LAKE: Located mostly in the N.W.T., but dipping slightly into Manitoba and Saskatchewan, Kasba is a superb trout lake. In 1983, there were 351 trophy trout (over 18 pounds), in 1984, 317 giant lakers and in 1985, 346 trout weighing from 18 to 42 pounds landed. Obviously, Kasba is a very consistent lake trout spa. During 1985, 330 Arctic grayling weighing from 2 1/2 to four pounds were caught from nearby Kazan River. Northerns are generally ignored by Kasba guests, but 27 over 18 pounds were taken in 1985.

The fly rodder generally needs a pocket calculator before the week is over to keep track of all the catches. Norm Strung, the prolific outdoor writer, fishing flies, landed 600 lakers in various sizes during his stay at Kasba.

Doug Hill's Kasba Lake Lodge has developed into a very comfortable, but not luxurious, camp and is the only one on the lake. From the outset, Hill instituted a catch-and-release program that has paid off through the years. A weekly stay, which includes the Saturday charter flight from Saskatoon, Sask., costs $1,995 per person.

VICTORIA ISLAND: High Arctic Lodge provides fairly comfortable accommodations at its main lodge as well as at its three outpost camps on Hadley Bay. There are two particular advantages to fly fishing at Victoria: (1) The fly rodder has a great chance of hooking numerous char in the lakes and rivers where they are very plentiful and can be taken on flies more readily; (2) there are places where one can wade rivers, or near the mouths of rivers, and hook lake trout.

To illustrate the fun one can have wading for lake trout, here's camp owner Don Hamilton's description of one party's experience and baptism: "I'll always remember when Bob and Eve Goplin brought their daughter Jodi to camp. I flew them to a hot spot for the day's outing. Here you must wade out on a sandbar in a small river where it flows into a lake. The big lake trout lay in the shallow water and are hungry. On their first casts, all three hooked big lake trout and you should have heard the yelling and whooping. It's a wonder that all the caribou and musk oxen weren't frightened right off the island. Each one had on trout weighing between 18 and 25 pounds! Jodi went in over her waders, and then I saw her sitting on a boulder where she dumped out all the water and wrung out her socks. Back into the freezing water she went. I asked her if she was cold and she said it wasn't too bad once her body temperature warmed up the water in her boots! I think she'd have gone out there without the waders.

"I don't believe there was a time that one of them wasn't fighting a fish and often all three were hooked up. All the lakers weighed in excess of 15 pounds and the largest was 28 pounds. Everyone I've taken to this spot has said he had never experienced fishing as spectacular..."

While we assume that the Goplins used spoons and spinners, the fly rodder's potential at this spot is also enormous. As reported earlier, Dr. Elmer Rusten leads the fly fishermen with his 18-pound, 2-ounce Arctic char, which is the present IGFA World Record for the eight-pound tippet class. The largest on hardware is John Taulborg's 24-pounder.

The season starts around the second week of July and terminates at the end of August (best fly fishing is generally the first two weeks of the season). The expense of operating a lodge in this desolate area is enormous, so the weekly rate of $2,295 per person from Cambridge Bay (Victoria Island) including a two-day outpost camp is a "bargain".

HENIK AND DUBAWNT LAKES: Dr. Ron Trunsky and his party reported fast fishing during their visit to Henik Lake Lodge: "We rated it as excellent. I computed that we averaged a fish for every 20 minutes of fishing time. The trout were not huge, mostly seven to 10 pounds, but they were certainly plentiful. More importantly, these fish really fought much harder than the lake trout I have caught elsewhere. All our fishing was done in shallow water...There was a river near the fishing camp. Fishing there was excellent for lake trout and grayling, only 300 yards from the lodge. On the last afternoon, our party of five caught 40 fish in less than an hour. There are larger fish at Dubawnt, but we opted for the shallow water fishing at Henik where casting can be successful." The accommodations, while not luxurious, are clean, pleasant and comfortable. The staff, meals, equipment were all excellent. The 1985 rate for Henik Lodge was $1,695, which includes five days' fishing, plus the round-trip charter from Thompson, Manitoba. The Dubawnt Lodge rate is $2,345. Arctic char trips can also be arranged.

MACKENZIE RIVER: Northern pike is the headliner here, and it just may be that Brabant's Lodge, at the mouth of the Mackenzie, provides the most consistent pike fishing in the Northwest Territories. Pike of over 15 pounds are fairly common. How good is the pike fishing? Dr. Charles Veith and his party of five in one week landed approximately 1,000 pike. Twenty-five were over 18 pounds, and every angler caught at least one fish of over 20 pounds. This was on regulation casting tackle, but the veteran fly rodder can be kept very busy, too. Dr. Elmer Rusten, on one trip to Brabant's, landed 150 pike on flies.

There's more to fishing than catching; these Inuit children found fishing and fishermen fascinating.

The secondary species here is the Arctic grayling. They are found fairly close to camp and will average about two pounds. Dry flies such as the Royal Wulff, Disco Trout and Black Gnat are effective.

There are also walleyes in these waters, but they are sometimes difficult to find and consequently not a good species for the fly fisherman. However, when located, these walleyes are generally considerably larger than those found in other Canadian waters.

Brabant's Lodge is considered among Canada's best resorts in terms of management, cleanliness and personal service. The season starts in mid-June and terminates in mid-September (you can include some duck shooting along with a September fishing trip). The weekly rate is $1,735 per person, which includes everything from Hay River, N.W.T., except the guides. At Brabant's, guides are not necessary because the fishing takes places close to the lodge (though they are available).

CHANTREY INLET: There's a 50-pound lake trout mounted in a coffee table in my office. It was contributed by Jerry Tricomi, who caught the giant on a spoon at Chantrey Inlet. Many huge lake trout of over 35 pounds have come from Chantrey. When Jerry fished there, accommodations and meals were quite spartan; happily, today Chantrey Inlet Lodge offers fairly comfortable facilities and excellent boating equipment for up to 18 anglers. It's located about 200 miles north of Baker Lake, where the huge Back River empties into the Arctic Ocean.

The season is among the shortest of any Canadian lodge: It commences in early July and terminates around mid-August. In addition to the lake trout, there is good fishing for Arctic char (24 1/2 pounds is the camp record) and Arctic grayling up to four pounds. The char fishing is best during the first couple weeks of the season, whereas the best lake trout fishing is at the end of July and the first half of August. When the char are running, lake trout are very common, but the big lakers are generally caught later on. Grayling are plentiful during the entire season.

Because the lake trout are found fairly close to the surface, Chantrey's fly fishing potential is immense but not proven. Big streamer flies should be the ticket here for lakers, whereas smaller, flashy streamers should work for char. Dry flies and wets are very successful for grayling. The six-day package is $2,300, which includes the 1,500 mile flight from Fort Frances, Ontario.

BAFFIN ISLAND: This huge island hasn't received the publicity that other sections of the Territories have acquired, and it still needs some development. There are a number of small fishing camps, operated mostly by the Inuit under territorial supervision. For the most part, Arctic char is the primary sporting species, and at some places it's the only one. There are four camps that offer char fishing that we know of: Clearwater Fiord Fishing Camp, Hall Lake Fishing Camp, Lake Hazen Lodge and Tongait Arctic Char Camp. Dr. Ron Trunsky fished at Tongait and reported good success for Arctic char up to 12 pounds via fly fishing. The rates range from $2,000 to $2,800 per week.

AND FINALLY... No other fishing area is more sparsely populated than N.W.T. Consider this: The Territories consist of over 1,300,000 square miles and the most populated city is the capital, Yellowknife, which has a population of 12,000 and roughly represents 20 percent of the total population. Talk about casting room! There are thousands of lakes and rivers that probably have never been fished. There is certainly room for exploration here. There's practically no industry, so one need not worry about polluted waters. While the potential of fly fishing will never be fully tapped—because of its tremendous vastness and unexplored waters—N.W.T. represents an ideal destination for the angler who enjoys fast fishing, exploring and challenges in a land that hasn't changed much in centuries.

And, you can pack a lot of fishing time during a day in the Territories, because in the summer there's an average of 22 hours of daylight.

Alberta

Classic Dry Fly Fishing for Browns and Rainbows

A river that flows right through Calgary happens to be among the best for classic dry fly fishing; where 20-inch rainbows and browns roam and are caught with regularity; where you can fish during the day and dine at Calgary's best restaurants by night; Kim Dayman's point-by-point strategy will make your next trip to the Bow more productive.

Bob Miller's photo captures a trout just after it inhaled a natural from the surface.

Chapter 4

ALBERTA

MY 1979 BAPTISM to the Bow River was a disappointment, despite the fact that there was a fine blend of ingredients: Stu Apte and Tim Clark, two delightful angling companions; Pete Skonsberg, a knowledgeable, dedicated, hard-working guide; basically favorable weather despite some rains and strong gusts of winds; and hatches that were sporadic but in sufficient quantities to periodically attract some of the trout to the surface.

On the debit side, we encountered an almost endless flotilla of weeds that floated down the river. Often it was virtually impossible to negotiate a 12-inch drift because the dry fly would quickly snag on a weed, or the leader would hang up, creating immediate drag. (A few weeks later, when the weeds weren't as bothersome, Lefty Kreh and Charles Brooks descended on the river and caught so many trout that only a computer could keep track of numbers and sizes.)

When we found open patches of water, we received solid responses mostly from rainbows and the occasional brown, but the best places were difficult to fish. We landed a number of trout, 16 to 18 inches, and each of us busted a few tippets, presumably on bigger fish; thus the bottom line of our trip didn't reveal a deficit after all.

Our disappointment stemmed from the fact that our expectations were extremely high, buoyed by a conversation I had with Al McClane, the writer who was most responsible for the Bow's popularity. In essence, Al claimed that the Bow was one of North America's best dry-fly rivers. And he had tried most of them.

Virginia Pierrepont has fooled numerous Bow River rainbows and browns.

Wayne Vinson landed a 22-inch brown from the Bow. It was his first fly fishing trip!

"In 50 years of trout angling," Al wrote in the March, 1980, issue of *Sports Afield,* "I can't recall many rivers that consistently produced 16- to 24-inch-long rainbows and browns to tiny dry flies, and these are ancient history now. Bear in mind, I am talking about a two- to five-pound average. I counted just four out of a collective 60 that were less than a pound in size on the one day I bothered to keep score..."

Other fishermen who had fished the Bow underscored Al's comments and classed this river in the "can't miss" file, reserved for the rare, elite fishing places.

The development of the Bow River trout fishery is fairly spectacular, considering that the river flows through Calgary, a modern, sprawling metropolis with a population of 620,000. Prior to the 1970s, it wasn't a very productive river (although it yielded some trout to the persistent locals), and the Bow would never have been listed on any experienced angler's "Top Ten" trout list. The transformation into a top river was mostly accidental.

The river originates in the Alberta Rockies of the Banff National Park. It's fed by glacial drainage and melting snows from the high country. The river changes in character considerably below Calgary, where it becomes almost a prairie river instead of the alpine stream that it is above Calgary.

Calgary shifted from a "cowboy town" to a bustling city when oil was discovered. Sewage disposal became a severe problem, and a secondary treatment was instituted. This treatment poured phosphates and nitrates into the Bow, which resulted in lush weed growth and ultimately created a fantastic environment for aquatic insects. The trout grew big and healthy, and the Bow suddenly became one of North America's finest trout rivers from Calgary to the town of Carseland about forty miles downstream.

Russ Thornberry, an enterprising Texan who moved permanently to Alberta, decided that the best way to fish the river was via float trips, because much of the bordering land was private so public access was difficult. He started the Bow River Company, which provided skiffs, knowledgeable guides, a daily shore lunch and transfers to and from the river. The guests stayed in Calgary, so a big investment in a resort wasn't necessary. (Russ has since sold his business; it is now operated by Pete Chenier, and today there are a number of excellent outfitters that serve the Bow.)

The Bow is an attractive trout fishing destination for many reasons: (1) There is frequent and excellent flight service to Calgary from many North American cities; (2) Anglers stay in Calgary, which offers fine hotels, a variety of good restaurants and other entertainment values that score high with nonfishing family members; (3) The fishing rates are exceptionally reasonable; (4) There are a number of different sections of the Bow that can be floated, which adds variety; and, (5) above all, it happens to be one of the best trout fisheries.

There was some concern by Bow River regulars and biologists that the trout population was hurt considerably by the 1980 and 1981 floods. The biologists claimed that the heavy spring waters scoured and silted the rainbow spawning beds and that the number of yearling and two-year-old fish had dropped dramatically. This information was derived from extensive electro-shocking of certain river sections from Calgary to Carseland.

In 1980-81 the census revealed that there were approximately 800 rainbows per kilometer of river, but in 1982 the rainbow population dropped approximately 25 percent. There were plenty of big fish, but the concern was for one- and two-year old rainbows.

The electro-shocking results indicated that the brown trout population remained stable for the same three years at 200 to 300 browns per kilometer. The biologists explained this by pointing out that the brown trout spawn in late fall and, therefore, were not affected as were the spring-spawning rainbows.

Simultaneously, the biologists conducted an intensive creel census. These results indicated that anglers fishing from the banks had a lower per rod/day catch but that the guided, float trips remained stable.

The fisheries department issued new regulations, including one that trout measuring *over* 15-3/4 inches must be released but that the creel limit remain at two fish per day (which must be less than 15-3/4 inches). This didn't affect the visiting anglers using the float-trip outfitters because the guides promote catch-and-release fishing and nearly all trout are returned. Bait fishing was also prohibited in the Special Fisheries Area (Calgary to Carseland).

It was hoped that these corrective measures, coupled with some luck (i.e., absence of tremendous floods), would preserve this great trout river. The recent quality of fishing delivered by the Bow, especially in 1985 and 1986, indicates that the fishery not only remains stable but that larger trout are being caught, especially browns.

There are forty miles of prime trout fishing water between Calgary and Carseland, and five to 10 miles of water can easily be floated and fished in a day. The average width of the Bow is about 400 feet, and the current flows a comfortable seven to eight mph. There are some narrow, rocky parts where the current is faster, but mostly it's a very pleasant river to fish. The terrain varies from lush pastureland to steep, heavily-timbered canyon walls and wind-sculptured sandstone bluffs. Canadian geese nest on the islands and one sees a variety of ducks, falcons, partridges and pheasants.

Recently I had an opportunity to visit with Kim Dayman, the energetic owner of Alberta Drift and one of the Bow's finest outfitters. His educational background was in Resource Management, majoring in water quality, wildlife and fisheries. Kim has fished the Bow for more than 20 years and has served as Federal Fisheries Officer, but he now concentrates his efforts entirely on his float-fishing trips.

I first heard of Alberta Drift through Stuyve Pierrepont, who rated Kim as "easily one of the premier trout guides." In one day, Stuyve landed two trout over 20 inches, a brown and a rainbow, on a No. 20 fly, which earned him a membership in the informal 20/20 Club.

Bill Morgan also sings the praises of the Bow and Kim. "The first fish we landed was a 21-inch brown. My son and I landed 18 trout on that day and two-thirds of them were over 18 inches."

PanAngling's Paul Melchior took a group of anglers to the Bow in 1986 using Kim's Alberta Drift as their outfitter. "He is undoubtedly one of the most knowledgeable guide's one could expect to find. He is a most pleasant companion. But it should also be pointed out that we found all his guides knowledgeable and dedicated," says Paul.

In six casts, Paul landed three fine trout, each over 18 inches, and lost a big fish that snapped his tippet. Wayne Vinson, Paul's partner, released a 22-inch brown and this was Wayne's first fly fishing trout trip.

I interviewed Kim on tackle, tactics and technique applicable to Bow River:

DAYMAN ON THE BOW

Q. Let's start with tackle for the Bow River. What type of fly fishing gear do you recommend and how many outfits?

Kim: An angler can get along nicely with two outfits: No. 5 or 6 weight rod for dry fly, and a No. 8 for streamer fishing. The reels

After a spirited fight, this trout is about to be landed under critical observance.

need not be expensive but should have very smooth drags, which are particularly important when using light tippets. The reels should have sufficient capacity to take a full fly line plus at least 50 yards of Micron or Dacron 20-pound backing.

Q. What about fly lines?
Kim: Naturally a floating line is used for dry fly fishing. It can be a double tapered line, but many anglers prefer the weight-forward tapers. For streamer fishing, a sink-tip line (like the Hi-D 10-foot wet tip) is recommended—you don't need a full sinking line.

One thing I should mention: Load an extra reel spool with a No. 8 floating line. Sometimes there can be strong, slashing winds and an angler might want to switch to the heavier outfit for dry fly fishing.

Q. What about a shooting head? Is distance needed on the Bow?
Kim: It's not needed. Of course if someone is comfortable in using a shooting head, it's fine, but it's not at all necessary. You don't need a lot of casting distance on the Bow.

Q. What about leaders? What length? Tippet size?

Kim: Most of the time an angler with a soft presentation will do well with a nine-foot leader, although sometimes a 12-footer might be better if the trout are particularly sensitive. But again this depends on the casting ability and presentation of the angler; there's no sense in using a very long leader, say 16 feet, unless the fisherman can straighten it out over his target. For most people, a nine to 12 foot leader will do fine. Now, of course, if the day is very windy, a shorter leader will work better. As far as tippet sizes, leaders should taper down to 4X, 5X and 6X. The 6X is used primarily for the tiny flies. For the hopper fishing, you can use a shorter leader, 7 1/2 feet, with a heavier tippet, 2X or 3X. For streamer fishing, more and more, anglers prefer a very short leader of a couple of feet; really it's just a tippet. The reason is that you want that streamer to sink fast.

Q. What about dry flies? What are your suggestions?

Kim: For most dry fly fishing, Pale Morning Duns and Caddis, No. 14 to 18, are fine. When the smaller hatches are prevalent, the Tricos and Blue Wing Olives, 18 to 22, will take care of your requirements. I think for most anglers the No. 14 to 16 dry fly works well for many conditions. You're not exactly matching the hatch. The bigger fly, however, means greater visibility, and it's important for the guest to see his fly at all times. This becomes critical if there are a number of trout sipping flies on top. The inexperienced angler may set hook even though the trout is taking a natural instead of his dry fly, simply because he can't see his fly. Now there are going to be times when one simply must use the smaller flies, especially if the trout are taking Tricos. So there can't be any hard and fast rules, but there are guidelines. To sum up, if an angler has some Light Cahills, Duns and Caddis imitation in No. 14 to 18, and some Blue Wing Olives and Tricos in 18s to 22s, he is well equipped for most fishing situations. Throw in a few Goofus Bugs, Royal Wulffs and Adams in 16s and 14s, too.

Q. Okay, but if you were going to break down the various patterns more extensively on a month-to-month basis—what are your suggestions?

Kim: Let's start with June. Pale Morning Dun imitations (Light Cahill and Cahill Quills) from 14s to 18s with 16s being most popular. Caddis in brown, tan and olive colors (Elk Hair, Henryville or Goddard patterns) in 14s to 18s, are also good. In July there is a continuation of the Pale Morning Duns until mid-month and an increasing emphasis on the caddis patterns. Sometimes hoppers appear in late July. In August, caddis are prevalent, but fish also move toward the banks and begin to feed on hoppers. Tricos appear at the end of

"Trout fishing on the Bow can be simplified or complicated. It depends on the angler..."—Kim Dayman.

August and continue to October. Tricos and Blue Wing Olives hatches are particularly heavy in September and continue into October.

Q. And streamers? Nymphs?

Kim: Wolly Buggers and leech patterns in black, in sizes 2, 4 and 6, are particularly effective. Sculpins tied on No. 2 hooks are also good, and some anglers have had good success with Matukas. Nymphs? The old reliable, Hare's Ear, in 12 to 16, plus Black and Yellow stonefly nymphs in 4s and 6s, will be sufficient.

Q. Are terrestials important patterns?

Kim: Unquestionably, terrestials are important, and the hopper is our most effective pattern. As you probably know, there were tremendous quantities of hoppers in Alberta in 1984 and 1985, so fishing with this pattern was very good. Most hopper patterns are successful, but I like the ones tied with a yellow body, on No. 8s to 12s. Whitlock's, Joe's and the Letort are three good patterns. All patterns should have legs for maximum effectiveness.

Beetles are also productive. Then we also have good fishing with ant patterns. Incidentally, during the Trico hatch, we've noticed that the ant patterns (tied with a touch of red for better visibility) work well. I believe one can make it (selection of fly patterns) as complicated as he wants to on the Bow, and some anglers enjoy this, or he can reduce his inventory to several dry fly patterns, nymphs, a few streamers and hoppers in several sizes and not feel inadequate.

Q. What about other gear? What are your recommendations?

Kim: You need chest-high waders with felt soles! Make sure they don't leak. Polaroids are necessary for seeing trout because a lot of our fishing is visual. Wide-brimmed hat, a light rain jacket and any of the assorted 101 items that trout fishermen find essential can be included. Take warm clothing but also some lightweight shirts, as weather can vary.

Q. Let's talk about casting. Some novice anglers are very interested in fishing the Bow, but are hesitant because they aren't confident of their casting. Do you have to have a 60-foot cast in your repertoire to succeed?

Kim: When the fish are feeding, if you are careful in wading, you can get fairly close to those trout, so only relatively short casts are necessary. You can get by with 30-foot casts, and even shorter presentations, at times. All things being equal, you try for the shorter casts. First, you can generally pinpoint your cast; second, you can proceed to work methodically on the fish that are closer to you; third, it's easier to set hook with a minimum of line bellying in the current; and, fourth, you can usually avoid drag. This doesn't mean that at times you aren't going to need a longer cast of, say, 50 feet. It's good to have the longer casts in your arsenal.

Q. What about during the hopper season? What type of casting is necessary at this time?

Kim: Actually, during the hopper season, when the trout are "on the make," you don't need long casts, and some fine trout have been taken on 20-foot casts. As a matter of fact, it helps at times for that fly to splash on the surface. It's more effective because it is easily noticed by the trout. This is true when there are several fish in the area, and these trout have gulped a few hoppers as appetizers. Well, they know there's competition, so the next thing that falls in the water that resembles a hopper, they are going to smash! Get there first. That's why some of the strikes on hoppers are quite explosive!

Streamer fishing requires a little longer cast. And you are fishing from the skiff and sitting down. But with a little practice, guests pick up the technique quickly. No, our casting is not as difficult here as say on some of the spring creeks of Montana.

Q. You like to work upstream with a dry fly or nymph. On some of the big western streams, there is a tendency to work across, or diagonally upstream. Your thoughts?

Kim: I really emphasize upstream fishing on the Bow for dry fly fishing. There are a number of reasons. First, I believe that most anglers, especially those with poor eyesight, can see a rise better if they are fishing upstream, though this depends on light conditions. Second, on the Bow you often find a pod of fish, maybe six to eight trout. If you are fishing across or even slightly downstream, you may hook the top fish, and this may put down the rest.

With the upstream approach, however, you can observe the feeding trout and mark their locations. Then you can proceed and take the bottom fish first and possibly hook several from the same group.

Ideally you want to show the trout the dry fly first, with a minimum of tippet. Naturally, you don't want that fly line landing on top of a trout's snout. So it's observation, location, then presentation and systematically working on the bottom fish first. You can hook several fish from a pod instead of just one.

Q. Let's talk about streamer fishing. When is it done? Best methods for success?

Kim: Most of the time we use streamers while drifting or rowing downstream, moving from one dry fly place to another. Most people prefer dry fly fishing, of course, so we fish select places by wading. But between these wading areas, the enterprising angler casts a marabou leech or Wolly Bugger pattern. Or if there's little surface activity, then we may fish streamers or nymphs. Some purists simply won't fish streamers and instead rest or check out the scenery as we drift from one dry fly spot to another. In streamer fishing, you want that cast to land as close to the bank as possible. Without hanging up! Then you want the streamer to sink fast; that's the reason for the sink-tip line and short leader. You also want to strip in so that the trout (facing upstream) see the streamer broadside. Finally, you want to keep "in touch with the streamer" by having a relatively tight line so that you can feel the take.

Q. What about winds on the Bow? Are they a problem?

Kim: They can be. Sometimes we have some strong winds swirling on the river, and they can be a problem, especially to the novice caster. A couple of things: We can often find fish in an area that is relatively quiet and, of course, in the evening, usually the winds calm down. Also, this may be the time to use the heavier outfit—either a

In six casts, Paul Melchior caught three trout, each over 18 inches: "Every serious angler should fish the Bow."

No. 7 or 8—with the dry fly line that I mentioned earlier. Yes, we can have windy conditions, but we do whatever we can to produce the best results under the circumstances.

Q. Lately, and especially in 1985 and 1986, you have had excellent seasons. There are more outfitters and, therefore, more fishermen. How do you explain this?

Kim: Well, the Bow is primarily catch-and-release. And we have also placed a daily limit whereby only one or two trout under 16 inches can be kept by the locals. Then, of course, it depends on the weather conditions during the previous seasons. Were the conditions favorable for spawning? For fry? The Bow is a natural food factory, so it can support quite a number of big trout. The rest is in conservation and, thankfully, outfitters and guests understand this.

Q. This question may be difficult to answer, but make a stab at it. On an average day, how many trout would an average angler land?

Kim: It is difficult to answer because there are so many variables. But I think I know what you mean. Hmmm...I would say perhaps 15 trout. There is a tendency to state a higher number because sometimes an angler can release five fish fairly quickly from one spot and still have the rest of the day to fish. I think "15" would be an accurate answer. Obviously, some good rods take 15 trout fairly quickly, but we're talking "average angler" here. Look, there are days when an average angler has taken 35 trout in a single day!

Q. What about the size of these fish? The guy who lands 15 fish—what's the largest he may catch that day?

Kim: Wow! I should have brought my crystal ball with me. Actually, I think that if a fisherman takes 15 fish in a day, he'll probably have landed one or two trout 20 inches or close to it. And several 16- to 18-inch trout.

Q. The Bow is primarily a rainbow trout stream. What about the browns?

Kim: The studies indicate that the ratio is about 70 rainbows to 30 browns. Some think it's a 60-40 ratio. The browns are more difficult to fool, hence some anglers feel that it is entirely, or close to being, a rainbow river. The larger fish are definitely browns.

Q. What about competition? Years ago, when A.J. McClane first popularized the Bow, there was only one outfitter. Now there are several. Plus competition from local spinning fishermen and some private boats. Your comments?

Kim: When you add boats, you add fishermen. No question about that. But the Bow is a big river and there are several floats. The local anglers fish primarily in one section, above a bridge where we often put in. Basically, I don't think that there is a problem; I think this point is driven home nicely because last year was one of the best seasons. One thing that helps is that we have two daily fishing schedules. Some clients (and guides) prefer an early session, starting in the morning and fishing until late afternoon. Others prefer starting at noon and fishing until dusk. Of course, the decision as to which period to fish is based on the hatches and the preference of the anglers. There is good cooperation among the established outfitters. Sure, each year there are a couple of new companies that enter the "market," or so it seems, but after one season they find it isn't so easy; they don't like the long hours and they give it up. We do need an association of established outfitters.

Q. There's talk about a dam going up on the Bow. Your thoughts?

Kim: I don't think that there's a chance of it going up. The locals, the outfitters and our growing Trout Unlimited chapter would all be upset. Very upset. Yes, I know there is talk about it, but I don't see it going up.

Q. Your season starts in June and terminates in early October. What are the best times, or is it fairly consistent throughout the season?

Kim: It's a consistent river provided—and that's the key word—that the weather and water conditions are "normal" and consistent. There are many variables that go into it. Heavy rains can swell a stream. Unusually cold weather can delay hatches. A scarcity of grasshoppers hurts the hopper season a little. But that's true of any river, anywhere. Our outfitting service, as well as the other established ones that serve the Bow, will do our utmost to show visiting anglers why we're so proud of our trout fishery.

BOW RIVER MISCELLANY

The guide selects the river section that he feels will be most productive. While most float trips start about 9 A.M. (to take advantage of the day's hatches), there is some flexibility. If the day's hatches are sparse, or if the weather is unusally bright and warm, the guide may suggest a later start and include some evening fishing.

Fourteen-foot flat-bottomed Jon boats are used. They are large enough to accommodate two fly fishermen and the guide who controls the boat with oars (motors are not used). Periodically, the boat is beached to allow anglers to wade a number of excellent places.

The normal procedure is as follows: Anglers fly to Calgary and check in at the Best Western Hospitality Inn-South (135 Southland Drive S. E.). A twin-bedded room runs about $70 per night. The cost of the hotel, breakfast and supper are the anglers' responsibility. The assigned guide contacts the guests that evening and briefs them. The next morning he picks them up and trails the boat to the selected part of the river to be floated. He provides a hot, tasty lunch during the midday break, and the fishing is continued until evening. In the mean-

Seth and Stuyve Pierrepont have enjoyed great trips on the Bow. This magnificent brown is about to be released.

time, his assistant moves the pick-up truck to a predetermined place. The clients are then transferred back to their hotel. It's all very convenient.

There are several excellent fishing tackle stores in Calgary, including the Country Pleasures (an Orvis shop), where equipment and fishing licenses can be purchased.

RATES AND SEASONS: Alberta Drift (as well as other outfitters) operates its float trips from June 15 to early October. The entire season offers productive fishing, when weather conditions are normal.

The cost for skiff, guide, transfers and lunch is $125 per person, based on two anglers sharing, or $200 for a single angler. A minimum of three days is suggested.

AND FINALLY...The Bow is an outstanding place to learn fly fishing as the guides are excellent teachers. Cam Dobbins, a skilled plug caster, was in Calgary for a few days and decided to fish the Bow. He learned to fly fish "on the spot" and succeeded in taking several fine trout. Obviously it is much better to pick up the fundamentals of fly casting prior to the trip, so that one can concentrate entirely on fishing.

The '86 season proved to be a banner year. Among the outstanding catches of 1986: Virginia Pierrepont—25-inch brown; Deb Eldridge—25-inch brown; Bob Jay—24 1/2-inch brown; Seth Pierrepont—24-inch brown; Tony Perry—24-inch brown; and, R. S. Pierrepont—23-inch rainbow.

Most fish by an angler in one day? Stuyve Pierrepont—36 trout (six of which were over 20 inches)!

The Mid-Canadian Provinces

Saskatchewan, Manitoba and Ontario: Thousands of Lakes, Dozens of Challenges

The dedicated fly fisherman has ignored these centrally-located provinces because they offer mainly lake fishing. But there is a world of fly fishing challenges for such denizens as northern pike, bass, muskies, lake trout and walleyes.

The author took this northern pike from Lloyd Lake Lodge in northern Saskatchewan. "They're a fun fish."

1985
STATE OF MARYLAND

Chapter 5

MID-CANADA

SASKATCHEWAN, Manitoba and Ontario are Canada's most popular fishing provinces for several reasons: (1) There are thousands and thousands of lakes, as well as numerous rivers. (Many waters are seldom fished because they can only be reached via arduous portages or by float plane.) (2) These provinces offer hundreds of camps that range from deluxe resorts to inexpensive housekeeping cottages to outpost cabins to tenting or camping trips. (3) The list of available species is extensive and includes: bass, northern pike, walleyes, muskies, whitefish, lake trout, Arctic grayling, brook trout and even rainbows. (All species are not found in each province.) (4) Furthermore, one doesn't need a high degree of fishing skill or knowledge for modest success; if one can hang on to a rod and twirl a casting or spinning reel, chances are that the guide can troll him over some productive waters for a score. So the plug caster, the spin caster, and the trollers too, find "mid-Canada" much to their liking, for they are usually able to satisfy their piscatorial ambitions.

Fine for the hardware anglers. What about the fly rodder? Is mid-Canada worthy of his consideration? Are there any fly fishing challenges?

Absolutely! Saskatchewan, Manitoba and Ontario not only provide the fly fisherman with many unique angling opportunities but also some of the toughest challenges. As an example, it's difficult to fool an adult muskie on any type of tackle, but on fly fishing gear the odds are greatly increased. It can be done, of course, but not consistently and never without difficulty.

Taking whitefish on dry flies *on a lake* is another remarkable achievement. During calm evenings, schools of whitefish can be seen dimpling the water's surface as they feed on small natural flies. "Duck soup," boasts the fly fisherman upon first observing this...until he tries it. He finds out he can get just so close with a boat to these traveling whitefish, but they always seem to be beyond casting distance. One must first decide on the fish's direction and then cast considerably in front of it. It's challenging. In fact, it is more difficult to take whitefish from a lake than bonefish on the flats!

Even the walleye, one of the most popular species among midwest anglers, is a challenge to the fly rodder. The walleye can usually be fooled by a variety of small lures or baits, but via fly fishing, it's a different matter.

There are many other challenges in mid-Canada available to those anglers who insist that fly fishing is supreme only when it's difficult. On the other hand, the fly fisherman who measures the success of a trip by the number of fish he is able to subdue also will find mid-Canada much to his liking, for there are a number of excellent gamefish that are usually in a cooperative mood when weather conditions are normal. So the mid-Canadian provinces offer opportunities for the guy who prefers challenges, as well as for the fisherman who wants action, action, action.

Let's first look at some of the species that are evenly distributed in all three provinces.

NORTHERN PIKE

One of the best targets for the fly fisherman is the much maligned northern pike. Unjustly, it is called "snake" or "hammerhead" or "slime devil," and it's obvious that in some quarters this fine species strongly needs the services of a clever public relations agent. I've fished on northern Saskatchewan waters where some of the guides detested the northern pike so much that upon landing the fish, they violently bashed its brains against the gunwale and tossed the pike on shore. (As far as I'm personally concerned, this happens only once; then the guide and I have a chat, and if he continues to do this, I ask for another guide.) Ironically, in another section of the same province, the northern pike is a coveted species.

I asked one guide why he disliked the pike. "They are slimy devils," was his only explanation. I'm not sure whether the pike has any more protective slime than the muskie, for example, its highly touted first cousin. "They eat up all the walleyes," another guide rationalized. It was obvious that this guide was not a student of nature's delicate aquatic balance. "Northern pike don't taste good," a fisherman, who had a dislike for this species, told me. Perhaps this is true in some warm, muddy, weedy waters, but on most Canadian lakes, where one can dip a cup and drink the water right from the lake, the pike is a delicacy. Menus of some four-star European and American restaurants offer a sumptuous dish, *"Quenelles de Brochet,"* which is northern pike.

The northern pike is one of mid-Canada's most valuable assets because it is very plentiful and nearly always cooperative. In addition, it is usually an excellent fighter.

I recall fishing with Jerry Tricomi, who at the time owned Camp Manitou, a popular Ontario fly-in fishing camp. We portaged to a seldom-fished lake where Jerry hooked a big northern—perhaps 14 to 16 pounds. After a couple of short-spirited runs, the fish rocketed clean out of the water by the outboard, arced across the surface and reentered his aquatic habitat near the bow of the 12-foot skiff. Jerry and I were amazed. We estimated the distance from the point at which the pike broke water to the point of re-entry to be about 10 or 11 feet. It was truly the most spectacular leap of any freshwater North American species that Jerry and I have ever witnessed. True, this was a most unusual leap, far from the norm, but pike are active fighters and sometimes their jumps are amazing.

One of the criticisms heard on some lakes where northerns are smallish (two to five pounds) is that they aren't much sport on plug casting tackle. This is true. A three-pound northern pike that tries to gobble down a four-inch spoon at the end of a 20-pound test line is not going to be much fun. The tackle definitely overpowers the fish. The fly rodder can enjoy his sport tremendously, even with small pike, simply by scaling down his tackle. A light fly rod that takes a No. 5 or 6 WF line

Bill Fontana pioneered houseboat fishing in Ontario, but shorelunches have been an institution for decades.

and a leader tapered to six pounds (with a small shock leader), and some streamers, are all one needs for increased sport.

The fly fisherman revels on waters where there are large pike: fifteen-pounders and over. Recently I fished at Lloyd Lake Lodge in northern Saskatchewan for pike on a very shallow (two to three feet) clear bay. On this sunny day, one could see northerns for quite a distance. The guide paddled the boat while we searched for big northerns. When one was located, I would make the presentation, watch the entire strike develop and enjoy the ensuing fight. It reminded me somewhat of bonefishing. The best northern that I landed on that trip was 18 1/2 pounds, but most of them were in the eight- to 12-pound class, ideal fish for the No. 7 graphite fly rod that I was using. I caught most of the fish on streamers (with a floating line), but I coaxed a few northerns to take surface poppers.

On some waters that are practically blanketed with lily pads, I cast a weedless popper right on the pads. The pike would follow the retrieved popper from below, waiting for a clearing, whereupon the northern would pounce on it with gusto! On open water, pike fishing with a surface popper is also fun. You cast, pop it a few times and retrieve it fairly quickly in jerks. Then you see the V-like wake develop as it zeroes in on the popper. You strip faster and faster, but the wake eventually catches up and devours that morsel.

Dr. Elmer Rusten has been fishing for northern pike for 35 years and now concentrates on them entirely with a fly rod. He has landed well over a thousand pike on a fly rod, and his largest is a 25 pounder. His best week was 125 pike (released) that ranged from seven to 21 pounds. He guesses that he has landed at least 40 pike in the 15- to 25-pound class, and perhaps he has caught more big pike on a fly rod than anyone else.

Since he particularly enjoys large pike on a fly, he uses a nine-foot fly rod for a No. 10 line in order to cast the bigger streamers. He is convinced that the large pike are attracted to bigger flies, and you can't very well drive a bulky No. 2/0 streamer into the wind with a light rod.

"I use a short leader, no longer than three feet most of the time, as long leaders usually are not necessary." Dr. Rusten relates. "For a shock leader, I use 20-pound mono. Depending on situations, I use both weight-forward fly lines and shooting heads. My streamers are tied on a No. 2/0 hook, and my favorite colors are red and white, white with Mylar, and black sculpins. I do use large surface poppers earlier in the season in weedy areas. Most of the time, I prefer slow, undulating retrieves with streamers, but naturally I experiment with various retrieves when fishing is poor."

Other northern pike enthusiasts prefer longer leaders, from 7 1/2 to nine feet, tapered from 30 to 10 pounds. "The longer leader may not mean a darn thing insofar as strikes are concerned, but I'm against using real short leaders for an aesthetic reason. I've been brought up on long leaders and I can't use those shorties," explains Miles Redgel. While Dr. Rusten apparently has no problem with the 20-pound mono shock leader, other anglers feel more secure in using a 30- or 40-pound test shock, and some merely attach about 10 inches of 27-pound test wire.

While the joy of pike fishing lies mostly in casting the shallow bays, at times northerns are found in deep waters where the use of sinking lines is paramount.

"When pike are not found in the normal weedy places, I like to troll the deeper waters with spoons until we find some northerns," says R.J. Ottoweigh. "Then I have the guide anchor or keep us in that vicinity while I probe the waters with a fast-sinking line and large streamer. Pike aren't necessarily a school fish, such as walleye, but they often do congregate together, and usually they are about the same size. It's sort of 'birds of a feather flock together' association. If you catch an eight-pounder, it seems that the rest of the pike in that area will be eight-pounders. If you are catching small pike (two- to four-pounders), every so often there will be a very large northern pike in the vicinity. I don't know why this is, but some guides tell me that the big pike will sometimes feed on the small fish. I have had this experience several times."

What's the best length for a northern pike streamer? "As large as one can cast," seems to be the opinion of experts. A streamer tied with five-inch saddle hackle certainly is a seductive morsel. (It is, however, air-resistant, and one needs a No. 10 fly rod to kick it out.) Some anglers use FisHair (a synthetic bucktail material) instead of hackle because it casts better and is more durable. Streamers of smaller sizes should be included because they are easier to cast in windy conditions. I encountered very strong winds one day on Lloyd Lake and had only a No. 7 graphite rod in the boat. It was difficult belting out the big streamers, so I switched to a smaller size (No. 2 hook with 2 1/2 inches of FisHair), and it worked. It was pike after pike, including an 18 1/2-pounder which, incidentally, was an exceptionally active fighter. So while large streamers are preferable, small versions can be productive.

Poppers are not as effective as streamers, but they are fun to use. Red and white or red and yellow are the favored colors, and most fly rodders use the larger saltwater models as opposed to bass-sized lures. Fish them slowly, with an occasional "kerplunk" to get the pike's attention.

LAKE TROUT

This denizen of the deep recalls memories of wire lines, big reels, heavy weights, giant spoons and endless hours of trolling. True, at the beginning or toward the end of the season, lake trout can be found in the shallows, especially after ice break-up, and can be taken by casting spoons and spinners. However, lakers are not the exclusive property of the hardware and trolling fraternity. Fly fishing for lake trout can be very effective if one picks the right time and place. Lakers have a preference for colder water, and generally seek temperatures in the 40- to 44-degree range. Thus, trout in the more northern zones are more likely to be found in shallow waters than those in southern Ontario because of the cooler water temperatures.

Some of the most enjoyable lake trout fishing I've ever encountered in mid-Canada occurred on Ontario's Manitou waters, just east of Highway 71. I had spent the entire season at Jerry Tricomi's Camp Manitou fishing mostly for muskies and bass. Jerry had told me that some of the shallow, rocky bays of Dogfly Lake (easily reached from Manitou via a portage) contained hundreds of lake trout toward the end of September. He was right.

I visited Dogfly on September 22, found the bays and was amazed to see hundreds of lake trout milling about in three to five feet of transparent water. What a sight! Using a light fly rod and a No. 2 Platinum Blonde streamer, the action was practically uninterrupted during the entire day. What was most fascinating was that I could locate the trout, which were mostly in the three- to eight-pound class, make a cast, retrieve the fly right by their noses and watch the take and, in fact, most of the fight. Because of the shallowness of the water, they streaked away at surprising speeds and often into my backing. In deep water, lake trout often "dog it" on the bottom. But this was different.

I returned to Dogfly, this time equipped with a six-foot fly rod that took a WF 5 line. I could get fairly close to the lakers, so long casts weren't necessary. It was one of the most enjoyable experiences I've ever had in Ontario. I had heard that sometimes lakers can be taken on top with small poppers or bushy dry flies, but I had no success with surface flies; however, streamers fished just below the surface produced exciting bulging strikes.

I was also successful in taking lakers in very deep water on a fly rod during that summer, but this required a different technique which wasn't as appealing as the autumnal Dogfly experience. "Hot weather" lake trout fishing entails using a fast-sinking fly line and much patience. The Manitou waters have a number of spring holes, close to shore, that attract numerous lakers. The water is about 40 to 60 feet deep and the trout hang close to the bottom. I would cast a streamer as far as I could, allow the fly line to sink and at the same time, pay out mono backing from my fly reel in order to get the fly close to the bottom. When I was convinced that the line had sunk sufficiently, I would retrieve slowly at first. If that didn't work, I would strip in line as fast as I could so that the fly zoomed to the surface. It was a method that Jerry Tricomi discovered by accident. Often the lakers would chase the fly, no doubt interested in the escaping "minnow," and sometimes the trout would grab it only a few feet from the surface! I had always been told that lakers seldom leave the deeper waters because of the difference in water pressure. Again the ensuing fight wasn't as exciting as the Dogfly encounter since it was almost entirely vertical. Up and down. We used to term it "yo-yo fishing."

That's in Ontario. As one proceeds to northern Manitoba and Saskatchewan, he is more likely to find lakers in shallow waters, especially near spring holes, but it becomes important to know where these holding waters are, so the services of a knowledgeable guide are essential. You can cast your arm off on a big lake and not hook a single trout with a fly rod if you are fishing in the wrong places. If guiding services are unavailable or insufficient, it's highly advisable to deep troll with spoons—but not with that Orvis or Leonard fly rod! Take a casting or spinning rod for this purpose. Once several lakers are hooked in a particular area, the fly rod can be brought into play. Remember to mark that spot accurately by lining up various landmarks so that you can return to it.

The lake trout available to the fly rodder will generally run from five to 10 pounds. This doesn't mean that a 20-pounder is not a possibility. The chances for a trophy laker are greatly increased in the northern parts of Manitoba and Saskatchewan.

Tackle is relatively simple to put together. An 8 1/2- or nine-foot fly rod (for No. 8 to 10 lines), a smooth-running single action fly reel, seven- to nine-foot leaders tapering to an eight- or 10-pound tippet, an assortment of streamers, and weight-forward fly lines are the requisites. The most important ingredient of fly fishing for lake trout is an assortment of fly lines. As mentioned earlier, there are times when one can fish for lakers successfully with floating lines, but most of the time, the angler will be using sinking types ranging from slow to the fast-sinking or lead-core lines.

Lake trout seem to have a penchant for white streamers with several strands of silver Mylar, tied in, on hook sizes ranging from No. 2 to 2/0. Purple and white or blue and white patterns are also productive, and be sure to include weighted and unweighted streamers in your fly box.

WALLEYE

The two most commonly voiced criticisms regarding the walleye are that it isn't a good fighter and that it isn't very bright upstairs. True, the walleye is not a particularly dashing fighter. It runs, it struggles, it resists, but not with the same oomph or style as other gamefish. By the end of the second or third round, it is tuckered out on the canvas. Intelligence? I don't know where it would rank in a Stanford Binet I.Q. test among gamefish. Yes, at times it is easily caught because the walleye is basically a school fish, and once the student body is located, an angler can land a number of them in quick order. But at other times, this fish is difficult to locate or fool, and even the expert walleye anglers (and there are thousands of them) are totally befuddled when their electronic gadgetry and wide assortment of lures and freshly-stocked minnow buckets aren't seducing this "easy" fish.

The Disco Trout is a superb pattern for Arctic grayling and other species. See page 116 for dressing.

So the fly rodder in pursuit of walleyes is challenged, and it is this challenge that makes fly fishing for walleye appealing.

My fishing ego is bruised continuously, but one of the most deflating experiences occurred recently in northern Saskatchewan on Lloyd Lake. It's one of the province's best walleye waters. Lloyd is a relatively shallow lake, and walleyes are found off gravely or rocky bars where the water is scarcely five or six feet deep, which presents an ideal situation for a medium-sinking line. The plug casters and spinners were catching many large walleyes. After I satisfied myself that the fish were definitely there by catching some on spinning gear, I switched to a fly rod. My fly fishing results were very meager by comparison. Originally I thought that the fly rodder might have an advantage because the walleyes were feeding on small minnows, which are easily imitated with any number of streamers.

One reason for the ineffectiveness of fly fishing is that a walleye is a light hitter; usually it doesn't smack a lure or fly hard. I suspect that I received a lot of strikes that I was unaware of, because these hits were not perceptibly transmitted through the line. On other trips, however, I have had far better success with walleyes, especially on waters where there were some weed beds near rocky bars.

White streamers with Mylar are generally effective, but on some lakes I've found that long black marabou flies are sensational (undoubtedly because they are a close imitation of leeches). The emphasis in selecting the right type of sinking line can't be overestimated. While one would think that a fast-sinking line would always be the answer, bear in mind that it may cause numerous hang-ups if the lake's bottom is cluttered with obstructions.

Some of the most delightful fly fishing for walleyes I've enjoyed has been on rivers with an average or fast current. River walleyes are used to having their food swoosh by them rapidly, so they must make an instant decision whether to grab a morsel or not. In lakes, walleyes probably take their time and investigate a lure carefully. Also, the river's current gives the fish an advantage; thus the fight is more stimulating.

Is the walleye a fly rodder's species? On a scale of one to ten, my answer lies somewhere between three and four. There are much better gamefish, but there is some interest in this species because it is a persnickety feeder. And speaking of feeding, in the gastronomical category, the walleye is a solid "10" all the way! Nothing can beat a shore lunch of golden fried walleye fillets, baked beans and homemade bread, while the coffee is simmering on crackling logs.

SMALLMOUTH BASS

I have a particular fondness for the smallmouth bass that stems back to preteen fishing expeditions to local waters. The smallmouth is a beautiful fish, but, more importantly, it is a tremendous fighter, an excellent leaper and it will attack a variety of lures.

Immediately, the smallmouth conjures up a personal experience that remains somewhat embarrassing even today. When I was 16, I fished Ontario's Kishkutena Lake, which is just east of Highway 71 between Fort Frances and Kenora. I had a chance to fish it for only two days and I quickly concluded that Kishkutena had to be the best smallmouth bass lake in the world. I wanted to return there the following year, but limited funds were a major problem. I belonged to a sportsman's club that was mainly composed of successful, affluent sportsmen, and why Paul Brewer, another teenager, and I were allowed to join always escaped me. At any rate, I baited two anglers, who had fished most of the fine smallmouth waters of Canada, into a bet. To win, I would have to land 50 smallmouth bass on a fly rod during one selected day. If I did this, the two older (and more affluent!) members, Wally Bolland and Bob Feldtman, would have to pay for the entire two-week trip. If I failed, Paul Brewer, whom I implicated in this bet, and I would have to pay. Paul wanted to fish this lake but was highly reluctant: "I don't have the money. What if we lose?" He was understandably concerned.

"Neither do I, so we can't lose," I countered. The folly of youth. The first fishing day was beautiful and I decided that this was the day to try to win the bet. The intricate rules stated that the other anglers could not fish but could observe from a separate boat.

It was one of those fantastic days. We started at dawn, and by 11 A.M., I had landed 37 bass on flies. Bob and Wally conceded the bet, as they were anxious to fish this Shangri-la. Obnoxiously, I insisted that the bet be completed, and it was. Paul and I were able to relax and enjoy one of the best fishing vacations imaginable. Although the rest of the trip provided good fishing, I doubt that on any other day I would have been able to catch 50 smallmouth on a fly, and I'm sure that Paul and I would have lost our bet. Today, many years wiser, I wouldn't have accepted a similar bet for six fish under any circumstances!

What makes the smallmouth an ideal fly rod species is that it can be taken on top with poppers, or on large bushy bivisible dry flies, streamers, muddlers and big wet flies. The smallmouth is primarily found in lakes but also inhabits streams and rivers.

Ironically, the smallmouth was not native to northwestern Ontario but was an introduced species. Lakes like Kishkutena contained huge populations of native largemouths, but the planted smallmouths eventually took over. The late Ernie Calvert, one of the pioneers in the camp outfitting business on Lake of the Woods, once told me that he had placed only 13 (his lucky number) smallmouths in Kishkutena (and other lakes) and was amazed that such a small planting took hold.

Sadly, for unknown reasons, smallmouth bass fishing has declined in many northwestern Ontario waters, and this has numerous camp owners puzzled. This fish is very hearty, durable and pugnacious, and it is hard to believe that it is losing its battlegrounds to other species. Even Kishkutena Lake is experiencing a downspin despite the fact that there are no fishing resorts on these waters, only a few outpost camps.

In Ontario, Lake of the Woods, the Pipestone chain, Manitou, Eagle Lake and dozens, if not hundreds, of other waters still produce good smallmouth bass fishing, but not of the same quantity or quality as in previous decades. In Manitoba, the fish's distribution is limited, but Crowduck and George Lake (east of Winnipeg) are two of the most productive waters. In one of Manitoba's annual contests, for example, 45 of the top 100 bass entered came from Crowduck (largest 5.7 pounds) and 17 were caught from George (6.2 pounds was the largest). George is fished much less than Crowduck. The Winnipeg River is another fine choice. Saskatchewan, to my knowledge, doesn't have any smallmouth lakes.

Just about any type of good fly tackle is usable on smallmouth. When the bass are selective, I prefer to use longer leaders (nine feet) tapered down to eight- or sometimes six-pound test, and switch to smaller streamer flies. Any color combinations seem to work, though if action is slow, the wise angler continually changes patterns until the right one is discovered. If a bright Mylar streamer doesn't produce, switch to a somber brown or black fly. If underwater flies are not productive, a popping bug fished slowly could be the answer.

THE ARCTIC GRAYLING

There are a number of northern Saskatchewan and a few Manitoba waters that contain this fine sporting fish.

If one were to name a species specifically invented to satisfy the dry fly fisherman, some consideration must be given to the

Arctic grayling. Usually it averages 1 1/2- to two-pounds, but on some rivers it grows larger. Because of the grayling's size, the fly rodder goes ultralight. A No. 4 or No. 5 fly rod is ideal, and leaders should be long and tapered down to 4X. An assortment of small dry flies completes the basics. Historically, the Black Gnat is the favored dry fly, but there are other patterns that I prefer, mainly because of the Gnat's low visibility. The Disco Trout is my favorite. It's tied as follows:

Hook:	No. 12 Mustad 94840
Tail:	Golden Pheasant tippet
Body:	Grayish or olive dubbing
Wing:	White calf tail tied down-wing fashion
Hackle:	Grizzly and brown

The Disco Trout is easy to see and floats well, but most importantly, it is very appealing to grayling, especially when caddisflies are prevalent.

While fishing Clearwater River (Saskatchewan) for grayling a few years ago, I found the action slow on some evenings. Yet the bushes and alders were loaded with caddisflies. So prior to fishing, I shook these bushes, which sent dozens of caddisflies cavorting over the stream and into the water. Invariably, the unmistakable large dorsal fins of grayling would cut the surface as they began to take these naturals. The initial topwater feeding by these few feeding fish aroused the appetite of other grayling, which finally resulted in superb action on artificials. On some grayling rivers, and the Clearwater specifically, it's important to place a fly on the exact channel of the fish's feeding lane. I have noticed that at times grayling will rise freely in a particular channel but will not budge more than a few feet to the left or right.

MUSKELLUNGE

This species is found in Ontario but not in Saskatchewan or Manitoba (except on Manitoba's Lake of the Woods). The muskie may very well be freshwater's most elusive gamefish and, frankly, cannot be rated as a top fly rod species. It is this elusiveness that creates a mixed reaction among anglers; fishermen either totally ignore this species or become so totally addicted to "muskie fever" that no other species can capture their interest. There's a special, inexplicable mystique that surrounds the muskie, and the fanatical pursuit of this species by a small segment of the angling fraternity borders somewhere between mania and madness, mostly the latter I suspect.

There are lakes that host numerous small muskies, usually from 25 to 32 inches, that can be enticed to smack a surface popper or a streamer fished close to the edge of a weed bed. On the right day, one can have a fair amount of action from these smaller muskies, even when fly fishing.

It's the adult muskies, the ones that are measured in pounds instead of inches, that provide one of freshwater angling's greatest challenges. And, logically, the bigger the muskie, the greater the challenge. Obviously, the 15- to 20-pound fish are more common than the over-25-pound trophies. The great muskieman, Len Hartman, who fished the St. Lawrence River in its halcyon days, landed a number of big muskies on a fly rod (using poppers) and his best was over 30 pounds. However, very few muskies of over 20 pounds have been caught on flies.

Muskies are difficult to fool on any tackle, but trying to fool a big muskie on a fly can devastate the ego.

The problem is that the number of adult muskies is greatly limited in any given body of water. One fisheries employee told me that he thought there were no more than 30 to 40 muskies of over 20 pounds in a particular lake of Ontario that is about seven miles long and about one mile wide. That's not a lot of fish.

Furthermore, when a muskie is hungry, it chomps on a sizeable morsel, and that may be the end of its feeding for the day. Back to snoozing. Muskies can be highly curious at times and will follow retrieved lures right to the boat. Again and again. They seldom hit them, and it almost appears that these tactics are purposeful—to antagonize or to drive anglers into a frenzy. The image of a 35- to 45-pound muskellunge slowly appearing from out of the darkness of a deep weed bed to follow a bait right to the boat will always send shivers up my spine.

For the masochistic fly fishermen interested in hooking a large muskie, there are two types of flies that can entice this ornery critter: a large saltwater fly rod popper that creates a lot of surface disturbance and a long streamer. The fly fisherman should retrieve the popper as erratically and as quickly as he can across the tops of weed beds or along rocky shoals or reefs. It's usually a first-cast proposition; if a muskie ignores the popper on the initial cast, chances are that it will ignore all future presentations. The boat must be paddled quietly (no outboards!) to the muskie's haunt, where the angler unleashes a long cast. Just as the popper lands, he begins the fast retrieve, stopping the popper now and then, but only for an instant. It's a tiring exercise in futility for the most part, but occasionally the persistent angler is rewarded with a strike. Sometimes the strike is so explosive that it will shatter the angler's nerves as well as the stillness of the water; other times the muskie merely grabs it with its jaws without much surface disturbance.

Big, long streamers, five- to seven-inches long, tied on a 2/0 hook, can seduce a big muskie. A medium-sinking line is very desirable, and while streamers can be effective off reefs and shoals, the edges of weed beds are also productive places for muskies.

I haven't had much success with big muskies on a fly rod, but I recall one afternoon fishing a big streamer in a weedy bay of

Ontario's Grant Lake. The weeds were sparse but long, perhaps ten feet. I hooked a very good muskie, but even the No. 10 fly rod was not a strong enough deterrent to prevent the fish from swishing all around the weeds before the hook came loose. The fly line cut many of the weeds, and after resting this bay for a couple of hours, I duplicated the experience with the second muskie. I got only a glimpse of each fish, but I suspect that both were in the 25- to 35-pound class.

Although one can fish a streamer in sparsely-weedy waters without continually hanging up, it's recommended that a supply of streamers tied with mono weedguards is included.

BROOK TROUT

You'll find brook trout in Manitoba and Ontario, but its distribution in these two provinces is not extensive. The largest brook trout from mid-Canada come from Gods River in Manitoba, where each season specimens of six pounds or larger are landed. The biggest brookie that I know of scaled 8 1/2 pounds. Another river that has produced good brook trout fishing is Island River, at Island Lake. Here a four-pounder is considered a fine trout.

Ontario has several excellent brook trout streams that are probably most conveniently fished from Miminiska Lodge, just north of Thunder Bay. Jim Cook, midwestern outdoor writer, fished the Suzanne River out of Miminiska in 1986 and reported fast action. "In two hours, Troy Huggins and I landed 11 brook trout that scaled up to four pounds, but we lost a real trophy that probably weighed over six pounds."

I've fished and explored some of the waters north of Sault Ste. Marie, MI., in the White River area of Ontario. The late Bill Blades, one of the the greatest fly tiers of all time, described great fishing adventures for squaretails when I was a kid. When I was able to make the trip later, as a teenager, Steve Primis and I loaded up our jalopy with camping equipment, food that we swiped from our cupboards, and our canoe. We emptied our small bank accounts and spent practically a month fishing this region. We portaged from lake to lake and never saw another person, but our results were indeed very meager, as sometimes we were lucky to get a few trout each day for the pan. I believe it was our total inexperience that accounted for our poor results. For one thing, I know we spent more time paddling and portaging than in actual fishing, for we always assumed that the next bend, river or lake would be loaded with big speckled trout. "Let's get away from civilization," Steve would say. He was a powerful, energetic person and sometimes carried our Old Town canoe a mile or two before setting it down. I trudged behind him, always encouraging him, carrying a few essentials and rods. We were rewarded with a three-pounder for all our foolishness. Okay, a 2 1/2-pounder.

But the famed Gods River, Miminiska's rivers to the north, Island River and a few other places deserve a shot. Unquestionably, the spinner man does well at Gods River, but some fly rodders confess that they don't do well on feathers. So the fly fisherman logically confines his energies to Labrador and some rivers in Quebec, if his main target is *Salvelinus fontinalis,* and especially if he is looking for a trophy brook trout. (Forget about ever breaking Dr. W. J. Cook's all tackle brook trout record of 14 1/2 pounds, caught from the Nipigon River, Ontario in 1916. That record will be with us forever!)

FISHING CAMPS

It would require several volumes to cover most of the fishing camps in Ontario, Manitoba and Saskatchewan. There are probably several hundred fishing facilities in Ontario's Lake-of-the-Woods area alone! Let's look at a few representative resorts in each province.

ONTARIO

CANADIAN WILDERNESS FLOATING LODGES: Bill Fontana provides a fleet of houseboats, ranging from 35 to 55 feet, on Ontario's sprawling Rainy Lake. Anglers live aboard the houseboats and fish from small outboard-powered skiffs. Guides and cooks are available for all houseboats (and are mandatory for the larger craft) for an additional surcharge. The "Wayfarer" (42-foot houseboat) sleeps four comfortably and costs approximately $1,000 per week, plus incidentals and food; thus, for about $250 plus per person per week, one can enjoy one of the great bargains in Canadian fishing. Maps, consultation and food lists are thoughtfully provided by Bill Fontana. Rainy Lake is one of Ontario's favorite smallmouth waters, but one can also fish for northern pike and walleyes. Muskies are seldom caught at Rainy Lake, but when they are, they tend to be big.

CAMP MANITOU: This comfortable American-plan resort is reached via a 35-minute float plane charter from Fort Frances, Ontario (across the border from International Falls, MN.). The camp offers smallmouth bass, lake trout, northern pike and muskies on the extensive Manitou and at a number of jewel-like lakes reached by short portages. A week's fishing with guide and charter plane service will run about $800 per person.

HAWK LAKE LODGE: Until recently, this extremely comfortable fishing lodge was owned by a major international corporation and used as a retreat for its executives. It was purchased by Garry and Sandy Delton and was opened to the public. Hawk Lake Lodge is located a scant 28 miles from the Kenora airport and accommodates up to 24 guests.

It is also one of the best smallmouth lakes in this region, and bass of over four pounds are caught each season. The waters are crystal clear, and the gravel bottom provides an ideal habitat for bass. Guests also have access to a half-dozen lakes which contain boats and canoes. In addition to bass, these waters also provide good fishing for lake trout and northern pike and walleyes.

Because the main lake is only five miles long, guides are not needed. All guests receive a two-hour tour of the lake and are provided with large accurate maps (guides available optionally). The rate for six-nights and five days fishing is $625 per person from Kenora.

CARIBOU FALLS LODGE: It's located on the English River, just north of Kenora. A lodge often reflects the personality of the owners, and in this case, it's class. Mr. and Mrs. Dutch Ackerman insist that the camp is immaculate, that the meals are the best that they can provide and that the camp's staff is attentive and polite. Smallmouth bass, walleyes and northern pike are featured, and the quality is nearly always determined by weather conditions. Dutch also knows a number of small lakes to which he flies his guests; included in his repertoire is Manitoba's Crowduck, famous for its smallmouth. You can charter a float plane to Caribou Falls (from Fort Frances or Kenora) or you can drive to the camp. About $180 per person per day plus incidentals.

MIMINISKA'S SPORTSMAN LODGE: A little-known lodge, which is a short charter flight from Pickle Lake, Ontario (served by commercial service), offers good fishing for northern pike and walleyes and is also a fine place to fly fish for brook trout. William Embry and his daughter, for instance, caught a number of speckled trout ranging from two to six pounds, mostly on streamers but also on dry flies, with the Humpy being the best pattern. A number of fly-out and boat trips are available on Miminiska (for a surcharge). Count on $160 per day per person.

KEYAMAWUN LODGE: A posh resort located at the western end of Deer Lake, the headwaters of the Severn River system. Deer Lake, about 120 miles north of Red Lake, Ontario, is 60 miles in length and has numerous rivers and streams flowing into it. Fishing is for walleyes, northern pike and lake trout. In addition to the main fishing grounds, Keyamawun owns a Beaver float plane, which may be chartered for side trips to other lakes.

Keyamawun Lodge was built in 1979 by the Weyerhaeuser family and nothing was spared for the comfort of its guests. It was recently sold to Stu and Kathy Loten who are dedicated to carrying on the fine tradition of offering superb accommodations, exquisite meals and excellent service. A week's trip runs $1,655 per person, which includes the round trip flight from Winnipeg, Man., via the lodge's own Grumman Goose, meals, accommodations, guide, boat, motor and fuel.

RESERVE-A-RESORT: This a consortium of approximately 20 fishing resorts that are mostly located in northwestern Ontario. Mark Duggan heads the organization which is headquartered in Kenora, Ontario. All camps selected have been graded "three stars" or higher and offer a variety of fishing facilities that range from housekeeping cottages to the deluxe fly-in resorts. Reserve-A-Resort has an excellent brochure which profiles each camp, provides rates, travel information, and, in fact, all details for booking a successful fishing trip in Ontario.

MANITOBA

PINE ISLAND LODGE: PIL is located on the Winnipeg River, about 100 miles northeast of Winnipeg. Two of its important advantages are that the camp is very accessible and Pine Island Lodge also provides some excellent fishing opportunities. Guests fly to Winnipeg, are transferred by car to Pointe du

Fishing for lake trout with a fly rod is fairly easy once you locate them and fish at their level.

Bois, and after a 20-mile scenic boat trip, arrive at the lodge. The total trip takes about two hours. Thus, overnighting in Winnipeg is avoided.

Smallmouth bass (late May and most of June and again in late August and early September), walleyes (June and July) and northern pike (any time) are the main species. In addition to the Winnipeg River, guests fish Crowduck, one of Manitoba's finest smallmouth lakes, or Echo Lake for walleyes. These waters are reached by float plane or by a short portage. George Lake is a "fly-in" hotspot for big smallmouth bass, but also offers lake trout. This American Plan camp has a capacity of 32; accommodations are in modern cottages and the five-day package, including guide, is $895.

SICKLE LAKE LODGE: Brian McIntosh's relatively new camp (1980) is a short plane hop from Lynn Lake and is one of Canada's premier northern pike camps. Brian instituted a trophy policy (only one large northern pike can be kept by a guest), so the ecology of his lakes remains mostly undisturbed. That's why in 1986, 122 pike weighing over 20 pounds were landed (and most of them released) by the camp's clientele. Capacity has been increased to 28 guests, but the lodge now offers 14 different lakes, some reached by portages. Walleye fishing has taken an up-turn and there is also some lake trout fishing. However, Sickle Lake Lodge is a place where the fly rodder can cast those long streamers for giant *Esox lucius*. The weekly rate, including charter from Winnipeg, guides and meals, plus two fly-outs, is $1,895 per person/week.

LITTLE CHURCHILL LODGE: Mike Dyste's well-organized camp is located where the Little Churchill River pours into a 75,000-acre lake with the unpronounceable name of Waskaiowaka. This is northern pike country, and the fly rodder can be kept busy hooking, landing and releasing pike on a continuing basis. While most pike will run well under 10 pounds, there are plenty of trophies (18 pounds and larger) that will occasionally chomp at a streamer. Often it's shallow-water fishing where the angler first spots his quarry and then makes his presentation. If Lake "Wawa" is windy, there's no problem because the Little Churchill River is always fishable.

There is also fast fishing for walleyes. This resort offers a number of outpost housekeeping cabins (you do your own cooking) on four different lakes. The main camp is $1,580 per week (American Plan) which includes the charter plane service from Thompson, Manitoba.

BIG HOOK LODGE: Island Lake is a biggie—it's 60 miles long and contains over 3,000 islands, numerous inlets and tributaries. Northern pike up to 20 pounds are taken each year. The best walleye in 1982 was a very respectable 7.9 pounds, and in 1985 a brace of 7-lb., 7-oz. walleyes were landed. The camp also offers lake trout; though trophies aren't commonly caught here; periodically a very big laker (of over 30 pounds) is taken from Island Lake. One of the more interesting side trips offered is for brook trout on the picturesque Island River which is about 12 miles north of the lodge and is reached by boat. Brookies reproduce naturally, and while the average size is 1 1/2 to two pounds, each year trout of over four pounds are taken. The accommodations are excellent, meals are tasty, and owners Tom and Sue Brotherston, who purchased the camp recently, are constantly making improvements. Guests are flown to Big Hook Lodge by scheduled commercial service (prop plane) from Winnipeg. The weekly rate is $1,190 per person, which includes guides, boats, motors, meals, accommodations and the round-trip air service between Winnipeg and the lodge.

GODS COUNTRY LODGE: Gods Lake was the place to fish in the 1950s. The "Abercrombie and Fitch types" raised their voices slightly every time they mentioned Gods Lake. It's still a good lake to fish. It gained enormous fame because of its giant lake trout (up to 53 pounds), but it also has a fine reputation for huge brookies (up to eight pounds) that are caught at Gods River. Speckled trout probably average in the three-pound class, lakers and northerns average 12 to 15 pounds and walleyes will weigh three to four pounds. All respectable sizes. The weekly rate at Gods Country is $1,500 per person, which includes the charter plane from Winnipeg.

TONAPAH LODGE: Walleyes, northern pike and lake trout are featured at this modern, drive-in fishing lodge located on the east end of Lake Athapapuskow, a scant 20 miles from the

Crowduck and George Lakes are two of Manitoba's outstanding smallmouth waters—for numbers and size.

Flin Flon airport. This lake has 1,500 miles of shoreline plus 500 islands, so there is plenty of casting room. Athapapuskow produced a world-record lake trout of 63 pounds, which has since been eclipsed by a 65-pounder from Great Bear Lake, N.W.T. The fly rodder, however, will undoubtedly concentrate on lakers under 15 pounds. Walleyes can provide fast action, and while most will run 2 1/2 to four pounds, there are numerous six- to eight-pounders taken each season. There are also hefty northern pike that will interest the fly rodder and elusive whitefish to challenge his patience. A week's fishing, all inclusive, costs $1,285 per person (based on double occupancy).

GUNISAO LAKE LODGE: Jim Gulay's camp has gained considerable fame for its big walleyes during the month of June, but there's also fast northern pike and some lake trout fishing. The lodge also offers two outpost camps on Trout and Bennett Lakes. The season starts in late May and continues to early October. The weekly rate is $1,300 per person, which includes the charter from Winnipeg.

SASKATCHEWAN

LLOYD LAKE LODGE: This comfortable fishing resort is located in northwest Saskatchewan. Lloyd Lake is relatively small, shallow and rocky and is possibly the best walleye lake of this province. It's also a good place for northern pike, but the emphasis is definitely on walleyes. There is superb grayling fishing at one of the rivers, but it's limited to two small areas and cannot take fishing pressure. Lloyd Lake Lodge also offers lake trout fishing at nearby Preston Lake, reached by portaging. Additionally, there is a pothole lake close to camp, which is spring-fed and deep, so a number of years ago rainbow trout were introduced here and the planting took hold. Today, rainbows up to five pounds are taken each year. Obviously Lloyd Lake offers considerable variety, and with owners Mary Jean and Richard Pliska looking after the guests' needs, Lloyd Lake Lodge is an appealing destination. Most clients fly to Ft. McMurray, Alberta, and then take a one-hour charter to the camp's private strip. The daily camp is about $175 per day, guide and meals included.

SPORTSMAN'S LODGE: Tom Pierce's camp, located on the south end of McIntosh Lake (50 miles north of La Ronge), is one of Saskatchewan's old standbys. The big attraction for the fly fisherman is probing the numerous weed beds for northern pike. There are also several whitewater chutes and rapids where walleyes congregate, and much of the time these places are very reliable. Nearby lakes also offer lake trout fishing, and the best times for this species are early and late in the season.

Sportsman's Lodge features a large recreation room with a big fireplace, carpeted dining room, a well-stocked tackle shop and cocktail lounge. Anglers are accommodated in individual cabins and meals are rated as outstanding. A five-day fishing trip, including the charter plane service from La Ronge, costs approximately $1,200 per person.

WOLLASTON LAKE LODGE: Located in the northeast part of Saskatchewan, Wollaston is unique in that it offers direct DC-3 flights from Minneapolis. Wollaston offers the gamut: big northerns, lake trout, whitefish, walleyes and Arctic grayling. For those who like to fish other nearby waters, there is a float plane stationed right at camp and fly-outs can be arranged to Murphy, Big Stone Rapids and other lakes.

Wollaston can accommodate over 50 anglers, but generally limits the capacity to a manageable 30. Sleek, 16-foot aluminum boats with a front deck and swivel chairs are featured. The camp's record for northern pike is a hefty 31-pounder, lake trout of over 40 pounds have been taken from these waters, and the top grayling is four pounds. The four-day fishing trip, including the round trip charter from Minneapolis, costs $1,395 per person.

HATCHET LAKE LODGE: Hatchet is an 18-mile-long lake, about 100 miles from the Northwest Territories border, that offers lake trout, walleye, grayling, northern pike and whitefish. The northern pike is primarily responsible for the camp's fishing reputation, but, frankly, the big draw is that owner George Fleming operates one of the smoothest camps in mid-Canada.

The accommodations and service would be top-rated anywhere, but when one considers the remote location of this lodge, it's doubly appreciated. Besides Hatchet, George can arrange for short fly-out trips to a half-dozen other lakes, including some grayling waters.

The weekly rate is $1,795, which includes the charter plane service from Winnipeg.

REINDEER LAKE LODGE: This camp was recently purchased by Wayne Gangler, who immediately began a renovation program. Today, RLL is a delightful lodge, strategically located near some of the Reindeer's finest fishing grounds. In addition to northern pike (up to 30 pounds), walleyes and lake trout, one can also enjoy Arctic grayling fishing with a fly rod ("some evenings you can see them dimpling near the dock"). The weekly rate is $1,195, which includes the round trip charter service from Lynn Lake.

WHEN TO GO

Ontario's waters are usually free of ice in mid-May and most camps stay open until early or mid-October. Usually, Ontario waters are more productive during early June and late

September. Manitoba and Saskatchewan camps are open in late May in the southern part of the provinces and early June as one progresses north. They generally close sometime in late September, depending on the latitude.

While the emphasis is on early and late fishing in Ontario by the majority of anglers, it should not be construed that these are the only times these waters are productive. I've had some of the best possible fishing in late July and early August. Manitoba and Saskatchewan, especially the northern sections, provide consistent fishing during the entire season.

ON WINNIPEG

Many of the Manitoba and Saskatchewan and some Ontario camps use Winnipeg as the gateway city. Invariably, the angler fishing north finds it necessary to spend at least one night in Winnipeg either prior to or after his fishing trip.

There are a number of good hotels in Winnipeg and among the top rated are: International Inn (adjacent to the airport), the Winnipeg Inn (2 Lombard Place) and the Holiday Inn (350 St. May Avenue).

Favorite restaurants include Hy's Steak Loft (216 Kennedy Street), the Rib Room at the Charter House, the Factor's Table (in the Fort Gary Hotel), Olivers (185 Lombard Street) and Chez Andre (426 Main Street).

For nightlife with a disco beat: Studio 44, Bogart's and Left Bank.

AND FINALLY... While the mid-Canadian provinces are not the favorite among dedicated fly fishermen, the potential of Ontario, Manitoba and Saskatchewan can't be ignored. Most of the species are challenging and the fly rod can be a very efficient instrument in the hands of an accomplished angler.

But to me, there is another special dimension, because these provinces feature the famous Canadian shore lunch: golden fried fish, baked beans, coffee brewing over a log fire. This ritual, followed by a half-hour snooze under rustling pines, can certainly make every world problem disappear. At least temporarily.

Labrador

Home of the World's Largest Brook Trout

Where brook trout fishing remains almost as good as it ever was (would you believe a 5-pound trophy average?). Some of the better Atlantic salmon rivers, and how to tip the odds for success in your favor. About a place where four anglers landed over 2,000 Arctic char in a week...And why Labrador will remain the same for decades to come.

Harvey Smith probably has landed more big brook trout than anyone else. This trophy weighed 8 1/4 pounds!

Chapter 6

LABRADOR

THE FLIGHT wasn't that long from Goose Bay to an unnamed river, which the bush pilot insisted was loaded with brook trout, big trout. From the Twin Otter, one's imagination was quickly activated as shimmering lakes and silver ribbons of streams and rivers appeared one after another, and you wished you had an unending, carefree summer to try many of them. Much like Lee Wulff's legendary exploratory trips of the fifties.

Surely many of these waters, tucked so far away from the tentacles of organized civilization, have seldom been fished. Perhaps never. And while you know, deep inside of you, that virgin waters aren't a guarantee for great fishing, you choose not to think of this. Not now, anyway. Instead, you prefer to fantasize that maybe in that pond, just below the plane's wing, maybe there's a squaretail so big that it might even challenge Dr. Cook's world record brook trout.

And see over there? Where that river pours, oh so angrily, into that boulder-studded pool? Surely there are dozens of energized Atlantic salmon, possibly hundreds, nervously awaiting the ideal condition that will make their swim upstream for the mating ritual easier. You picture yourself standing right there, next to the flat boulder. You would place a Royal Wulff at the top of the sluice of water and watch it dance teasingly into the pool. And you know that one of those Atlantics surely would rise for your fly. Maybe not on the first cast. Or the fiftieth. But you just know that it would happen.

Lee Wulff explored Labrador years ago. This Adlatok river salmon action was photographed by Ted Rogowski.

The plane finally landed on a small secluded lake, taxied close to the river's mouth, and four very anxious fishermen jumped into ankle deep water. As we unloaded our gear, we could see J.C. Campbell—a member of our party who flew in earlier in the day—fighting a hefty brook trout, and another, Bardon Higgins, releasing one. It wasn't long before Dr. Dan Moos, Art Thrun and the rest of us had our tackle together, slipped into our waders and began to catch trout.

J.C. said that he had landed a couple of dozen brook trout that morning, and we believed him. Maybe he landed 50 or 60 or 70 during that entire day, but whatever the number, it would be impressive. These were two- to four-pound brookies flaunting their most fantastic orange colors.

Minutes after assembling his fly gear, Art Thrun (who never fished for brook trout before), tied on to a 4 3/4-pound brook trout that he beached, admired and released. "There is no such thing as a bad fisherman on these waters," he muttered.

The pilot never told us the name of the river, but then we never really asked him. You can't blame him, of course, because this was the sort of place that a man keeps to himself and shares with a few paying guests, but only if he is convinced that they will appreciate it and never abuse the stream. The pilot wandered off to another section of the river, and sometime later during that glorious day, when maybe even I had enough of fishing, I caught up with him.

"There aren't many salmon here. This isn't a good salmon river, although a few come up. I've rolled one twice," he allowed. He changed to another fly pattern, then another size, then still another pattern, his fingers deftly tying them on to his wispy leader quickly, with spider-like precision and agility. In one sense one could say he was a very patient man: He had stood at this particular pool for over an hour without testing his fly rod even once. In another sense, he was impatient: He seldom allowed more than three or four casts to float over the salmon's domain before changing the fly. The presentations were delivered swiftly, but accurately, and he kept insisting that on this day, the fish would be taken on a dry fly. He was right, for he did just that. He killed that salmon and trudged back with it to his plane. It would be supper that night for his family, he said.

Labrador's brook trout fishing is probably the world's best. Catch-and-release fishing is one reason why.

THE LABRADOR MYSTIQUE

This was my first trip to Labrador. I've been back, of course. It's a corner of the angler's world that, periodically, one is compelled to revisit, not only for its salmon and the colorful brook trout, but also for its seclusion. Much of Labrador is desolate, almost stark, and one feels an inexplicable magnetism, a mystique.

It's true that many fishing places change through the years, but I can't imagine Labrador will ever undergo a major facelift. A tuck here and there—when a bridge or dam is built, or a new road is constructed—but much of Labrador will remain untouched. I'm sure.

It will never be overrun with fishermen, like some other Canadian areas have been. There are reasons for this. For one, Atlantic salmon can only be fished for with a fly rod in Canada. That eliminates the plug casters, the spinning men and the bait fishermen. Even some of the trout resorts have established "fly fishing only" restrictions, and several outfitters allow for the killing of only one brook trout either for mounting or for food, which eliminates those fishermen who insist on going home with a cooler full of fish for domestic consumption. (Or is it ego satisfaction?) Furthermore, there aren't any deluxe fishing camps in Labrador; the anglers who insist on every comfort of home will be attracted elsewhere.

While Labrador's brook trout fishing rates among the best in the world, it's unfortunate that the Atlantic salmon population has diminished here, as it has in many parts of Canada, as well as in the entire world. There was a time, certainly in my lifetime, when one could go to the Pinware, or the Forteau or the Eagle and catch many salmon; even the novice scored well. Outstanding catches are made today, of course, but they aren't as frequent—not by a long shot—and one has to be more skilled, more patient and lucky enough to have selected the best run of the season. It's the commercial netting that has hurt, here and elsewhere.

BROOK TROUT FISHING

It was Lee Wulff, more than any other person, who attracted and focused the angler's attention on Labrador's superb brook trout fishing. Flying his own float plane, he explored many promising waters and uncovered the best brook trout waters in North America. In 1966 Curt Gowdy and Lee produced a film for the "American Sportsman" television series featuring Labrador brook trout. Although the specific area was initially kept a secret, eventually the location was discovered. Ray Cooper, with considerable help from Robert Albee, constructed two camps (Anne Marie and Minonipi Lodges) on the Minipi River watershed. These men, with Lee's input, however, implemented strong conservation measures in order to insure that this phenomenal fishery would survive. One of the first policies established was that only fly fishing would be permitted, and that only one big trout could be killed per guest. It's probably for these reasons that this watershed of Central Labrador continues to be as productive as ever. Ray sold his camps to Jackie Cooper (no relation) who enforces these conservation measures with equal fervor.

Jackie reports that the average trophy brook trout weighs a hefty five pounds, and the largest was a nine-pounder! Bear in mind that a brook trout of over 12 inches in Michigan and Wisconsin is practically a trophy!

During 1981, Lex Hochner, Jr., on his first brook trout trip, fished Cooper's Anne Marie camp and reported: "The average weight of the trophy fish was 5.4 pounds, and our party of three landed 18 trophies. The largest trout was 7 1/2 pounds. I had a fish which I had estimated in the range of 8 1/2 pounds, but he straightened out a No. 18 fine wire hook in subsurface vegetation. I also saw one cruiser which I'm sure would have weighed at least nine pounds."

THE SEASON AND HATCHES

The season starts June 15 and closes September 15. In June, mayflies emerge in the early afternoon; success is achieved by fishing those shallow areas where the water moves slowly and is quickly warmed by the June sun. As the season progresses, the main hatch (Hexagenia) is so heavy that on calm days the lakes can be blanketed with insect life, so the fishing is concentrated on lakes. This "main hatch" occurs in late June or July, and if the weather is warm and dry, it will last for a week to ten days; but if the weather is coolish with considerable cloud cover, it can continue to mid- or late July.

When the water temperatures warm up during the latter part of July and early August, the fishing emphasis shifts to the rivers and the inlets, outlets and riffles, and often one can enjoy dry fly fishing from morning until dusk.

In late August and early September, dry fly fishing is limited mostly to the mornings and early evenings, and the streamers become important during much of the day. It's the evening fishing that's most spectacular. Trout seem to be divided into two characteristic groups for the evening rise: Some trout seem to select one particular location and primarily feed in that vicinity; other trout, "cruisers," move purposefully along the streams looking for food. The angler must first ascertain the direction of the fish by the series of rises, and then adroitly place his cast ahead of the trout. Fishing for cruisers demands a high degree of casting skill coupled with some guesswork.

Wading and boat fishing are effective during the entire season, although during June and early July, there is more boat fishing on lakes where casting to cruising trout is practiced. Aluminum boats and canoes powered by small outboards are used, and there is an experienced guide provided for every two anglers.

While the brook trout is the foremost reason for going to the Minipi region, these waters also harbor Arctic char and northern pike. The char are landlocked, and average about six pounds, with an 11-pounder (1978) reigning as the camp record. Most of the northern pike will average four to five pounds, but in 1978 a 29-pounder was taken! No doubt this fish had been feasting heavily on smaller trout.

ON TROUT TACKLE

According to Cooper, eight- to nine-foot fly rods that handle a No. 6 to 8 weight fly line are fine for these waters. Leaders need not be much longer than 7 1/2 feet tapered down to four or six pounds. There is seldom a need for sinking lines, and nearly all fishing is done with floating tapered lines. The possible exception is fishing for Arctic char, when a sinking line is occasionally preferable. Any good, single action reel will suffice, and it doesn't require large line capacity. About 25 yards of 20-pound backing, plus the fly line, is sufficient.

The Wulff series of flies, plus the Irresistible in sizes 10 through 16, will accommodate most of your requirements. The Muddler Minnow (or any other pattern with a head of clipped deer hair) is exceptionally effective. The Mickey Finn, Hornberg, Little Brook Trout, Black Nosed Dace and Yellow Marabou are also good streamers. Wet fly patterns include the Coachman, Dark Cahill, Hare's Ear and Wooly Worms. Gray Nymph, Hare's Ear, Montana and Golden Stone tied on 8 to 10 hook sizes are effective nymphs.

Many anglers insist that the big trout are only attracted to large Wulff flies (No. 8 and 10). Not entirely so, says Lex Hochner: "I had one magnificent day where in a matter of 1 1/2 hours I caught four big trout on Elk Hair Caddis, Fluttering Caddis, Blue Quills, Blue Duns and small Wulffs tied on No. 14 and 18 hooks."

THE CAMPS

The angler looking for big brook trout would do well to concentrate on the Minipi watershed. There are dozens and dozens of trout lakes and streams that offer splendid possibilities, but the Minipi is a superb choice.

The Upper Minipi complex consists of a chain of small lakes that form two main water systems, which flow south on parallel courses and empty into Big Minipi Lake (about 65 miles southwest of Goose Bay).

Joan Salvato Wulff—one of the world's premier fly casters—landed this hefty trout from the Minipi.

ANNE MARIE LAKE LODGE: Cooper's large self-contained building was constructed of peeled logs and houses four double-occupancy bedrooms. The bathroom has hot and cold running water, shower and flush toilets. A dining room, sitting area and kitchen complete the lodge. The weekly rate which includes the helicopter service from Goose Bay is $1,995.

MINONIPI LODGE: A ranch-style bungalow with four double-occupancy bedrooms, Minonipi is situated in the center of a great trout area at the very headwaters of the western branch of the Upper Minipi River. The weekly rate is $1,995 (including the helicopter transfers). The lodge features a dining room, kitchen and modern plumbing facilities.

Both of Cooper's camps are serviced by helicopter and are booked on a weekly basis (Saturday to Saturday).

LITTLE MINIPI BROOK TROUT CAMP: Peter Paor, another pioneer of sport fishing in Labrador, built his lodge on Little Minipi Lake, immediately adjacent to the main outlet. This camp accommodates six anglers and offers all the necessary amenities. Lake fishing is available right in front of the camp, and for those who enjoy wading, the Little Minipi outlet is a charming, medium-sized brook trout stream. Fishing technique and quality are similar at all three camps.

ATLANTIC SALMON FISHING

Although Labrador has a number of excellent salmon rivers, the Pinware, Forteau, Eagle and Big rivers are among the most popular. Most Labrador rivers predominantly feature grilse (Atlantic salmon that have spent one year at sea and weigh under seven pounds); however, all rivers have runs of salmon that have spent two years at sea and, therefore, will generally weigh nine to 14 pounds.

At one time Labrador's salmon fishing rivaled all but a handful of rivers in the world. Alex Parsons, who pioneered salmon fishing in Labrador and Newfoundland, stated in his 1949 brochure: "Every day you fish, you are sure to hook your eight salmon (10 to 25 pounds or more). Or if your interest lies in sea trout, you can depend on getting your limit of 24." At that time

Alex operated a 50-foot cabin cruiser, and thus had access to many rivers. Robert D. Price Jr. remembers his trip with Parsons: "Four of us went on this trip in 1949. We released over 50 salmon and their average weight was about 16 pounds. And there were loads of sea trout. All you wanted to catch." He also mentions that the cost was $22.50 per person per week. Ah, for the good old days.

One can't turn back the calendar, and realistically, Labrador's salmon fishing today is just a fraction of what it was several decades ago. As the market price of salmon rose dramatically, commercial fishermen became more active. By depleting the rivers of adult salmon (fish that spent two or more years in the ocean), they significantly reduced future stocks of big fish, since there is some evidence that genetically big salmon tend to reproduce offspring that also will remain at sea for several seasons. Hence the greater populations of grilse today.

This is not to say that the grilse is a slouch. These little bundles of dynamite frequently rise to the surface, and once hooked will streak across the river in fast, sustaining runs and repeatedly break water, often with high graceful leaps. It becomes obvious, then, that by scaling down the strength and weight of one's tackle, the angler derives all the fighting pressure of a grilse.

What results can be expected on a Labrador salmon river? The statistics of the Forteau River may serve as a good starting point, but bear in mind that the catches from river to river may differ widely; furthermore, catches can fluctuate from season to season. Like imported wines, there are good and bad years, with the occasional vintage year popping up.

Month	Year	Salmon Landed	Rod Days	Salmon per Rod/Day
July	1981	351	283	1.24
July	1982	345	631	.54
August	1981	203	283	.71
August	1982	202	431	.46
September	1981	53	79	.67
September	1982	(figures are unavailable)		

This averages to .68 salmon per angler per day for the two seasons—hardly a statistic that will send a fisherman who insists on plenty of action streaking to Labrador! The activity can come in spurts. Dr. Joe Car raised and hooked 11 salmon in less than two hours on the Forteau, while Paul Melchior hooked eight salmon the next afternoon. This sort of action compares very favorably to any Atlantic salmon fishing in the world.

Monitoring a half-dozen rivers in Labrador indicates that Atlantic salmon fishing was not as productive in 1984 as during the previous season. But this is hardly shocking news because salmon fishing was off in '84 just about everywhere in the world. Here are the results for a number of rivers in 1984:

River	Rod Days	Grilse	Salmon	Fish per Rod/Day
Big	297	349	78	1.44
Eagle	1,309	875	84	.73
Forteau	1,336	402	18	.31
Pinware	2,661	585	167	.28
Sandhill	225	180	13	.86
Hunt	484	287	133	.87
TOTALS	6,312	2,678	493	.502

The best results (based on number of fish per rod/day) were turned in at the Big River, which yielded 1.44 salmon. The Hunt was the best producer as far as salmon vs. grilse is concerned: one-third of the fish were "adult" salmon. The Pinware delivered disappointing results after a fine 1983, but the fish were larger in 1984. In 1983, the Pinware had a 1+ fish per rod/day.

George "Bus" Duhamel has been fishing Labrador continually since 1954, and most of his trips have centered on the Eagle River where he and friends have a private camp. It's possible that he has landed more Labrador salmon than any other visiting angler. How does he compare today's fishing with the 1950s?

"I believe that fishing today on the Eagle and elsewhere in Labrador is probably about 25 percent as good as it used to be.

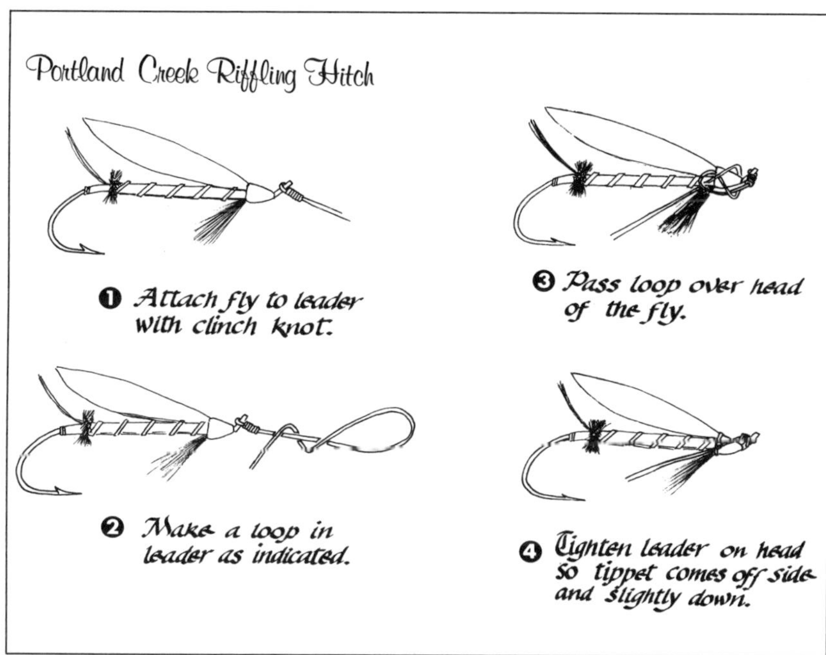

Here's how to tie Portland Hitch. It's an exciting way to fish salmon. —Illustrated by Paul Melchior.

In the earlier days you could sometimes see a dozen or more salmon porpoising simultaneously. What a sight! I don't know what caused the diminishing salmon runs, but everyone points to the commercial netting.

"Today the Eagle can still provide excellent fishing compared to other countries or areas. When the salmon are in, a good angler can land five fish in a day, and maybe play another six or seven. And that's a fair amount of action for a day. A good angler will land probably 30 to 40 salmon during a very good week. I believe that today an angler is far more knowledgeable, but equally important are the great advances made in the tackle field. With glass, then graphite, and other composite rods, anglers are able to cast farther, easier and with less effort. Even leader materials have been so improved that one can use a stronger tippet and not alarm the fish. Our records on the Eagle indicate that there is one adult salmon to every 20 grilse landed, and our camp record for the Eagle is 22 pounds,'' Bus reflects. His best salmon, incidentally, was an 18-pounder.

It is most challenging to take these smaller salmon on the surface. Casting a dry fly repeatedly over a productive area does work, but skittering a fly across the surface is much more effective on some Labrador rivers.

To accomplish this, the angler throws a half-hitch around a standard salmon pattern (not a dry fly), just below the head of the fly. The leader should come off to one side and slightly down. This tie is known as the Portland Creek Hitch because it was on this Newfoundland stream that the method was popularized. It is important that the leader comes off the left side of the retrieved fly when the current is against the left side of the fly. And vice versa. The hitched fly is cast, and by raising the rod tip, the fly, when retrieved, should skitter on top. If it splashes across the surface, the retrieve is too fast, and if it sinks, it's too slow. The fly should travel across the surface, leaving a barely discernible V-like wake.

The method works, and works well. A number of years ago, Stu Apte and I tried it on the Pinware, and in a very short time we had numerous salmon takes. The rise is exciting. A silver torpedo shoots from the depths and slashes at the fly, much like the brown trout rise to an emerging caddis.

The disadvantage of using the hitched fly is that the angler must be able to discern the right time to strike. Some fishermen claim that hook setting should be done quickly, as soon as the jaws of the salmon close on the fly. Others feel that the angler should wait until the salmon turns with the fly. Use whichever method is most effective for you.

ON SALMON TACKLE

Because the majority of salmon taken from Labrador streams are going to be grilse, lighter tackle should be utilized so that maximum sport is derived. Fly rods should be 8 1/2 to nine feet for a No. 8 line. A single action reel that accommodates the fly line and about 150 yards of 20-pound Micron backing is fine. Leaders should be about nine feet and tapered down to eight- or 10-pound test tippets. Most of the time floating lines will be used, but the wise angler brings a sink-tip line as well. Obviously, adjustments to this tackle may be necessary, depending on the type of waters to be fished and wind conditions. If fishing is very good, for example, one might put together a No. 6 fly rod to increase the challenge. On the other hand, if one encounters exceptionally windy conditions, and long casts are needed, a No. 9 rod might be more practical.

All camps will provide a list of effective fly patterns, and most stock the popular flies and sizes. Among the favorites are: Blue Charm, Silver Tip, Silver Doctor, Green Butt and Cosseboom, tied on No. 6 and 8 hook sizes. Hair wings are exceptionally popular, not only among anglers and guides, but also with salmon. For dry fly fishing, the Grey and White Wulffs, Bombers and Rat-Faced McDougall (or Irresistible) on the same hook sizes are among the effective patterns.

THE SALMON CAMPS

PINWARE LODGE: Located on the Pinware River (not far from Blanc Sablon, Quebec) this lodge accommodates six to eight anglers in fair comfort, which means electricity, heat, two tiled bathrooms with showers, main dining room and a lounge area. A guide is assigned to every two anglers. In addition to the Pinware, guests also fish County Cat River (which joins the Pinware) and the Forteau River, an excellent salmon river about an hour away from the lodge. The lodge furnishes car transportation. The Pinware River is not "private," and there is some local fishing pressure; happily, several game wardens make sure that limit regulations are observed. The Pinware Lodge accepts bookings on a weekly basis (5 1/2 days fishing). Guests fly to Deer Lake, Newfoundland, are driven to St. Barbe, take a ferry across the channel and finally are driven to camp. July and the first two weeks of August produce the best salmon fishing.

EAGLE RIVER SALMON CAMP: The Eagle is one of Labrador's most productive salmon rivers, and although most of the fish will be grilse, there are a fair number of bigger salmon (one out of 20). This camp is owned by Peter Paor and is located at one of the most strategic points of the Eagle. The permanent camp comfortably houses up to six anglers, and guides and boats are part of the package (there is little wading opportunity here). The camp is almost 100 miles due east of Goose Bay. July and August are the best months for salmon and just about any week during these months can be highly productive, but the last two weeks of July and the first week of August may be best.

BIG RIVER SALMON FISHING LODGE: Bob Skinner's permanent camp is located 120 miles northeast of Goose Bay. It comfortably accommodates 10 anglers. The camp record salmon is a 22-pounder. Grilse average 5 1/2 pounds, and there is a fairly high percentage of "adult" salmon that average about 10 pounds. Salmon enter this river around the second week of July, and the runs continue until late August. Grilse enter this river in August. (Incidentally, there is also excellent fishing for sea-run brook trout that average four to five pounds, with the largest being a seven-pounder. The peak time for the sea-run trout is from August 10 to September 7.)

FORTEAU SALMON LODGE: This camp (which accommodates up to 10 anglers) is located on the Forteau River (near Blanc Sablon, Quebec) and offers mostly grilse (five to seven pounds), but there is always the possibility of a large salmon. The camp record is slightly over 20 pounds. In late July and August, there is also sea-run brook trout that range from one to five pounds. Guests fly to Deer Lake, Newfoundland, and from there they fly to Blanc Sablon via Labrador Aviation. Bookings are on a Friday-to-Friday basis and July and August are the favored months for salmon fishing.

MICHAEL RIVER LODGE: Located 144 miles east of Goose Bay, this camp began its operation in 1967 providing only tent accommodations. Later a modern lodge was constructed at the river's mouth. In addition to salmon and grilse, there is sea-run brook trout fishing (camp record is seven pounds) and Arctic char (five to 10 pounds). Much of the fishing is via wading or from shore, but the lodge also provides 23-foot cargo canoes for the upstream pools. July and August are the best months for salmon.

SANDHILL RIVER LODGE: This modern lodge on the Sandhill River accommodates up to 10 anglers. One licensed

Labrador's fishing will remain stable for years to come. Stu Apte does his thing on a Pinware salmon.

guide and a 14-foot river boat is provided for each two fishermen. The camp's largest salmon is a 17-pounder, and while the season is from late June to mid-September, the peak season is mid-July and most of August. Brook trout will average four pounds and a 7 1/2-pounder is the largest taken from these waters. Trips are booked on a Saturday-to-Saturday basis.

ARCTIC CHAR FISHING

Although the Atlantic salmon and brook trout are the featured species, Labrador also boasts excellent Arctic char fishing. The char, however, do not grow as large as they do in Canada's Northwest Territories, but Labrador char can readily be taken on fly fishing tackle.

One of the best rivers for char fishing is the Umiakovik, 300 miles north of Goose Bay. These are sea-run char averaging around five pounds, but there are a number of 10- to 15-pounders caught each season.

How good is the char fishing on the Umiakovik? Dr. Ron Trunsky, who fished it with four companions in 1976, reported: "Dr. Arnold Zuroff must have taken over 100 char in one day. I landed seven char in seven casts, had two unproductive casts, and then took five more fish in five casts, and after two more casts, I took five more char in five additional casts. That's 17 char landed in 21 casts! We took many char on both spinning and fly fishing tackle, and I would suspect that our group of five landed more than 2,000 char in the six days of fishing."

Peter Paor, who operates several trout and salmon resorts in Labrador, also offers a canvas/plywood camp on Umiakovik. It's not luxurious: it consists of separate quarters for staff and guests, and a larger facility that houses the kitchen and dining room. One must bring his own sleeping bag, towels and, above all, very warm clothing. Because conditions are often windy, a No. 8 fly rod (with floating and sinking lines) is ideal. Char seem to prefer brightly-colored streamers, though muddlers and sculpins also work well. August is the favored month.

As good as the fishing is on Umiakovik, Peter Paor ironically has not found tremendous interest in his char camp. Part of the reason may be the long flight (about four hours) to this desolate area, and long charter flights are expensive. "The Arctic char is a first-rate game fish. It's unfamiliar to most anglers because its range is limited to the more desolate geographical areas of the world," Paor explains. This frontier will no doubt remain untainted for a long time.

LABRADOR NOTES

Weather Conditions: The following temperatures registered at Goose Bay will be helpful to the angler in selecting clothing for his Labrador trip.

	TEMPERATURE F			PRECIPITATION	WIND IN MPH	
Month	**Mean Max.**	**Mean Min.**	**Mean Mo.**	**Mean Rainfall**	**Mean Speed**	**Prevailing Direction**
June	61	42	51	3.1″	8.6	NE
July	70	50	60	4.0″	8.9	NE
Aug.	66	49	58	3.6″	8.9	WSW
Sept.	57	41	49	2.9″	10.1	WSW

The Insect Problem: Labrador is mosquito and black fly country. At times these insects are extremely pesty, while on other days, when there is wind, they may be practically nonexistent. With modern-day repellents, insect problems are easily combatted. Anglers who are especially allergic to insect bites should take along a mosquito head net and lightweight gloves for emergencies. Some fishermen claim that mixing Muskol (a powerful repellent) with Vicks VapoRub increases the effectiveness of the repellent.

AND FINALLY... Labrador is part of the Newfoundland province. Goose Bay is the gateway town for most of the fishing camps. There is very little in terms of sightseeing in Goose Bay (or nearby Happy Valley), so anglers limit their stay here to essential overnights. The Labrador Inn (P.O. Box 58, Goose Bay, Labrador) is popular with many anglers.

Whereas in the mid-fifties there was only one sportsman's lodge in all of Labrador, today there are more than 20. Labrador has come a long way since Lee Wulff's exploratory trips in the early fifties. Thankfully, it will not be overrun with fishermen—not for the next decade or two. And maybe never.

Bahamas

Classic Bonefishing at Its Best

Winston Moore, one of the most accomplished bonefishermen, unveils his secrets—from tackle selection to presentation to fighting the fish. What are some of the most popular (and productive) places in the Bahamas? When is the best time to go? And the recipe for one of the most deadly bonefish flies ever devised!

A. J. McClane, of McClane's Fishing Encyclopedia fame, is one of the world's most knowledgeable bonefishermen.

Chapter 7

BAHAMAS

"If it weren't for bad luck, I wouldn't have any luck at all."

I don't know who coined this gem, but I kept muttering it as I waded the knee-deep flats of Great Harbour Cay, in the Berry Islands chain.

It wasn't as if there weren't any bonefish around. Au contraire. The flats were loaded with them. School after school of bonefish, some that numbered in the hundreds, continuously swam past me. To an inexperienced bonefisherman this at first appeared like a sweet dream, a fantasy of sorts, for these bones were not only plentiful, they were also fairly large. This dream turned into a sour nightmare as the short trip progressed.

I cast to my left where a school of several hundred bonefish were approaching. The shrimp fly I was using landed somewhat on target, but I had not noticed a few other bonefish between the school and me. When I accidentally lined these fish, they spooked, and immediately flushed the big school. Suddenly all the water in front of me erupted with dozens of thrashing, streaking bonefish, scurrying for deeper waters. It was depressing, I'll tell you.

But no matter. Another platoon was coming up on my right. This time I didn't lead them sufficiently, and again the chain reaction. Dozens of bones spooked in all directions. This happened repeatedly.

A good bonefishing guide is important to angling success—especially for the first-timer to the Bahamas.

"If it weren't for bad luck, I wouldn't have any luck at all."

It was time to outwit them. No more Mr. Nice Guy. I made a long cast to my left where there were no bonefish in evidence, and let the shrimp fly sink to the bottom. Surely a school of bones would be arriving at this area momentarily. By making the presentation well in advance of their arrival, I wouldn't have to worry about spooking them on my cast. If and when the fish approached the fly, all I would have to do would be to touch it up once or twice. I know I had a Cheshire cat's grin, and I giggled over my cleverness as a school approached my sunken fly. Just at the right time I moved the fly slowly, and one bone became interested and peeled off the school. I moved the fly again and he was about to take it. But another bonefish's dorsal fin rubbed against my floating fly line, and the fish flushed, sending all the other bones crashing across the surface. Swish! They were gone. So much for this stratagem.

"If it weren't for bad luck, I wouldn't have any luck at all."

This experience would not have been so devastating if I were alone on this trip, for I'm sure that I would have buried this fiasco so deep in my subconscious that only a skilled hypnotist would be able to retrieve it.

But on my left, and somewhat behind me, was Al McClane, the master of the bonefishing flats, and a sort of hero of mine stemming back to the days when he first wrote articles for *Field and Stream*. Perhaps no angler has more fishing information stored in his brain than Al. And on my right was Bing McClellan, another superb fly fisherman, not only on trout streams but on the flats as well.

While they occasionally experienced similar problems of flushing bonefish, it is also true that they were fighting fish constantly. I would look to my left and see Al's rod arching, and I was close enough to hear his reel screeching, no, singing, for this is a melodious riff to an angler's ears. And Bing, he was on to this big bone, I remember, and that fish whizzed right by me and then circled around me and was about "to rope me." No way was I going to allow this! I jumped over Bing's line, and it occurs to me now how humorous it would have been if I had tripped on his line and bellyflopped on the water.

"If it weren't for bad luck, I wouldn't have any luck at all."

Anyway, I've never been drunk in my life but I came very close that evening when I quaffed several tropical drinks at the now defunct Great Harbour Cay Club. We discussed the problem at supper and at breakfast too, and the solution offered, which should have been obvious, was to find small groupings of bonefish or stragglers rather than to attempt to take a fish from these huge moving schools. Or, it was suggested, one could cast at the very edge of the school after ascertaining the size of it, but never, never cast to the "student body." It's ironic that in "battle" the obvious sometimes escapes the angler.

So the next day I moved out of the "bonefish alley" and set out to stalk singles or doubles. I nicked a couple of fish and fought a few others for several runs, but in my euphoria—or was it hysteria?—I lost them. That morning, fishing took a downturn and the large quantities of bones weren't evident. We only had about an hour of fishing left that morning, before we'd be flying back to Palm Beach, and the fact that I was fishing some of the most prolific bonefish waters in the world, under favorable conditions, without scoring once, preyed on my mind.

Furthermore, the wind picked up considerably, making accurate casting difficult if not somewhat impossible. I noticed that Al and Bing were heading for the skiffs, so I didn't bother to repair the wind knot that developed in my tippet. I could squeeze in maybe a few minutes of fishing before I would have to join them.

There in front of me, just 60 feet away, was this great big tail, sticking clear out of water, an obvious indication that the big bone was grubbing the bottom. As I waded a little closer I judged this fish to be nine or ten pounds. Maybe even larger! The cast unfolded just beyond and to one side of the fish, and while the bonefish submerged briefly, perhaps somewhat alerted, the tail popped right back out of the water as it apparently continued to grub. Excitedly, and nervously, I touched up the fly slightly. Then again. I felt something solid, set the hook several times and watched the big fish streak across the surface. I knew I was on to the largest bonefish I'd ever hooked or, in fact, ever seen. It was an exhilarating moment; the song of

John Donohue captured this magnificent bonefish while fishing at Andros. Estimated weight? 15 to 16 pounds.

the whirling reel was so sweet. Out of the corner of my eye I saw that Al and Bing had noticed that I had hooked a big fish. Now it was simply a matter of landing it, and then I would display the huge bone for them to see it before releasing it. It would have been the biggest bonefish of the trip.

I survived the first run easily. But the second run, while not as long, bellied the line tremendously, and it was this added pressure that caused the tippet (with the wind knot) to snap. I returned to Palm Beach without landing a single bonefish.

"If it weren't for bad luck, I wouldn't have any luck at all."

Happily, most bonefishing trips to the Bahamas under favorable weather conditions provide much more satisfying results, for there is probably no better place in the world for both quantity and quality.

The late Ralph Ward's trip to Charlie's Haven on Andros Island illustrates the vast potential of the Bahamas. True, he was a skilled fly fisherman, but this was his very first bonefishing trip. During his week he landed exactly 100 bonefish (all by fly fishing), a tremendous angling accomplishment. Now it's possible for an accomplished fly fisherman to take 100 bones on his first trip, as there are several places on this earth where huge numbers of small, unsophisticated bonefish can be found. They are mostly two- to three-pound fish, and at times one can ignore many bonefishing rules and still score.

These Andros bones, however, are not only very sophisticated, but they run big, too. Ralph's largest fish was a 12-3/4-pounder and he took four other bonefish in the 10- to 12-pound class as well as dozens of other fish over six pounds! His results, though, are not at all typical of bonefishing, and the angler considering a trip to the islands would be highly disappointed if he expected to duplicate Ralph's phenomenal success.

A good fly fisherman, with fair weather conditions, would probably average four or five bonefish a day (and fight a few others). If weather conditions are ideal, faster fishing could be experienced, but conversely, poor weather can produce blanks.

In no other type of fishing is keen eyesight more important than in bonefishing. A combination of a cloudy sky and a choppy water surface creates a low visibility factor, which is the curse of the bonefisherman. Thankfully, most guides possess superb eyesight and can direct a less gifted client to a bonefish by using an imaginary clock."Three o'clock, 50 feet!" means that the angler casts 90 degrees to the right of the bow of the skiff and approximately 50 feet. It's not foolproof but it works often, and a number of myopic anglers are successful mostly because of their persistence and their use of this system.

It's a stalking game. First, the angler and the guide search the bottoms of the flats for a shadow or a puff of marl, or really any movement at all. If this sign is identified as a bonefish, the angler quickly delivers the fly in front and somewhat beyond the fish. The fly is moved slowly but lifelike, and the angler hopes that the bonefish will not change its course. Tension mounts when the bone sees the fly, approaches it and then decides whether to mouth it or ignore it. This species is among the wariest of all marine species (only the permit tops it), so the approach, the presentation, the retrieve must be done exactly right. If all goes well, the strike is followed by a blazing run that may melt 50, 100 or even 150 yards of line from the reel. With each repeated dash, the runs are not as long or as far. The fight is especially spectacular in very shallow water where the fish often whizzes across the surface, and the fish's wake will excite even the most jaded angler. Most experienced fishermen claim that the stalk, presentation and the take are the most challenging aspects of bonefishing; the fight is anticlimactic. But it's all good—from the stalk to the release.

BEST TIME TO FISH?

That's easy. Anytime that visibility is excellent (clear, bright skies), there's a minimum of wind and the water temperatures of the flats are from 70 to 85 degrees. Ideal conditions can crop up just about anytime during the year. Most anglers, especially those who live in the northern climes, fish the Bahamas during the winter months, but unfortunately, cold fronts are common at this time. April, May and June are generally excellent months and so is November. Weather conditions are likely to be stable during these months. July and August tend to be very warm and if the water temperature of the flats is extremely high fishing can be poor. It's important to realize that bonefish spend most of their time in deeper water and come to the flats on a flood tide to feed, but if the water temperature is too cold (low 60s) or too warm (high 80s), they may avoid the shallows.

However, according to Don McCarthy, who for years was the Bahamas' fishing information director, the period of January to April produces many big fish. He claimed that this is the spawning season, the females may have an additional one to three pounds of roe and the big bones come to the shallows to spawn. (Other experts disagree and feel that the bonefish spawn in deep water and the tides and currents carry the eggs to the shallows.)

November is also a good month in the Bahamas probably because the water temperatures are often ideal and because the hurricane season is over.

BONEFISH STRATEGY

While gear and technique are purely subjective, I interviewed Winston Moore, a brilliant bonefish tactician, for his thoughts and recommendations:

ON EQUIPMENT:

Q: What type of a fly rod do you use for most of your bonefishing?
WM: Day in and day out I use a 9 1/2-foot Sage graphite rod for a No. 10 line. There are rare days when the wind isn't blowing and a person could get by with a lighter outfit. But wind is often a problem in the Bahamas and elsewhere, and the heavier line simply allows you to make a decent cast into the wind. Also I find that a person really can make a delicate presentation with a No. 10 if he simply aims his cast to straighten out about three feet above the surface, then gently lets it settle onto the water.

Q: What about fly lines? What type do you prefer? And what about color?
WM: Generally, I use a WF10F (weight-forward, floating) line. A full floating line seems to work much better than a sink-tip or intermediate, because it's easier to pick up. All of my lines are dyed a medium shade of grey. I use Rit Dye. I have tried all colors including sky blue, green, beige and white. But grey seems to be the least likely to spook the fish during the cast and when the line is on the water.

Q: What about backing? What type, pound test and how many yards?
WM: I use 20-pound Micron. I've never had any problem with Micron and I especially like it as it is smaller in diameter than Dacron, thus you can load more line on a reel. Occasionally you hook a big fish that practically cleans your reel of backing. I would not consider fishing the flats where large bonefish are found without at least 200 yards of backing.

Q: Fly reels are important in bonefishing. What's your preference?
WM: I personally use the Seamaster MK I and the MK II. Both are direct drive, single action. Of course, there are other good serviceable reels available in a wide range of prices. The brake must be silk-smooth.

"I use the Agent Bonefish about 90 percent of the time..." says Winston Moore who devised the pattern.

Q: What are your thoughts on leaders? Length? Tapers?

WM: I build my own leaders and use Maxima Chameleon exclusively. The tippet usually is eight pounds, but if there are any permit on the flats I change to 10 pounds. My leaders are seldom shorter than 16 feet for every day fishing. However, if the wind is really howling I shorten them to 12 feet so I can get the tippet to turn the fly over. Here is the formula for my leaders from butt to tippet:

Length (feet)	Pound test
4	25
3	20
2	15
1 1/2	12
1 1/2	10
4	8

Q: You've developed your own bonefish fly, "Agent Bonefish." How successful has it been? How is it tied?

WM: The "Agent Bonefish" has proved to be so deadly that I use it 90 percent of the time. Sometimes I'll switch to the "Bonefish Special" when I get a few refusals on "Agent Bonefish" to see if it is the pattern or the mood of the fish. Very seldom does the pattern change seem to make any difference. Both Ivan and Charlie (guides at Andros) swear that "Agent Bonefish" is the most effective fly they have ever seen for Andros. The late Ralph Ward took almost all of his 100 fish in one week at Andros on the "Agent Bonefish," and five bones were over 10 pounds. I use this pattern in Belize most of the time, and I've not found a flats area where it is not deadly, although I understand that at Christmas Island, bonefish seem to gobble up "Crazy Charlie" patterns almost exclusively. In the Bahamas the largest hook size I use is No. 4. Most of the time I use No. 6, but in extremely shallow water and on a totally flat surface during a windless day I'll go to No. 8. If I could carry only one hook size it would be No. 6. In the Bahamas I use an unweighted fly for tailing fish and a weighted fly under all other conditions. However, I've found that if you make the right presentation, you can use weighted flies even on the tailing fish. Here's the formula:

	"Agent Bonefish"
Hook:	Mustad 3407 or 34007 sizes 4, 6 and 8
Weight (optional)	No. 1 fuse wire (front portion of the shank)
Body:	Orange chenille
Wing:	Fluorescent orange FisHair 2X length of shank. Tie the wing in on bottom of shank so fly rides point up.
Cheek:	Grizzly hackle tips reaching 1/2 way up wing
Head:	Red thread

ON CASTING:

Q: What's the average length of your casts? What about the maximum?

WM: My casts probably average 40 to 60 feet. Maximum length cast? Occasionally, I find that I'm into my backing on a given cast, which means that sometimes I'm casting well over 90 feet. Obviously it's hard to achieve pinpoint accuracy with a long cast and it's more difficult to make a soft presentation, so I never use it on tailing fish except when you just can't get any closer to a fish due to a variety of circumstances.

Q: What about false casts? How many?

WM: To moving fish, one false cast is all I usually make. I keep enough line on the bottom of the boat or in a wide loop beside the boat in the water. I simply roll cast the line into the air, come back with the back cast and fire on the forward. However, when I am stalking tailing fish and wading I find that I may need three or four false casts. This is always done at right angles to the fish so that the false casts do not spook them, and then when I'm ready, I simply change directions and let go. Certainly the fewer false casts, the less chance of spooking fish because not only the line and leader can alarm them, but a lot of arm and rod waving will also scare the bones.

Q: Where do you cast when a bonefish is spotted?

WM: This is a tough one as there really isn't any constant formula. If it is a single tailing fish I like to cast right on its nose, just as close as I can. Otherwise, it may not see the fly. On a school of tailers, which will kick up more mud than a single fish, I like to cast about three to four feet beyond them but right in the middle of the school. In other words, the leader will settle into the school while the fly is a few feet beyond; hence the long leaders. Casting to moving fish, again depends on a lot of variables: How deep is the water? How fast is the fly going to sink? How fast are the fish moving? If a fish or school is just moving, and not randomly stopping to feed, I try to cast ahead of them by maybe 10 feet, let the fly settle, then wait for the fish to get close to the fly before any stripping. If they are kind of rambling around, tails up, then moving, then up again, I try to get the fly quite close, two to three feet from the fish. However, if the fish are coming toward me then I try to determine how fast they are moving and usually put the fly about five feet in front of the fish, wait for them to "get there," and then show them the fly by stripping. Again, there are so many variables. For me the toughest cast is to a fish going straight away. You have to cast before it is out of range. This usually means a hard cast with the fly coming down to the water not quite as delicately as one would like. But one thing I've learned is that as long as any fish is within your casting range, even though it may appear to be spooked, you should keep casting. I've had some takes from fish that I just knew were aware of the boat, or had been spooked, or were not originally interested. If a fisherman is to make an error in his casting to an approaching fish, it should be a cast that is too short as opposed to one that is too long. A short cast can be picked up and recast, or if the fish does not change course, you can just wait for it to get to the fly.

ON RETRIEVING:

Q: Some anglers believe that a fly should be retrieved very slowly. Others impart more action. What are your thoughts on this?

WM: Wow! This varies so much. Some fish will take the fly lying dead or motionless on the bottom. What I try to do is watch the action or reaction of the fish to my fly presentation. If the fly is close enough for the fish to see, generally you will notice some slight positive reaction. It may be subtle but you can see it. If it does not take it, I simply *twitch* the fly, moving it maybe an inch or two, just a very slight movement of the fly with the hope that it will be seen. I've found that if the bone is close to the fly and does not see it and you make a hard strip, it will almost always scare the fish. If I am casting to and beyond a school of tailers I let the fly settle to the bottom very slowly and then delicately strip the fly into the middle of the feeding school. Again a long hard strip will send the school running. But a series of one-or two-inch strips will not scare them and is usually the retrieve that not only gets their attention but causes them to strike. My observation is that if there is one prevailing mistake that bonefishermen make it is stripping too fast and in strokes that are too long. Granted once in a while those fish like something that is really moving. But if you were able to observe the little crabs, shrimp and other critters that they feed on, you would note that their movements are subtle, short and crisp as opposed to long strokes. Watch a bunch of those bonefish tails and many times they won't move from a very small area for several minutes. Rarely, if ever, have I seen a bonefish chase something across the flats.

Day in and day out the bonefish fisherman will have greater success with very subtle twitches, very short strips, just enough to get the fish to see the fly, as opposed to the longer, faster strips.

ON HOOKING AND PLAYING BONEFISH:

Q: How about setting hook? What's your procedure?

WM: Assuming that I can see the fish, and that I think it has the fly, I simply strip line *slowly* until I feel it "on," then give a fast hard strip, and if it is still there then I come up with the rod tip. Here again the usual mistake, especially for freshwater fly fishermen, is to come back hard with the rod tip as the first step in setting the hook. But if, in fact, the fish does not have the fly, or, if it just barely has it, you take it out of its mouth. You don't get a second chance as you have now pulled the fly several feet away from it, and undoubtedly it has been spooked by this very unnatural movement. However, by taking up slack until you feel the fish, then making the one short hard strip, if you do miss it, the fly is still in the vicinity and you can resume whatever strip is appropriate for a given fish and given situation.

Frankly, having been weaned on freshwater fishing, mostly dry fly, my instinct today is still to come back with the rod tip when I think

Dr. Rod Neubert tamed this 11-pound, 12-ounce bonefish on a two-pound tippet for an IGFA world record. He was fishing from Charlie Haven's resort.

the bone is on. Rarely do I make a trip for bones without lousing up a few good chances by setting the hook with the rod tip.

Q: How much drag do you have on your reel?

WM: Just enough to keep the reel from overrunning. I do not fight the fish with the drag. This holds true for the first run as well as any subsequent runs.

Any drag I need is applied by pressure on the line with my fingers. You can respond *immediately* in this manner to any sudden movements of the fish.

Q: Often bones go into the mangroves. What do you do?
WM: I've never found a guaranteed way to work a fish out of the mangroves. One of the benefits of heavier tippets is that if a bonefish wraps the leader around a mangrove you may be able to go in after it and hopefully unwrap the leader. Usually, by the time you catch up with a mangrove-wrapped fish, it is totally worn out and is not inclined to break off. Some anglers apply all the pressure the tackle can withstand in order to prevent a fish from going into the mangroves, but with some bonefish the more heat you apply, the more inclined they are to run faster and longer. I've found that, depending upon an individual fish, sometimes when they are headed for a mangrove if you give them a lot of slack they may stop running. Then you can gradually get them turned away and back into open water.

ON WADING AND SKIFF FISHING:

Q: When fishing from a boat, how do you prefer to be poled?
WM: If we are fishing the shoreline, I like to be within easy casting distance of the shore. More often than not, the fish that are working the shore are very close to the beach and I would rather be certain of being able to see those fish. I have to remind some guides to keep me within *easy* casting distance of the actual shoreline. Quite often we'll find fish so close to shore that their backs are out of the shallow water. Because light conditions are so important in bonefishing, obviously the sun should be at your back. Sometimes there is the wrong combination, i.e., the wind in your face and the sun at your back, and if the wind is strong, then you just have to find another place to fish. Your guide can't pole into a strong wind nor can you cast well. The guide gets worn out, and with many skiffs there is the continual "plop plop plop" against the hull that definitely warns the fish that a big bad boat is in the area.

Incidentally, that plopping noise does alarm the fish for great distances. For many reasons poling into the wind does not make sense. To have conditions just right (tide, sun and wind) is tough but the optimum would be: Pole with the wind, sun at your back and an incoming tide (that is, moving with the tide).

Q: What are your tactics for wading?

WM: One thing I've found, which is no great discovery, is that when wading you can get a lot closer to tailing fish if you will do some of the wading on your knees. I do this all the time and most guys can't believe what they are seeing. Remember, softer presentations are easier to make with shorter casts. So I wade just as close as I think I can without spooking the fish, then I very quietly drop down on my knees and continue to get closer to the fish while moving on my knees. Your body profile or silhouette is much smaller, much less visible to the fish, and you can get almost on top of them if you wish. Of course, you cannot cast as far kneeling, but obviously your cast will be short anyway. And again those false casts have to be away from the fish. This knee wading is fine on sand, but when you are on the coral flats you absolutely must wear some kind of protection for your knees. I've tested knee pads used for gardening, basketball, etc., but have finally found those used by cement finishers really work well. They stay in place while wading and fully protect your knees and pants from being cut all to pieces. I still have a couple of very tiny pieces of coral in my right knee from a trip to Belize several years ago. I much prefer to wade as opposed to being in a boat, but obviously you can wade only certain flats due to soft versus hard bottoms. Also, unless the fish are tailing well and unless you are on a flat really loaded with fish, wading is not as productive because you cannot see nearly as well being so low to the water. Furthermore, you cannot even begin to cover as much water by wading as you can from a boat.

There is no way that I can stand in one spot and wait for fish to show up. I don't have the patience and I feel certain that if I keep moving I'll find the fish. Whether wading or boat fishing, if I don't find fish within a short time I'll just move to another flat.

IN SUMMARY:

Q: You are obviously an enthusiastic bonefisherman. What attracts you to bonefishing?

WM: I think that bonefishing *generally,* but not always, is the ultimate challenge for the serious fly fisherman. In places where the fish are inclined to be larger and, accordingly, smarter or more wary than in some other areas, this fishing is especially challenging, for there is little margin for error.

Consider all the necessary steps required in bonefishing, in addition to proper tackle and selection of an area:

1. You have to find the fish and be able to spot them.

2. You have to get close to them without spooking them.

3. Your casts have to be "right on" (in terms of accuracy and delicacy).

4. Your strip or fly action must be just right.

5. You have to learn to see and/or feel when the fish has taken the fly.

6. You have to tighten up and set hook without blowing a chance that you may have worked hours to achieve.

7. You have to apply the right amount of pressure during the fight, and, of course, very little during the initial run.

Above all, it's important to release the fish carefully. They are an important resource.

So much for bonefish. God bless them as they are truly worth spending a lot of time with!

WHERE TO FISH?

Next to weather conditions, the most important facet of successful bonefishing is the proper backdrop or location. There are hundreds of excellent bonefishing flats and many have resorts near them. Here we'll cover several representative resorts that generally offer superb bonefishing.

DEEP WATER CAY CLUB: Deep Water Cay Club (DWCC), on the East End of Grand Bahama Island, is a favorite of many seasoned anglers who have had an opportunity to fish some of the world's best bonefishing flats. Novices, too, find the waters of DWCC productive, and many anglers have caught their very first bonefish from these flats. Clearly the flats of DWCC are among the most extensive found anywhere in the tropics.

DWCC's location is ideal. It's only a one-hour charter plane hop from West Palm Beach, Florida, or a 15-minute flight from Freeport, Grand Bahama. Within a boat ride from camp, there's more than 200 square miles of the most fertile and strikingly beautiful bonefish flats imaginable. Additional flats can also be found further north and east of the lodge, making DWCC's territory virtually limitless.

Most fishing, especially in February and March, occurs in the many "creeks" that slice through the East End of Grand

Bahama Island. Each creek is really an extended "flat," with deeper cuts and channels throughout permitting boat navigation and fish movement from flat to flat. Here an average flat runs over a quarter of a mile but may extend over a mile.

The creeks are mostly composed of marl and soft sand bottoms, with patches of turtle grass, clusters of mangrove and other plant life. This enormously rich environment provides an ideal habitat for shrimp and crabs, two of the bonefish's favorite staples.

Flats are found at the mouths of many of the creeks, but there are also several very productive areas located offshore. Offshore flats, such as Spencer's Rock, seem to rise out of nowhere at low tide and can be extraordinarily productive for bones.

Because of the complex makeup of the creeks, tidal flows are intricate and often can be used to the angler's advantage. Areas just 30 minutes from the main lodge may be a couple of hours behind in actual tidal flow; thus anglers can often fish rising and falling tides throughout the day by moving from place to place.

Bonefish are not generally found in large schools but rather in groups of four to a dozen, with an occasional cluster of 25 to 30. Bones average three to four pounds, although there are many five- to seven-pounders. Occasionally, bonefish of over eight pounds are taken, and the lodge record stands at a hefty 12 1/2 pounds!

In addition to bonefish, permit are present at Deep Water Cay. Taking a permit on light tackle is one of angling's toughest accomplishments, and some of the best permit flats anywhere are within reach of Deep Water's skiffs. A favorite place, Burroughs Cay, is to the east of the camp. It's a long, white sandy flat where spotting cruising permit is easy, though hooking them is always difficult.

Permit will average 15 to 30 pounds in these waters, with some over 40 pounds sighted each season. The lodge contains several mounted permit of over 35 pounds. A live crab is by far the most productive bait. Fly fisherman have made many valiant efforts, but fly fishing for permit is perhaps angling's biggest challenge at DWCC, or elsewhere.

Barracuda are often encountered on the flats, and for the angler who has never seen a cuda devour a rapidly retrieved fly, there is angling adventure ahead. Cuda in the five- to 10-pound range are commonplace, with far larger specimens possible year-round. The barracuda's swift runs are often punctuated by spectacular jumps.

Skiffs utilized at Deep Water are 16 feet long, constructed of fiberglass and powered by 35-hp outboard motors. They have padded seats, rod racks, dry storage, an ample casting platform in the front and are fully carpeted. They are ideal for thin-water fishing.

Local guides know these waters intimately. They are avid anglers and are familiar with all approaches to shallow water fishing. Many have been guiding at Deep Water for over 10 years.

Winston Moore landed 156 bonefish in nine days while fishing at Charlie's Haven. "It's a great area!"

DWCC is a comfortable oasis in an attractive setting. Double occupancy cottages are standard, each with a private bathroom, full electricity, air conditioning, comfortable twin beds and even a front porch. Two deluxe cottages are also available for a nominal additional charge.

The main lodge faces both the ocean and an inside creek. More than one meal has been interrupted by the sight of a bone tailing on the flats just beyond the dining room window. The lodge has a full bar, large lounge area complete with fireplace and library plus dining facilities. Meals are superb (a lunch can be taken along in the boat if additional fishing time is desired). *Rate:* $1,015 for five nights, and four days' fishing, per person, double occupancy. This includes the round trip charter plane service from Palm Beach.

CHARLIE'S HAVEN: In the last few years, Andros Island has earned a tremendous reputation for big bonefish and some experts, who have fished the world's most productive flats, are convinced that Andros has the largest bones. Earlier we mentioned that Ralph Ward landed five in the 10- to 12-3/4-pound class via fly fishing at Charlie's Haven on his first bonefishing trip. Dr. Rod Neubert landed an 11-lb., 12-oz. bonefish on a two-pound tippet for an IGFA world record. Winston Moore, on his first trip to Charlie's Haven, landed 156 bones during nine days of fly fishing, including several in the 10-pound class and one over 12 pounds. Clearly, these are big-league waters. Says Winston:

"One morning Charlie and I were poling along and saw one of the 'monsters' cruising toward us. We waited for it, got off a good cast, it took the fly, and I was well hooked to the largest bonefish I could ever imagine. Would you believe that after I fought the fish for perhaps 20 minutes, a shark showed up and took it away from me?

"We got just the head back and it weighed over four pounds. We had the fish close to the boat several times, and that bonefish had to be in the 15-pound class or larger," Winston recalled.

He went back to Charlie's Haven a few months later. He saw three tremendous bonefish together and hooked and landed the smallest of the trio. It was no less than 14 pounds and possibly over 15. He took a snapshot and released it even though it would have been an IGFA fly fishing world record. "The largest one had to be somewhere in the 17- to 20-pound bracket by comparison."

Paul Melchior, who fished Andros briefly, saw a number of bones over 10 pounds. "On one day my guide and I saw a huge bonefish that he said could go 18 pounds! I made three presentations to the fish, but it wasn't impressed or or even slightly interested. I get the jitters just thinking of that monster!"

John Donohue has fished most of the outstanding bonefish flats of the world. He has invested countless of hours meticulously searching the sandy and marl bottoms for a trophy bonefish.

Fishing Charlie's Haven in 1986, he was richly rewarded with a huge bonefish that stretched 32 1/2 inches in length and a hefty 19 1/2 inches in girth. Sadly, he had no scale with him. Most knowledgeable bonefishermen estimate that John's fish weighed between 15 and 16 pounds!

While most Charlie's Haven guests concentrate on bonefish, occasionally one can also enjoy excellent tarpon fishing at an area known as "west side." It's about 50 minutes away from camp but one needs calm weather.

"Tarpon fishing on the flats is mostly done on a rising tide," explains Paul Melchior, "so you fish the creeks first, then follow the fish to the flats. The tarpon are usually in the 50- to 75-pound range, but there have been some fish of over 100 pounds hooked. It's not fast action on the flats—on a good day you may jump four to six tarpon—and I suspect that casting the creeks is more productive, though not nearly as fascinating as stalking the silver king on the flats."

Unfortunately, Charlie's Haven was totally destroyed by fire in 1983; however a new, more comfortable, camp was completed in 1985.

Ironically, Charlie's Haven was not as overrun with fishermen as one would suspect. There are two reasons: (1) The anglers who have fished Charlie's kept their results in the "top secret" file and shared them only with a few close friends; (2) Charlie's Haven is not a posh resort by any means, and numerous things can go wrong. In the past, it was certainly not the place for the angler who wanted and expected everything to go according to schedule. Charlie's Haven is for the angler who is looking for big bonefish, but has the patience and resiliency to fend off the pesty gremlins that can pop up from time to time. A sense of humor may be one of the most important ingredients needed here.

Owner Charlie Smith understands that better logistics are necessary. He started the camp from scratch, with just enough money to buy some cement and materials to begin construction. Each season he improved his camp or purchased a boat or a motor. It has not been easy.

Guests fly to Andros Town airport (from Nassau) via Bahamas Air. From Andros Town they are transported by vehicle to camp about 25 miles north of the airport. It is essential that all guests bring their own tackle with them, as there is virtually no gear available on the island. *Rate:* $1,095 per week per person based on double occupancy.

OUT ISLAND INN: The above two resorts are strictly fishing camps. They cater exclusively to fishermen. There are many resorts or small hotels that offer a number of water and recreational activities, among them bonefishing. Although Out Island Inn is that type of a resort, owner Ken Bowe is dedicated to establishing his spa as an outstanding bonefishing place. Located on Exuma, Out Island Inn recently spent more than a half-million dollars in renovation, and it is indeed a sparkling jewel. More important to the fishermen, Ken has purchased new bonefishing skiffs and trained additional guides. As a result, his resort is becoming a favorite among some bonefishermen. Unfortunately, not all goes smoothly in the Bahamas, and some trips have unfolded badly at Out Island Inn. The number one nemesis seems to be the lack of experienced guides. The "old-timers" understand what bonefishing is all about. The younger guides apparently need more experience. One angler puts it best: "The younger ones (guides) don't take it as seriously as the veterans. Any obsessed bonefisherman or guide knows it's not quite 'do or die,' but darn close to it! Bonefishing is serious stuff, and not the casual recreational activity that a few new guides make it out to be."

Deep Water Cay Club, near Freeport, is a very comfortable lodge catering strictly to fishermen.

I fished Out Island Inn in May, 1984, for a few days. The first day was slow. Cloudy. Strong winds. Threatening skies. We still took a few bones. But on the second day my guide, Neville, took me to a special spot. There were three small mangrove tidal "creeks" that flowed into a center area which formed a pool.

I looked up the left "creek." There must have been several hundred bones, "lined up" like soldiers, impatiently waiting for the tide to rise just a little more so that they could invade the mangroves for a lunchtime feast. The center and the right creeks may have contained even more fish and the "pool" just in front of me was also thick with fish. How many bones? I wasn't about to conduct a demographic study. It was sufficient for me to know that wherever the fly would land it would surely fall right on the snout of a bonefish. To hell with the wind that had cursed me the day before, in which well-intended casts were blown far off the targets.

Actually, at Neville's special spot, I was more shocked if the fly returned without being attacked. Why couldn't all bonefishermen, especially those with my amateur status who have invested thousands of unproductive casts, experience this at least once in their lifetimes?

Amazingly, I think four of my first 20 casts produced nothing. The way this game should have been played was to see if one could actually cast into this area and retrieve the fly *without* getting a hit. That's where the real skill was! I giggled and laughed and giggled some more.

"There's more fish than water," I exclaimed to Neville, and he nodded. I landed more than my share of bones, and some broke off in the mangroves, and I lost a few at the end of the fight, and all of this frenzy would have continued except that one bone, much heftier than the others, deftly needled my fly line through a maze of mangroves. Ultimately, it required my wading right through the pool, among the bonefish, and up the creek to recover the line. They moved off, but didn't flush.

Ironically, a few bones followed me only a few feet away, which puzzled me, until I realized that when I nervously (or clumsily) waded on "their table," I had kicked up puffs of marl and sand, and surely a few tidbits. After I retrieved my fly line, re-tied a tippet and fly, I actually made several casts with only a couple of feet of fly line beyond the rod tip and hooked but lost a bonefish. Eventually these bones disappeared. Had I scared them? No, Neville insisted, they moved up into the mangroves and would now gorge themselves silly. "We'll look at other places—there are many flats." And we did.

Now don't for an instant conclude that the entire trip was like this. The above experience was unique. There were tough times. Very tough times. On a particularly thin flat, even 16-foot wispy leaders that unfurled high above sent bones scurrying for deeper water before the fly would enter the surface. A sudden movement...the plop, plop of the skiffs...a hard cast ...a1l flushed bones. I was convinced that some fish were unapproachable unless one possessed the distance casting skill of a Steve Rajeff. After the first day of fishing—which was cloudy and very windy and therefore with visibility (and my score) close to zero—I was wondering very privately how

Exuma developed its lofty reputation as one of the best bonefishing places in the Bahamas (and therefore in the world). On the second day my score increased considerably, and so did my confidence, and on the third and final day I was convinced that this may just be the place for frustrated bonefishermen. For out of a dozen different flats areas, only one failed to reveal a hefty number of bones.

On that third day, on the flats, Neville and I saw a very big bone approaching us. Surely it would veer off but, no, it came on closer and closer. When it was almost within casting distance I hurriedly cast into the wind, for I was convinced that the skiff or Neville or I (we were wading) would scare the bone off. The cast landed in a slop of curves and the fly was well off the intended path of the bone, but the great fish heard the plop of the fly, became curious and went over to investigate it. Anxiously, I retrieved in long strips, instead of twitching the fly inches at a time as Winston Moore had taught me. Nonetheless, the fish kept coming and coming—and Neville and I thought that it had mouthed the fly a couple of times, but dropped it before I could tighten up. Now the bonefish was only about 25 feet away but kept following, though somewhat nervously. It saw the skiff, or the guide or me—or all of us—and with a sudden flip of its giant tail it produced a cloud of powdery sand. When the sand settled, the great fish had disappeared. Presto. Like a magician. Neville said it was nine pounds. Maybe ten. I thought it was bigger...but then, how many bonefish do I see on Chicago's Michigan Avenue?

I saw another huge bone on the flats—one that I'm sure would scale well above 10 pounds—but it was on the move. I chased it diligently, but not gracefully, for a hundred yards hoping to get off a cast, for occasionally it would stop briefly. But as I got closer to it, almost within casting distance, the great bone would move off. It eventually tired of the "carrot" game, fluidly shifted gears and I'm sure chuckled as it easily eluded me and submarined into deeper, if not safer, waters.

There were several other big fish that broke off heavier leaders in the mangroves, but most of the bones in the area that I fished were in the three- to five-pound bracket. The week before I arrived, one guest had landed an 11 1/2-pound bone.

I was told that there are other areas on the Exumas where big fish are more prevalent. But on a three-day trip you want to pack more casting time and less traveling time.

While quality of fishing is the main magnet, Out Island Inn also incorporates a high degree of comfort: Spacious, modern, air-conditioned rooms that overlook the beach, pool, tennis courts, a dining room constructed at water's edge, gourmet meals, plus a courteous, friendly, competent staff. The lodge has runabouts, bicycles, windsurfing boards, sailing boats, scuba equipment and a private sandy beach. While the fisherman may not give a hoot about all this, bear in mind that this facility is one of those rare places where the angler can practice his art (in peace) while his nonfishing family is well entertained. In the evening you can slow-dance with your wife to ballads or boogie to a combo's upbeat tempos.

Owner Ken Bowe tries to run a smooth operation. An example of his fastidiousness: He firmly exclaimed his displeasure to a guide because when we arrived at the landing, the guide's outboard wasn't started. "I want the outboards purring, ready to go. I want the guides to immediately help the clients into the skiffs with a 'good morning' and a handshake, and be off in a flash." But life in Exuma is slow-paced, and Ken may be fighting a losing battle.

He dreams of an outpost fishing camp in years to come. Perhaps offering cruiseboat fishing a la Vic Barothy in the pre-Castro days at Cuba's Isle of Pines. "If we have the main ingredient, *fishing,* which I think we have, all the other things will come. It won't be overnight...but we will get there." With Bowe, it's an obsession.

Rate: Approximately $200 per fishing day per person based on double occupancy. This rate is applicable during the main bonefishing season from May to December. This includes accommodations, meals (including box lunches), skiff, guide, motor, gas and transportation between Out Island Inn and the landing. You can fly to Exuma via Fort Lauderdale, FL., on Aero Coach (1 hr. 40 min.) or fly Bahamasair via Nassau.

BIMINI BIG GAME FISHING CLUB (BBGFC): This extensive resort owned by the Bacardi Rum company has gained a fine reputation through its usually reliable marlin fishing. However Bimini also happens to offer excellent fishing for very big bonefish. Jim Orthwein set a new IGFA world record at BBGFC during March, 1983, by landing a 15-pound bonefish on a four-pound tippet. As a matter of fact, it's the largest fly-caught bonefish listed in the IGFA records. Currently there are two other world record bonefish, 15 and 16 pounds (caught on spinning gear), that were caught at Bimini, and a number of other bones in double-digit weights. So clearly these waters can be seriously considered if one is searching for big bones. BBGFC is also for the angler who enjoys trolling for big game as well as bonefishing on the flats.

One can expect good to excellent fishing during the entire season (if weather conditions are favorable) but the time for the big bones here appears to be March and April.

Jim Orthwein's 15-pound bonefish taken from BBGFC is a current IGFA world record for a four-pound tippet.

One of BBGFC's strong assets is that it has working agreements with about eight excellent bonefishing guides who through the years have acquired tremendous experience. They provide skiff, motor, fuel (and their great eyesight) for approximately $170 per day. If there are two persons in your party, the cost is half.

Hotel rooms (European plan) cost about $98 per night. Meals can be ordered at the hotel's restaurant or taken elsewhere in Bimini.

PITTSTOWN POINT LANDING: There is another type of accommodation available for bonefishermen in the Bahamas. Basically, it's the small resort that has a maximum of up to ten twin rooms and features the usual water sports, including bonefishing. It differs from the above hotels in that it is much smaller and has a very casual atmosphere with few planned activities. Pittstown Point Landing is one example. This resort is located on Crooked Island (southern end of the Bahamas), which is serviced only twice a week from Nassau. Usually only one or two guides with skiffs are available on this island, so fishing arrangements must be made well in advance.

Don Jones, an obviously enthusiastic Pittstown fan reports, "There were more big schools of bones than anywhere we've fished. Most days we boated 12 to 25 and the average "bad day' produced 10 bones. On our best day we landed 30 bonefish that averaged 1 1/2 to four pounds. The largest bone that we landed was in the five- to six-pound class. Obviously, there are places where bigger bonefish are found, but we also hooked one fish in the 10- to 12-pound bracket so there are some big bones too. The disadvantage is that the best flats are one to 1 1/2 hours away and if the water is rough it can be a tiresome ride."

ABOUT THE ISLANDS

There are more than 700 islands that compose the Bahamas, which stretch from Florida all the way down to Haiti and Cuba. Freeport on Grand Bahama Island, Nassau on New Providence and nearby Paradise Island represent three very "touristy" centers that offer everything: posh hotels, golf courses, shops, casinos, fine restaurants, calypso and glittery entertainment. One can easily arrange a stopover at these towns either prior to or after the "main event" (bonefishing). Occasionally, a tourist encounters less than cordial treatment, but most of it seems to take place at the larger tourist centers and is sometimes indirectly provoked by the tourist who demands instant service. The experienced traveler avoids political conversations, and realizes that he is a guest of the Bahamas and acts and speaks accordingly. It's seldom that impolite treatment is accorded to the visiting fishermen at camps or resorts away from the big centers.

Documents and Entry Requirements: To enter the Bahamas, proof of U. S. citizenship is required. A valid or expired passport, birth certificate or U.S. voter's registration card are all acceptable. A driver's license is not. Up to 200 cigarettes and one quart of liquor may be brought into the Bahamas.

Weather Conditions: The average low temperature for the year is 70 degrees, the average high 82 degrees. The following chart provides monthly temperatures and number of clear days per month. June through October is the wettest period, and hurricanes can occur from July through October.

Weather in Nassau:

Temp (F)	Jan	Feb	Mar	Apr	May	Jun	Jul	Aug	Sep	Oct	Nov	Dec
Av. Low	65	64	66	69	71	71	75	76	75	73	70	67
Av. High	77	77	79	81	84	87	88	89	88	85	81	79
Days no rain	25	23	26	24	22	18	17	17	15	18	21	25

*AND FINALLY...*The Bahamas represent one of the best places for the experienced or novice fly fisherman to stalk the bonefish. While the quality of bonefishing is paramount, the Bahamas scenic value can't be overestimated. As Cam Dobbins puts it: "Perhaps nowhere on earth are you going to find more shades or hues of green and blue than in the Bahamian waters. The white sandy beaches, the numerous cays and islets, often transcend the actual fishing experience, recreating visions of Robinson Crusoe days; this seance in our pressure cooker life may be equally as important as catching bonefish. Or almost."

Mexico

Fast-Paced Fishing, with a Latin Beat

You can fish the Yucatan flats for bonefish or permit, the channels at night for cubera snapper and the mangroves for snook and tarpon. Or slap a fly next to a hungry sailfish or angry striped marlin, and, don't forget Guerrero's bass fishing. It's all there, at mostly bargain prices.

April and May are the best months to fish the Yucatan peninsula for its high-leaping, energetic sails.

Sport Fishing
SOLMAR
ANGLER ED RICE
FROM VANCOUVER, WA.
FISH STRIPED MARLIN
TACKLE FLY
TIME 45 MINUTES
WEIGHT 88 LBS.
BOAT OSO NEGRO
CAPT
DATE 27-DEC-85
PHOTO MARIO

Chapter 8

MEXICO

I JUDGED that first day's fishing at Pez Maya (Yucatan) as "great," and it would have been "perfect" had it not been for a particularly greedy, snot-nosed bonefish.

It was one of those rare days when all the necessary elements for superb flats fishing come together: the high, blue sky, the bright but not blinding sun, the placid waters, the light puffy breezes that cooled us but hardly ruffled the water's surface. And bonefish, the most important ingredient, were everywhere and easy to spot.

No matter where my guide Carlos took me, we saw bones. Often we found them lined up, in pods of six or eight, but sometimes in schools of 20 to 50. Occasionally we would see a single or a double, but mostly they were in packs.

The bonefish must have had a bad night, I suspect, because they were very truculent, angry at the world, and they gobbled anything that whisked past their noses. Sometimes they would even rush right to the top as the fly splatted on the water, grabbing it only inches from the surface.

Before this trip, Bing McClellan, who fished Pez Maya before, had advised me that a small Pink Shrimp pattern tied on a keel hook was just the ticket for these Yucatan bones. "Take your pliers and offset the hook to one side. That's important, especially on the keel hooks. If you need another pattern, try a white fly on a keel," he prescribed with precision. The only time I changed flies was to replace the chewed up models that bore little resemblance to the original pattern.

Ed Rice (left) landed this striped marlin on a fly. Less than 10 anglers have ever accomplished this.

Pez Maya is a delightful fishing resort on the Yucatan. Its nearby flats are excellent for bones and permit.

Since I only had 1 1/2 days at Pez Maya, I asked the guide to show me as much of the water as he could. We fished the camp waters and then headed south to Ascension Bay, stopping often along the way and nearly always picking up a bonefish or two.

At one place, near Ascension, the guide took me to a spot that was just short of amazing. A couple of hundred bones continually circled our boat. Round and round they went. I tried to find the largest bonefish, but Carlos urged me to cast. He spoke little English, I spoke no Spanish, so it was difficult to convey my strategy, which was to pick out the largest bone. Surely the school would disperse on the first hook-up. All Carlos would say is "Cast, cast, cast!"

And I did. To my surprise, the school didn't disappear after the first hook-up, or the second, or the third. They would flush, yes, but they would return to circle our boat. We must have released a half dozen bones from this school.

It was right after this experience that I came across that greedy, snot-nosed bonefish that spoiled my perfect day. Carlos spotted a tiny wake on the surface some distance away and, after observing it carefully, he concluded it was a permit. The fish was moving, but it would pause briefly from time to time. Carlos poled that boat as fast, but as quietly, as he could, hoping to get us within casting distance.

We chased that fish for a long time. Sweat poured down Carlos' face, but he poled harder and faster. Occasionally Carlos would stop, cussing under his breath I'm sure, for he would lose sight of the permit. Then he would pick up the fish again, and the chase continued. But the permit was always beyond casting distance. Finally the permit stopped, apparently to grub. Now Carlos edged the boat slowly, quietly, carefully. He turned the craft slightly so I would be in better casting position. It was not an easy cast, but Carlos didn't want to chance getting any closer. He had done his work. And done it well.

Normally I would have botched up the cast, but after the way Carlos had poled for probably 20 minutes, his shirt drenched with perspiration, I just had to make a good presentation. The fly unfurled safely in front and just beyond the permit, which I judged to be 10 to 12 pounds. I hadn't alarmed it. I could see the fly, and the permit began inching closer to it. It was at least intrigued. I was sure that it was about to take the fly when that greedy, snot-nosed bonefish appeared from nowhere grabbed it and scooted off, flushing the permit, and ruining my first presentation I had ever made to this elusive species. We cursed that bonefish alright! Carlos in Spanish, and probably in Mayan. I cursed it in English and in Greek.

We had a very early start that day and in addition to the bonefish, we caught barracuda on large streamer flies, several jacks, and one small tarpon on a popping bug, although we probably raised a half-dozen. We saw some very big cudas in the cuts that probably weighed over 20 pounds, but they were not interested.

Carlos could not have planned a better itinerary, concentrating on bones but mixing it up with other species. We took only a 10-minute lunch and he worked hard from morning to dusk.

After a superb supper, the camp manager told me about some good cubera snapper fishing that sometimes takes place at night at the channel that links the flats with the Caribbean. This was also a good snook place with plenty of jacks as well, he said.

It must have been 10 P.M., when I wandered to the cut armed with a No. 10 fly rod and plenty of large sailfish-type poppers. The almost-full moon, shone bright and clear, so it was not at all difficult to fish.

A seven- or eight-pound snook started the nocturnal session, after which I must have hooked a half-dozen jack crevalle, but then the action stopped for awhile. I could sense, however, that something unusual was about to occur. You just know it.

The popper was doing its thing. Kerplunking. Gurgling. Splashing in moonlit water. Pausing for a bit. And then kerplunking, gurgling and splashing again. I was almost mesmerized by the popper's moonlight dance.

The strike wasn't particularly explosive, but what ensued was certainly dramatic. The fish, undoubtedly a big cubera, started off slowly, and then realizing its danger, increased its speed, gaining tremendous power. All I could do was hang on to the fly rod with both hands, giving out line stingily. The fly line was beyond the tip, and now yards and yards of backing melted off the reel. I tried to get an angle on the fish, to turn it by applying all the pressure I could to one side. But the cubera swam on and on, and I trudged along the bank to save whatever line I could. The fish made it beyond the mouth and there was no way of stopping it. The leader snapped. Good-bye.

Okay! Chalk up one for the cuberas. I beefed up the tippet to 15 pounds, tied on another shock leader and popper. The results from the second and third fish were carbon copies of the first. So was the fourth fish, which was probably the largest of them all. They all did the same thing: they swam beyond the mouth and into the ocean.

After Pez Maya, I was scheduled to continue to Club Pacifico de Panama for a shot at sails on poppers. My supply of poppers suddenly was down to an alarming few, and there would be no way to replenish my stock. So when the cubera action ended, I was relieved in a sense. No use feeding those cuberas any more

Atlantic or Pacific sails on a fly offers high-voltage fishing. Mexico provides both species.

of my poppers. The stillness of the night enveloped the channel again, a mist appeared on the surface and I know I slept with a smile that night. It had been a great day.

It would appear, then, that anyone who is searching for a bonefishing utopia, coupled with some variety of fishing, would do well to book Pez Maya. But problems developed in the past. Some of the locals discovered that they could make money selling bonefish on the market. So nets captured huge quantities of bonefish, and this region, known as Boca Paila, suddenly was just another bonefish spot.

The camp owners of Pez Maya and the nearby Boca Paila Fishing Resort protested the illegal netting to officials. Finally, after several seasons, the authorities began to patrol the flats, and made a number of arrests. Most of the netting ceased, and today, the flats of Boca Paila have recovered to a point where, once again, outstanding catches are being made.

When this region first became prominent, some mind-boggling catches were recorded. Ted Williams, the baseball great, once landed 70 bonefish in a single day's fishing. Stan Levy probably holds the record for a one day's catch with 84 bones while staying at Boca Paila Fishing Resort. Don't expect to even remotely approach these catches today, for you would surely be disappointed. A dozen bonefish in one day is good, and if conditions are right, a skilled fly rodder can probably hook 30 in a day.

Boca Paila (which means "mouth of flat dish") is about 90 miles south of Cancun, that famous Yucatan resort town built from scratch in the late '60s. Boca Paila consists of a series of lagoons, mangrove islands, extensive flats and several bocas, or mouths, that lead into the Caribbean.

Most of the Yucatan bones will weigh between two and 3 1/2 pounds, smallish in comparison to those taken from the Florida Keys and Bahamas. Larger fish are usually landed during the course of a trip, but fish above six pounds are considered exceptional.

While the Boca Paila region gets most of the play because of its close proximity to Cancun, there is another fishing area that is more productive and contains larger bonefish. It's Ascension Bay, which is about 25 miles south of Boca Paila. This huge lagoon is about 10 miles long by five miles wide. There is a camp (Punta Pajaros) on the southern edge of the bay that can accommodate up to eight anglers, but from what I understand it is now closed to the public.

The guests of Pez Maya and Boca Paila Fishing Lodge consider these waters so productive that they are willing to spend the two to three hours' boat ride or the 30-minute charter flight necessary to reach Ascension Bay. This area is also a superb place for permit (largest on spinning gear is Ed Boese's 27 1/2-pounder), and, at times, snook and tarpon fishing can be a bonus.

THE CAMPS: The two camps, Boca Paila Fishing Resort and Pez Maya, are fairly similar and therefore a common description should suffice. Guests are housed in rondavels, circular cottages that contain two independent units. Each unit has twin beds, modern showers and plumbing, small patio, screened windows for ventilation, thatched roof and stone exterior. The main lodge incorporates dining/sitting room and kitchen.

Fiberglass 16-foot skiffs are used with one guide assigned to two anglers. Pez Maya's rate is $1,139 per week; Boca Paila's is $1,275 (both rates are based on double occupancy).

THE SEASONS: Good fishing can be expected any time from November through July, but usually late April through July provides the best possibilities because the winds are less frequent at this time.

THE TACKLE: Probably the best all-round fly rod here is an 8 1/2 footer calibrated to take a No. 8 WF floating line. Leaders up to 12 feet, tapered down to six pounds, will suffice for most bonefishing and permit. Nearly all the standard bonefishing flies are productive here, but the Pink Shrimp pattern is particularly effective.

Since the tarpon are small in this area, one can get by with the same rod (most tarpon are under 25 pounds). You can use similar gear for barracuda and most other species, but if you try for cubera snappers at night with poppers, a No. 10 or 11 rod is needed.

YUCATAN'S SAILFISHING

In May, 1984, I had the privilege to fish the Cancun area from Steve Sloan's boat (the "Double Header") with Larry and Gloria Furman, two of the best light tackle anglers I've come across. The Furmans spend a great deal of time in Panama fishing with gossamer lines for sails, black and blue marlin.

The fishing for sails was nothing short of fantastic. In three days of fishing the Furmans landed 72 sails on trolling gear. In 1 1/2 days, I managed nine sails. Obviously the potential of the Cancun region for sailfish can't be overestimated.

Unfortunately, my fly rods were lost between New Orleans and Cancun, so I had no chance to try for sails with flies. I've taken my share of Pacific sails on a fly, but not an Atlantic, and I would have liked to compare them.

From my brief observation, I believe that it is probably more difficult to tease up Atlantics. The Pacific sails can be teased up

The bonefish, the phantom of the flats, is once again plentiful along the Yucatan Peninsula—especially at Ascension Bay.

for a longer time and a greater distance, which serves to aggravate the fish to such an extent that they will usually hit a fly if it is presented properly. The Atlantics aggressively attack a bait, but on this trip, it also appeared that if they missed it, their interest would wane.

The Atlantics seem to be tougher fish than the Pacific sails, pound for pound. Most of the fish we hooked were 40 to 60 pounds, almost half the size of the Pacifics, but even on regulation tackle, they were not easily subdued.

There was one time that I'm sure I would have had a hook-up with an Atlantic on fly gear. Capt. Tom Furtado noticed some diving birds and immediately headed to that place, where at least a dozen sails were feeding voraciously on small bait fish. I suspect that any streamer or popper tossed amidst these fish would have received immediate attention. We had a triple-header on our trolled baits at this spot.

The two most productive months to fish sails in the Yucatan are April and May, while the three best areas are Cozumel, Isla Mujeres and Cancun.

There are dozens of resort hotels to choose from at Cozumel and Cancun. At Cozumel, the El Presidente, Sol Caribe Sheraton, Mayan Plaza and Cabanas del Caribe can be considered. At Cancun, the Camino Real, El Presidente, Sheraton and the Cancun Caribe Hyatt will satisfy most tastes. At Isla Mujeres, the selection is limited and service is generally substandard. The Zazil-Ha-Bojorquez, Posada Del Mar and the Berny are the best possibilities.

Years ago it was very difficult to obtain a sportfisherman boat at these places. Many American anglers would move their boats from the U.S. to Cozumel for the sailfish season. Today, however, there are a number boats that are available for private charter ranging from $300 to $800 per day.

WEST COAST'S BILLFISHING

There are at least a dozen excellent sportfishing centers on the Pacific side of Mexico that attract thousands of anglers each year. Let's look at two major destinations:

MAZATLAN: Located in the state of Sinaloa, Mazatlan probably gives up 3,000 to 5,000 billfish each season. This one-time sleepy village has grown into one of the most popular tourist centers on the west coast, and while it will never rival Acapulco for pure glitz, Mazatlan has a variety of hotels ranging from inexpensive but clean to deluxe and expensive.

At $230 per boat per day, Mazatlan private charters are among the best billfish bargains in the world. Nearly all anglers at this and other west coast mainland fishing centers use trolling gear exclusively for billfish. The supplied tackle generally includes 50- or 80-pound line, Penn reels and a heavy rod. Since most of the billfish are striped marlin or sails that weigh considerably less than 200 pounds, the gear used easily overpowers the species. But these charters thrive on satisfied customers, so SOP is a photo that includes the fish hanging from the gallows, the smiling tourist and, of course, the ever-present sign of the charter company's name. By using heavy gear, and by having the mates set the hook before handing the rod to the tourist sitting in the fighting chair, the charters deliver a high success ratio.

Is the light tackle guy completely out of the picture here? No. Most private charters will fish light tackle if they are informed well in advance. Fly fishermen can be accommodated, but it is necessary to go over the game plan with the crew—teasing up the fish, yanking out the teasers, throwing the motor into neutral and other details—before making the presentation. It's best for an angler to take along a friend who is also interested in fly fishing for billfish. They can alternate in handling the teaser rod and casting to the fish.

It's important that the captain and mate understand the project on hand, and this is best discussed prior to departing from the dock. Most captains and mates speak little or no English, but the owners of boat liveries are usually very fluent, so the whole procedure should be explained beforehand. Actually the captain needs to know just a few words, "slow down," "speed up" and "neutral," and these instructions are probably best delivered through hand signals.

I've fished Mazatlan on several occasions and these trips were highly successful. The last time I was there, it was a relaxed, nonfishing vacation with my wife, but at midweek I decided to charter Gil Aviles' boat for the day. I had no tackle with me, so I had to use what was onboard. It's a long run to the marlin waters from the port (about two hours each way) so I had about four hours of actual fishing time. I landed two stripeds, hooked two others and teased up a couple of more. I've had slower fishing in my life! If I had my fly gear with me, there probably would have been a chance of a hook-up with a striped marlin on a fly because the fish were very aggressive that day, and in a couple of cases, they were teased up for some distance.

Mazatlan has two distinct seasons as far as the fly fisherman is concerned: December to about mid-March for striped marlin; May through July for the sails. Of the two periods, the fly rodder is more likely to be successful if he chooses the summer months for sails. Striped marlin are indeed very difficult to tease up. Furthermore, Mazatlan is less crowded during the summer months, and some boat liveries even offer a discount.

Dolphin or "dorado" as they are known in Latin America are excellent fighters...especially on a fly rod.

That summer run of sailfish can be something else. One angler told me that he raised over 40 sailfish in one day. He was using trolling gear, but after taking a few fish, resorted to the light casting tackle that he brought along. Obviously, that day was tailor-made for the fly rodder.

There are three disadvantages to Mazatlan fishing: (1) the billfishing waters require about a two-hour run each way from the port, (2) there isn't much variety fishing, so if billfishing is poor, there aren't "lesser" species to save the trip and (3) you miss the fishing camp atmosphere (in Mazatlan you stay at one of the hotels and transfer by taxi each day to the fishing dock).

The advantages are: (1) Mazatlan is one of the best billfishing bargains in the world, (2) it's a "touristy" town, so it's a superb place for an angler to take his nonfishing family members and (3) it's relatively easy to get to from most U.S. cities.

The Hotels: Mazatlan is blessed with dozens of excellent hotels. The Camino Real is posh and well-operated and probably at the top of the list. The Holiday Inn is a notch or two below but also highly rated. Anglers who are interested in a good, clean hotel that's inexpensive can book the older Playa Mazatlan.

The Restaurants: Nearly all top-rated hotels have excellent dining rooms. Among the best are the Laffite (Camino Real) and the Marina del Sol (Holiday Inn). For continental cuisine, Fellini's, Sr. Pepper and Casa Loma are recommended. For a fun time, Mr. Frog or the Shrimp Bucket should be included.

BAJA CALIFORNIA: One of Mexico's most prolific fishing areas is Baja California where, according to Ray Cannon, author of the popular "The Sea of Cortez," there are more than 700 varieties of fish. Of particular interest to the fly rodder are the billfish, roosterfish and the dolphin (dorado).

As is the case in Mazatlan, the majority of fishermen are tourists who charter a day's fishing and are satisfied to land a few fish on furnished tackle. However, the resorts strung along the east cape of Baja are also attracting a large number of excellent anglers from California, including light tackle anglers and expert fly fishermen, so some of the captains and mates are becoming aware of light tackle fishing.

Anglers, like the venerable Harry Kime, have been taming billfish with a fly rod for many years, so while not common, it's also not that unusual to see the occasional fly fisherman; in fact, there is a fly fishing cult developing, mostly composed of west-coasters, who continually fish Baja.

One such angler is Ed Rice, the sport show impresario, who has made numerous fly fishing trips to Baja. He scored particularly well in December, 1985, during a striped marlin bonanza by landing an 88-pound striped marlin on an eight-pound tippet. There are probably only a dozen anglers who have landed striped marlin on a fly; the list includes such luminaries Lee Wulff, Billy Pate, Winston Moore, Harry Kime and the man who started it all, Dr. Webster Robinson.

During the same trip, Ed's fishing partner, Ray Beadle landed a 111-pound striped marlin on a 15-pound tippet.

Mexico's Lake Guerrero is a very consistent bass lake and offers first class accommodations. Cam Dobbins does the honors on this largemouth.

According to Ed: "The striped marlin were everywhere. It was a matter of finding diving birds, heading to that area, identifying that there were marlin (as opposed to other species) and making a presentation. Sometimes I'm sure that as many as a dozen marlin were balling the bait. I had plenty of chances on this trip before succeeding."

In saltwater fly fishing, especially in billfishing, a considerable amount of the credit must be given to the captain and mate. Ed Rice and Ray Beadle were quick to acknowledge this: "Our captain, Didier van der Veecken, is among the best. He understands the challenge of fly fishing, particularly for billfish, and the necessity for the angler and crew to work smoothly as a team. He is highly recommended. It helps, too, that he is fluent in English."

Didier operates out of Cabo San Lucas. At present, he has a couple of center-console boats, which are ideal for the fly fishermen. However, he also acquired a new Spencer 28-foot fiberglass boat powered by a CAT 3208.

"There will be plenty of room aboard for the light tackle and fly fisherman," Didier reports, "I enjoy this type of fishing and all its challenges. This past season has been particularly good for the fly fishermen." The daily rate is $275 for the boat and up to three anglers can be handled although two fly fishermen, taking turns, is better.

Didier's concentration on fly fishing and light tackle is certainly a boom to Baja fishing. Not all captains and mates along the Baja strip have been cooperative with light tackle fishermen. Many captains feel that their main responsibility is to deliver as many billfish as possible, and if this means using heavy gear, then that's what they will provide and insist on using. Often I hear anglers returning from Baja complain about their captains: "They are fine if they are fishing for marlin or sails using heavy tackle and their methods, but when an angler suggests roosterfishing or fly fishing, some of the captains become surly."

It's unfortunate that most resorts, especially the posh, more expensive spas at Cabo San Lucas, do not own the boats and instead book boats and crews from the local marinas. There is little control and no effort in matching a crew with the angling party, so it becomes a pot luck situation. This, however, is slowly changing, and Didier van der Veecken's commitment to light tackle and fly fishing is not only highly welcomed but I suspect will induce other captains to follow suit.

The Hotels: At Cabo San Lucas, the swank Twin Dolphins, Hotel Cabo San Lucas, Hacienda and Finisterra are all excellent, with the Twin Dolphins probably rated slightly higher than the others. However, many anglers prefer the smaller, less pretentious but still first-class Solmar Hotel. At San Jose del Cabo, the Palmilla is top-rated but the El Presidente is worth considering.

As one proceeds north to Buena Vista and La Paz one finds more cooperative captains who are willing to try something new. There are a half-dozen excellent resort hotels between Cabo and La Paz that seem to care more about the angler's desires. Hotel Club Spa Buenavista, Las Palmas, Punta Colorada and Rancho Buena Vista are good examples. Most of these resorts own the boats and hire the crews. Another tremendous advantage is that these hotels are out of the high-rent district and if the angler wants to save money and concentrate on fishing, these resorts are highly recommended. As an example, a five-night, four-day fishing trip, which includes accommodations, all meals, and private charter (28-foot cruiser), captain and mate costs approximately $550, based on double occupancy, at Club Spa Buenavista (the other nearby resorts offer similar rates).

Roosters and Dolphin: The Buena Vista/La Paz area is also excellent for its roosterfishing. This species, while fairly easy to take on live or dead bait, and sometimes on artificials, presents quite a challenge to the fly fisherman.

The smaller roosters, up to a dozen pounds, once located, often can be taken on poppers, but the big fish, are very difficult to fool. Giant roosters, along Baja, will grab bait, especially mullet, while totally ignoring poppers and swimming streamers. The late Lew Jewett of 3-M had figured out a way to interest larger roosters on fly gear and offered to demonstrate his method. We planned to fish Baja together, but we never did, because a few months after our conversation, Lew died.

Some of the west-coasters have been fairly successful with roosters and have numerous ideas on the subject. A few feel that the flies used by many anglers are too big, and that small streamers are better. Others claim that to be successful, one must find their exact feeding level, by using various density lines. One angler who scores often along Baja, fishes very early in the morning—from around daylight to 9 A.M.— because he feels that once the light is bright, the big roosters are not apt to take flies or poppers. My experience with roosters has been confined to plug casting for them in Central American waters. At times, I've caught them on top, with big lures and on bright days. I've never read a definitive piece on taking roosters on flies, but I suspect that there are a number of west-coasters who do it fairly consistently.

Another species of interest to the fly rodder is the dolphin, or "dorado." This aggressive, very cooperative species can be taken consistently on poppers once a school is located. Fly rodders along the Baja coast have made amazing catches. Once a school of dorado is located, the action is practically endless, as the school will congregate close to the boat as long as a hooked fish is kept near it. Catching the big bull dolphin on flies is a different matter, and often a matter of luck. The big dolphin are almost always loners.

FRESHWATER FISHING

What about freshwater fishing? Is this of interest to the fly rodder? Mexico has tried to introduce rainbow trout in some waters, but from what I understand, it hasn't been very successful.

The country has a number of largemouth bass lakes that have been very productive. The best from the fly rodders' standpoint might be Lake Guerrero, which has produced tremendous catches on casting tackle when weather conditions were normal. Some anglers claim that Guerrero is strictly a "quantity" lake, and that a largemouth of over five pounds is a rarity. However, since December, 1985 several huge bass have been taken via plug casting, including a 12-lb., 2-oz. trophy, and three other bass of 10 pounds plus.

I haven't fished Guerrero, but several anglers have told me that they watched fly fishermen work these waters and their results were fairly good. With the great numbers of flies available, from poppers to streamers, plus the variety of fly lines including fast sinkers, there's no doubt that the fly fisherman could score well on Guerrero.

There are several excellent resorts on Guerrero, and undoubtedly the most comfortable is the Alta Vista. The rate per person, based on double occupancy, is $760 for five-nights and four-days' fishing. Anglers fly to Harlingen, Texas and from there are transported to Guerrero by car (about a five-hour drive) or by charter plane. The best times to fish Guerrero are the winter and spring months.

Required Documentation and Currency: To enter Mexico, U.S. citizens need a tourist card, obtainable from any Mexican Tourist Office or airline that services Mexico, upon presentation of proof of citizenship (birth certificate, voter's registration card, valid or expired passport). Note: Minors (under the age of 18) traveling with one parent, must have written permission from the other parent. This letter must be notarized and in duplicate.

Mexican pesos, the official currency, are easily obtained from banks, American Express offices, hotels and at airport currency counters.

AND FINALLY... Yes, there's Montezuma's revenge to contend with, but the smart tourist can often avoid this by staying at the best hotels, eating at the better restaurants that primarily cater to tourists and taking such precautions as drinking only bottled water.

Mexico offers the fly rodder numerous saltwater challenges, from bonefish in Yucatan to billfishing at Baja. It is unfortunate that a number of excellent tarpon waters have succumbed to pollution, for in years past some of the largest tarpon in the world were landed from the Panuco and other rivers that pour out into the Gulf of Mexico.

With two extensive coastlines, plus Baja California, Mexico offers the saltwater fly rodder a lifetime of challenges.

Belize

The Caribbean's Most Varied Fishing

Extensive bonefish flats, a better-than-average chance for a permit, tarpon that come in small to large packages, classic snook fishing, barracuda that jump sky-high—and snappers, jacks and ladyfish that can enliven a slow day. These (and so many other) reasons are why hundreds of fly fishermen flock to English-speaking Belize each season.

Frank Wentink landed this 18-pound permit while fishing from The Piper. Belize's permit population is growing.

Chapter 9

BELIZE

IT WAS A HELLUVA TRIP. It was exciting, comical, frustrating, satisfying, educational, fun, adventurous. I've caught more tarpon elsewhere, but no other tarpon expedition proved more stimulating than my first trip to El Pescador, on Ambergris Cay.

Talk about comical. Pancho, my guide, was racing across the bay, looking for some new flats. When he found them, he throttled down to a crawl and meticulously and efficiently surveyed the flats ahead. Then he started shouting, pointing, yelling. "There's a big one! Over 100 pounds!" he insisted.

I mean the thing looked like a huge torpedo, slowly heading for our skiff. Naturally I grabbed my fly rod, quickly stripped line and began to cast. But the fly line wouldn't shoot through the guides.

"What the hell is going on?" Pancho demanded. He takes his guiding seriously. He wants his sports to do the best.

The line was strangely wrapped around the rod tip. In my hurry to make a cast, I yanked the rod across the boat seat, popping off a rod guide near the tip. There's no way I could cast without it, and I didn't have a spare tarpon rod in the boat. Thankfully, we found the guide on the skiff's bottom. I wrapped it tightly to the rod with mono and applied a coat of clear fingernail polish, which I carry in my tackle bag for such emergencies. All I could do then was wait for it to dry.

The emotional Pancho couldn't control himself. "There's another tarpon, maybe bigger! There's two more! We've hit tar-

Fishing the mangroves for small tarpon is electrifying sport—Bob Stearns captured this action at KCS Lodge.

pon heaven and we're waiting for nail polish to dry. No wonder guides die early." Oh, he could get carried away. I like emotional guides.

The nail polish dried, and there were plenty of tarpon that day, though none as big as those two behemoths Pancho spotted at the outset.

I landed three fine tarpon that morning that took 30, 35 and 65 minutes to subdue. They were very tough fish to land. I jumped probably another 15 tarpon that day. In other words, I was casting to, or fighting tarpon, most of the day.

At Ambergris, when the water is clear and not particularly ruffled, and if the sun is shining brightly, visibility can be extremely good. You (or more likely, your guide) can pick out the silver-sided targets at distances of over 50 yards. Just like in the Florida Keys. This is vastly different from other tarpon experiences that I've had in Latin America, where you are primarily blind casting in murky waters.

When a tarpon is located, the guide poles the boat swiftly but quietly, hoping to intercept the fish and provide you with an advantageous casting angle. The presentation is made, and much of the time the tarpon's strike will be dramatic, sometimes even explosive, because of the shallow water and because the fly is traveling close to the surface. The ensuing fight is spectacular. And these fish are very powerful. I found that 30- to 40-pound fish here fought as well as tarpon twice as large elsewhere.

During the two days I fished the tarpon flats, we saw probably a total of 200 to 250 tarpon. They were primarily in groups of two to four fish; thus I was able to cast to fish continuously. On the second day, the longest time we spent looking for a target was probably twenty minutes. I fished El Pescador in early October, which was considered an off-period, but I wonder if there is such a thing as an off-period when weather conditions are right. I must emphasize that we had close to perfect fishing conditions, with tremendous visibility, which is so vital to this hunt-and-cast type of fishing.

Let me tell you about lunch one day. Having fought tarpon most of the morning, I was totally exhausted. My arms refused to make another cast; my hands refused to reel in another yard.

I told Pancho to find a spot where there would be no tarpon to disturb our lunch. I was played out. When he was convinced that he had indeed found such a place, he proudly stuck the pole in the flats and tied up. Sure enough, there were no tarpon around, so we started to eat our lunch. But in the midst of munching a pork chop sandwich, I noticed one tarpon approaching our boat. Then three others. To my right there were a pair of 60-pounders. I spotted a few more. During that 40-minute break, we must have seen 30 tarpon swim within, or close to, casting distance. I could take it no longer. I convinced my arms that they weren't nearly as tired as they claimed. I was in an experimental mood so I tied on a big fly rod popper and flung the whirling bird in the direction of a 60- to 70-pounder. The tarpon seemed bored with the surface bait and turned away from it. I looked for another target, when suddenly the same tarpon turned again and smashed angrily into the popper. He was on for a few exciting close-to-the-boat jumps before the hooked pulled out.

The fish were exceptionally aggressive in the morning but skittish in the late afternoon. I'm sure that the position of the sun had something to do with it. Again, in order to fish the tarpon flats effectively, one must have a number of special conditions come together. Among them: bright sun, calm surface, clear waters, the right water temperatures and, of course, tarpon on the flats. You need to provide fast, accurate casting, and on those days when everything comes together, it helps to have the arm strength of a blacksmith.

HOW IT ALL GOT STARTED

This tiny Central American country (it's smaller than the state of Vermont) gained prominence in the angling world in the early 1960s when the late Vic Barothy started a modern camp on the Belize River. Previously, Vic had operated a fishing resort on Isle of Pines in Cuba, but after the Castro coup, he and his wife loaded two of their cruisers with whatever possessions they deemed most valuable and at dusk, sailed to Belize (known as British Honduras in those days).

Belize is the only country in Central America that offers tarpon fishing on the flats.

In addition to establishing a main lodge in Belize, the Barothys also offered cruiseboat fishing, just as they had done in Cuba. Anglers could live aboard these large boats and fish from smaller skiffs. Thus, the many flats, islands and river mouths that were too distant to reach from the main lodge became convenient to those anglers who were willing to trade some comfort for the privilege of fishing practically virgin waters.

Outdoor writers spread the word quickly through their articles, and soon fishermen flocked to Belize to sample some of that great fishing that Tom McNally, the late Joe Brooks, A. J. McClane, Vic Dunaway and others had described. Barothy's main camp and cruiseboat fishing became so popular that Vic constructed another camp on the Turneffe islands. Because of illness Vic sold his camps, but the new owners carried on his fine tradition. Other smaller resorts eventually were constructed, although most of these featured other water sports along with fishing.

In the early seventies, the angling press de-emphasized Belize, not because fishing had somewhat declined, but because there were other emerging fishing areas in Central America.

The pendulum of Belize's popularity is fortunately ascending again. Fishing in Belize has matured and now commands the angler's attention for several reasons: (1) There is a long list of species available; (2) rates are comparatively reasonable in today's inflationary times; (3) English is the main language; and (4) it's basically a safe country, politically.

Belize is an excellent destination for the fly fisherman. Among the species offered are bonefish, tarpon, permit, snook, jacks, barracuda, snapper and ladyfish. There are a dozen other species, including wahoo, tuna, kings, sails and even blue marlin, but these aren't considered prime targets for the fly rodder because they are usually hard to locate. Let's look at those species that do challenge the fly fisherman:

Bonefish

Most Belizean bonefish weigh 2 1/2 to four pounds, so bonefish of over six pounds deserve an honorable mention. Bonefish weighing over 10 pounds have been taken from these waters (primarily at the Turneffe islands), but this is a very rare occurrence. The angler who is contemplating a trip to Belize should not pin his hopes on big bones or he will surely be disappointed.

Here are some some above-average catches that indicate what can be accomplished under ideal conditions: Henry Bryer and his son landed 50 bones in one morning's fishing. Don and Chan Coffey released 31 bones in one afternoon. Jerry Gerson landed over 30 bones in one day by following a large school. Lex Hochner, who has fished many of the world's most outstanding waters with a fly rod, found one school that contained more than a thousand bones. He had superb fly fishing.

The most outstanding fly rod catch from Belizean waters that I know of was delivered by Winston Moore. He took 258 bonefish during his 12-day fishing trip in 1982 while living aboard a KCS cruiseboat. This comes to a fantastic 21 1/2 bonefish-per-day average!

"Most of the bones are smaller here than those found in the Bahamas," Moore admits. "Mine averaged 2 1/2 to three pounds, although we took some in the four- to five-pound class and a few that were six to seven pounds. The previous year I landed some in the seven- to eight-pound bracket, which is about maximum for the area. I did cast to some individual fish that I feel might have been in the 10-pound class.

"Probably 95 percent of the bonefish I cast to were tailing fish. It was not unusual to see 20 to 40 tails at a time and to see as many as 10 to 12 different schools tailing simultaneously. My best day was 32 bones, and my slowest was seven. Sometimes five or six fish would rush to the fly first.

"Because the waters are so shallow I used only unweighted flies and a 16-foot leader. Nearly all the fish were taken on the 'Agent Bonefish' fly." (See "Bahamas" chapter for dressing.)

Bonefish can be taken year-round in Belize *provided* that the weather and water conditions are suitable. When a cold front chills the flats, bones simply remain in deeper waters. Furthermore, poor weather conditions or choppy waters can obscure the angler's vision, and he may not detect them even if they are on the flats. On very low visibility days, the wise angler will tackle other species, unless he is blessed with extraordinary eyesight.

April through October is usually the best period for bonefishing in Belize, though again, good fishing can occur at any time.

"To my mind, one of fishing's ultimate thrills is the stalk of a bonefish," says Bill Cullerton, a frequent visitor to Belizean flats. "To see moving bonefish a great distance away, decide where they are going and slowly approach them, stalking them, crouching low, not unlike the stalk of a lion, and finally making a presentation, is an unbeatable angling adventure."

Permit

Easily the most wary species of them all, permit are periodically spotted in Belize when weather and light conditions are favorable. Mexico's Yucatan Peninsula probably has more permit, albeit they are generally small. Deep Water Cay Club in the

Bahamas is the place for big permit (some over 30 pounds), but they are hard to fool. Thus Belizean waters serve as a good compromise: Permit here are larger than the Yucatan permit and more cooperative than their Bahamian counterparts.

I recall fly fishing for bones at the Turneffe islands. Suddenly Elkins, my guide, whispered excitedly, "There's a huge permit to your left. Big fish. But be careful."

I began my back cast and made one false cast away from the fish so that I wouldn't spook it, but my arm motion sent it scurrying to safety. When it was over the guide said that the permit was in the 30- to 35-pound class. "That's the biggest permit I've ever seen," he claimed.

A couple of other similar encounters with permit convinced me that this species is practically impossible to catch. I gave up on permit. Then in October, 1984, while bonefishing out of Ambergris Cay, I was busy untangling a snarl in my fly leader. "Permit!" my guide pointed. There was no time to replace the leader or unsnarl it. With a what-the heck attitude I cast the fly, snarls and all, in the path of the fish. The permit grabbed the

El Pescador is a delightful resort on Ambergris. Kathy and Juergen Krueger are outstanding hosts.

bonefish fly and we landed it. It was small, but a permit is a permit is a permit. Later that day I hooked another permit, much larger, but finally lost it. Luck is a very important ingredient in permit fishing.

Sy Rosenthal fished the Turneffe islands hoping to take a large permit on a fly. Lots of rain and an overcast ceiling seemed ominous, but during a slight break in the weather Sy hooked two permit on a fly, both in the 20- to 25-pound class. Although he fought them valiantly, both fish cut the leader against the coral.

Drs. Henry A. Anderson and Sam Milham, fishing from the live-aboard Piper, encountered horrible weather conditions that made fly casting impossible so they used spinning gear. "In the five days of fishing (September 1986), we were able to cast to 50 permit, landing three out of the seven we hooked. Many of the permit we saw were large for Belize (over 20 pounds). Either the small fish were not on the flats, or we couldn't see them because of the poor visibility," relates Dr. Anderson. The largest landed? A 35-pound permit!

Success often comes to the persistent. Winston Moore recounts, "I tried to catch a permit on a fly for 15 years; then on one day in Belize I took one and on another day I landed two. They were small, perhaps six to 10 pounds. I saw and cast to some huge permit in the 30- to 50-pound range but with no success. The three small permit, on the other hand, were very aggressive and charged the fly. When I stopped stripping in line, they actually tailed and dug the fly out of the bottom."

So Belize represents an above-average place to try for a permit on a fly, but bear in mind, they don't come often and they certainly don't come easy.

Tarpon

Tarpon probably can be found somewhere in Belizean waters just about year-round, but the catchword is "somewhere." In the rivers? The islands? The flats? The cuts? The fly rodder, in order to be successful, needs plenty of aggressive targets, so spotting a few lazy tarpon in a week will not result in fast-paced fly fishing. The obvious solution is to go to Belize when tarpon are more plentiful. April, May and June historically are the three best months for tarpon, but July through mid-

October can be great, too. Manatee Lodge, however, considers the months of September to June as its prime time.

Belize offers three sizes of tarpon:

(1) Baby tarpon: These fish weigh from a few pounds to under 20 pounds. When hooked, they leap high and often and are spectacular adversaries on light tackle; they aren't as tiring as the "biggies." They are usually found along the mangrove shorelines, small lagoons and at the mouths of creeks.

(2) Medium-sized tarpon: These will weigh 20 to 70 pounds. Heavier gear is needed, of course, and the fight takes much longer. They are found in cuts, larger mangrove-lined lagoons, channels and flats.

(3) The "grande" tarpon: Big fish, over 70 pounds and sometimes over 100 pounds, provide a tremendous challenge to the angler and his tackle.

To the best of my knowledge no other place consistently offers all three sizes of tarpon.

The largest fly-caught tarpon that I know of, that was weighed, was taken by Tom McNally, outdoor editor of the *Chicago Tribune.* Fishing out of Barothy's main camp on the Belize River, he hooked the tarpon in the late afternoon and fought it until total darkness. His fishing partner, Bill Cullerton, was finally able to grab the leader carefully and gaff the fish. It weighed 135 pounds and, because the Belize River is quite deep, and because of darkness, Tom obviously had his hands full.

There have been a number of other tarpon taken on a fly that may have been larger but were not weighed. Winston Moore has taken several on his numerous jaunts to Belize that he feels would weigh well over 135 pounds. Bill Cullerton Jr., who has caught many tarpon, insists that he saw a fisherman play one that could have exceeded 175 pounds. There have been other reports of fish estimated at well over 150 pounds.

My experience with Belize tarpon is basically limited to small tarpon (under 25 pounds) and medium-sized fish (up to 70 pounds). Hooking big tarpon, 80 pounds or more, is a spectacular experience, but I also love to catch small tarpon because a lighter fly rod (No. 8) can be used, and after I enjoy all those fantastic jumps, I can finish off these smaller tarpon without the tremendous amount of work that's necessary to subdue the biggies. Unfortunately, there are very few places in the world where one can find the smaller tarpon. Belize is possibly the best.

I fished the Turneffe islands at the end of May when the lodge first opened up, and I was ecstatic to see so many small tarpon working the cuts and the open water. We spotted the schools and motored close to them; then my guide paddled quietly within casting distance so that we wouldn't disturb them. I was using a light fly rod and a white streamer, and I enjoyed some of the finest tarpon fishing imaginable because conditions were perfect. It's unfortunate, however, that one doesn't come across this type of fishing more often. When it comes, take advantage of every precious moment.

Paul Melchior fished KCS Lodge on the Belize River in November and caught a number of baby tarpon (up to 15 pounds) on light fly gear. "I used a variety of streamers similar

Belize's bonefish aren't big, but they are plentiful and capable of taking 100 yards of line off your reel.

to Lefty's Deceiver. The wing was yellow and grizzly while the collar was calf's tail. While fishing the bonefish flats, we suddenly saw a school of baby tarpon. Their backs were sticking out of the water. After some adjustment on my terminal tackle, I began to hook these fish and land some of them. Fly fishing for baby tarpon—eight to 15 pounds—is a super thrill."

It appears that in the clearer waters of the islands and the Caribbean itself, smaller, sparsely-dressed tarpon flies (similar to those used in the Florida Keys) work well. In the rivers, where clear water is rare, the darker, bulkier dressed patterns, such as the Cockroach, are more effective.

Barracuda

I've had some fast cuda fishing while wading the flats of Belize and also at Honduras' Bay Islands, using a white streamer with Mylar strips and retrieving it fast. My experience, however, is limited to small barracuda.

To catch the big cuda, anglers use large streamers constructed from blue and white FisHair. Prior to use, they dab a little Pliobond on the hair and mold it so that the fly resembles a small needlefish. After sighting the barracuda and casting, they retrieve the fly as fast as they can and observe the fish's response. If the barracuda yawns, they change the retrieves and/or flies until success is attained. Occasionally, when the streamer flies are not productive, the anglers may tie on a large chugging fly rod popper. Again it must be retrieved rapidly. Cudas love fast traveling lures.

Some of the most spectacular jumps I've ever witnessed have come from barracuda; many of their leaps are truly awesome. It's an excellent game fish, although some fishermen still need to be convinced.

Barracuda are found year-round in Belize. Good places to look for them are the cuts, the deeper holes near mangroves and the flats, but it's on the flats where barracuda fishing is most exciting.

Snook

One will not find "Costa Rican-sized" snook in Belize (or elsewhere for that matter); most of the snook taken here will run up to 15 pounds, but, again, this is an ideal size for a medium fly rod. Furthermore, anglers can catch Belizean snook in the classic way, by casting a streamer or a popper close to the mangroves. The skill lies not only in accurate casting but also in selecting the places that deserve probing. Unlike tarpon and bonefish, snook seldom show themselves, so the angler must rely heavily on his instinct, his knowledge of the fish's habits and some luck. (Occasionally, you see a V-like wake cutting the surface; this usually denotes a snook.) Once snook are located along a particular mangrove-lined bank, the angler is likely to have continuous action for several hours.

It's important that the fly lands as close to the mangroves as possible (inches make a difference). The retrieve is equally important. If a streamer is used, some experts like to strip it very fast for about six feet after it lands and has a chance to sink a little. Then they vary the rest of the retrieve until the successful formula is discovered. With poppers, a different type of retrieve is used. After it plops next to the mangroves, the popper should be twitched and vibrated, mostly with the rod tip, to show plenty of life, but without moving it too far away from the bank. If a strike doesn't occur, then it should be stripped in more actively back to the boat. It's not an easy technique to learn, but it's deadly.

During October, 1984, I visited KCS Lodge for a couple of days, hardly enough time to sample these potent fishing grounds. Guide Richard Smith decided on Hick's Cay. We quickly spooked one tarpon and didn't see another, so we fished the mangroves for big snook. There's snook fishing and there's snook fishing. This was the ultimate! Visual fishing. The snook were right in the mangroves, in a couple of feet of gin-clear water. I was primarily equipped for fly fishing, but I had a light spinning outfit along. The fly rod poppers and streamers were of no interest to these snook, but a yellow Darter cast with spinning gear got their attention. The plopping noise of the Darter obviously interested the snook, but it's also easier to make an underhanded flip cast with a spinning rod. The lure had to be placed right in the open holes of the mangroves. Period. Since I wanted to try for snook via fly fishing, we developed a plan, which was to cast Darter lures right in the mangrove tunnels (to get their attention), tease the snook out of the mangroves and then quickly switch to a fly rod and a streamer. It almost worked, too. A couple of snook mouthed the streamer, but I wasn't able to set hook. In some cases I had the snook following almost to the boat, inches behind the fly, before they would spook back into the mangroves. These fish were mostly in their low 'teens, but one hefty model may have scaled 18 or more pounds. Another snook that was particularly quick grabbed the Darter and weaved 50 to 70 feet of light spinning line around the mangroves. I didn't land any snook via fly fishing, but it was one of the most enjoyable snook experiences I've had. I think the plan would have worked had there been two anglers: one to tease the snook out of the holes with a hookless casting lure, while the other entices them to the fly.

The success of snook fishing in the mangroves is predicated on placing the lure right against the vegetation, but not in it. The novice fly rodder becomes overly concerned about hanging up, lest he arouse his guide's anger. Everyone hangs up occasionally, but don't overdo it; otherwise, your guide may keep the boat too far from the bank. Practice your casting *before* you go on your trip. You will find your fishing much more satisfying, and your guide will appreciate it.

Jacks, Snappers and Ladyfish

There is a great resemblance between the jack crevalle and the permit. If you land a permit on any type of tackle, your angling prestige is elevated considerably (and if it is done on a fly, you've earned the right to hold your head just a little higher than your fishing partners). If you land a dozen jacks on a fly, however, you will probably receive a "That's nice, Charlie" comment and the subject will be instantly changed. Jack crevalle are very strong fighters, and anyone who tries to land one on light tackle finds this out quickly. Even the smaller fish are tough. The main difference is that permit are exceptionally scarce, and it's very difficult to entice them to hit any type of lure. On the other hand, jacks will smack most lures or flies, for they appear to have an insatiable appetite.

At times jacks can be a nuisance because often they are intermingled with the highly-coveted tarpon. You cast for the silver

Al Schaefer landed this snook while fishing at Manatee Lodge—a fairly new facility on the mainland.

king, but the more aggressive jack swipes the fly, and by the time you land it, the tarpon school disappears.

PanAngling's Al Schaefer enjoyed two mornings of fast-paced snook fishing, casting from a beach near Manatee Lodge. But on the third morning a school of jacks moved in. It was impossible to hook a snook because the jacks were more aggressive. It can be frustrating.

But then there are times when jacks are a blessing. You've searched everywhere for a tarpon or a bonefish tail without success. You need a fix, a "pull-back." Finding a school of jacks proves to be a soothing balm for agitated nerves.

There are several varieties of snapper in Belize, but the most interesting species is the cubera. This snapper can grow to over 50 pounds and has one of the most menacing sets of choppers this side of a shark. Fishing for cubera on the reefs and on big rivers is generally a deep-water proposition, which means fast-sinking lines and large streamers. You need a 12-inch wire shock leader (45-pound test) so the cubera won't cut your tippet. The big fish are exceptionally powerful on any type of tackle, but they represent a particularly satisfying (or frustrating) challenge to the fly rodder.

Occasionally cubera will come to the surface and whack a popper during the day, but they are more inclined to do this at dusk. I've had spine-tingling action with cuberas on poppers under moonlight. It's not reliable sport, it's a now and then thing, but if it could be done more consistently, night fishing for cuberas on poppers would be among angling's best adventures.

I've had super fishing for small snappers while fishing out of KCS. My guide paddled along a mangrove stretch while I cast a smaller popper. The trick was to cast it right next to the mangroves, move it a little, let it rest and—Wham! We must have hooked dozens of snapper during a short period.

The ladyfish is a superb fly rod target when located. Paul Melchior, on his '84 trip to El Pescador, found them. "Daryl Freeman and I had a sensational day of ladyfishing when conditions prevented us from going onto the tarpon or bonefish flats. Ladyfish are slim, silvery fish with the running ability of a bone and the acrobatic skills of a tarpon. They inhabit the wide 'creeks' of Ambergris, travel in large schools and appear in the distance like moving dark patches. Once you locate them, the action is fast and furious on both fly gear or light spinning gear and small grubs or jigs. We fished one school for hours, motoring up to it, making the cast, then watching with a mixture of glee and amazement as 10, 15 or more ladyfish would converge on the fly. Once hooked, even a four-pounder rips off 50 yards of line, then arcs in a tarpon-like leap. Most of the fish ran two to four pounds, though I did take one that approached seven pounds...maybe larger.

"White streamers with some Mylar strips are effective flies, but when these fish are on a feeding spree, just about any brightly-colored streamer works well. In these waters ladyfish mostly weigh from three to six pounds, so suitable light tackle should be used. Don't overpower these fish by employing a heavy fly rod such as a No. 10. It would be a mismatch, akin to putting a heavyweight fighter in the ring with a lightweight. A No. 7 or 8 fly rod is ideal."

There are other species available in Belize, but these fish represent the more important targets for the fly rodder.

THE CAMPS

The angler who is contemplating a trip to Belize is fortunate because there are diverse facilities in various locations from which to choose, and the rates are reasonable. Here are some possibilities:

KCS CAMP: After Vic Barothy had operated his camp on the mainland (Belize River) for a number of years, poor health caused him to sell Barothy's Lodge. Fred Keller bought the camp, renamed it Keller's Caribbean Sports (KCS), continued the tradition and made numerous improvements. He finally sold it to three Californians, and additional renovations were made. Bob Johnson and his wife have done an admirable job in managing the resort. KCS today is a very charming fishing camp.

Up to 16 fishermen can be simultaneously accommodated in attractive cottages that feature comfortable beds, modern plumbing and overhead fans. The air-conditioned main lodge houses the kitchen, dining room, lounge, bar and tackle shop.

All-time fishing great Lefty Kreh did his number on this fine barracuda while fishing in Belize.

The customized 16-foot fiberglass boats are powered by 20-hp engines and a local guide is provided for each two fishermen. The guides are excellent; they know their waters and species intimately. Besides fishing the Belize River, guests can venture out into the Caribbean for bones and other species found on the flats and also ascend several other nearby rivers for a change of pace or scenery.

Rates: A five-day trip costs $875 per person based on double occupancy. This includes the accommodations, meals, guide, boat, motor and fuel. If one wants to fish beyond the five days, there is a $175 daily surcharge.

KCS CRUISEBOATS: KCS also offers live-aboard fishing trips from two cruisers, The Christy Ann and the Blue Yonder. They are 50-foot yachts that can accommodate four guests plus crew. All meals are prepared by a skilled cook and served on board at the convenience of the guests. Both cruisers have refrigeration, showers, modern plumbing and provide sufficient privacy so that even couples can be accommodated comfortably (but not luxuriously). The obvious advantage of cruise-boat fishing is that the anglers can explore and fish places that logistically aren't available to camp guests. Furthermore, fishermen can stretch their day considerably because the boat is moored near the fishing places. If the guides and crew work abnormally long hours, don't forget to tip them accordingly, especially if a return trip is contemplated. Guides may forget a name; they never forget a poor tipper!

Rates: A five-day cruise/fishing trip costs $1,075 per person but there must be four persons to a party; if less, the price per person is proportionately increased. The rates include captain, guides, cook, all meals, use of skiffs and, in fact, just about everything but drinks, incidentals and gratuities.

TURNEFFE ISLAND LODGE: This was Barothy's outpost camp located on Caye Bokel at the southern edge of the Turneffe islands. Because of illness, he sold this camp to Bill and Dolly Haerr, who eventually sold it to Phillipe and Andre Job, who in turn passed on the baton to Dave Bennett. With each change of ownership, new improvements, new ideas and new concepts were introduced.

The extensive flats, a short distance from the lodge, are prime bonefishing waters, and many outstanding catches have been recorded within 30 minutes or less from the lodge. Occasionally permit are sighted on these same flats, and just about all species found in Belize can be taken from this lodge. (Snook, however, are not commonly caught here.)

The camp's capacity is limited to 14 persons. They are housed in individual cottages, and there's a main lodge that contains the kitchen, dining room, tackle store and sitting room. The lodge generates its own electricity and stores over 100,000 gallons of fresh water. In effect, Turneffe Island Lodge is practically self-supporting, which is one of the camp's charms.

In addition to skiff fishing, Turneffe Island Lodge also offers a variety of larger craft including the "Grand Slam"—the 38-foot sportfisherman cruiser. It can be chartered for day trips, but also used for overnights.

Turneffe Island Lodge also offers scuba diving (including the famous Blue Hole) for those anglers who not only wish to view fish from above the surface but from below as well.

Rates: The weekly tab is $1,400 per person. In addition to the accommodations, meals and fishing arrangements, the price also includes the round-trip transfers by boat from the mainland (about 2 1/2 hours).

EL PESCADOR: There are a number of small resort hotels that offer fishing along with other water sports. El Pescador ("The Fisherman") is located on Ambergris Cay, a 21-mile-long island in the northern portion of the Belizean Barrier Reef. Guests fly the 36 miles from Belize City to San Pedro on Ambergris Cay via Maya Air's scheduled daily flight. This resort is three miles from the village of San Pedro.

El Pescador offers ten twin-bedded rooms (all with modern plumbing and electricity), a very attractive dining room and a small bar. It's a very comfortable, charming beachfront resort. El Pescador uses local guides who provide their own boats and motors (it's best to reserve the guides well in advance). These guides have an excellent idea of what saltwater fly fishing is all about. Among the best guides at El Pescador are: Romel, Pancho, Erlindo, June and Carlos.

El Pescador, owned by Kathleen and Juegen Krueger, has developed a tremendous reputation for its tarpon fishing on the flats among knowledgeable fly rodders. It's easily the best tarpon flats fishing in Central and South America.

Rates: A six-night, five-day fishing trip, including all accommodations, meals, fishing arrangements and round-trip airfare from Belize City, is $789 per person based on double occupancy.

THE PIPER: This is a relatively new "cruiseboat fishing" operation that started in 1982. The Piper is a 38-foot Egg Harbor yacht that provides berths, galley, plumbing, refrigeration and other creature comforts, but few luxuries. Fishing is from smaller skiffs, and the captain and mate double as cooks, guides or mechanics. Most of the trips have been successful (there were a couple of interruptive break downs), and much of the credit must be bestowed upon Captain Junior Eiley, who earned his wings as a guide from the "Barothy Days." He knows these fishing waters intimately and is considered among the best captains in Belize. Lately, he has been particularly successful in permit fishing.

Rates: At $725 per person, double occupancy, for six nights (five days of fishing), the Piper represents one of the best fishing bargains available. Anglers should understand that breakdowns do occur, which, of course, is true with any boat. While the Piper can accommodate up to four persons (in which case the rate is lower), it's advised that parties be confined to two. Staples are brought along, but the crew doesn't hesitate to dive below and procure some lobster for dinner. Talk about fresh seafood!

Three essential fly patterns for Belize tarpon: Cockroach, Stu Apte Keys' fly and Lefty's Deceiver.

MANATEE LODGE: This relatively new fishermen's lodge is operated by Jamie Claiborne. It's located at Gale's Point south of Belize City, about 25 miles by road and via inland waterways. Gale's Point is the slender finger of land that extends into Southern Lagoon, which is fed by the Manatee and the Main rivers and connects to the sea via Bar River. These waters are particularly good for tarpon, snook and cubera snapper; generally the camp doesn't offer bonefishing. Most of the fishing takes place very early in the morning, from daybreak until about 10 A.M. and in the late afternoon until almost dark. Manatee is one of the very few camps anywhere that arranges "its day" around the prime fishing hours. The best fishing months are from September through June. This comfortable camp accommodates eight anglers.

Rates: The weekly rate is $950 per person based on double occupancy. The single occupancy rate is $1,150, and is recommended to fly fishermen because there is one angler to a boat and guide.

THE TACKLE

Basically, two types of fly gear are necessary for Belizean fishing:

Light Outfit: A No. 8 or 9 fly rod will take care of all bonefish, snook, jacks, baby tarpon, mackerel and permit. Load the appropriate-sized reel with about 150 yards of 20-pound Dacron or Micron backing. Leaders tapering down to six pounds are ideal for bonefish, but heavier tippets will be needed for other species.

Heavier Outfit: For medium-sized tarpon of 40 to 60 pounds, a No. 10 outfit is ideal. There's sufficient backbone to not only punch out the air-resistant, bulky streamers or poppers but also to control most tarpon during the ensuing fight. This same outfit can be used for cubera snapper, big barracuda, large permit and bonefishing for those windy conditions when a lighter rod is unsuitable. Reels should be loaded with 200 yards of backing, and tarpon leaders can be of basic saltwater tapered construction: four feet of 25-pound mono, two feet of

20-pound, about 18 inches of tippet material (either 12- or 15-pound) and a 12-inch shock leader (60-pound mono, or 27- or 45-pound test wire). For big tarpon, of over 80 pounds, a No. 12 rod is recommended.

Snook fishing at mangroved-lined rivers present a superb challenge. Accurate casting and patience are important ingredients.

Flies: Winston Moore's "Agent Bonefish" is a must for bonefish. Other good patterns include Crazy Charlie (in deeper waters), Bonefish Special and Pink Producer. The white and brown inverted keel flies tied on No. 4 and 6 hooks are deadly bonefish patterns, but they are also effective for permit.

For tarpon, the splayed-wing flies or Stu Apte pattern (such as used in the Keys) are recommended for clear water conditions, but the bulkier-dressed patterns are more successful for discolored waters. Lefty's Deceiver pattern is also highly recommended.

Cubera, barracuda and other toothy denizens are rough on flies, so the more durable FisHair is a better material than hackle.

Fly Lines: While floating lines are preferable for bones, permit and flats fishing, sinking lines should be brought along for deep-water fishing. For tarpon on the flats, an intermediate (slow sinking) WF line is recommended.

BELIZE, THE COUNTRY

Belize (British Honduras) was a British Crown Colony, but in 1964 Britain granted its people the right to seek self-government. In 1981, Belize became almost totally independent of Great Britain.

Belize's most remarkable natural characteristic is the Great Barrier Reef, which is composed of numerous islands and cays and extends the entire length of the country. It's the world's second largest barrier reef (Australia's Great Barrier Reef is longer).

Belize's population is only 140,000, and English is the primary language. Until the mid-sixties, this land was almost totally unknown among tourists; even the itinerant traveler who prided himself in the number of off-the-beaten-path places he had toured was only vaguely familiar with Belize. It was the fishing camps first, and then the small fun-in-the-sun resorts, that eventually attracted whatever tourist trade exists today. Belize will never make the international jet setter's, "Ten Most Desirable Places to Visit" list, but then that's good news for the angler.

Belize City has a population of 7,000 and is the least interesting of all Central American capitals. As far as the fisherman is concerned, Belize City serves one primary function: It's the gateway "airport" to some of Central America's most varied light-tackle fishing. Period.

Hotels and Restaurants: If one must overnight in Belize City, the Fort George Hotel is the logical choice (though expensive); if it's solidly booked, the Bellevue Hotel should be considered. The best restaurant in Belize City is the Fort George Hotel restaurant. There are a number of night spots, discos and dance places where the energy level (and the volume) is on high, but the wise angler avoids these places.

For Gifts: Try the National Craft Centre on Vernon Street, the Cottage Industries on Albert or the gift shop in the Fort George for wood carvings, coral and tortoise shell items. The carvings are by far the best buy.

Climate: It's subtropical, with a brisk easterly wind off the Caribbean blowing mostly from November to early March. The temperatures range from 67 to 88 degrees. The rainy season is from July to December, but even during this period, half of the days of each month are dry. When it does rain, it pours, and rivers can take several days to clear up after a storm.

Required Documents and Currency: A passport is not required to enter Belize for U. S., Canadian or British citizens. However, proof of citizenship, such as a birth certificate or voter's registration card, must be presented to obtain a tourist card. (Valid passports may be required in the future.) Vaccinations or inoculations aren't needed. U. S. dollars are freely exchanged in Belize, so currency conversion is unnecessary.

Getting There: From the U.S., there's frequent jet service to Belize City, mostly from Miami, Houston or New Orleans, offered by SAHSA, TAN and TACA airlines.

AND FINALLY... Belize offers many fishing thrills, but none greater than stalking a tarpon on the clear, sandy flats. Perhaps the following letter written by Sam Clements, Amarillo, TX, to a fishing pal states it best and most accurately:

This is what it's all about. When a tarpon takes a fly the world's problems disappear.

Dear Tom,

You asked me a minute ago what happens when a tarpon takes a fly. Oh, Boy! Roughly stated and in round figures—here's what happens.

Maybe it is the eleventh hour of your trip and for 12 days you have fought the rigors of high winds, muddy flats, heat, bugs, even fire, floods, feuds and flu. Maybe your feet are swollen and hurting, your head is pounding, your neck and back ache and you are going crazy trying to scratch yesterday's 'no-see-ums' bites on your left foot with your right foot, and maybe—just maybe—you wonder just why you ever thought this was such a hot idea in the first place. Most likely your mind will wander with heat 'deliriums' and you will wonder what the poor folks are doing. Probably, you will conclude, the poor folks are sitting around some lush cantina, fraternizing with a gorgeous woman, sipping a Rum Collins and smoking a big, black cigar. The poor, dumb slobs; and here you are—a rich cat—out in the middle of the bleeding ocean and having fun. Suddenly you will feel the boat quiver and you will hear the seldom-spoken word from the guide: "Fish!" Fish, indeed! There it is. A dark shadow over white sand. Eighty pounds of fighting silver—100 feet at 12 on the imaginary clock and coming at you. You probably will take a deep breath to brush away thoughts of panic as you mentally run down the check list: Is the brake set properly? Is the line coiled correctly on the deck? And, how in the hell did I end up with a No. 10 rod in my hand when I need the 12?

Then.

Without regard for the high wind, right to left, left to right, tailing wind or head wind, you roll the first 30 feet of line into the air, haul a little while casting the line behind you, haul again on the forward thrust, which somehow catapults the fly some 70 feet in front of you and four feet in front of the fish. The guide undoubtedly is impressed. So are you!

The great mouth opens, then closes, the fish starts to turn and you hit it—about five horizontal jabs—little, hard, quick jabs straight.

Then, it happens.

The tarpon, the great silver king, comes roaring out like an upside-down bomb, water flies all over the ocean, the great mouth opens, its gills rattle. The fish hangs up there for two eternities, finally crashes back into the water and the race is on. A great, sizzling race.

And how do you feel about all this? Well, you feel like maybe you just backed into a hot branding iron. You can jump and fly like the fish. There comes over you a mighty feeling. A feeling of fulfillment.

You have suddenly come closer to understanding the mortality—or is it immortality of a great fish—and possibly yourself, than you ever will again.

You couldn't possibly kill the fish for the sake of a little 'dock-ego', so you will in the end, revive it, throw it a kiss and in the words of Winston Moore, say "Thanks. Now, go have babies."

Sam Clements

Costa Rica

Where the Sun Rises in Tarpon Country... and Sets on Marlin Waters

This banana republic offers some of the world's finest tarpon fishing and record snook on the east coast, fantastic fly fishing for Pacific sails on the west coast, and there's some rainbow trout fishing in the interior, too. Friendly, easy-to-get-to and comfortable fishing camps have made Costa Rica one of the favorite fly fishing destinations of Central America.

Stu Apte "froze" this tarpon in midair. Costa Rica's fame is largely due to its tarpon.

Chapter 10

COSTA RICA

CARLOS BARRANTES missed his calling. He should have become a public relations man for a dynamic Madison Avenue advertising agency or PR firm. Carlos, a Costa Rican sportsman, almost single-handedly promoted sportfishing in his country, and he did it with practically no budget.

"I love fishing—it's sort of an obsession—but it was equally important to share it with sportsmen from all over the world," Carlos explains. He began by converting a small school building, on the edge of the Parismina River, into a fishing lodge that later evolved into Parismina Tarpon Rancho. Then, with considerable assistance from American Don Dobbins, Carlos constructed another lodge on the Rio Colorado, which was named Casa Mar Fishing Club. He invited writers from major outdoor publications, television crews and influential anglers to enjoy (and publicize) the beauty and fishing of Costa Rica. He quickly transformed a little-known country into one of the most famous fishing places in the world. "In those days, most Americans were unfamiliar with Costa Rica. It was known as a 'banana republic' or 'the place that grows coffee'. Yes, we grow bananas, and I think we make the best coffee, but Costa Rica today is equally known for its great fishing."

Once the plug casters became aware of Costa Rica's volatile fishing, Carlos focused his PR efforts on Costa Rica's fly fishing potential. He invited some of the best fly fishermen to his camps: Stu Apte, Billy Pate, Ted Williams, Tom McNally, Al McClane and many others.

Rip Cunningham landed this fine sail on a fly rod while fishing at Gulf de Papagayo.

While he originally promoted the east coast's superb tarpon and snook fly fishing potential, he also explored the Pacific side and even the interior jungle trout streams.

Carlos sold his camps a few years later; today he operates a sporting goods store but continues to promote his country's sportfishing with vigor. True, Costa Rica's great fishing would eventually have been discovered by anglers, but Carlos' dedication and enthusiasm hastened the recognition. In effect, he explored it, developed it and served it on a silver platter with all the trimmings for sportsmen from around the world to enjoy.

EAST COAST

Tarpon Fishing: The veteran fly fisherman, who has chased tarpon on the Florida Keys, initially is likely to be disappointed here. There are no extensive sandy flats in Costa Rica, and the stalk of an individual tarpon is rare. The river and lagoon waters are murky and deep, so most presentations are "blind" in various "holds." Casts are often made to a school of rolling fish, seldom to a specific fish.

Then why should an experienced fly fisherman bother with Costa Rican tarpon? Florida Keys' fishing is mostly confined to late spring and early summer. In Costa Rica, however, the fly fisherman can tackle tarpon from January to mid-May and from late August to late October; thus the angler can considerably extend the tarpon fishing season. It's difficult to compare the fishing quality of the Keys and Costa Rica. Both will range from poor to excellent depending mostly on weather and water conditions, but many anglers who have experienced both areas feel that Costa Rica can provide faster fishing under optimum conditions.

Several years ago, fishing the ocean from Parismina, I made a total of 14 casts during the entire morning! On all but one cast I hooked and fought a tarpon.

One fish inhaled the fly and, after a few furious jumps, threw it. I began to strip in to prepare for another cast when a second tarpon hit the streamer. It mouthed it and threw it after a 10-minute fight. A third tarpon grabbed it only a few feet

Angling's biggest thrill? A big, angry tarpon crashing on the surface is certainly among them. It's an awesome sight!

from the boat. On its initial jump it smashed right on the gunwale and only the guide's deft, backpaddling maneuver prevented this green tarpon from coming right in the boat. Several plug casters have reportedly hooked as many as six tarpon on a single cast. This doesn't happen at many tarpon places. On the flipside, if weather and water conditions are poor, the angler is most likely to challenge the veracity of the hundreds of articles touting Costa Rica's great tarpon fishing.

It's seldom that one lands a tarpon under 50 pounds in Costa Rican waters, but it's also true that few tarpon of over 100 pounds are hooked. The average is probably in the 60- to 70-pound range. Anglers, especially fly rodders, have explored the intricate network of rivers hoping to find places that harbor "baby" tarpon (under 20 pounds), for these fish are extremely sporty on light gear. They haven't been successful. I doubt that more than a few dozen "babies" have been landed during the past 15 years. Clearly, Costa Rica mostly offers tarpon in 50- to 90-pound range.

There are basically two types of waters that are fished in Costa Rica: the freshwater (or brackish) rivers and the Caribbean itself. Each offers a unique appeal. The "inside" or lagoon fishing provides a special allure, enhanced by a lush, impenetrable jungle backdrop, the eerie cry of the howler monkeys and sightings of alligators and other fauna. The guide paddles the 16-foot aluminum skiff looking for that familiar, slow roll that is the tarpon's signature. When the guide locates a concentration of fish, the angler delivers the streamer repeatedly to the area and hopefully is rewarded with a strike. For the most part, fast-sinking fly lines are used, but if these lines do not bring results, the anglers may change to lead-core lines (which sink faster). Although the tarpon may show on the surface, they sometimes refuse all offerings except those that move close to the bottom, as these waters have large quantities of shrimp. It's a high-voltage experience to first feel a "bump" at the end of your line and then to watch a tarpon, the silver king of all marine fish, explode in a series of spectacular jumps, momentarily disturbing the jungle's serenity.

Undoubtedly the fastest, most consistent tarpon fishing occurs in the Caribbean. This is why knowledgeable "regulars" ask daily if the sea is calm enough to fish it from the small skiffs. The fascination of Costa Rica "ocean" fishing cannot be overstated. It's explosive. First the guide searches the sea for moving fish and when a school is located, he speeds to that area. He must accurately gauge the school's direction in order to place the skiff strategically in front of the oncoming tarpon. A school can consist of dozens of big tarpon. Or hundreds. Sometimes thousands of these silver torpedoes can be seen smashing into bait fish. The surface commotion, the splashing and the rolling of hundreds of tarpon, is a sight seldom seen in other fishing. Glenn Lau, the brilliant outdoor cinematographer, described a tremendous school of tarpon beyond the mouth of the Rio Colorado: "I wouldn't even try to guess how big the school was! It seemed to be a mile long and possibly a quarter of a mile wide. What was amazing was that the fish were stacked in tiers. It was mind-boggling."

This, of course, doesn't mean that all one needs is to "fish the ocean" for a guaranteed tarpon bonanza. Schools of tarpon are not always spotted near the coastline and sometimes, even if found, they may be uncooperative.

We once located a school of possibly a hundred tarpon. They had coralled thousands of bait fish and were on a voracious feeding orgy. The tarpon totally ignored the streamer fly. It was a frustrating experience. We found it difficult to understand how so many tarpon in one small area could ignore a fly.

"Keep casting!" guide Eduardo Brown insisted. "There are so many sardines that the fish are swimming with their mouths open. Maybe a tarpon will accidentally take the fly." He was right and the tarpon did just that. Incidentally, it was an unusually strong fish. He was hooked north of the Rio Colorado and was landed at the mouth of the Samay River. That's a distance of about seven miles, according to Eduardo.

There's another type of fishing that's successful, but it's debatable whether it falls into the realm of fly fishing. Just inside of the mouth of the Rio Colorado, anglers cast lead-core lines from anchored boats and allow the current to swing the line. They continually jig the fly rod tip and hope that a tarpon hits. If unsuccessful after an hour's fishing, they move to another spot.

Snook Fishing: Whereas the success of fly fishing for tarpon is quite high, similar results aren't enjoyed by fly fishermen who are after big snook. By now just about every follower of international fishing knows that Costa Rica has the largest snook in the world. The all-tackle world record 53-lb., 10-oz. snook came from Parismina (on casting equipment), but few large snook have been landed by fly fishermen.

There are times when one can fish for small snook (two to six pounds) with a fly rod and take dozens of them. I was fishing with Carlos Barrantes one September day in Samay Lagoon (Rio Colorado). Our guide paddled us along the east bank, which was loaded with small snook. Between us we probably released close to 100 snook on streamers. Action was continu-

Dr. John Finch pours it on! You need a strong rod, smooth-running reel and well-tied knots to subdue the powerful tarpon.

ous, provided that the casts were made right next to the bank. Ironically, we tried the same place several times later, but never found it productive.

The late Ted Bates used to fish Casa Mar during the second and third weeks of January, and he enjoyed tremendous fly fishing for snook. Often he would average 40 or more per day. Most of the fish were well under 10 pounds, but he preserved all the sport and challenge by using light tackle.

But what about the "grande" snook for the fly rodder? The best snook that I know of is a 26-pounder taken by Bill Barnes during the month of October. The fish is an IGFA world record for 16-pound tippet. There was another snook, a 32-pounder, taken by Marshall Finkelman via fly fishing, but it was never entered for a record. "One of the reasons why more big snook aren't taken on a fly rod is because not many anglers attempt it.

During the fall season most of the snook men use casting or spinning gear," one of the guides explains.

During September and October, giant snook in the 20-, 30- and sometimes 40-pound class cruise the shallows along the sandy coastline. Fishermen are placed knee-deep at strategic places and fan-cast the waters. The plug caster can cover the water easily, but the fly fisherman is definitely at a disadvantage for he must make long casts, usually into the wind. If he has not mastered the double-haul casting technique, it most likely would be an exercise in futility. Furthermore, when the fly fisherman strips in the shooting line, the waves quickly carry the loose line behind him creating a tremendous drag on the next cast. A stripping basket, such as those used by steelhead fishermen, should work, but the chances for successful snook fly fishing along the beaches are not high.

Fishing for snook in the inside lagoons can be productive. Snook will sometimes crash a popper but usually a white streamer with strips of Mylar cast right next to mangroves is more effective. These fish tend to be in the six- to 14-pound class; occasionally a huge snook is hooked.

Other Species: There are several other species, indigenous to tropical climes, that should appeal to the light tackle fly fisherman. The machaca resembles a shad and fights much like a smallmouth bass. A good leaper, the machaca runs up to eight pounds. The guapote is similar to the largemouth bass in temperament: pugnacious, tough, challenging. Most of the guapote are two to four pounds but can grow to eight pounds or more. The mojarra has a similar configuration to the bluegill or sunfish but grows much larger. All these species take small poppers at times, but white or yellow streamers are generally more productive. This type of fishing takes place in the freshwater lagoons. The guide paddles the skiff along a bank and it is important to cast close to obstructions or pads. Twitch the popper a couple of times, let it rest, twitch it again—a la bass fishing. If that doesn't work, retrieve faster in 12-inch strips. If that also fails, try streamers and vary the retrieves until you discover the successful formula.

These waters also contain a number of other species including king mackerel, tripletails, snapper and huge jack crevalle.

Bob Miller's IGFA world record. The jack crevalle is easily one of the toughest marine species to land—especially on a fly rod!

Bob Miller landed a 44-pound jack crevalle on a fly rod from the Tortuguero River while fishing out of Casa Mar. This is the present IGFA world record for 16-pound tippet.

EAST COAST CAMPS

There are three major river systems that empty into the Caribbean: Parismina, Tortuguero and Colorado. There are excellent, comfortable fishing lodges strategically located at each of the three river systems.

PARISMINA TARPON RANCHO (Parismina River): Costa Rica's first fishing lodge, located on the edge of the Parismina village, was originally a schoolhouse. In its conversion to a fishing camp it has been vastly modernized, so that today there are a number of duplex cabins, each with private bathroom and shower. The main building occasionally accommodates some clients upstairs, but basically it contains the dining room, kitchen and sitting area. There are two advantages to Parismina: It's the only camp on its network of lagoons and waterways including two river mouths (Parismina and nearby Pacuare); and it's located about 800 yards from Parismina's "boca" or river mouth. Thus, anglers can extend their normal day by fishing the mouth prior to breakfast or after supper. The night fishing is sometimes excellent but offers limited fly fishing potential.

Rates: $1,275 per person (double occupancy). Includes: the round trip charter from San Jose, Costa Rica to camp; seven nights' accommodations; fishing two anglers to a skiff, motor, fuel and guide. Saturday to Saturday.

TORTUGA LODGE: (Tortuguero River): The development of this lodge was hampered by a number of changes in ownership and lack of funds. Happily, Axel Mehnert purchased it, completed it and today, Tortuga is a fine, well-managed, modern camp. It is strategically located near the mouth of the Tortuguero river, the only camp on this waterway. The Tortuguero is a very productive water system for tarpon and snook; its advantage is that it doesn't muddy up as much as the the other east coast rivers. There are also some excellent back lagoons that harbor big snook along with tarpon.

Rates: $960 for a full week's fishing, including the round trip charter plane from San Jose, and two nights' accommodations in San Jose.

ISLA DE PESCA: This lodge is located about 1 1/2 miles from the mouth of the Rio Colorado. As the name implies, the camp is on a small island. Twenty-four anglers are comfortably accommodated, two to a room, in modern duplex cottages that are equipped with overhead fans, modern bathrooms and comfortable beds. The main lodge is composed of two large buildings, one housing the dining room and kitchen, while the other has a small bar, tackle counter and rec room. Isla de Pesca is very attractive and has all the conveniences an angler could reasonably expect from a jungle fishing camp. Isla de Pesca is managed by the very capable Pete Magee.

Rates: $1,375 per person based on double occupancy per week. Sunday to Sunday. Includes: round-trip charter plane service from San Jose; seven nights accommodations and all meals at camp; 6 1/2 days fishing (two persons to a skiff, motor, fuel and guide).

CASA MAR FISHING CLUB: This camp accommodates 24 clients in fully-modern duplex cottages. The dining room, sitting room and kitchen facilities are found in the main building. Casa Mar features an extremely attractive rec room, which, among other things, offers fly-tying facilities. Casa Mar was carved out of a jungle and represents one of the more popular Central American fishing camps. Owner/Manager Bill Barnes is a superb fly fisherman, a fine operator and undoubtedly has taken more Costa Rican tarpon and snook on a fly rod than any other man.

Rates: $1,450 per person per week based on double occupancy. Includes: round-trip charter plane service from San Jose to camp; seven nights' accommodations; all meals at camp; and 6 1/2 days of fishing (two persons to a skiff, motor, fuel and guide). Saturday to Saturday.

RIO COLORADO LODGE: This is the newest fishing camp on the Colorado and was constructed by Archie Fields. While not as comfortable as the other two camps on the Colorado, it has all the conveniences of a fishing camp and offers flexibility in that anglers can start and terminate their trips on any day of the week. Accommodates up to 24 anglers.

Rates: $1,125 per person per week, based on double occupancy, including the round-trip charter plane service.

When to go? There are two distinct periods to consider. The winter/spring and fall season. The winter/spring season begins in early January and terminates mid-May. During a typical 20-week season, four or five weeks traditionally deliver very good to excellent results; five or six weeks will provide average fishing; and the remainder can be classified as poor. Unfortunately, there is no way of predicting when the good or great weeks will pop up since weather and water conditions are the determining factors, and the weather can change quickly. Heavy rains occur along the east coast where the average annual rainfall is about 180 inches! The ideal conditions would be dry weather with a westerly wind (which would calm down

In one day's fishing, Gerald Almy landed six tarpon out of the nine he hooked on a fly rod. Talk about tired arms!

the Caribbean near shore). In the past, the second and third weeks of January and the first two weeks of May have provided the best periods for the fly fisherman, but, again, it all depends on the weather. You pick your week and take your chances.

The fall season runs from late August to late October. This is the time when the big snook invade the shallow coastal beaches and eventually enter the river mouths. While the fall season primarily belongs to the snook fishermen, it is also a super time for tarpon fishing, mostly because the Caribbean is often calm so the small boats can safely venture out to sea. Historically, the last two weeks in September and the first ten days of October have been very productive.

Rio Colorado Lodge is opened year-round. Owner Archie Fields admits that sometimes it rains very hard during the summer and late fall months when the other camps are closed, but heavy rains can come at any time during the year. Gerald Almy, *Sports Afield's* talented hunting and fishing editor, reports:

"I always thought that the tarpon action slowed down on the east coast of Costa Rica in mid-May, since that is when most of the camps close.

"However, I fished Rio Colorado Lodge the last three days of May and the guides and lodge personnel assured me that the tarpon are there and can be caught year-round. And it doesn't always rain in the rainy season. You may luck out, as I did, and miss the rains entirely.

"As for fishing several weeks after the 'peak' season ended, I jumped 40 to 50 tarpon in three days, boated nine that averaged over 80 pounds (a 110-pounder was the largest). All were caught on a No. 12 fly rod and fast-sinking lines. I landed six of the nine on my last day, which made it hard to leave camp."

EAST COAST TACKLE

Rods: For tarpon, a fly rod calibrated for a No. 11 to 13 line is recommended because tarpon will invariably run over 50 pounds. Whether one chooses fiberglass or graphite, or one of the new graphite/boron composites, several factors must be considered. Rods should have sufficient backbone to drive a 1/0 to 5/0 hook into the "concrete-hard" mouth of a tarpon.

Rod butts should be hefty in order to lift a sulking tarpon from the 15-foot-plus depths of the river lagoons. Rod guides must be strong enough to withstand plenty of strain and reel seats should be double-locking so that reels don't come loose during the energetic fights. Lighter-weight graphite is an advantage because "blind" casting is often practiced in this area. Fiberglass, less vulnerable, is the choice for many and is far less costly. Sage's GFL 1296 RP, Fenwick's WCF 9012, Fisher's F-2139 (glass), Shakespeare's Ugly Stick for No. 11 line or similar rods are recommended for these waters.

Reels: Reels should be sturdily constructed from materials that resist saltwater corrosion. They should have a capacity of at least 200 yards of 20- to 30-pound Micron or Dacron backing, plus fly line. Drags should be widely adjustable and smooth. Large Fin-Nors and Seamasters and Billy Pates are top-of-the-line choices. The Pflueger Medalist 1498 has withstood considerable service in these waters and has become an inexpensive favorite for many.

Lines: As the tarpon tend to hold deep in the lagoons and river mouths, super-fast-sinking lines are a necessity. Advances in fly line technology allow anglers to fish Costa Rican waters with far greater efficiency than ever before. Scientific Angler's Deep Water Express shooting heads sink with the quickness of lead core, yet cast more easily. The 550-grain size can be used uncut on a No. 11 to 13 fly rod, but the 750-grain heads must be shortened to suit your rod. Shooting heads can be attached to several types of running lines; Gudebrod Super Shooter in 30-pound test is one favorite. Cortland and Scientific Anglers offer shooting lines that handle exceptionally well with heads but do not allow the greater distances possible with the mono type lines. In either case, about 30 feet of shooting head and 80 feet of running line is standard, with the running line attached to 30-pound Dacron or Micron backing via a nail or Albright knot.

Leaders: Leader tippets should test no greater than 16 pounds and at least 15 inches in length in order to comply with IGFA regulations. Some anglers recommend short leaders with sinking lines, as longer constructions tend to buoy the fly above the level to which the fly line sinks. They use only three feet or so of tippet tied directly to the fly line and shock leader. Others prefer a more elaborate set-up: A six-foot butt section of 60-pound mono is nail-knotted to the fly line. (Two coats of Pliobond are applied to the knot for added protection.) This is coupled via a Stu Apte Blood or Albright knot to a class tippet. The tippet should have several inches of doubled mono at its front end, which is used to attach the shock leader via an Albright or similar knot. The shock leader can be no longer than 12 inches, and is usually 80-pound mono.

Flies: They should be dressed on plated hooks, in sizes 1/0 to 5/0. Color combinations such as red/white, red/yellow and

Costa Rica's angling popularity also stems from the number of well-operated fishing resort that are located on both coasts.

black plus standard patterns such as Cockroach, Lefty's Deceiver, and Barred and Black are also effective. Tarpon feed on both large, dark shrimp that reach up to five inches long and silver-sided "sardinas" common to these rivers. Flies should be fully dressed and weighted to sink rapidly. Hooks should be triangulated to a sharp point to aid in setting, and touched up with a stone or file after each fish.

Tackle for Other Species

Snook run large in Costa Rica and the potential for trophy fish is there. Lighter tackle than that recommended for tarpon can be used for big snook, such as a No. 9 or 10 outfit. Medium-sinking fly lines will handle most requirements in fishing the beaches or the interior jungle lagoons. Streamer flies with a touch of red in them, tied with darker colors, are recommended for snook. Use a 12-inch shock leader (30-pound mono).

For machaca, guapote, mojarra and small snook, a light fly rod outfit (No. 5 to 8) should prove ideal. Floating lines are suitable, and you will want an assortment of bass-sized fly rod poppers and streamers (yellow and white). Leaders should be about 7 1/2-foot tapered to eight pounds.

WEST COAST

Because of a lack of fishing lodges, most of Costa Rica's Pacific coast from Nicaragua to Panama is virtually an unexplored fishing resource. Until recently, there were a few small fishing camps, but they primarily focused on river fishing and only occasionally fished the Pacific because they didn't have the large sportfishermen cruisers needed to fish the ocean safely.

But in 1976, Henry Norton, former owner of Isla de Pesca on the east coast, constructed Bahia Pez Vela in the province of Guanacoste, close to the spectacular fishing grounds of Gulf de Papagayo. He purchased a number of 26-foot sportfisherman boats and for the first time, Costa Rica had a very comfortable, well-equipped fishing camp on the Pacific ocean. The fishing results in the ensuing years were often sensational. It started during Bahia's inaugural week: Stu Apte, one of the world's premier anglers, landed a world-record sailfish (102 pounds on 10-pound tippet). With each succeeding year it became more apparent that the Papagayo waters are among the best sailfishing waters of the world.

Sailfishing: While the Gulf of Papagayo offers numerous species of interest to the saltwater fly rodder, the Pacific sailfish is definitely the main target. Until the last decade, probably less than a dozen anglers had successfully landed Pacific sails on a fly rod. Today, membership to this once exclusive club is growing rapidly, and probably 200 fishermen have successfully landed a sail on a fly rod.

Interest in fly fishing for sails is increasing. The Pacific sail provides all the ingredients for a challenging adventure: Sails generally weigh from 70 to 120 pounds and are spectacular fighters: they can thrash and tail-walk across the surface and unwind a series of sensational aerial acrobatics that truly defy the laws of gravity! The sail makes long, reel-screeching runs that would empty even the largest fly reel of its precious backing, so the captain must follow the fish quickly while the angler recoups his precious line as fast as possible.

Naturally, you don't pick a spot out of the vast Pacific and start fly casting. The fish must first be teased to the top, which is done by trolling hookless teasers—lures or bait. It becomes a waiting game, yes, but if it is any kind of a good day, eventually a fin cuts behind the lure, then a bill slashes at the bait and that's when the captain hollers, "Sailfish!" and the action unfolds. The mate grabs the teaser rod and retrieves the bait away from the sailfish, but not so far away that the fish loses interest. Occasionally, he allows the sailfish to mouth the bait. It's a cat-and-mouse game. The sail becomes angrier and angrier by the minute. It can't quite devour that meal. The fish is frustrated, for it is one of the fastest marine gladiators of them all! It lunges for the bait repeatedly but can't quite grab it. You know it is mad because its powerful body changes colors, to a neon blue or bright purple. When the fish is "cooking real good," madder than hell, you yell "Neutral!" and the captain throws the engine out of gear (to comply with IGFA rules), the mate literally yanks the teaser bait out of the water and you, the angler, cast the fly rod popper or streamer to the fish. If all goes according to plan, the sailfish grabs it, you set hook and immediately it takes off in a long run, punctuated with some of the greatest jumps you've ever seen. The captain skillfully follows the fish with the boat now and all you can do is reel, reel, reel. And bow to the fish each time it leaps by quickly lowering the rod so that the sail's power and weight won't snap the tippet. And hope. It can take ten minutes or fifteen or an hour or two. It depends on the fish, but it also depends on you! With luck, the fish is brought boatside, the mate bills it, removes the fly and you feel darn good about it, for you have conquered one of the great gamefish with a fly rod.

AN EXPERT TELLS ALL

Winston Moore, one of the world's most skilled and persistent fly rodders, has landed more Pacific sails on a fly rod than any person in angling history. At the time of this writing, he has landed 138 Pacific sails from various trips to Panama and Costa Rica. During his 1982 trip to Costa Rica, he landed an amazing 23 sails on a fly rod! He even landed a striped marlin, making him probably only the sixth angler ever to land this species on fly gear.

Here are some of his thoughts on tackle, technique and theory:

MOORE ON TACKLE

"It's pretty much standard. I use a nine-foot fiberglass rod for a No. 12 line. I gave up on graphite rods for heavy fish a long time ago as they simply don't have the lifting and moving power that I seem to need when those big fish sulk 50 feet below the boat and just dog it. I feel most comfortable with fiberglass, and I seem to be able to whip and work a fish better with these rods. My rods have large guides all the way up.

"I have used John Emery fly reels and both anti-reverse and single-action Seamasters, and they all work very well. I prefer 30-pound Micron backing, loading the reel practically to capacity. To the backing I attach about 33 feet of level No. 1 floating Cortland line, using a nail knot. On the other end I make a loop by first stripping the coating from the shooting line, then bending the core back over itself and whip-finishing it. My fly line is a Cortland No. 10

floating shooting head, but I cut about six to eight feet off the rear of this shooting head and make another new loop, for a loop-to-loop connection with the shooting line. The reason I cut back the shooting head is to have less large diameter line in the water in order to reduce the drag. Long ago I found it doesn't take much pressure to break the tippet when those sails start one of their long and fast runs, then come back at speeds up to 40 mph and create a tremendous belly in the line.

"I make a standard saltwater leader by attaching four feet of 40-pound Maxima mono as the butt section to the fly line using a nail knot and coating it with Epoxy. The rest of the knot system is not as

Although many anglers like to use large streamers on sailfish, Winston's preference is for saltwater poppers: "You see it all!"

sophisticated as those used by the pros. On the tag end of the butt section I tie a perfection loop. I take several feet of 12- or 15-pound Maxima for my class tippet. For the butt connection I use a Spider Hitch, then double it and use a surgeon's knot. This gives me a loop-to-loop connection that rarely, very rarely, gives me any problems. I use the traditional 12-inch shock tippet from 65-pound Maxima. I tie the perfection loop in one end and attach the class tippet by using a double Albright to the perfection loop, leaving me about 18 inches of tippet. Then I tie the fly to the shock leader with another loop. I realize that some of the pros would be highly critical of this leader system, but Woody Sexton taught it to me many years ago. I've had considerable success, and so very few failures, that I continue to use it."

MOORE ON TEASING SAILS

"Obviously, you can't cast to sails unless you raise them, and I think too many boats travel all day long dragging those teasers around without doing the one thing that raises more fish than anything else I know of. While fishing Club Pacifico de Panama years ago, I was with a young captain who had lived in Panama all his life and grew up commercial fishing with his father. He told me that he had learned that most of the billfish raised were coming up from the deeper water as opposed to cruising on the surface, and that they checked surface disturbances. So his M.O. for trolling teasers was never to troll more than five minutes without making several very tight turns and figure eights. This caused a lot of white water and surface commotion in a small area, and it has been most interesting to me how often it works. So when I'm looking for sails, we do a lot of tight turning and always seem to see more fish than others in the same area.

"My teasers are the standard plastic squid, Sundance made by Boone Bait Co., and others, and/or the classic bonito or dorado belly strips. If I'm using plastic squids, I always have two in tandem on each teaser rod and always use two rods. Both teasers on each rod are of the same color, but I use a different color on each side of the boat.

"Obviously, I have my fly rod set up. Being right-handed, I keep it in the port corner of the cockpit with all of the shooting head stripped on the deck. When we raise a fish I grab the 'live' teaser rod that attracted the fish while the mate or captain reels in the other teaser out of the water. Handling the teaser rod is very important. I've seen mates and others reel the teaser in much too quickly, and the fish is at the transom before you are ready. A fish teased to the boat too fast will not usually take the fly. So when I pick up the teaser rod, I drop the teaser back to the sail, let it take it, then jerk it out of his mouth and reel it in a dozen feet. Then I repeat the process again, letting the sail take it, then pulling it away. I'm never in a hurry to get the fish in close enough for a cast. I take plenty of time with each fish as I want that sail so 'hot,' so excited and frustrated, that you could probably throw your shoe at the fish and it would grab it.

"Then when I think I've got the fish lit up and ready, I give the teaser rod to the mate, captain or partner and let him keep the fish in the vicinity while I make a false cast from the port side. When I am ready, I scream loud and clear 'NOW', at which time, hopefully, three things happen: (1) the captain throws the engine into neutral; (2) the teaser is jerked completely out of the water; (3) and, finally, my fly is on its way to the fish.

"I want the fly to land beside the fish as opposed to in front of it so that the sail can see it better. I use poppers exclusively, instead of streamers, as I've found that by creating a surface disturbance with the popper you can attract the fish's attention better. When the sail sees the fly and charges it, I keep it away from him for a few seconds, just as I do with the teaser, because I want him to really inhale it. I pop the bug along the surface and finally, as the fish is attacking it, I let it lie motionless in the water which sometimes allows the sail to take it better. Then I let the fish turn and, as it turns, when it is either at right angle to the transom or headed straight away, I set the hook several times just as hard as I can without breaking my tippet.

"To summarize, I think that the important integrals to successful fly fishing for sails are:

- Fiberglass rods are, in my opinion, preferable to graphite. A surface popper is more effective than a streamer—more fun, too.

- Stir up the water while trolling the teasers to give the fish a reason to come to the surface.

- When a fish comes up, the captain should reduce the boat's speed.

- Use two teaser rods with two teasers on each rod. Each set should be a different color.

- Hooks should be triangulated and sharp!

- The fish must be teased properly. There is no hurry; if the fish leaves during the teasing process, he was not 'hot' anyway.

Outdoor writer and expert fly fisherman Tom McNally proves that roosterfish can be landed on a fly...but it isn't easy!

▪ Use a minimum length of fly line to reduce the water drag during the fight.

▪ Set the hook in the opposite direction from which the fish is headed.

▪ While fighting the fish, it should either be taking line out or you should be gaining line, but the fish should never be allowed to dog it as it will regain its strength and energy. Apply maximum pressure."

OTHER PACIFIC SPECIES

Although fly fishing at Gulf de Papagayo centers on the sailfish, there are a number of other species that will interest the fly rodder. School dolphin, ranging up to 20 pounds, are excellent targets. These sporty gamefish will grab a popper, leap often and are flashy fighters. The action with school dolphin can be extended if a hooked dolphin is kept near the boat. (Ask the mate to hook and bring a dolphin close to your boat, but to leave it in the water.) The other dolphin, or "dorado" as they are called in Latin America, will remain in the area for a long time.

Roosterfish will take surface lures, but they are difficult to hook via fly fishing. The best method is to have someone cast a hookless lure (such as Arbogast's Scudder) and chug it to attract the roosters to the surface. When they appear, the chugger is yanked out of the way, and the fly rod popper is quickly delivered to the fish. It's not easy, but it works. Sometimes.

Cubera and other snappers are attracted occasionally to the surface by bait fish. They have been taken on a fly rod, but one needs ideal circumstances to accomplish this.

Another species that responds to a streamer fly is the wahoo. First, find a wahoo school, hook one on heavy gear and "control" it near the boat. Other wahoo will follow the hooked fish, much as is the case with dolphin. The streamer fly is cast near the hooked wahoo and stripped quickly. Another wahoo will sometimes peel away from the school, inhale the streamer and be off on one of its patented 150- to 200-yard runs. (See "Panamà" chapter for technique.)

WEST COAST CAMPS

The province of Guanacoste in the northwest section of Costa Rica is the finest area for fly fishing. There are other resort centers down the coast that offer fishing arrangements but the emphasis is on heavy-gear trolling. The lodges near Gulf de Papagayo offer the best possibility, by far, for fly fishermen.

BAHIA PEZ VELA: This one-time delightful camp, built on a knoll over-looking the Pacific accommodates 12 anglers (two to a room) in fully modern cottages. There is no air conditioning but there are overhead fans; most of the time they aren't needed. The main lodge contains the dining room, kitchen and an attractive sitting room. An outdoor patio offers anglers a

Don Dobbins who contributed so much to Costa Rican fishing was the first to land a snook of over 30 pounds at Casa Mar.

relaxing spot to congregate after a day's fishing and to share adventures. Bahia is located near the town of Liberia and clients are transferred there by charter plane from San Jose. Although Bahia is open from February to December, the best time for fly fishing is from late April to mid-September. At the time of this writing Henry Norton had sold Bahia Pez Vela, and the future of this facility is not known.

EL OCOTAL: This posh resort was completed in 1981 and provides a very luxurious facility for anglers who want to fish the Papagayo waters. It features modern, spacious accommodations, a fine dining room, a breathtaking view, swimming pool, tennis courts, horseback riding and other activities. It is ideal for the angler who wishes to take his nonfishing family along. El Ocotal has several excellent twin-engine sportfisherman boats and the captains know these waters intimately. Rick Wallace, who was Bahia's first manager, oversees the El Ocotal operation and understands the challenges of saltwater fly fishing.

Rates: $1,650 per person (double occupancy) per week, including seven nights' accommodations, all meals, boat, captain and mate.

There have been attempts to develop other fishing camps down the southern coast, but so far they have failed for numerous reasons. The best place, with tremendous potential, is Isla de Cano. Today one would need a live-aboard cruiser to explore these waters efficiently.

TROUT FISHING

Rainbow trout were not native to Costa Rica. However, about 25 years ago a successful stocking program took place and today there are a number of good trout rivers, although the better streams are practically inaccessible. One outfitter will offer organized trout fishing trips in 1987 to the Savergre River. Additional information may be obtained from Carlos Barrantes' Gilca Tackle Store. Here's how Carlos reviews the trout fishing potential:

"Right now the Costa Rican rivers offer rainbow trout fishing. Some thought has been given to importing brown trout.

Sometimes a hooked Costa Rican tarpon leaps into the angler's boat! Usually this results in considerable damage.

The best time is usually the rainy season, which is June through October, but for fly fishing on the Reventazon River at Tapanti, March through May is best. The trout fishing season is closed from November through February."

What is the largest trout taken? What's the average? "The largest rainbow was taken from the Humo River and weighed 10 pounds. This river, however, is practically inaccessible. Forget it. It's not for the tourist. The Tapanti (Reventazon) is second best and the average trout downstream is two pounds. Upstream, trout are more numerous but smaller in size—mostly in the 12- to 14-inch category. In the other rivers they average about the same size, with an occasional larger fish. I've heard of one rainbow that supposedly weighed 13 pounds, but I haven't seen it. The ten-pounder is mounted and displayed in my store," Carlos explains.

In addition to the Reventazon at Tapanti, Carlos rates the Parita at Copey, the Savergre at San Geraldo and the Cotton at Mellisar as the best rivers that can be fished by visiting anglers.

Fishermen must be prepared to rough it to some extent. Some of the rivers are as far as a two-hour drive from San Jose and there's plenty of walking involved. The Cotton River is near the Panamanian border and takes about an eight-hour drive to reach. Most Costa Ricans fish for trout via spinning or casting tackle, but some of them have become interested in fly fishing. Dry flies sometimes work, but weighted dark nymphs and wet fly patterns in various sizes are more productive. A No. 4 to 6 fly rod outfit with floating lines and nine-foot leaders tapered to 4X is suitable for this fishing.

Part of the Costa Rican trout fishing appeal is the spectacular scenery which includes ferns, orchids and other flora mostly associated with a jungle habitat.

COSTA RICA, THE COUNTRY

Costa Rica is one of Central America's best developed and most democratic countries. A country of about two million people, it is bordered by Nicaragua on the north, Panama to the south, and the Pacific and the Caribbean on the west and east coasts. Costa Rica enjoys the highest literacy of any Central American country. Spanish, of course, is the national language, but English is heard often in San Jose at restaurants, hotels and other tourist centers. There is no language problem at any of the fishing camps as most guides understand some English, and several are exceptionally fluent. Costa Ricans are among the friendliest people and this country welcomes Americans.

The Costa Rican currency is the colon. U.S. paper currency is readily exchanged in Costa Rica so one need not purchase colones in advance. U.S. silver coins have no value in Costa Rica.

The Capital: San Jose, Costa Rica's capital of about 350,000 residents, is near the geographic center of the country, and since elevation is 3,500 feet, the weather is very comfortable year-round. December to May is the "dry season" in San Jose. San Jose is one of Central America's most delightful cities, beautiful but informal; even at the most elegant restaurants, a sport coat will suffice.

Hotels in San Jose: No matter which area you plan to fish, you will have to overnight in San Jose. There are more than a dozen good hotels to choose from. Among them are: *Deluxe:* At the top of the list is the swank Hotel Cariari and Club, which features an 18-hole golf course, tennis court, swimming pool and, of course, air-conditioned, modern rooms. It's ten minutes from the airport and there is frequent shuttle bus service to San Jose. Also in the deluxe category is the huge Corobici Hotel complex. *First Class:* The Herradura is right next to the Cariari and shares some of the resort facilities. For old world atmosphere and a downtown location, the Gran Hotel Costa Rica is recommended. It's a renovated hotel, full of charm, and right across from the National Theater. The Bougainvillea is also recommended. *Moderate:* The Presidente is small, pleasant and centrally located. The Europa is also recommended.

Restaurants of San Jose: Le Mirage features French cuisine (Lobster Provincale is one of their specialties) in an elegant but not overly decorated atmosphere. La Bastille is an intimate French restaurant known for its seafood specialties. The Suisse Chalet is a favorite among visiting anglers who are looking for an informal place that serves good food; the same applies to the Van Gogh. The restaurant in the Royal Dutch Hotel has been top-rated for years. There are dozens of other excellent restaurants featuring French, Italian, Mexican and other cuisines.

Entertainment in San Jose: Don't look for glamorous and glittery nightclubs in San Jose, but most of the major hotels do offer entertainment and dancing. The "liveliest" nightclubs include Leonardo's, Le Club and Coco-Loco. Most Costa Ricans rely on providing their own fun and entertainment, and much of it goes on until dawn and beyond.

Getting There: From the U.S. there are excellent connections from Miami, New Orleans and Los Angeles. It's a 2 1/2-hour

Frank Woolner, *Salt Water Sportsman,* was possibly the first to popularize fly fishing for machaca. It's a good "fill-in" fish.

Fishing columnist Bob Stearns (center) landed this IGFA record sail on a 10-pound tippet and popper from Gulf de Papagayo.

flight from Miami to San Jose, and there are a number of bargain excursion airfares available. Upon arrival in San Jose, you will be met by a camp representative who will take you to your hotel and arrange to pick you up the next day for your charter plane trip to the camp.

Required Documents: In addition to a valid passport you will need a tourist card. This is issued at the U.S. airports by the international carrier that will fly you to Costa Rica. Costa Rica also maintains a number of consular offices in major cities that can provide a tourist card for $2.00. No vaccinations or inoculations are necessary.

You will also need a fishing license ($10), and these are readily available at all fishing camps.

AND FINALLY...Carlos Barrantes has to be pleased with the great number of anglers who come to his country not only from the United States, but from France, Germany, England, Italy and even the Orient. Yes, Costa Rica is famous for its bananas and its coffee but, at least in angling circles, it's more famous because of its tarpon and snook and marlin and sails and other denizens of both oceans and its inland rivers. Sportfishing here has matured, but there is much to be explored in the future, especially on the Pacific side, and it will be done. In time.

Panama

Fish Bowl of the Pacific

Panama's Pacific side provides an unending series of fly fishing challenges for numerous species. Here's a novel method for taking wahoo on a fly consistently (heretofore considered an almost impossible feat); what happens when a man hooks a huge marlin (over 300 pounds) on a fly rod; a foolhardy attempt to land a sail on a 6-pound tippet; a place where peacock bass are so plentiful that only a couple of days of fishing is recommended.

When a sail first feels the barb, it unleashes an awesome series of leaps.

Chapter 11

PANAMA

I THOUGHT the idea was insane. Stu Apte thought it was worth trying. Bob Griffin, the owner of Club Pacifico de Panama fishing camp, was convinced that it would definitely work. He should have been. After all, it was his idea.

The Problem: How do we catch a wahoo on a fly? Sure, we could troll a streamer fast, especially in the productive waters of "Wahoo Alley," and no doubt wahoo would whack it. But trolling a fly isn't exactly fly fishing. We tried making long casts and stripping in the fly as fast as we could, but this didn't work to anyone's satisfaction, the wahoo's or ours. What we were searching for was a better idea that would greatly increase our odds of hooking these speedsters on a fly.

The Target: First, a little background on the wahoo. Foremost, it is one of the fastest of all species, and when it takes a lure, it can strip out line faster and longer than any bonefish. And this fish is a lot larger and stronger than a bone. Since the wahoo inhabits deeper water, one can't merely spot the fish and make a presentation, a la bonefishing. Wahoo are primarily taken by fast trolling.

On the other hand, the smaller species, under 30 pounds, definitely school up. That's helpful, for once one is located, there may be other wahoo in the immediate vicinity. Furthermore, wahoo are similar to dolphin in that once a fish is hooked and fought, others will follow it and congregate curiously near the boat. An obvious solution would be to hook a wahoo on heavy tackle and try to control it near the boat, allowing another angler to make a presentation to any other wahoo

Bill Cullerton landed his first sail with a fly rod at Club Pacifico.

spotted. We tried it, but even on heavy gear, these fish would speed quickly for other parts of the ocean, or rip the hook off. It didn't work.

Bob's Solution: We would troll a heavy jig very rapidly over prime wahoo waters. This jig would be attached to a wire leader, which in turn is tied to a 1/4-inch nylon rope. The rope would be securely fastened to a boat cleat so that the jig was no more than 50 to 60 feet behind the stern. Now according to Bob, after the fish struck the jig, the rope would keep the wahoo "under control" and within casting distance. The engine would be thrown out of gear (to comply with IGFA regulations) and we would then make the presentation to any trailing fish.

The Results: The problem with the initial setup quickly became evident. The wahoo grabbed the jig and immediately started off on its first powerful run. Because of its tremendous burst of energy, the hook quickly tore out of the fish's mouth. This happened several times, so Bob went back to the drawing board. The revised version employed several feet of bungee cord at the end of the rope that would provide the right amount of cushion during the first few minutes of the fight. We were anxious to try it.

The first hooked wahoo on the rope was lost to a shark, and another one became unhooked, but on the third try, it worked like a charm. The fish settled down after a frenzied struggle and Bob was able to control it on the starboard side. There were two wahoo that followed the hooked fish and Stu released a quick, accurate cast. He stripped line in quickly, and the blue and white streamer darted enticingly in front of a wahoo. He hooked the fish, and the wahoo whooshed all over our part of the ocean. It was eventually landed, and just to make sure that it wasn't a fluke, Stu proceeded to land several other wahoo.

Only a few fly rodders have landed wahoo, but by using Bob's system, it can be a most challenging angling encounter. The cast must be accurate, the strip must be fast, and the ensuing jolt on the initial run must be cushioned. This means a minimum drag on the reel, and of course, all knots must be well tied. Meanwhile, the person who is handling the rope with the hooked wahoo must be able to control the fish within casting

Taking a wahoo on a fly is a tremendous challenge; but Bob Griffin and Stu Apte devised a successful method.

distance (ideally on the starboard side). Furthermore, once the fly rodder hooks a wahoo, the "rope" man must land his fish quickly so that the lines don't tangle. It's fast, furious and exciting action, I'll tell you.

The equipment is basically simple: a No. 9 or 10 fly rod; a very smooth running reel that holds at least 200 yards of 20-pound backing; a sinking shooting head; a nine-foot leader with a 12- or 15-pound tippet; and a 12-inch shock leader (27-pound, coffee-color wire) for the sharp-toothed wahoo. Attach the wire to the fly with a haywire twist knot and the other end to a very small swivel (haywire twist). Make sure the swivel is dull black (a shiny swivel will attract houndfish or other species that will surely cut you off). Tie the tippet to the swivel with an improved clinch knot. The wire shock leader works very well, as wahoo are capable of cutting even very heavy mono leaders. We found that streamers tied on 5/0 hooks (sharpened) with blue and white FisHair were very effective on these waters.

I tried a yellow popper on wahoo and I was surprised—no, shocked—to have a 30-pound wahoo smash it. I was so stunned that I never bothered to set hook and goofed up that fish.

"That fish should sue you for malpractice the way you played him," Apte admonished me, somewhat jokingly. "And he'd win." He was right.

Stu returned to Club Pacifico in October, 1975, and set four IGFA world records, three in one day! The largest was a 20-pound, two-ounce wahoo on 15-pound tippet, but the most impressive catch was a 17-pound, 10-ounce wahoo on a flimsy six-pound tippet. Landing wahoo on six-pound line on plug casting or spinning gear is quite an accomplishment, but it becomes doubly difficult with fly tackle. Remember that the wahoo swims very fast and doubles back quickly, so the thick diameter of the fly line bellies in the water, which puts heavy pressure on the tippet. Stu used a 16-foot lead-core section instead of a standard fly line on this trip for two reasons: the thinner diameter of the lead core cut through the water better (less belly); and, he found out that wahoo became more interested in a fly if it emerged from the deeper water to the surface.

The wahoo will never have a large following among fly fishermen because he is not a particularly good fly fishing target, but Stu Apte's experience illustrates that most species can be landed on a fly rod provided the angler's persistence is coupled with ingenuity.

FLY FISHING FOR SAILS

Most fly fishermen who book Club Pacifico are attracted to this area by other species, and the Pacific sailfish tops the list.

It was at Club Pacifico, many years ago, that I landed my first sailfish on a fly rod. At the time it was estimated that no more than 10 anglers had landed a Pacific sail on a fly rod, but today this circle has been expanded to possibly 200 members.

Prior to my trip, I read everything available on fly fishing for sails, but the information was somewhat limited. On numerous occasions I called Stu Apte who patiently answered my unending flow of questions; he was exceptionally helpful, divulging every piece of information he had acquired the hard way, through personal experience.

On the first fishing day, camp owner Bob Griffin accompanied me. We were going to fish the island of Jicaron because Bob said those waters were loaded with sails. On the way there, I reviewed in my mind over and over again what Stu had told me. How to tease up a sail. How to tell when the fish was ready. Where to cast the popper. When and how to set hook. At least 101 "do's and don't's" pelleted through my mind. When we arrived at the area, Bob and I again reviewed the procedures. He would handle the teaser rod; we got our signals straight.

Within five minutes a sail came up, crashing behind the trolled hookless teaser. "Sailfish!" someone yelled, and a crescendo of excitement prevailed. The fish was aggressive. It slashed at the bait several times, each time appearing more angry, and Bob handled the teaser rod perfectly. He would pull the plastic squid just far enough from the fish so that the sail couldn't quite grab it, but not so far that it would lose interest. The fish was frantic, furious, frustrated. It turned an electric blue, an indication that it was, to put it mildly, upset.

"The sail is hot now. It's cooked! Ready?" Bob asked.

"READY!"

The engine was thrown into neutral, Bob yanked the squid totally out of the water, and just an instant later, my popper plopped to the right side of the sail. It grabbed it, turned and swam nonchalantly away from the boat. More instinctively than by design, I set hook several times, with short jabs, just as Stu had explained many times. In the next few seconds I was treated to a series of incredible leaps, tail-walking maneuvers and head-shaking convulsions that made one wonder how that 15-pound tippet held together. Those magnificent jumps were close to the boat, and the boat was less than 100 yards from the island of Jicaron. A sail flopping out in the middle of the ocean is a dramatic sight, but it becomes doubly spectacular when the action occurs near shore. To my mind anyway. Words of encouragement flowed constantly from Bob and from Mike Bolton, who served as mate on the boat that day.

In 18 minutes the sail was brought to the boat. Mike billed it, Griffin congratulated me and I must admit that I felt damned proud, though I tried to assume a casualness, as if I do this sort of thing all the time. Of course, no one was fooled. Mike spent 20 minutes trying to revive the sail, which was totally enervated, but to no avail. Just below, a white-tip shark cruised back and forth, waiting patiently for his breakfast, though now and then he would come closer to the fish for an inspection.

"It's not going to revive," Mike said, "and the shark will get it."

"Best we bring him into camp. The people on the island could use this fish," Bob directed.

When that sail leaps (especially near the boat) lower the rod tip swiftly to reduce the tension on the tippet.

And we did. I was only sorry that the fish couldn't be revived and released. It would have been the finishing touch to a most satisfying experience.

The rest of the trip was devoted almost exclusively to fly rodding for sails. They were everywhere, and were they aggressive! We were down to only one plastic squid teaser, and we had just teased in a big sailfish. Bob was breaking in a new kid, Jose, on the teaser rod, and the young man was doing an admirable job. But this time he teased the fish so close to the boat that I couldn't cast. Jose removed the teaser from the water and held it a couple of feet above the surface, hoping that the sail would back off.

"Swing that teaser on board," I told the kid. "It's our last teaser."

"No problema," he grinned. Suddenly the sail came out, grabbed the hookless teaser and broke it off from the frayed leader. Jose was stunned. I was mad because we had lost our last teaser. We didn't even have any fish strips, which make excellent teasers, on board.

Bob was amused. "There are so many sails out here that if we troll anything, we'll probably raise them." The enterprising Griffin took out a handkerchief and tied it on.

And it worked. We teased enough sails for the rest of the day by merely trolling a piece of cloth.

I don't know whose crazy idea it was—Bob's or mine—but we decided to try for a sail using a six-pound leader tippet. No one had ever landed a Pacific sail on that weight tippet.

"Hell, man, I'm not in that class. I can't handle these sails very well on 15-pound tippet," but Bob was insistent, and, frankly, what did we have to lose?

We must have raised over 30 sails. Most of them got off quickly, because it was impossible to set hook. A few were hooked for an instant or so, but would break off, or immediately they would disgorge the popper.

We came close to controlling one sail that was especially active, but just as we were developing our confidence, a school of porpoises moved into our area.

"Damn it," Bob was upset, and began to pound his gaff against the side of the boat in an attempt to scare them off. "All they have to do is rub against that light leader and that's the end." And that's exactly what happened.

Later we hooked up with another sail on six-pound tippet. It was an exceptionally active jumper, and the sail cooperatively fought near the surface. There's no way you can budge a sailfish if it decides to sound.

The fight lasted over three hours, and I remember that it rained twice, very hard, but in between the sun came out and I dried out. Somehow, someway, the leader didn't part, and now the fish was a few feet from the boat, tired, exhausted and on its side.

Bob Griffin was very confident during the last 10 minutes. "We've got this baby," he kept repeating, as he nervously sharpened the gaff hook.

"I think we can try to gaff him now," I said.

Bob reached with the gaff as far out for the fish as he could. "I can't quite make it." He was short by about a foot or so. "We'll back up the boat."

"I think I can ease it just a little closer," and I carefully tried to move the sail. It seemed to be moving, but all of a sudden the fish shook its head, in one last gasp, and the leader popped. The fish slowly submerged. Bob was quiet. The captain and mate shook their heads and muttered something about bad luck in Spanish.

"We were close, Chapralis. Very close," Bob said. "You can't come any closer and lose."

Sure, I would have liked to have landed that fish. It would have been a record. I also knew I was totally lucky. These types of catches belong to the experts: the Stu Aptes, the Lefty Krehs, the Winston Moores, the Billy Pates, and all the others who have paid their dues throughout the years. Heck, I pop six-pound leaders on medium-sized trout when I'm overanxious. This fish was in the 90-pound class. It was nice to come close, so the trip back to the lodge wasn't so painful after all. I think I smiled much of the way. Naw, all the way.

Many anglers have taken their first sail at Club Pacifico. I encouraged Bill Cullerton to try and he succeeded on his second attempt. The late Ralph Ward did it on his first trip to Club Pacifico, and so did his wife. (In fact, she may have been the first woman angler to land a Pacific sail on a fly rod.) One needs some luck, of course, and plenty of aggressive fish, as well as patience and perseverance.

And endurance, too. Stu Apte had urged me to practice reeling in order to increase my speed and endurance. About a month before that trip, I had practiced each evening so that I could reel for a half-hour, or 10 minutes at full speed. I attached the reel to the butt section of a fly rod for convenience.

Hooking and landing a Pacific sail on a fly rod is one of the great fishing challenges available to the angler today. Winston Moore's advice and tips (see "Costa Rica" chapter) should be carefully studied by anyone interested in sailfishing with a fly rod.

"You have to completely play out a sail on a fly rod before the captain can bill it..." W. Moore.

Winston has taken many sails at Club Pacifico (he caught his first and his 100th sail from these waters). He prefers the first couple of weeks in January. During his 1982 trip he raised 82 sails to the teasers, was able to cast to 57 of them, hooked 27 and landed 19. An incredible accomplishment. Pacific sails will weigh from 75 to over 150 pounds, but the majority of the fish are in the 80- to 100-pound bracket. He landed one sail in seven minutes, but had some fights that lasted over three hours with a 15-pound tippet. Fish are individuals.

During his numerous Club Pacifico trips, Winston has had a number of encounters with black marlin. Since these marlin weigh from 300 to 400 pounds, understandably the odds of landing one are insurmountable.

But he came close in 1982. He cast to a fish that took the popper. It immediately leaped. To Winston's astonishment, it was not a sailfish. It was a marlin estimated at 350 pounds! After a 45-minute fight, the marlin appeared whipped. It was on the surface, perhaps only a dozen feet from the boat. While Winston releases all billfish, even those that would surely become IGFA world records, he admitted later that possibly he would have kept this marlin because of the historic significance.

There was only a small hand gaff aboard his boat. The captain radioed one of the other fishing boats and explained the predicament. The other boat had a large gaff and raced to Winston's aid. It was about a 15-minute run, and this was more than sufficient time for the marlin to recover. Winston fought the revived fish for a total of four hours and five minutes. By now they had drifted a considerable distance from camp; Winston realized that his chances were nil and finally broke off the fish.

"I wanted to land that marlin, of course. But we were a long way from camp and it was getting late. Obviously, it was a tremendous thrill to fight a large marlin on a fly rod," Winston related.

OTHER TARGETS

There are other fish that are attractive to the fly rodder. The school dolphin is one of the most interesting (and most cooperative) species, and when a school is found, the action is fast-paced. Most of these dolphin will run from eight to 12 pounds, and they will attack a popper with gusto. Dolphin are excellent jumpers, fast swimmers, beautiful fish and, of course, great eating. Fly rodding for dolphin certainly can break up the monotony when other species are uncooperative.

The waters of Club Pacifico are also known for big snapper, although not many anglers try for them with a fly rod. The ideal time would be during the "crab hatch," when snappers come to the surface and gorge on these delicacies. The water at this time takes on a dark red hue because there are so many mutton snapper or cigueros. The hatch, however, is unpredictable. It lasts about 10 days, occurring any time from late February to early April.

Club Pacifico guests hook cuberas on surface plugs during the entire season by casting the lures to the turbulent waters around rocky islands and points such as Hermosa (not far from the camp). I say "hook" because it's one thing to hook them and a totally different matter to land them, especially from these spots. Cubera have incredible power, and once hooked, they go where they please, generally back to their rocky homes. And they go when they please, usually immediately. They can easily chafe the line against these rocks. When they are found in open water, landing cubera or other large snapper species is still not a piece of cake, but somewhat easier.

I recall fishing with Bob Griffin one summer near the island of Jicaron. It was one of those great days when the ocean was alive with feeding fish. Sails were everywhere. The eagle-eyed Griffin spotted a floating log some distance away that was moving peculiarly. The waters were placid, and he insisted that we move closer.

"Unbelievable! There are big snappers, huge snappers, underneath that log, and they are bumping that log and rolling it," Bob announced from his vantage point. "They seem to be rolling that log and grabbing some food. Maybe the snappers are feeding on crabs. I've never seen anything like that!" And Bob has seen plenty.

When we got closer, I witnessed this remarkable phenomenon. These snappers looked huge. They were over 30 pounds.

The author lucked out on his first presentation to a sail. "I listened to Stu Apte and followed his advice."

"This may be the best possibility for a big mutton snapper on a fly rod. It's like falling off a log," and Bob laughed at his pun.

It appeared that way. I cast the fly rod popper right next to the log and braced myself for the strike. I envisioned the gaping jaw of a big mutton smashing the lure. But nothing happened. I made a dozen casts with the popper and even switched to a brown streamer, but to no avail. Bob had a plug casting outfit handy, and his large gurgling surface lure wasn't intercepted either.

Some large snappers have been taken on a fly at Club Pacifico. Jim Lopez landed several on 10-, 12-, and 15-pound tippets; the largest was a 30-pounder.

Roosterfish is another challenge for the fly rodder. They have been taken on a fly in Costa Rica, Baja California and other places. Many fine specimens up to 50 pounds have been caught by plug casters at Club Pacifico, but the fly rodders have virtually ignored this challenging species.

Sometimes roosters will come to the surface and feed voraciously for a short period of time, but one needs to have some luck, first in finding feeding roosters, and second, in enticing them to hit a fly.

Anglers who have been successful elsewhere tell me that they initially attract the roosters to the top by casting and retrieving big surface hookless plugs. In effect, they are teasing the fish to the top. The man handling the spinning or casting rod continually pulls the plug away until the fish's anger is fierce. Then the fly fisherman casts a popper or a streamer and hopefully hooks the roosterfish. This system obviously requires a team effort, but if one doesn't have a fishing partner, most guides or captains can handle a plug rod.

Club Pacifico has numerous jacks, amberjack, rainbow runners, Pacific barracuda, and other species, but the fly fishermen who book this camp spend most of their energy pursuing sailfish.

In addition to Club Pacifico, Panama also offers fishing arrangements at Tropic Star, a very posh resort that caters to anglers from all over the world. Tropic Star earned its fame primarily because of its fine black marlin population, so most of this fishing is via trolling. During May and early June, Pacific sails invade these waters in unbelievable numbers. This in turn has attracted some fly fishermen, and many newcomers to the sport have taken their first sail on a fly.

When's the best time to fly fish for sails at Tropic Star? In 1981 over 130 sailfish were landed during a week in May by a dozen fly fishermen. In 1982 the May sailfish run was somewhat disappointing, although the fish did appear in heavy numbers in June. In 1986 there was a tremendous run of sails during the first week of April, and 257 were landed and released by light tackle anglers using regulation gear. In fishing, one quickly discovers there are few hard and fast rules.

There are other species such as dolphin, snapper, roosterfish and wahoo that can be taken on a fly rod, but usually the fly fishermen who book Tropic Star have the sailfish almost exclusively in mind.

Tackle for Club Pacifico and Tropic Star: The suggested tackle list for fishing Costa Rica's west coast (see "Costa Rica" chapter) is highly recommended for Panamanian saltwater fishing.

The Caribbean: A New Frontier?

An angler has two excellent choices (Club Pacifico and Tropic Star) if he intends to fish the Pacific Ocean. What about the Caribbean side? According to Bob Griffin, who has explored this area, there is certainly good tarpon and snook fishing; in fact, it is so good, that he decided to construct a fishing camp. He ran into considerable red tape, however, and his highly placed political scissors wasn't able to cut it. It seems that the local Indians had a treaty from way back when, and while the majority of residents were highly in favor of the camp because, after all, it would mean jobs and money for their community, the chief was against it. Reluctantly, Bob had no recourse but to dispense with his plans, despite the fact that this area offered fabulous fishing. Is there a future here? Maybe.

Fishing The Interior: Lake Gatun

There's another type of fishing that ought to interest the fly rodder: pavon fishing on sprawling Lake Gatun. The pavon, more popularly known as peacock bass, is a sporty fighter that's indigenous to the northern part of South America. Many years ago the Panamanians planted the pavon in Gatun and they took hold. And how. Some of the areas of Gatun are so overrun with this species that anglers are encouraged not to release them. Most of these peacock bass are in the one- to two-pound class, and anglers often land 40 to 60 fish in a day. Warren Brewster set out to see how many pavon he could land in one day on a fly. He topped 200!

At times, pavon are so easy to catch at Gatun that fishermen search for a lure that won't catch fish. Out of desperation, one fisherman devised a lure using a McDonald's straw and a hook. It caught dozens of pavon (presumably a Burger King straw would also work).

Although Gatun appears to be a fisherman's utopia, boredom may set in after a couple of days. The angler looks for that

Club Pacifico's waters are known for its roosterfish; getting them to take a fly is a tremendous challenge.

bigger pavon, the six-pounder (or larger), or perhaps a snook to interrupt the unending series of "two-pound clones." One wouldn't book a whole week at Gatun (unless he doesn't mind the consistent size of these fish), but one or two days of Gatun pavon fishing in conjunction with a major trip to Club Pacifico or Tropic Star is recommended. While all reports that I have received indicate very fast fishing, I'm sure there are also slow periods on Gatun.

Tackle for pavon: A light fly rod, such as a No. 5 or 6, is desirable for this type of fishing. A lightweight reel (you don't need much backing), weight-forward floating or sinking lines, 7 1/2- to 9-foot leaders, (tapered to six-pound tippet), an assortment of streamers tied on No. 2 and 4 hook type, and bass sized poppers complete the basic outfit.

THE CAMPS

CLUB PACIFICO DE PANAMA: This jewel of a fishing camp is located in a protective cove on the island of Coiba, which is

Club Pacifico is comfortable but not an elegant fishing camp. It's located on a secluded cove on the island of Coiba.

about 180 miles west of Panama City. Coiba is about 25 miles long, and there are numerous other islands that provide a lee-side to fish.

The camp accommodates up to 12 anglers in duplex cottages that are fully modern, air-conditioned and offer a magnificent view of the Pacific. The main lodge contains dining room, kitchen, sitting room, and tackle bar. Very attractive, very comfortable.

The standard boat at Club Pacifico is 23-feet, inboard-powered, with a center console. The convertible canvas top is ideal for fly fishing because the top can be dropped quickly, allowing anglers easy maneuverability all around the craft while fighting a fish. A captain (no mate) is provided; he knows the waters well, but speaks very little English.

Club Pacifico is open from December through April, which is prime fishing time.

The Rate: A week's fishing at Club Pacifico costs $1,895 per person based on double occupancy. The rate includes seven nights' accommodations, six days of fishing, all meals, the

For sheer luxury, Tropic Star Lodge can't be beat. This is the famous El Palacio cottage located on a knoll.

round-trip charter flight from Panama City, all tips at camp, and even the necessary two nights' hotel accommodations in Panama City, one prior to and one after the trip.

TROPIC STAR LODGE: Tropic Star (originally called Club de Pesca) was constructed by the late Ray Smith, a Texan who wanted to build a very plush fishing resort near his favorite marlin waters. Located in the Darien Jungle, near the Colombian border, Tropic Star is a testament to Ray's perseverance, for he accomplished his goal under unfavorable odds. The posh jungle resort changed hands several times, and is presently owned by Conway Kittredge but managed by daughter Terri, a very accomplished light tackle angler.

Guests are accommodated in duplex, air-conditioned cottages while the main lodge incorporates the dining room, bar and sitting room. Gourmet meals are served elegantly by formally-attired waiters. For those anglers who insist on the finest (and don't mind paying for it), they can reserve the "El Palacio," a sumptuously-appointed cottage that is constructed on a knoll. Tropic Star also has a freshwater swimming pool.

Anglers fish from twin-engine, 31-foot Bertrams that are old, but have been exceptionally well-maintained through the years. The crews consist of an experienced captain and mate. While sportfisherman cruisers aren't the best type of boats for novice fly fishermen, they are certainly adequate, provided the angler is conscious of any obstructions that could prevent a trouble-free back cast. Outriggers should definitely be removed for fly fishermen.

The primary season is mid-December through June, but the fly fisherman who is interested in sails ought to consider May and early June. Historically, the second or third week of May has been the most productive.

The Rate: A week's fishing costs $2,500 per person based on double occupancy. It includes all accommodations, fishing arrangements (two persons to a boat), all meals and the round-trip charter plane service from Panama City. The captain and mate are generally tipped $100 to $150 total per week.

CLUB LAGO: This is the name Bob Griffin gave his fishing arrangements on Lake Gatun (for peacock bass fishing). Actually, there is no club at all; clients are accommodated in a first-class hotels in Panama City. They are driven to the fishing grounds each morning and returned to Panama City in the late afternoon. The drive is about one hour long and quite scenic. Bob provides hotel accommodations, round-trip transfers by car to Lake Gatun, tackle (even fly fishing gear), 16-foot aluminum skiffs powered by outboards, guides and box lunches. The cost is approximately $190 per person, per day based on double occupancy.

Lake Gatun is the world's largest man-made lake and covers about 165 square miles. It is the reservoir that operates the Panama Canal. The lake has many small islands and one can take a short boat trip over to the main channel and watch the ships negotiate the Canal.

PANAMA, THE COUNTRY

Panama's most famous physical feature is the Canal, but there is a great deal more to this country. It has some of the most beautiful coastline one can find anywhere. There are also mountain ranges, lush jungles, many islands, fine resorts, a tropical climate and an abundance of flora and fauna. Its population is about two million, but approximately 700,000 live in Panama City.

Panama City, although informal in dress code, is a very cosmopolitan, bustling, energetic city. It contains over 100 international banks, museums, a national theater, excellent restaurants and hotels, numerous casinos and night spots.

Climate: It's tropical, but the trade winds keep the temperature down. In Panama City, the average low is 70 degrees, and the average high is 90 degrees. The summer, or dry season, is from December through April. Fall brings heavy rains, but even in September and October there are about 13 or 14 days a month with no rain.

When fishing the ocean, one should realize that the sun is exceptionally intense, even when there is some cloud cover. This means long, lightweight trousers, long-sleeved shirts, wide-brimmed hats, sunglasses, and a good supply of a powerful sunscreen (such as Eclipse 15) that is liberally applied from

Winston Moore whipped this huge sail; but it wasn't easy. He has landed 138 Pacific sails in Panama and Costa Rica.

time to time. Even anglers who spend a great deal of time outdoors, and are well-tanned, should take precautions.

Required Documents and Currency: Valid passports are necessary for citizens of the U.S. and other countries. No vaccinations are needed.

The Panamanian currency is the Balboa, which is on a par with the U.S. dollar. U.S. dollars are exchanged freely, so one does not need to obtain local currency.

Hotels: There is a plethora of hotels in Panama City. Among the best in the deluxe class: El Continental, El Panama, Holiday Inn, Marriott and La Siesta. First-class hotels include: El Ejecutivo, Granada and Internacional.

Restaurants: Panama City has dozens of excellent restaurants. For starters, consider these: Belvedere (expensive, on the top floor of the Holiday Inn), Panamar (at the end of Calle 50), Casa del Marisco (for seafood, on Balboa Avenue) and El Dorado (Calle Colombia No. 2). In addition, nearly all major hotels generally have excellent dining rooms.

After Hours: Panama City probably has the most active nightlife of any Central American city. The casinos and the brassy nightclubs are the big tourist attractions but just about every form of entertainment is available.

Shopping: Panama is a shopper's mecca because goods made all over the world are imported free of duty. Everything from cameras and stereos to tableware to Cuban cigars is available. Among the popular gifts made locally: silver and gold jewelry, embroidered linen and molas (which make excellent wall hangings).

AND FINALLY... Panama's fishing potential is immense. While some of this potential has been realized, there are still other areas that need further exploring, more specifically on the Caribbean side. The Panamanians are very much aware of the importance of sportfishing to their country, not only because of the financial income but also for the prestige the country reaps through articles in major outdoor magazines and from national television exposure.

Colombia

Land of Pavon, Payara and Piranha, Jungle Fishing at its Best

South America's newest fishing discovery offers trophy-sized pavon, payara, piranha and other exotics in a lush, jungle environment that heretofore was practically inaccessible. A description of the main species... What to bring... Where to stay... and numerous tips.

Butterfly pavon of up to 20 pounds have been landed from the Orinoco watershed.

Chapter 12

COLOMBIA

SOME fishermen endure inconvenience and even risk danger for the opportunity to cast a stream, a lake, or an ocean that perhaps no one else has fished. True, we all have our favorite, more predictable places that we cherish for their escape value and to which we return regularly for sustenance and to renew relationships that grow stronger with each visit. Yet there are those times, when lured by the possibility of a new adventure, that we follow our curiosities to frontiers. Logistics, accommodations and equipment may be poor in comparison to our treasured haunts, but fishing is infinitely more intriguing.

So when Al McClane penned those fine articles on the Ventuari, Orinoco and other Venezuelan rivers and wrote of exotic species such as pavon, payara and picuda, there was a powerful urge by his readers to penetrate this newly discovered fishing frontier. (Never mind that Al accurately described the hazards of jungle fishing: "It was so hot I thought my brains were being fried.")

Anglers quickly discovered that these prized jungle rivers were tightly wrapped with a red tape that was practically impossible to cut. Simply, the Venezuelan government was not at all interested in allowing anglers or other tourists into the interior unless, of course, there was a scientific reason, or if someone possessed political connections of the highest kind.

Of course, even red tape wasn't going to stop some of the more fervent, or perhaps masochistic, anglers. Several went to Caracas, Venezuela, and pleaded for the opportunity to fish these waters. Kay Brodney, who spent more time fishing South American jungle rivers than anyone I know, invested over a

It was A. J. McClane's fabulous articles on the Orinoco that primed the well.

week's time in Caracas trying to arrange the necessary permission. She was unsuccessful and returned home. (Today, however, interior fishing in Venezuela has opened up considerably and camps may be constructed.)

So this fishing was not tapped by many anglers (a few were successful but would not divulge their technique). While interest didn't necessarily wane, the Orinoco's heralded fishing potential was not immediately realized.

The breakthrough came a number of years later. *The PanAngler* (a monthly newsletter devoted to international fishing) repeatedly reported on the fantastic fishing potential of the Orinoco watershed and expressed hope that this area would soon be opened to anglers. These items caught the attention of Kjell von Sneidern and Erland (his son) who offer hunting and fishing arrangements in Colombia. They knew, of course, that they wouldn't be able to operate in Venezuela, but what about

In past years, the Orinoco Ark hosted hundreds of anglers. Today, a permanent lodge at Puerto Carreno has replaced the houseboat.

setting up a camp on the Colombian side of the Orinoco? (This river separates the two countries.) Surely, the pavon and other exotic species wouldn't be so parochial as to remain on the Venezuelan side!

Erland and several friends flew to Puerto Inirida, which is a tiny frontier town on the Orinoco River and began exploring some of the waters, using dugouts and whatever motors they could find. They slept in the bush and it wasn't an easy trip. But one fact quickly emerged: These waters were loaded with pavon and payara and the other exotics, and Erland was convinced that the quality of fishing would certainly be equal to that available on the Venezuelan side, and might actually surpass it.

Once he had located a number of excellent rivers and fishing places and was indeed convinced of the potential, one major problem remained: Where could he house his clients? Building a camp would be risky and very expensive...and time-consuming.

Erland purchased a large boat (85 feet) that he converted into an adequate houseboat. It could accommodate, in reasonable comfort, up to 12 persons in twin-bunked rooms and included two washrooms with showers. He topped it off with a thatched roof. Shades of *The African Queen,* without Humphrey Bogart and Kate Hepburn, of course. He needed a good name for the boat, and when someone suggested "Orinoco Ark," Erland quickly grabbed it. One has to sell romance, you know.

He acquired some skiffs, a few dugouts and several outboard motors and hung an "Open for Business" sign. A little publicity attracted anglers, and in 1981 the Orinoco Ark became headquarters for a few dozen adventuresome fishermen who were willing to risk the unknown for a shot at some fishing that heretofore was only available in Venezuela for a select few.

Glowing reports immediately filtered back—of pavon weighing in the mid-teens and of giant payara with jaws so powerful that even the large plastic lures were smashed to bits.

At this point it's best to briefly introduce the cast of characters that inhabit the Orinoco and other local waters, as I suspect that pavon, payara, and sardinita aren't household names. Not yet anyway.

The peacock bass (pavon) is an ideal fly rod species. Even the bigger models crash out of the water competely.

PAVON: These exotics closely resemble the largemouth black bass, not only in appearance but also in habits. Pavon are, however, a much stronger fighter, more colorful, and because of the year-round feeding season and tremendous food available, they grow rapidly. There are at least four subspecies, but I will describe the three that are found in these waters:

Peacock Pavon: Also known as "peacock bass," this is the most famous of the pavon. It's easily distinguishable from the other species because it has three (and sometimes four or five) very prominent black vertical stripes against a bronze, olive-greenish body coloration.

Butterfly Pavon: Three dark blotches, or rosette patterns, along the lateral line identify this species. The body coloration varies from olive-green at the back turning to a bronze or yellowish side. The fins are orange or reddish (colors vary from river to river).

Speckled Pavon: This is the smallest of the pavon, and in the opinion of a number of anglers, the most beautiful of them all. Basically, its back is a dark olive color that becomes lighter at the lateral line and takes on an orange hue just above the white belly. The fins are a reddish-orange. There is a black spot rimmed with white on the tail. The body is dotted with white speckles throughout most of the fish's length. The eye, as is the case of all the pavon, is black but rimmed with a fiery red. Colorful critter, eh?

PAYARA: This fish is easily the best street fighter in its neighborhood and uses every tactic at its disposal. The payara resembles a steelhead in coloration and configuration, and its most unusual characteristic is the two saberteeth that protrude from the lower jaw but fit neatly into two cavities in the upper

Dr. Rod Neubert probably has landed the largest payara on a fly rod. This one was estimated at 25 pounds.

part of its mouth. Furthermore, its jaw is lined with dozens of needle-sharp smaller teeth (similar to a northern pike's or muskie's). It's obvious to anyone who has gawked into a payara's open mouth that no baitfish ever escaped these teeth! The payara's disposition matches its menacing dentures. It is tough to set hook, not only because of its many teeth but also because its mouth is almost cement-hard, like a tarpon's, and even several hard jabs with the sharpest of all hooks is no guarantee that the fish will be solidly hooked. But when a payara is hooked, the angler is treated to spectacular leaps, reminiscent of small tarpon, and fast runs at breakneck speeds (though these dashes are not as long or as fast as the bonefish's). All of this happens in the Orinoco's fast current, amidst numerous boulders, some as big as a small cabin. And the payara knows how to wind your line around them.

SARDINITA: It usually weighs five to 10 pounds, and it not only resembles a small tarpon but also fights like one. It's found in relatively fast water, at the end of run, and when one locates a feeding school, fast-paced action is encountered.

PIRANHA: This fish has achieved its notoriety mostly through novels and Hollywood films rather than fact. Yes, it's a vicious little bugger, no doubt about that, but not to the extent of its publicity. Piranha usually grow to two to four pounds, but specimens of over seven pounds have been taken from these waters. Both the black and red varieties are available on the Orinoco. It can be taken on a fly, but after a few bouts with the notorious piranha, fly rodders tend to focus their attentions on other fish.

There are about a dozen other species, but those just described are of special interest to the fly rodder.

I went to the Orinoco during March of that maiden year (1981). Kay Brodney had fished the Orinoco the previous week but decided to stay another week. Until Kay's visit, most of the guests were plug casters or spinning enthusiasts. Kay, who fishes exclusively with fly rods, had taken a number of pavon and sardinita on a fly, and even several payara. Although her fishing was limited because of a painful shoulder, she pointed out that the fly fishing potential on the Orinoco was unlimited.

Our guide, Cuenca, took John Renk (my fishing partner) and me up the Matavani river and through a maze of small lakes. He selected one particular shoreline, obviously his favorite, picked up a paddle and urged us to cast. He only spoke about a dozen words of English (we knew about six Spanish words) but this was really no problem since fishing is an international language. We both started out with spinning tackle and almost immediately began to hook peacock bass. They were primarily in the four- to six-pound class, scrappy little devils and good jumpers.

The beauty of the jungle-lined lakes, the clarity of these waters and the remoteness of this area would appeal to any freshwater angler, but no doubt would overwhelm the largemouth bass fisherman. Except for the sound of feeding fish, birds and wildlife rustling in the bush, a total stillness often prevails. There is a strange blend of ruggedness, the survival of the fittest, mixed with an unexpected gentleness in the jungle.

The aluminum skiff we were using was quite small, but after assuring John that it was perfectly safe to fly cast, I picked up my fly rod. I used a No. 6/7 graphite rod and started with a blue and white streamer, which, frankly, I didn't change because the peacock bass gobbled it up. John took a lot more fish with his assortment of spinning lures, but I believe that day I landed 30 to 40 pavon, two to seven pounds, via fly fishing. What more could one ask for?

As the trip began to unfold, our group landed a number of trophy pavon, both peacocks and butterflies, on casting and spinning equipment. By the end of the week, there were at least a half-dozen pavon of over 15 pounds boated, topped by John Renk's 19-pound peacock bass. My best fly-caught pavon was about 10 pounds, but Bob Miller, of Toledo, Ohio, landed an 11 1/2-pound peacock pavon that gulped a yellow popper, and this fish is the current IGFA fly fishing world record for pavon.

That first season on the Orinoco was considered a tremendous success; the largest pavon (on plug casting) was a 21-pounder by Dave Orndorf, which was certified as the new IGFA world record. Most of the 1981 clients returned to the Orinoco the following year, and the 1982 results were incredible:

Dave Rose landed this giant payara on plug-casting gear during the maiden season. Weight? Estimated at well over 25 pounds.

More than 60 pavon of over 20 pounds were landed on hardware, topped by Rod Neubert's mammoth 26 1/2-pounder for a new IGFA record. Frank Zackary, and several other anglers, insist that they fought but lost huge pavon, some estimated at over 30 pounds. So the Orinoco watershed was now not only made available to fishermen, but, clearly, the quality of fishing surpassed their wildest expectations.

Most of the fly-caught pavon were taken on streamers, but bass poppers also worked well. Although the fly fishermen who have fished this watershed haven't even remotely approached the magic 20-pound class, it should be understood that only a handful of dedicated fly rodders have fished these waters to date. Furthermore, most of us have used smaller streamers (No. 2 hooks) because we prefer the lighter fly rods (No. 6 and 7) that are not at all suited for tossing saltwater streamers. I suspect that if fly fishermen were to use a No. 9 or 10 fly rod and giant streamers, the odds of taking trophy pavon would be greatly increased.

Pavon are very pugnacious and greedy and have a penchant for larger lures. To illustrate: Toward the end of the 1981 season, Dennis Wolters was fighting a small pavon (two to three pounds) when a huge peacock bass grabbed the smaller fish and tried to swallow it. Dennis fought it for a long time before the monster finally disgorged the small pavon. He and his guide obtained an excellent view of the fish and they both estimated it at over 25 pounds. Dick Winders, Dennis' fishing partner, had the identical experience the following day. It was these experiences that encouraged future guests to use unusually large lures (like the Rapala Magnum), and many anglers are convinced that the use of the big plugs was the main reason for the tremendous results realized during the following season. The fly rodder, then, who is bent on taking big pavon, should bring a heavier rod and some huge streamers.

While some fly fishermen will be obsessed with the idea of taking a trophy pavon of over 20 pounds, and you can't blame them, it should also be clearly emphasized that catching four- to seven-pound bass on lighter rods and smaller streamers is a totally invigorating experience. I recall fishing a small lake, very close to where the Orinoco Ark was moored. It was one of those super afternoons: The jungle was alive with noise, and the mirror-placid water was continually punctuated by concentric rings from feeding pavon. This was target casting at its best: sunken logs, bogs, fallen trees—all great places for pavon. It was simply a matter of shooting a streamer, or a popper, as close to these targets as possible, and invariably I was rewarded with a strike.

Of course I was interested in landing a trophy pavon, so one day I tried a large popper at Sema Lake (a longer run from the houseboat), as I was sure this was going to be the answer. There were big pavon, right in the pocketed bogs, feeding voraciously; they sounded like a bunch of sloshing pigs. I had several tremendous strikes from pavon that I'm sure were over 15 pounds, and although I failed to either hook or land these fish, it was certainly exciting fishing.

While the pavon is an ideal species for fly fishermen, there are other fish that are challenging too. The payara is the most intriguing and easily the Orinoco's most spectacular fighting species. It's caught mostly in boulder-strewn areas of the tepid Orinoco, where swift currents angrily swirl around these rocks as they race hurriedly downstream. So the angler must not only battle a very powerful fish, but he must also contend with the fast waters that the payara use advantageously.

Payara will weigh anywhere from seven to over 30 pounds (the camp plug casting record is a 33-pounder taken by Dr. Tom Stark), and there are reports of payara over 40 pounds having been landed by locals.

Bob Miller, Bert Ellison, Kay Brodney and others have landed payara on a fly, with most of their fish weighing seven to 10 pounds.

Relates Kay Brodney: "One evening we found a whole school of smaller payara. They attacked just about every cast but would throw the fly quickly. It was fast action. I think one of the problems in fly fishing for payara is that the fly is momentarily caught among the fish's teeth, and after a few head shakes, the fly comes lose."

Because this area is so new, there have been very few fly fishermen at camp; thus, information is scarce. I'm convinced, however, that dedicated fly rodders will consistently land payara in the 20-pound class. No doubt, the key will be large streamers with super sharp hooks. First it's necessary to find the right type of fly to attract the payara's attention, and then it's a matter of developing a technique to increase the number of successful hook-ups. Should one strike quickly, as in trout fishing? Should one let the payara turn with the fly before setting hook and hope that the barb penetrates the corner of the jaw? Would a double hook help? These questions must be answered before fly fishermen are able to take big payara consistently.

I had some success plug casting for payara with a huge surface lure (the Arbogast Scudder). The fish certainly attacked it repeatedly, but again I had trouble hooking them. This experi-

Dave Orndorf's one-time IGFA world record 21-pound peacock on conventional gear created tremendous interest.

ence may indicate that large saltwater poppers could be used effectively with a fly rod. Even if one doesn't solidly hook many payara, the slashing, dramatic surface strike of this species is worth the invested time and energy. Perhaps only the dorado (caught in Argentine rivers) is a better fighter than the payara—and I'm including all freshwater species.

Another fine gamefish is the sardinita, the small tarpon-like species that is caught mostly at the tail end of a fast current. Kay Brodney said she preferred the sardinita to all other Orinoco fish. They average five to 10 pounds, will aggressively grab a streamer, are fairly easy to hook and will entertain any angler who enjoys light tackle fishing. The problem is that the sardinita are hard to locate; some days you find them, but mostly you don't.

My week of fishing flew by so fast that the 101 things that I would have liked to try will have to wait for another trip. I strongly feel that an angler is wise to book two weeks instead of one, especially if he likes to experiment with different methods. In addition to the mighty Orinoco and a number of smaller rivers that flow into it, there are so many little "oxbow lakes" that have hardly been explored (and some that haven't been fished at all) that a week is insufficient time.

The Orinoco safari was not without inconveniences. While most trips unfold fairly smoothly, there are any number of problems ready to ambush the angler. One can't lose sight of the fact that, until very recently, this fishing area was only available to a few hearty souls who managed to acquire locally a skiff and a motor of undetermined vintage and didn't mind sleeping out and eating off the land. This is frontier fishing. Once the angler understands and accepts this, he is in a much better position to cope with the numerous disruptive gremlins.

To my mind, the most frustrating aspect of the trip was the long, arduous flight from Bogota to Puerto Inirida. It can be three hours or longer, depending on the number of stops it makes along the way. Satena Airlines, which flies this route, consists of DC-3s or DC-4s that aren't particularly well-maintained. The flights are usually crowded, not only with passengers, but sometimes with live chickens, produce, bicycles, whatever. Remember, this is Colombia's "outback."

But there's good news. Erland von Sneidern has decided to discontinue the use of the Orinoco Ark and future guests will be housed at his Orinoco Fishing Lodge. He purchased a large house at Puerto Carreno on the Orinoco and converted it to a fishing camp.

"It won't be featured in *House Beautiful,* but it is vastly more comfortable than the Ark. We will provide much better service, because the problems in operating the houseboat via Puerto Inirida are beyond comprehension," explains Erland. "Although we had back-up generators, often they broke down and there would be no ice, no refrigeration or electricity until they could be repaired.

"Furthermore, we can fly our clients to our new lodge via jet service from Bogota right to the airport at Carreno. The flight time is about one hour."

What about the fishing? "We fished it during the 1986 season and our largest pavon was 18 pounds, but we had only a limited number of anglers. There is no doubt in my mind that larger pavon will be caught here. The payara fishing is far superior from our new location, because the best payara rapids are closer to our new lodge. If I were not confident that these waters are as good as the Matavani area I would not have bothered to establish this camp. Most importantly, the safety factor in flying modern jets instead of those old DC3s made us decide on the Puerto Carreno location.

"Yes, I know, a lot of the clients who fished from the Orinoco Ark are sad to see us give up on the houseboat for nostalgic reasons, but I also remember that many people complained about the houseboat. 'Why don't you build a permanent lodge?' they would ask. Well, I have done just that, and all things considered the new location will prove more productive, convenient and, of course, comfortable."

Rates: A week's stay at the Orinoco River Lodge costs $1,495, which includes accommodations, all meals at camp, six days' fishing, (boat, motor, fuel and guide) and local transfers. The round-trip jet transportation from Bogota to Puerto Carreno and ground transfers to camp is $220. Cost of the license ($10), gratuities and personal purchases (including soft drinks and

"The speckled pavon is the most beautiful, but it doesn't grow as large as the peacock or butterfly,"—Erland von Sneidern.

beer) are additional. Other costs include air transportation to Bogota, two nights' accommodations in Bogota and personal expenses.

What about jungle hazards? Snakes? "Ferocious" animals that may pounce on the unsuspecting angler? The answer is yes, there are some dangers, but they are easily avoided. True, if one were to take a "walk" through the jungle, he probably would encounter a snake or two that could destroy the serenity of his promenade. But one doesn't walk through the bush. John Renk and I spent a considerable amount of time trying to locate an anaconda snake that reportedly lived up a river, but we weren't successful (it was his idea, not mine!). Jungle creatures are not that easily spotted without some luck. They are there, but they are equally as fearful of us as we are of them. Without a doubt, the most beautiful animal of the South American jungles is the jaguar; sadly, this creature is on the endangered list because of poaching and excessive hunting. After numerous jungle trips, I've yet to see one, although one night a jaguar attacked von Sneidern's chicken coop on shore near the houseboat and left nothing but feathers and a few bones.

The two jungle hazards that should be most worrisome to the angler are the sun's intense rays and the no-c-ums or other insects; but the wise angler prepares himself to minimize the effects.

Here's how to effectively combat the sun: Most important, take along an ample supply of a powerful sunscreen (which blocks out most of the harmful rays). Sunscreens come in various intensities and are rated 5, 10 or 15. The higher the number, the greater the screening value. I used Eclipse 15 and have had excellent results. What you don't want to apply is a suntan lotion, which increases tanning. It's important to apply the sunscreen continuously, perhaps every two hours. A few fishermen also apply a coating of zinc ointment to their noses and use a sunscreen lip ointment on their lips. Long-sleeved, lightweight shirts, trousers, (not shorts!), wide-brimmed hat and Polaroid glasses provide the additional protection. Furthermore, I recommend wearing golf gloves to those anglers who have super-sensitive hands.

Here's how to effectively combat insects: A powerful insect repellent will help discourage the no-c-ums. The effective ingredient in most insect repellents is a Diethyl compound, so the higher the concentration of Diethyl, the better. I use Muskol,

"The payara is a powerful, leaping fish that empties a reel quickly," says Steve Orndorf, a veteran of many jungle fishing trips.

and while it is expensive, it's a very powerful deterrent since it contains a high concentration of Diethyl. Some anglers insist that by mixing Muskol with Vicks VapoRub, a more effective repellent is derived.

Joe Mainous, who fished the Orinoco, told me that he wasn't bothered at all by insects. His secret? Avon's Skin-So-Soft! This is a hand preparation available from Avon, but why it repels insects is best left to chemists.

TACKLE FOR THE ORINOCO

Two types of fly tackle should be taken for Orinoco jungle river fishing:

Medium fly gear: Ideally this outfit consists of a No. 7 or 8 fly rod (either 8 1/2- or nine-feet), floating and sinking weight-forward lines, 7 1/2 to nine-foot leaders tapered to eight or 10 pounds and a smooth single-action reel with some backing. This will be used for small pavon, sardinita, piranha and other species up to 10 pounds.

Heavy fly gear: The fly rodder should also bring a No. 9 or 10 fly rod (nine-feet), floating and sinking lines, a larger reel that accommodates at least 150 yards of 20-pound Micron backing and heavier leaders that taper to 12- or even 15-pound test. This outfit will be used for payara and large pavon. The backing is primarily for the payara (pavon do not usually run great distances).

Flies: An assortment of streamers tied on No. 4 to 2/0 (or larger hooks) in various color combinations should be taken along as they are unavailable in Colombia. Blue and white seem

The author fights a peacock pavon in Sema Lagoon. "There were some 'pigs' sloshing in the bogs, but I didn't connect."

to be effective colors with a few strands of Mylar included for flash. Medium and large (saltwater size) poppers can be effective.

Miscellany: Since payara, piranha and several other species have very sharp teeth, use a few inches of heavy mono (60 pounds) or copper colored wire (27- or 45-pound) for shock leaders. If wire is used, a small black swivel will connect the wire to the tippet.

COLOMBIA, THE COUNTRY

Colombia's population is 24 million; 3 1/2 million people live in the capital city of Bogota. While Spanish, of course, is the main language, English is widely spoken in the larger cities. Colombia's topography is varied and ranges from tropical sandy beaches to verdent valleys to mountainous ranges to dense, lush jungles. Just about every type of tropical flower can be found in Colombia, and probably no other country in the world hosts so many different species of birds.

Climate and temperatures: Climate varies, just as the country's topography. On the Caribbean coast the temperature averages in the low 80s. In Bogota, because of the elevation (8,678 feet), the weather is coolish. The average low is about 50 degrees while the average high is in the upper 60s. On the Orinoco, the weather will be somewhere between 80 and over 90 degrees. January through most of April is the dry period on the Orinoco, although there is a chance of a rainburst during these months. The weather is mostly sunny with blue skies and occasional clouds. Incidentally, the sunsets on the Orinoco can be breathtaking.

Hotels in Bogota: Two overnights in Bogota are required in order to make connections to and from the Orinoco. The Tequendama Hotel is huge (800 rooms) and practically an island to itself with all the conveniences located right on the premises. After using it for several seasons, the von Sneiderns recommend the smaller Continental Hotel on Avenida Jimenez because they found that better service was provided to their clients.

Dining in Bogota: Bogota's many restaurants offer international cuisine. The Monserrate Dining Room on the roof top of the Tequendama is a favorite among tourists, although expensive. Le Toit Supper Club and the La Hacienda at the Hilton International Bogota can also be recommended as can the Unicorn Club (Calle 94, 7-75), also a first-class restaurant.

Shopping in Bogota: The central shopping area is on Carrera 7 and Carrera 15 between Calles 72 and 100. Clothing, shoes, and linen shirts are relatively inexpensive. Although Colombia is known for its emeralds, the von Sneiderns advise that caution should be used even if the shopper is somewhat familiar with gemstones. The jewelry shops in the larger hotels (Tequendama and Hilton) are no doubt reliable but may be somewhat more expensive. For silver and leather goods, the government controlled store, Artesanias de Colombia (Carrera 10, 26-50), is a good suggestion.

Documents And Entry Requirements: A valid passport and two passport-size photos are required in order to obtain the necessary tourist card to enter Colombia. The tourist card is issued by the international carrier servicing Colombia. No inoculations or vaccinations are necessary but consult your physician on this. (There are very few mosquitos in this area, so the threat of malaria is little or nil.)

AND FINALLY...There's something very magical in fishing and exploring the jungle rivers of Colombia for pavon, sardinita, payara and other characters. Unfortunately, in today's shrinking world the opportunity for fishing new waters is limited. Colombia's vast Orinoco watershed provides that total jungle fishing experience.

When I decided to visit the Orinoco, I didn't feel any special magnetic attraction, but I needed to increase my knowledge of the area and to obtain a first-hand experience with these exotic species. After fishing this watershed for a few days, I decided that I would return for a much longer stay. Two weeks would be good, three weeks would be better.

It's just that type of a place.

Argentina

From Leaping Rainbows to Sea-Run Browns to Tackle-Busting Dorado

Bariloche—the Swiss-like town that serves as the starting point for classic rainbow and brown trout fishing; Tierra del Fuego—where sea-run browns of under 10 pounds seldom rate a handshake; Parana River—where the tough, rough, brawling leaping dorado earned its reputation as the strongest freshwater species of them all!

A. J. McClane—one of the greatest fishing wordsmiths—and a fine Argentine rainbow.

Chapter 13

ARGENTINA

MAYBE I will never fish Argentina again.

Just like I never returned to Paris, my favorite city. I stay in touch with a few Parisiens, and, yes, they begrudgingly admit that Paris has changed somewhat in the past 25 years, but they also insist that the city's *joie de vivre,* the kinetic spirit, remains alive. I still don't think that I will ever go back. It would not be the same.

I probably won't go back to Argentina for similar reasons. One develops a fondness, perhaps it's an infatuation, for a place—a town, or a city, a lake or a stream—and I suppose I resent drastic changes in places that I cherish. It doesn't really matter whether these changes are positive or negative.

Seventeen years ago, when I first visited Argentina, the roads from the tiny Patagonian hamlets to the trout streams were dusty, gravelly and profusely booby-trapped with potholes that would abruptly jar anyone out of his private fishing fantasies. I remember driving with guides Count George Wenckheim and his son Laszlo to a trout stream. The aged vehicle, with the big heart, seemed to gasp for its last breath, a result of numerous minor and major mechanical surgeries that had left the car virtually drained of any spirit. Naturally it stopped. Many times.

So we pushed that machine, and we sweated and panted and groaned, and cussed a lot too. But by throwing the gear into first on the downslide, the vehicle would start, and we did manage to squeeze another trip from Wenckheim's car.

In the "olden" days, a first-rate fishing guide not only had to be knowledgeable in pointing out trophy trout to his "sports,"

Dr. J. Watt Shroyer fished Tierra del Fuego and landed many large sea-run browns.

but he also had to be skillful with a screwdriver, wrench and even bailing wire. Today, I understand, there are smooth black-top roads, service stations and even rental car agencies in Patagonia. They call it progress, but this progress made things so convenient that other fishermen began to appear in consistent numbers.

I remember driving with George and Laszlo alongside a number of streams for many miles. Occasionally we would see a lone fisherman. Sometimes two.

"Damn place is going to hell," the Count was fuming. "Too many bloody fishermen. And they keep most of the trout they catch."

While fishing several rivers, and wading probably a total 40 miles of water on that initial trip, I never saw another fisherman. Wenckheim should have been on one of the New York streams on Opening Day, I thought. He'd freak out.

Because the Count knew the landowners, I had the privilege of fishing on a couple of "estancias," huge ranches that rivaled even those Texas showplaces. In order to fish a special section of the Malleo River, we had to drive for hours, and we were still on the same owner's property. This part of the river was so beautiful that I thought there was no way it could be improved. I mean you couldn't move this rock over there, or widen that pool, or add a few more boulders to improve it cosmetically. It's that kind of a river. And to top it off, there in the background is majestic Mt. Lanin. Its peak is a long way from my favorite pool, but the air is so pure that it appears to be much closer.

Perhaps my infatuation with the Malleo River developed because this river was kind to me. It was very forgiving of my numerous angling blunders, but at the same time, when I got a little fat-headed with my accomplishments, it brought me down to size, quick-like, with a series of challenges and occasional frustrations. So it kept me on my toes.

Mt. Lanin is still there. And so is the pool, of course. But other aspects have changed. Several anglers have told me that they have fished my favorite sections of the Malleo recently, and although the trout are still there, they are smaller and not as numerous. That's because access through this estancia has been liberalized, and other anglers have discovered this part of

Try the small creeks that flow into the larger streams or rivers; often they are overlooked, but can contain big trout.

the Malleo. Furthermore, I've heard that the local fishermen weren't as generous in releasing their catches as the foreign visitors, especially during the highly inflationary period that tragically devastated the Argentine economy. I suppose you can't blame them. First they had to feed their families; conservation was of secondary importance.

The Malleo holds mostly rainbows. The Malleo trout seem much more acrobatic than their foreign counterparts, partially because the stream is shallow (so the fish often become airborne), partially because of the food (they feed mostly on pancora—a large freshwater shrimp that is loaded with protein), but also because the strain, which was introduced in the early 1900s, has not been tainted through interbreeding with hatchery types. Some of the trout of the Malleo (and other Argentine streams) can unwind 10 or more magnificent leaps—none of these halfhearted jumps you encounter elsewhere. I'm talking about the kind of jumps that you see on calendars or in artwork. And when you hold them gently to release them, you can feel that they are solid, all muscle, not a gram of excess fat on these fish.

I accompanied a number of angling friends on my second trip to Argentina, and, of course, I wanted to share the Malleo River with them. George and Laszlo Wenckheim guided most of our group downstream, but I played "guide" and took Bill Wanke upstream to my favorite place. The river flows gently there, though it quickens its pace as it tumbles down a small chute and swirls around several boulders; it finally settles down where it widens into a small pool. It was here that Bill landed 33 rainbows that morning without moving more than a few yards. The trout were mostly in the two- to four-pound class though a couple of fish may have scaled over five pounds. I left Bill to enjoy what surely must have been his best day of trout fishing and explored an untried section further upstream. Several fine trout became interested in the Honey Blonde streamer I was using, and then, perhaps looking for a further challenge, I switched to an Irresistible dry fly despite the fact that everything I had read indicated that Argentine trout were seldom interested in surface flies. Perhaps I cast 70 times, or maybe 100, to the same glide before I saw a fish flash underneath the fly, and now, buoyed with the knowledge that these fish could be enticed to the top, I continued casting. In effect, I had hoped to create an artificial hatch. And it worked. As I landed several trout, the surface disturbance seemed to encourage other rainbows to look to the top. It was a super day of unending fishing action.

While the Malleo is primarily a rainbow river, there are a few browns that lurk in the deeper pools. One day, Wenckheim told me of a big pool a long distance from our tent camp that contained a very big brown. "It sulks all day on the bottom. But in the evening it comes to shallow water, and no doubt it feeds on small trout. You might give it a go, but be back by dark. I'll have dinner ready."

I trudged off quickly, for there there wasn't much daylight left, and I sought Wenckheim's pool with the big brown. When I came to a widening of the river, I was sure that this was the pool. I walked carefully, quietly now, for browns, even in distant undisturbed areas, have that inherent wariness. Behind me I heard the unmistakable crash of a big trout. It startled me for an instant, but I quickly turned to mark the spot in the dim light. Snap! It was a sickening sound. I examined my Pezon et Michel split bamboo rod, and the tip section was broken. When I turned suddenly, my rod, caught in a branch, busted. There was no way I could cast it. Worse, there wasn't sufficient daylight left to return to camp to exchange rods and this was my last day on the Malleo. Sadly, I ambled back to camp. George was quick to note the broken rod tip: "I see you hooked the big fella. Too bad. Too bad because you lost it, but worse because you busted that Ritz rod. I sorta had my eye on it. Good, smooth action. A little soft in the butt. I had hoped that maybe you would have left that rod with me," the Count grinned. "It's a big fish, eh? Big brown?"

I nodded, but didn't bother to explain how that rod broke. "Yep, he is a big trout. Darn big."

We toasted Argentina, its trout and its beauty several times with Mendoza wine, and I think we both slept comfortably, though I felt shortchanged in not having at least a couple of casts at that giant; and, I'm sorry that the Count couldn't add that Ritz rod to his collection.

What about trout fishing in Argentina today? Does it still offer good potential? Is it worth the long, arduous flights?

Perhaps the sportsman who fished Argentina 20 years ago would be disappointed in the number of changes; but then how many places remain the same today? The angler who has never fished Argentina and therefore is not in a position to compare the present with the past, is likely to find Argentine trout fishing most appealing and productive, if not a total answer to his Utopian search. It's true that most of the trout fishing pressure is in the Bariloche/Junin/Los Andes region, but this is only a small portion of Argentina's fishing grounds, which extend all the way south to Tierra del Fuego. Today many more anglers fish Argentine rivers than when I fished the

Laddie Buchanan loves the challenges of Tierra del Fuego; however, he warns that better conservation among the locals is needed.

country years ago, but there's still plenty of fishing room. I suspect that on several remote rivers one could fish an entire day without seeing an angler. So Argentina is not overrun with fishermen today, but the total solitude that I experienced in those days on some of the streams is somewhat threatened.

BUCHANAN ON TROUT

Laddie Buchanan is one of Argentina's most knowledgeable fishing guides today. (Count Wenckheim is now more involved in hunting safaris.) His fishing expeditions not only cover the major trout areas but also dorado fishing on the Parana River. I interviewed the colorful Laddie and here are some of his thoughts pertaining to Argentine sport fishing:

Q: Do you think that Argentina's trout fishing potential is blown out of proportion in the outdoor press and by some fishing guides, publicists and outdoor travel agencies?

LB: In some quarters, absolutely. Why must travel agencies, fishing guides and others with vested interests give out such gosh-awful lies about it? I'm not saying half-truths or exaggerations, no, just plain, downright lies. Why try to attract fishermen by offering something that simply is not true? Let me illustrate. I saw a brochure that includes a photo of two damn big brown trout held by an angler. The caption reads: "Average size in Argentina." And naturally, somebody swallows this and is likely to book on the strength of this photo. Obviously he will be disappointed. I feel, based on total honesty, Argentina is an attractive trout fishing destination. I remember reading an article in a U.S. fishing publication in which the author stated: "I began to fear for my life as I stood belly button deep, knowing that there are creatures of such strength and magnitude swimming round my spindly legs." And he was referring to the Chimehuin River. Wow.

I've also read a brochure stating that on a normal day a good rod on the Chimehuin River can take up to 10 trout weighing five to 20 pounds. Can you believe that? It appears that 100-pound-trout days are quite normal unless you are a complete duffer. Now, once in a great while, at certain times and at certain places, one can have exceptional fishing, but these brochures dish out the information like it's normal, everyday stuff. Tierra del Fuego is an entirely different story, but only when conditions are favorable.

Q: I've personally fished the Chimehuin and there are some very big trout at the mouth of this river; but they are very difficult to fool, and it requires expert casting under adverse windy conditions. However, I understand that huge trout are sometimes easily taken at the start of your season right in the town of Bariloche. What about it?

LB: Our trout season begins in November, and I remember that in 1979, on the morning of Opening Day, anglers fishing the Limay River landed five big browns that weighed from 13 to 22 1/2 pounds. This is a short-term run that normally lasts about 10 days and is not at all totally predictable. In 1981 the run lasted almost 1 1/2 months and fly fishermen were taking very large fish right off Bariloche's waterfront promenade. Now this can happen at the inlet of the Correntoso River and at the outlet of Nahuel Huapi. But off the city front? Amazing!

So much depends on weather conditions. During the 1981/1982 season, there was a pronounced heat wave. This put down the fish in practically all rivers. There were plenty of small- to medium-sized fish, 12 to 16 inches, but very few over this size. Then it rained, weather cooled off considerably with light frosts in the morning and, bingo, the fish awakened and fishing improved. On rivers like the Malleo, Chimehuin, Collon Cura and others, a good rod I repeat, a good rod, could at times take up to 40 fish a day in from 12 to 22 inches, with some bigger fish thrown in occasionally.

You never know what will happen. At the end of the 1982 season, one of my clients was making the last casts of his Argentine trip. A very small trout was hooked and ran into a pool and around a log. Or so it seemed. The log started to move and you can guess the rest of the story. The "log" turned out to be a 7-3/4-pound big male brown, and it was landed on a four-pound tippet with a wind knot in the leader. So strange things happen.

Q: I've been told that guides have private waters and, therefore, are in a better position to deliver results for their clients. I've also heard that there is no such thing as private waters. Can you clarify this?

LB: I want to get this straight once and for all: There are no private waters in Argentina. The gospel truth. The only way that waters can be considered private is if they rise and die in one's property or if a lake is completely within private property. Otherwise, all trout waters are public because of an old law. What is private is the right of access to these waters over private property. If a fisherman can get on a stream at any public spot, and this means off a road running within 25 yards of it, he can then walk along its banks, right to the seas where it empties out if he so desires, and no one can legally forbid him this right. Many guides receive letters from potential customers who ask if they are among the elite who have private waters. Some answer "yes," and book the clients, who are really being fooled. If they truthfully answer "no," the prospective fisherman continues his search for the guide who has these private waters. When asked, I merely say that I have permission from the landowners to *cross* their properties. And sometimes, when we get to this super secret spot, I may find a couple of fishermen ahead of us who had walked in all the way from a road!

Q: Laddie, I know you are "high" on Tierra del Fuego's fishing. Let's discuss this region, for very little has been published on this. What is the best time, and what about those winds, rains and temperatures?

LB: The season at Tierra del Fuego (TDF hereinafter) starts on November first, but I advise late December through very early March. The 50-mph breezes turn into 60 mph after mid-March. So the very best time is likely to be from early January to the end of February. There is virtually no rain other than a few showers during this period;

most of it comes in March. January can fluctuate and be warm, mild or cold, but mostly it's mild. February usually ranges from mild to cold. March is always cold.

Q: How good is the fishing at TDF? What can be expected? And what are the major species?

LB: Under ideal conditions a good rod can raise or hook from five to 10 big fish per day. By "big" fish, I'm talking about trout approximately 10 pounds. These are *sea-run* browns. The resident browns and rainbows rarely weigh over three pounds and they aren't very plentiful. The sea-run fish, of course, gain their weight feeding out in the ocean.

On the Ewan River there are medium-sized brook trout, but there is another river, the Rio Claro, that often contains some very big brook trout at the outlet of Kami Lake. I have seen them over 10 pounds, but getting there and fishing this water is a real adventure. Very high winds. Enormous waves sweeping off the lake. Fishing is very difficult. In fact, even the hardiest of anglers who fish this place must be quickly placed in the "fools" category.

There is also some controversy concerning Atlantic salmon that have been planted in some rivers. Some anglers insist that they have caught Atlantic salmon whenever they land an unusually bright fish.

Huge sea-run browns like this one is what attracts anglers to the end of the world...Tierra del Fuego!

All scientific identifications are thrown into the winds and a salmon is claimed. In all my years of fishing TDF, I have yet to see an Atlantic salmon. As you know, or should know, browns that venture out into the ocean return bright silver.

Q: Back to the winds for a moment. Are they as strong as claimed?
LB: Are you kidding? When it blows here, there are no winds. They are GALES. Anything up to 50, sometimes 60 mph. But usually and normally, the velocity is about 20 mph. Obviously, it's hard to cast into these winds, but since wading is easy, you can get the wind at your back. Except for the wind and weather conditions, the Rio Grande area is just about the easiest fishing in the world. Fish are very close to the banks. There are no obstacles. Well, actually there is one pool aptly named "The Lone Tree Pool." Except for that single tree, the highest obstacle is grass about four inches high. Of course, with the wind at your back, there is a tendency for your fly to drop on the back cast into the aforementioned four-inch grass, making you wonder why in the hell did your moron guide make you cross the river in the first place. But I consider most of the fishing spots at TDF to be about the easiest; there are no slippery rocks, just gravel, so they are easy to wade.

Q: Then what about fishermen's wives on a TDF trip? Will they have problems?
LB: Women? Humpf! Much depends on the female of the species. If they know about the elements and can put up with them, then the only thing that worries me is that they generally do better than their male counterparts, something that upsets the menfolk, who in turn vent their anger on their guides.

Q: Considering all that wind, what about the effectiveness of the fly fishing versus spinning?
LB: Quite frankly, a fisherman using a spinning rod will do much better than the fly rodder. Those big browns go for medium-sized lures far more frequently than flies. As an example, last year I had a party who honestly couldn't put their fly rods together, let alone cast them. We tried flies for an hour. No soap. I told them to switch to spinning and in the same area of water we landed seven browns, one after the other. One weighed 16 pounds! This is not to say that the fly fisherman won't catch many fish. Remember, the fish are only a few feet from the bank, so he is assured of putting a fly over them.

Q: What about accommodations? Food? Creature comforts?
LB: What kind of accommodations does one want? The hotels down here are pretty much first class. Private rooms. Private bath. In

Ushuaia, the island capital, the hotels are tip-top. At Rio Grande, Les Yaganes is fairly good. It also has an excellent bar to lean against to offset all the leaning one must do against our winds.

Meals? The beef is not really top quality, but the lamb and mutton and chicken are excellent. Seafood, hot soups and desserts are good, too. No one will starve. Weather permitting, I like to barbecue steaks or lamb or serve broiled trout *a la Buchanan.*

Q: What about fishing hours?

LB: They are a lot more than the average fisherman can handle—anywhere from eight to 21 hours a day. But the cold evenings usually make even the most dedicated anglers yearn for the fireplace and something warm to drink. Some of the best fishing does occur late in the day!

Q: Where do most of your fishermen fly to? How far are the fishing grounds from the hotel?

LB: There are daily flights from Buenos Aires to Rio Grande. We drive about 30 to 45 minutes to reach most of the streams; the Ewan River takes an hour. You don't have to worry about the traffic jams here.

PATAGONIAN NOTES

Because of the variety of fishing waters, terrain and weather conditions, it's impossible to provide specific information on Argentine fishing, but here are some rules of thumb:

- ***Argentina's reverse trout season.*** Because Patagonia is considerably south of the equator, seasons are "reversed" (winter in the U.S. is summer here). This is of tremendous advantage to the northern trout fisherman who simply can't wait for his trout season to begin. If he has the time and the airfare, he can fly to Argentina and fish anytime from November through mid-April.

- ***Argentina is very windy.*** Laddie mentions the gales of Tierra del Fuego, but winds are prevalent on most Patagonian rivers. I remember fishing in the Junin area and the winds never let up for a week. You actually learn to lean into the wind. Some members of our party had very little fly casting experience, but surprisingly they became accustomed to the wind, and their catches were above average. Then, on one day, the wind ceased and it was dead calm. It was an eerie feeling. It felt as though the earth had suddenly stood still, or as if we were in a vacuum. However, the smaller streams like the Malleo, Alumine and tributaries of the Manso meander considerably, so one can find some protective waters. If you are not a good "wind" caster, inform your guide well in advance so he can make the proper stream selection.

▪ ***Argentine trout vary greatly in size.*** Most of them will run one to three pounds, but one hears consistently of very big fish—10- to 20-pounders—being taken from time to time. The big fish are nearly always migrating trout that gain most of their tremendous weight while feeding in the lakes (or in the ocean, as is the case at TDF), but they ascend and descend the rivers usually at the beginning or end of the season.

▪ ***Argentina's boca fishermen catch most of the big fish.*** Anyone who fishes Argentina quickly becomes acquainted with the term "boca," or river mouth. Outside of TDF, most big trout are caught at the bocas. Boca anglers are mostly interested in giant fish—the monsters that scale upwards of 10 pounds—so they plant themselves stoically at the mouths of rivers and continually cast big streamers using heavier equipment. The winds invariably come from the wrong direction and the anglers must withstand the occasional slap of a line or hook against their necks. Action is generally slow-paced (or nonexistent), and it may take several days before a big fish is hooked. The most famous boca is the Chimehuin. In addition to the wind, anglers often must contend with pounding waves that develop considerable power as they sweep across Lake Huetchalafquen. Is it worth it? It depends on the angler. If he wants a very big fish and is willing to invest hundreds or thousands of casts for a hit, he is most likely to find success at the boca. Most anglers, however, opt for the smaller trout and faster action.

▪ ***Argentina is mostly "wet fly fishing."*** Streamers, wet flies and nymphs are the most effective fly types, but dry flies do work at times. By casting to a particular run or glide continuously, one can "create a hatch" and invariably the trout come to the surface. I've also had success on some streams by shaking a few bushes or small trees next to a stream. If there are any may-

Giant wild brown trout are among the most difficult species to fool. But worldwide angler Billy Pate persevered and won. Again.

flies on them, the wind will deliver the insects to the water, and trout will sometimes come to the top. Most of the naturals I've found were white or light tan (imitated by White Millers, Light Cahills and caddis).

▪ ***There are few trout fishing camps in Argentina.*** Most fishermen are accommodated in small hotels or inns (hosterias) located fairly close to the fishing waters. A visiting angler can book a hotel room, rent a car and be "on his own," but I don't recommend this, especially if this is his first trip to Patagonia. True, he may be able to fish some of the streams, near bridges, but he would not have permission to cross private property; even if he were able to obtain the necessary permission, he probably would waste a lot of time before finding productive waters. Thus, he is strongly advised to obtain the services of an experienced guide who will not only put him on the right spot but also will offer the necessary counsel in terms of fishing techniques. Years ago, when hotels and inns were scarce in many areas of Patagonia, guides provided camping equipment and, while there was some sacrifice in comfort, their clients were often treated to a "50-yard seat" near the heart of the best fishing areas.

If one prefers to book a "pure" fishing camp in Tierra del Fuego, the Kau-Tapen Lodge is recommended. It's a very comfortable facility and efficiently operated. Kau-Tapen completed its first full season in 1985 and was highly rated by its guests. (Seven nights of accommodations, six days of fishing, all meals, transfers and hotels in Buenos Aires and other extras will cost $2,690 per person.)

▪ ***There is no dangerous wildlife in Argentina.*** One of the great pleasures of Argentine fishing is that the angler may amble along a stream without fear of poisonous snakes or of being attacked by animals. Of course, the usual precautions must be taken in terms of wading.

▪ ***Argentina's landlocked salmon fishing has deteriorated.*** The Rio Traful (about 80 miles north of Bariloche) was probably the world's premier landlocked salmon stream until the mid-fifties, but the lack of conservation has greatly deteriorated this and other streams. Salmon here averaged about seven pounds, and I'm told that in past years a fly fisherman could land eight to 10 landlocks in a day. The largest recorded was 22 pounds. These landlocks are exceptionally fine leapers, often jumping four feet out of the water. When we fished the Traful, we landed several salmon up to 12 pounds.

▪ ***Argentina's trophy salmonids.*** The largest brown trout recorded in Argentina is over 30 pounds (taken from a lake on hardware). The largest brown landed on a fly that I know of is a 24-pounder. Rainbows of over 20 pounds, brook trout in the double-digit weights and the aforementioned 22-pound plus landlocked account for Argentina's lofty position as one of the world's best trophy salmonid fishing places. It is unfortunate that some very large fish are not recorded (often because locals are not concerned with records). Amazingly, none of these salmonids is native to Argentina; they were introduced in the early 1900s.

DORADO FISHING

While the trout is the primary magnet for attracting many international anglers to Argentina, there is another species that provides a substantial amount of drawing power to this country. It's the dorado (Salminus maxillosus). This species inhabits the South American rivers and many experienced fishermen feel that the dorado is the strongest and the most spectacular leaper of all freshwater fish. While its frequent jumps are "high and mighty," one may fully appreciate the power and body contortions only by viewing slow-motion footage of a particularly active dorado. I viewed a film made by Jim Richardson and Frank Zackary showing a particular dorado making two full turns, two jackknifes and a complete somersault in one spectacular jump.

There are several subspecies and the dorado's distribution ranges from Colombia to Argentina. The largest dorado are found in the Parana River, which partly forms the border between Argentina and Paraguay. While dorado have been taken throughout the course of this river, the best fishing starts in the Upper Parana (province of Misiones) and extends to Esquina (Corrientes province), a total of over 500 miles.

The dorado has a dark-greenish back, which changes to an almost metallic gold on its side. It has reddish-gold fins with a black stripe in the center of its caudal fin. While dorado mostly range from eight to 12 pounds elsewhere, the Parana produces fish of over 30 pounds consistently. The record is 68 pounds.

The Parana region is subtropical and is vastly different from the Patagonian trout fishing terrain. The Parana is very wide, up to several miles across, and while its character changes considerably throughout its course, it maintains its subtropical flavor.

The most important factor controlling the quality of dorado fishing is water level. If the water is in flood and muddy, this usually means poor fishing.

I recall a number of years ago when Dr. R. W. Koucky and I arrived at an innocuous little fishing camp called Apipe Safaris. The owner Virgilio Magri was surprised to see us. "But I cabled a week ago to cancel your trip," he said, "The water is too deep. There is no hope for dorado fishing." We didn't speak Spanish, but we understood what he was telling us. "Go to Buenos Aires and enjoy yourselves. It's a waste of time here."

It looked like our investment of over 9,000 miles in round-trip travel would be a total waste. No, we would stay at camp, we told him.

As it turned out, the waters subsided quickly, and toward the end of the trip Dr. Koucky and I were hooking dorado with tremendous regularity.

In one day I landed two dorado (32 and 36 pounds) and Doc had a 29- and a 34-pounder, plus dozens of smaller fish. These dorado were taken on spinning or plug casting gear; the waters were too high and fast for fly fishing.

Virgilio was a very knowledgeable, highly spirited guide who lived life to the fullest. He was "streetwise," clever, highly entertaining and reminded us of Anthony Quinn in *Zorba the Greek.* His animations and gesticulations served us well for he was able to communicate even complicated thoughts despite

Parana guide Virgilio Magri—one of a kind—holds two dorado taken by the author. The smaller one was caught on a fly.

the language difference. Foremost, he was able to communicate his knowledge of dorado fishing to us, which was the main reason why our trip was so successful.

I expressed an interest in fly fishing for dorado. "Mosca? Malo. Agua muy profundo y no claro." And he was right, the water was much too deep, the current too strong and the river was certainly murky. However, I fished a streamer from a small rocky island where the water was not deep, and I managed to take several small dorado. Even on a No. 9 outfit, though, I wasn't able to overpower them. They leaped like little tarpon, and gave up only when their last gram of energy was expended. I would have loved the challenge of hooking a dorado over 20 pounds on a fly in the fast tricky currents of the main Parana.

I almost had an excellent chance one day when we found the dorado not in front of the rock piles where they generally hold, but in a pool just above an elongated island, but, alas, I did not have a fly rod in the boat for that session. We hooked a number of big dorado, including a 25-pounder, by casting large popping plugs. They were certainly aggressive. I'm sure that, under the right conditions, it would have been possible to hook big dorado on large fly rod poppers.

Kay Brodney visited Apipe Safaris the following year and fished with a fly rod exclusively. She was successful in taking a number of dorado on a red and white streamer, including a magnificent 20-pounder.

Dorado fishing on the Parana is almost entirely done from a boat. Because of the strong current, it is very difficult for the guide to keep the boat in position, either with oars or with the outboard; in some places it is difficult to cover the water by plug casting or spinning, let alone by fly fishing. When the water is low, and therefore the current not as swift, I believe that it would be possible to anchor the boat above the dorado holding spots and present a fly successfully. Most of the time it is essential that the lure or fly is fished five to 10 feet deep. The potential of this plan is highly increased today because of the availability of many super-fast-sinking fly lines (including lead core). Generally one doesn't have to make many casts to a specific spot; if a dorado is "home," it usually whacks anything that goes by its nose with gusto.

A few fly rodders have been successful on some of the smaller, shallow dorado rivers, but I haven't had the opportunity to try this.

The most successful dorado fly fishing trip I know of was the one that Bill Barnes and Billy Pate arranged, through Argentine friends, to the Rio Bemerjo near the town of Oran in the province of Jujuy. They stayed at a small hotel at Oran and drove to the river each day. The Bemerjo is a tributary of the Parana River and its headwaters are close to the Bolivian border. In September and October this and other rivers are often in fine shape: low, clear and wadeable. Both men are superb fly fishermen and once they got the hang of it, they landed many dorado via fly fishing. The largest was Billy Pate's 31-pounder followed by Bill Barnes' 24-pound dorado. They mainly used long streamers, with six-inch wings, tied on 2/0 hooks with plenty of Mylar. Argentine's golden fish is a fantastic species when fished from a boat, but when they can be fished by wading and stalking, this becomes one of angling's supreme thrills.

The best time for dorado on the main Parana is from August to early October, a period which unfortunately does not coincide with the Patagonian trout season (November to mid-April). It would make a perfect trip if one could combine trout with dorado fishing in Argentina.

However, Laddie Buchanan, who is not only an excellent trout fishing outfitter but a keen dorado guide as well, tells me that April can be a productive month for dorado.

"While the fall season is definitely the best, sometimes good dorado fishing is possible from late April until approximately June 10th. The quality of fishing depends on the water conditions, and sometimes river levels are predictable a month or so in advance. August and September are the best months normally, and although October is not quite as dependable, it should not be ruled out as it can produce good fishing," Laddie explains. Incidentally, he has found a new area near the town of Esquina that has been very productive even when the other hot spots along the Parana have been poor.

While the dorado may not be an ideal species for the fly rodder, it is a very intriguing fish and can be recommended to the angler who enjoys systematically overcoming challenges one by one.

What about other species in the Parana? While at Apipe, I noticed a small hatch emerging near the camp's dock and fish soon began to rise. The water was shallow here, and not very swift, so I waded it. I tied on a Irresistible dry fly that soon captured the interest of these fish. I missed the first few rises but then solidly connected on several fish. They resembled shad, fought well, but didn't jump, and the largest was about 10 pounds. Virgilio referred to them as "salmon" because they have a salmon-colored meat, but as far as I can find out, these gamey little fish are a member of the brycon family. The Parana also has pacu, surubi and other species that are indigenous to the area, but since they aren't taken by fly fishing, they won't be covered here.

FISHING RATES: Because of the volatile exchange rates between the Argentine peso and U.S. dollar, costs change enormously from season to season. Laddie Buchanan furnished me with rates for the beginning of the 1986 season. The rates are per person and are based on double occupancy. They include transfers to and from the local airport, accommodations, all meals with local table wines, beer and soft drinks, Buchanan's personal guiding service and local transportation.

Trout Fishing at Bariloche, Junin, etc.: $180 per person, per day.

Trout Fishing at Tierra del Fuego: $225 per person, per day.

Dorado Fishing Parana River: $180 per person, per day.

FISHING TACKLE

For most trout fishing in the Bariloche, Junin, San Martin and Manso regions you will need the following: a No. 7, 8 or 9 fly

The high-leaping, catapulting dorado struts its stuff. It just might be the best freshwater fighting fish.

rod; a smooth-running fly reel that is spooled with 100 to 150 yards of 20-pound backing; floating, sink-tip and sinking lines; nine-foot leaders tapered to six pounds (also tippet material of various sizes); and an assortment of streamers, nymphs, wet flies and dry flies. The Blonde series (popularized by the late Joe Brooks) are still deadly streamers. Muddlers, matukas, black marabou and sculpin patterns tied on various hook sizes (6 to 4/0) will find ample use. Nymphs on hook sizes 6 to 12 are effective. For dry flies, I suggest the Wulff series, Irresistible, Light Cahill and brown bivisibles tied on hook sizes ranging from No. 8 to 12.

Anglers fishing the smaller trout streams in the protected areas might want to include a No. 6 fly rod outfit.

For Tierra del Fuego, a No. 10 rod (remember, it's windy here) with a slow-sinking line will prove most useful. Since these trout prefer larger lures, include streamer flies with a wing length of four to five inches. There won't be much use for dry flies here.

For dorado fishing on the Parana, a No. 10 or even an 11 fly rod will be needed. Your reel should have a capacity of 200 yards of 20-pound backing. Include a few floating lines, but primarily you will need fast-sinking lines. Use the largest streamers (saltwater types) you can possibly handle and since the dorado has teeth, you must use a shock leader. I prefer the 27-pound coffee color wire (single), which can be tied to the fly with a haywire twist and affixed to the leader with a small black swivel. Large streamers, similar to Lefty's Deceiver but with a lot of Mylar and tied on 2/0 and 4/0 hooks, are effective, but you might include some large poppers just in case you find them feeding in shallow waters and in slower currents (sometimes you see big dorado surface-feeding).

Miscellany: Very little tackle is available in Argentina, though the guides develop quite a collection through the years. Best to bring everything you need with you, as Orvis doesn't have a shop at Junin (yet).

Felt-soled waders are advised (instead of hip boots), and be sure to include a patch kit. Take along warm clothing. In the Patagonian trout areas you are fishing in elevations of 2,500 to 3,000 feet and it can be chilly. Incidentally, excellent heavy wool sweaters can be purchased cheaply in Argentina. For Tierra de Fuego, be prepared for blustery weather; even on the Parana River in the north we found the mornings somewhat chilly in September.

Argentina doesn't have much rainfall but it's best to include raingear. There are very few insects in the trout areas but the Parana can be bad at times, so you should pack a powerful insect repellent. Furthermore, on bright days on the Patagonian streams apply a sun screen periodically to exposed skin.

ARGENTINA, THE COUNTRY

Logically, a land that stretches for more than 2,000 miles ought to provide a variety of terrain, climate, customs and interests, and Argentina does just that. The pampas, the colorful gaucho, the excitement of cosmopolitan Buenos Aires, the brooding mountain peaks and Swiss-like resorts of the lake country, the thousands of miles of unpolluted rivers, the mostly temperate weather combined with tropical climes to the north and ice-cold winds in the south, Iguazu Falls—more spectacular than Niagara or Victoria Falls—all combine to make Argentina one of the great tourist countries of the world. There are four times more cattle than people, and this sparsely-populated land averages four miles per person. Argentina is mineral-rich, it produces South America's finest wines (though the Chileans may disagree), it's industrial and agricultural at the same time and is oil rich. The literacy rate is the highest in South America. One would think, then, that Argentina would be among the wealthiest countries of the world. Sadly, this country has not achieved this lofty position to date, mostly because of mismanagement and a volatile political history.

Buenos Aires: It's called the "Paris" of South America, and rightfully so. It's bustling, it's vibrant, it's mysterious, it's a city that never sleeps. It has deluxe hotels, excellent restaurants, superb shops, fantastic promenades and much more. Anyone who fishes Argentina will find it necessary to spend at least one night in B.A., and even the anglers who are always in a hurry to be on the waters don't seem to regret this. If one has to overnight somewhere, this city is as good as any in the world.

Hotels and Restaurants: There are numerous hotels in Buenos Aires. Among the recommended are: The Plaza, Buenos Aires Sheraton, Claridge, El Conquistador and the Libertador. All have fine restaurants. Other good dining places are La Cabana, La Veda, Au Bec Fin and El Caldero. Most Argentines dine around 9:00 P.M., so plan accordingly.

Entertainment: Not much happens until 11:00 P.M. or so. The "boca" region (or Italian section) specializes in pasta dishes, unending quantities of table wine, a small (but loud) combo and entertainment that is generally provided by the customers. Usually a conga line develops that may include half of the patrons and a few waiters snaking around the tables to the beat of Latin rhythms. It's a fun place. The Spadavecchia and Sparafucile on Necochea are two famous boca restaurants.

The Hippopotamus is a spectacular nightclub, and so is the Cabaret. Actually, all the deluxe hotels have excellent entertainment. For those who want to hear the best tango music, consider the Cano or the Michelangelo. Argentina also has numerous casinos.

Shopping: Florida Street is B.A.'s most famous shopping center. There are also fine stores along Avenida Santa Fe. H. Stern and Ricciardi in the Plaza Hotel specialize in jewelry and precious stones. Argentina is famous for its leather goods and onyx carvings as well as furs. Shops are open until 7:30 P.M. and on Saturday mornings (most stores close during the lunch break).

Required Documents and Customs: A valid passport, a visa and a round-trip ticket are required of U.S. citizens. Two cartons of cigarettes, two liters of liquor, 50 cigars and other items may be brought in to Argentina duty-free.

Currency: Because of inflation and devaluation, the Argentine peso bounces up and down like a yo-yo. Check prior to departure for currency requirements, exchange rates and the amount that may be taken into Argentina.

AND FINALLY... Argentina represents a "must" for the itinerant fly fisherman. Whether it's stream trout fishing in Patagonia, a shot at Buchanan's sea-run browns off Tierra del

The late Frederick Galbraith loved Argentine stream fishing. This Malleo river trout fell to a tiny dry fly...hence the satisfaction.

Fuego or the challenge of the mighty dorado of the Parana and its tributaries, most anglers will find Argentina a most satisfying experience.

I have many fond memories of Argentina:

Like the time when George Wenckheim was fixing camp and he dispatched his dog, Perla, to guide me along the stream. She stopped at every good pool and if I blew a trout, she would shake her head. (Actually, Perla guided me to better areas than George did. Honest.)

Or the time I hooked a magnificent rainbow trout and just when it leaped sky-high, splashed by purple rays of sunset, a gaucho suddenly appeared on a cliff, dressed in his splendid, colorful outfit and riding a beautiful horse. He waved, bid me good luck and disappeared (it was a seven-pound rainbow).

And I recall fondly a particularly large Parana dorado that shot downstream at full speed. Magri, our guide, shouted excitedly in Spanish and I answered "Si" without knowing what he had said. My attention was directed to a malfunction in my reel, while he was rowing the boat furiously against the current. Later I found out that he had asked me whether I was willing to chance going down a set of rapids which he had never engaged before. The boat spun like a top as we pursued this wild dorado and Magri masterfully avoided the rocks. Well, all but one. (We dried out quickly and we did land the dorado.)

Maybe I will go back to Argentina. Someday.

New Zealand

A Tale of Two Islands

If you like your fishing "easy," you can catch rainbows on Lake Taupo by the dozens; but if you prefer challenges, those giant river browns will have you muttering to yourself. There are hundreds of trout streams and lakes loaded with trout; Tony Busch and Rex Forrester—two of New Zealand's best—tell you what it's all about in this land of friendlies.

Billy Pate (right) famous for his billfish and tarpon records is equally skilled on trout streams.

Chapter 14

NEW ZEALAND

I COULDN'T TELL YOU exactly where Ron Houghton moored his 38-foot cruiser on Lake Taupo, as I was too busy rigging tackle while we were underway. I know it was somewhere in Western Bay. In the three days we used his cruiser as our portable floating cabin, I don't recall seeing another boat or fisherman. I do remember that there were a number of small streams that fed Taupo and it was at the mouths of these creeks that I enjoyed some of the finest rainbow trout fishing this side of Argentina's Malleo River.

Initially, the fishing didn't come easily and was darn frustrating. During most of the day, Ron took hunting and fishing outfitter Leo Richardson and his wife harling (a form of trolling) on the big lake. I opted to fish the river mouths on my own and had the whole section to myself. Lots of wading room. And some of the largest rainbow trout I have ever seen were cruising a long cast away.

Dry flies didn't work. The rainbows were obviously feeding subsurface, and they weren't going to waste their time and energy to sip in a dry when they could feed voraciously on schools of smelt-like minnows they could easily corral.

"Okay, so they won't take a dry. Let's slip on a Honey Blond streamer and get some fighting experience," I muttered to myself. It was ignored. I changed pattern after pattern and finally tied on a New Zealand streamer that imitates Taupo's forage fish. The water was extremely clear, and the rainbows continued to ignore my feathers. Perhaps it was the reflected glint off the leader tippet? So I went to lighter and lighter tip-

As is his custom, Lefty Kreh out-maneuvered this fine New Zealand rainbow trout.

pets and probably settled on a 5X, which in those days wasn't anywhere as strong as the mono that Cortland, Aeon and others extrude today.

The lighter tippet was a partial answer, for now I was getting strikes. They weren't rises or "takes"; they were smashing strikes. There would be a flash, and in my excitement, I would hit the fish hard and break the tippet. When I eased up on the strike, I often sustained most of the first run before the tippet would break. I waded back to to my rod case on shore and replaced the stiff-action rod that I was using with a Charlie Ritz (Pezon et Michel Parabolic) split bamboo that was much softer.

I like to think that my ensuing success was the result of putting together the right mix: the correct fly, lighter tippets and most important, the soft-action rod that absorbed and cushioned the rainbow's hard strikes and powerful runs. Whether this was the reason for my success was not important to me at the time. All I remember is that I was able to land rainbow after rainbow, most between four and seven pounds. I savored those golden hours, but after notching more than a dozen large rainbows, I left this area, waded along the shoreline to search for larger fish, bigger challenges. Are anglers ever satisfied?

In crystal-clear Taupo, if one is patient enough and meticulously investigates all shadows with Polaroids, eventually he will see some very large shapes, so big that even the most optimistic angler may doubt that they are actually fish. Until they scoot off.

There was a shadow that seemed only slightly less than a yard long. I was mesmerized by the silhouette and wondered whether it was a fish. Only after long observation, straining my eyes to their limit, did I extend sufficient line to cover the distance between the great shape and me. I still wasn't positive. But the shadow moved slightly, and I know it opened its big mouth. I'm not so sure that it had engulfed my streamer when I set hook fast, and much too hard. The alarmed fish quickly disappeared for the safety of the nearby deeper water.

Those three days on Taupo were as productive and satisfying as I've ever enjoyed in terms of quality rainbow fishing—very few 'bows scaled under four pounds.

Mrs. Richardson, who had never fished before, caught over 20 fine rainbows trolling a fly from Ron's cruiser that day. Taupo is that type of a place: It can satisfy the angler who's looking for a challenge, and it can keep the novice busy fighting fish much of the day when conditions are right. This is also true of several other lakes on the North Island, but "easy fishing" is not the norm in New Zealand.

A visit to New Zealand's transparent streams on the South Island usually underlines this, for no matter how experienced the angler may be, brown trout fishing here tends to be as challenging and demanding in skill as is bonefishing. On a productive bonefish flat, an angler usually encounters scores of bonefish, but on most South Island trout rivers, spotting a half-dozen browns must be considered a good day. True, these trout are likely to be large specimens, but a half-dozen chances a day doesn't give the angler ample opportunity for a big score

Keith Gardner, world traveler and editor of *Fishing World*, is particularly fond of the Tongariro River on the North Island.

in terms of numbers. As in bonefishing, the important elements for success must incorporate the following: spotting the quarry, a stealthy approach, careful, accurate presentations and precise hook setting.

New Zealand's quality of trout fishing generally falls somewhere between extremely easy (trolling) and extremely difficult (stream fishing); it depends on where you are and what methods you are using.

FORRESTER ON NEW ZEALAND

Rex Forrester knows New Zealand fishing best. For many years he operated a very successful hunting and fishing outfitting business. Seventeen years ago, he accepted the challenging job as New Zealand's Hunting and Fishing Officer. He recently visited our office for the following interview:

Q: Some anglers who visit New Zealand for the first time are slightly disappointed with their results. What's the main reason?

RF: I think many newcomers to New Zealand are under the misconception that one needs to tie on a fly behind a tree or a brown trout will grab it. Such is not the case. New Zealand offers quality stream fishing, not "fast" fishing—and this is especially true in the South Island.

Q: There's quite a big difference between fishing on the North Island and the South Island. What are your thoughts on this?

RF: The North Island is primarily rainbow trout country and much of its fishing is in lakes, although there is excellent stream fishing and there are browns, too. The South Island is predominantly brown trout fishing and most of it is on streams. Browns are, of course, more difficult to fool.

Q: Let's discuss South Island brown trout fishing. What's it all about?

RF: We refer to it as Polaroid fishing because it is primarily sight fishing. Polaroid glasses are a must. The angler wades slowly and quietly up a stream and examines every foot of water. When he spots a trout, he must make a careful presentation. If the brown trout sees or hears him, it is gone. So this becomes a stalking game. It's much like your bonefishing.

Q: During an average day, under good conditions, how many browns can a good angler expect to hook on an average South Island stream?

RF: Probably three or four. Or none. They will weigh somewhere between 3 1/2 to five pounds. Some fish may be larger, of course, and some days can produce more fish, but the above is probably very representative. This is what I mean: We offer quality fishing. Another important point is that you can wade all day on some of the South Island streams and not see another angler. You can return to the first pool you fished and be reasonably confident that no one else has disturbed it that day. It's important to remember that a brown trout is a brown trout is a brown trout. One of the wariest and "smartest" of all game fish. And they are just as smart in New Zealand as anywhere else.

Q: What about the Mataura River? You always hear about that river in the South Island. Is it the best?

RF: It is an excellent stream. But there are many others just as good on the South Island. Years ago there weren't many fishing guides in the south. One of the best worked Mataura and that's how the river achieved its lofty reputation.

Q: What about fly patterns? There are a lot of New Zealand patterns.

RF: We do have our own patterns, mostly streamers, and the angler is advised to procure them locally. Nymphs are also effective, of course. I generally use one dry fly pattern in various sizes—the Royal Wulff!

Q: Helicopter flying is heavily discussed in various camp brochures. Is it essential to quality fishing?

RF: While a helicopter is certainly a great way of reaching the waters beyond, there is excellent fishing available without the necessity of hiring a copter.

Q: Let's talk about the North Island. Lake Taupo has to be among the best rainbow producers in the world. But I had noticed, when I fished it years ago, that the trout landed were seldom returned to the waters. Yet the lake is still good.

RF: Taupo is an unusual lake. The general feeling is that if all fish were returned, this would eventually lead to smaller fish, and even stunted trout. Many years ago, the trout averaged about two pounds. Today the average is probably three to four pounds, and you can catch a dozen of them and there won't be much variation. Sometimes we catch a very long fish—25 inches—and it only weighs a couple of pounds. We kill that fish or give it to our mothers-in-law! Taupo probably produces 400,000 fish a year and it is doing well.

I should add that Taupo produces very fast fishing with harling (trolling of streamer flies), and often a dozen trout can be taken quickly.

This giant brown fell for a No. 10 Hare & Copper weighted nymph. It was stalked to within 25 feet. One cast...and BOOM!

There are some excellent streams in the North Island, and Americans are most familiar with the Tongariro.

Q: What about seasons?

RF: There is some fishing available in New Zealand year-round. There are 26 different districts and each controls its season. The South Island has a shorter season, of course (limited usually from October through April), but Lake Taupo on the North is open year-round to fishing. There are too many variations to discuss here.

Q: Is it correct to assume that fly fishing is by far the most popular angling method in New Zealand?

RF: Yes. The English who came to this country were primarily fly fishermen, and our waters—especially on the South Island—are ideal for fly fishing.

Q: There aren't many fishing lodges as such. I know of the one on the Tongariro, Cedar Lodge and a few others. Mostly one hires a guide and stays at inns?

RF: This is primarily true. The main reason is that we have so much water, and the guides will select the stream that is likely to produce the best results for a particular client during the time that he is there.

Q: I know that some anglers visit New Zealand and hire a guide. They learn some of the waters and return the following season on their own, thus saving the cost of a guide. This has to irritate the guide who has shared some of his secret waters.

RF: True. But this doesn't always work that way. You can fish one stream, or a section of it, one year and it can be terrific. But the next year it may be poor, depending on water and weather conditions, so the long flight to New Zealand and other expenses go to waste. Look, there are times when even the most talented guide will have problems in providing quality fishing, and he has many places at his disposal.

Q: What about the costs of guides?

RF: Usually a guide for stream fishing charges $150 to $170 U.S. per day, and he can take two anglers who share the expense. If a guide supplies a boat, the cost is about $200.

Q: And some closing words?

RF: We think that our country offers an excellent fishing opportunity for the angler. We will do our best to satisfy him, but he should not look for a-fish-a-cast or he'll be vastly disappointed, I'm afraid.

THE NORTH ISLAND

One of the things that impressed me the most while fishing with Ron Houghton is the New Zealanders' constant emphasis on the *condition* of fish. Let me illustrate: We landed a fine rainbow, perhaps 25 or 26 inches in length, that I thought fought quite well. I wanted to release it, but Ron killed it and explained that it was not a healthy fish. From all indications it looked like it was in good condition, except that it was thin. Ron explained that all the guides and local fishermen practice this—the removal of "sick" fish from Taupo. To me, it appeared that this fish was a spawned-out trout, but let's face it: Lake Taupo is one of the healthiest trout lakes in the world. The average Taupo trout at one time was over two pounds, but today it's almost four pounds. How can you argue with success?

Taupo and nearby Rotorua are the North Island's most famous lakes, and it was these waters that did much to build New Zealand's fine reputation. More people who have never fished before have probably taken more big rainbows on Taupo or Rotorua than anywhere else in the world. As mentioned before, the harling method is basically trolling. Guides provide all fly fishing gear and often will use very long leaders of 20 to 30 feet, depending on the clarity of the water. The fly is trolled along dropoffs, ideally where one can see the bottom of the lake on one side but not on the other. By following this contour, a guide will often have his "sports" into fish. If the guest can turn a reel handle, he will undoubtedly catch numerous rainbows unless he has horrible weather conditions.

I must confess that I have a distinct prejudice against trolling with a fly rod. I am not at all opposed to trolling with conventional gear, and often I enjoy it. But a fly rod was made for one

Tony Busch—one of the South Island's premier anglers—is on to a big fish. For a close-up of his quarry see page 354.

purpose only: to cast a fly. If it is used for any other purpose, it does about the same thing to me as hearing someone scratch his nails on a blackboard. These first-timers who land dozens of big rainbows while trolling a fly, are, of course, delighted, and I'm sure that photos of huge Taupo rainbows are continuously flashed back home. That's why New Zealand has a "can't miss" tag.

But the serious fly rodder, who likes to catch fish on his own terms, finds other options that are more compatible to his skill. He can fish the mouths of streams as I did, or he can fish some of the rivers.

Taupo's average rainbow trout is 3.9 pounds, while brown trout average almost five pounds. Each season, browns and rainbows of over 8 1/2 pounds are taken from these waters. Taupo's season is open year-round.

Lake Rotorua's average rainbow is slightly over two pounds, while browns average five pounds. Lake Rotorua offers year-round fishing, but the streams are only open from December 1 to June 30.

Lake Tarawera rainbows average five pounds, and trout of 10 pounds are taken annually. There are no browns in this lake. Its season is from October 1 to June 30, but the streams that flow into it are open from December 1 to June 30.

During the summer months (late December through March), most of the trout have left the rivers and entered the lakes; some of the best fishing is found by wading the mouths of these rivers. The trout are attracted here by the great food supply and the cooler temperatures.

Many anglers, however, prefer to fish a river itself and not just its mouth; the North Island offers a number of outstanding streams. Among the most famous is the Tongariro River, which contains big rainbow trout in the faster stretches but also browns in the slower portions. There are two periods that are recommended: September to the end of December, when the trout are dropping down to the lake; and from April onward when the fish return to the river. There are some trout that remain in the river during New Zealand's summer months that can be taken on nymphs, but obviously this is not the preferred time.

Tongariro River fishing technique is similar to steelhead fishing in that shooting-heads are used, longer casts are required and wets or streamers are the effective flies (at times, dry flies also work).

What about other rivers for the dry fly addict? There are a number of excellent rivers near Taupo, including the Rangitikie, Ngarora and Mohaka. These rivers will produce rainbows up to five pounds, although in some stretches, usually near the headwaters, one can hook trout of over 10 pounds. The remote areas, where the bigger trout live, are difficult to reach except by helicopter, or in some cases, small planes.

There are dozens of excellent lakes, rivers and streams that can be considered on the North Island, and no matter what type of fly fishing an angler wants, he can be satisfied here.

NORTH ISLAND FISHING CAMPS

TONGARIRO LODGE: This recently constructed resort is located on the bank of the Tongariro River at the southern end of Lake Taupo. It can accommodate 20 anglers in good comfort. Tony Hayes—one of the most experienced North Island guides—overlooks the fishing, whereas Margaret Coutts, chef par excellence, is in charge of the meals and lodge. Tongariro Lodge offers a variety of fishing options (in addition to the river) including fishing on Taupo or nearby streams and optional helicopter trips to remote rivers. The cost per day is $170 (U.S.) per person, based on double occupancy, and includes accommodations, meals, transfers and guide.

SOLITAIRE LODGE: Reg Turner's posh resort sits on a private peninsula on Lake Tarawera and offers just about every amenity, including a penthouse suite, six junior suites, hot tub, tennis court, helicopter pad, sailing yacht, motor launches, sumptuous meals and impeccable service. Reg is one of Tarawera's most knowledgeable guides (the first fish he ever caught from these waters was a 10 1/2-pounder). The daily rate is $150 per person for meals and accommodations; guiding arrangements are additional.

HUKA LODGE: In the late '20s, Alan Pye emigrated from Ireland and found incredible fly fishing on the Waikato River between Lake Taupo and the Huka falls. He built a modest lodge, and after political and angling luminaries visited Huka, the word spread. Today, this lodge on the Waikato River offers elegant accommodations, gourmet meals, "old world" service and total attention to details. Yes, fly fishing for trout is still a main activity at Huka, but other interests from sailing to golf to riding can be pursued from this lodge. Meals and accommodations run $150 per person (based on double occupancy).

SOUTH PACIFIC SPORTING ADVENTURES: Simon Dickie, the youthful, energetic tour de force of this outfitting business, offers a variety of fishing arrangements. Here's what Simon reports:

"We operate three basic fly fishing trips:

1. Helicopter fly-in to remote Rangitikei and Agarurgro Rivers for trophy rainbows. The optimum time is three days. Access is exclusively by helicopter and we limit parties to one guide and two anglers. All camping equipment is provided. We don't use a standard base camp because we like to have flexibility over many miles of water. The angler can hook huge rainbows (10 + pounds), but it is essential to present a fly skillfully. Virtually all rainbow and resident fish.

2. Daily excursions to local rivers and streams, particularly Tongariro River, for both rainbow and brown on nymphs and dries. Overnight in a motel in Taupo. Optimum time is five days. We have a number of waters to which we have virtually exclusive access, all within an hour's driving distance from Taupo. Because of the vast variation in the size and nature of the streams around Taupo, the fishing methods are equally varied; however, most success comes with using nymphs. Both rainbow and brown average three pounds.

3. Live-aboard boat trips to inaccessible Western Bay of Lake Taupo to fish streamers and wets on feeding rainbows around lake edge and river mouths. The optimum time is five days. Large areas of Lake Taupo's shoreline are accessible only by boat. Here the cruising rainbows tend to feed close inshore, particularly around the estuaries and mouths of inflowing streams. While fly presentation is not that important, greater success is attained with longer casts, although at night, trout averaging five pounds are often taken very close to the angler. Overnight accommodation is aboard large charter launches with competent crew and all facilities."

SOUTH ISLAND

If the rainbow trout fishing is emphasized on the North Island, brown trout fishing is featured on the South Island. Here we have hundreds of rivers and streams providing fly fishing challenges seldom encountered elsewhere in this world. The man who fishes the South Island streams and scores consistently on large trout has much to be proud of, for he has learned his lessons and learned them well. Here on the transparent streams of the South Island, the angler must rely on careful approaches, good vision for spotting fish, accurate presentations and a good knowledge of brown trout. Except in riffles, the first-timer to New Zealand quickly discovers that blind casting is seldom productive and that he must spot his quarry first. But that's only the beginning. Click a couple of stones together, false cast over the fish or slop a cast on the mirror-smooth, surface and the spotted trout will scurry to safety.

Those rivers that can only be reached by helicopter provide faster fishing and bigger fish, and therefore success is generally obtained provided that weather and water conditions are favorable.

South Island's basic fishing season is from October to April, but this varies from district to district. The New Zealanders highly recommend avoiding the Christmas holidays because the waters are much more crowded at this time. If one can only fish at this time, he can avoid the "crowds" by fishing the more remote waters.

There are dozens of excellent rivers to consider on the South Island, including the Karamea, Buller, Mataura, La Fontaine, Arnold and others. There is no such thing as "the best stream" because so much depends on weather, water levels, personal demands and cyclical spawning years. But if one river is fishing poorly, another nearby stream may be excellent. Hence I recommend obtaining the services of a guide or counsel from a lodge owner.

How about fishing technique? What about methods and strategy? Tony Busch, the skilled angler who operates Sportgoods Ltd. ("The Corner Sports Shop") in Nelson, has put together some solid advice. While the following edited version of Tony's strategy for successful fishing is for the South Island, it also applies to North Island streams.

TONY BUSCH ON TECHNIQUE

The techniques employed in any particular period will be determined by the feeding pattern of the fish at the time. There is little point in placing a nymph in front of a trout that is enjoying an afternoon's snack of juicy dry mayflies.

It is imperative to understand and recognize feeding patterns to obtain good results. I elaborate:

1. The Dry Fly Rise: You can recognize it by the quiet manner in which the fish lifts to the surface and just breaks it with his mouth to suck in the fly. On a calm pool perfect rings will formed on the water surface, while in the rapids the fish will be seen lifting its head upward to the surface.

The Technique: Dry fly feeding fish should be approached, if possible, from behind, slightly to one side and no closer than 30 feet if in calm water, or about 20 feet in the riffles. Cast the appropriate fly about two feet to one side of the rise, insuring that your line does not lay over the fish either in the air or on the water. If you are fishing in moving water, be sure to strip in loose line with your free hand. You must strike the fish immediately after the take by moving the rod upward and simultaneously stripping in line with your free hand. This is a smooth, fast action but not so hard that the tippet is broken.

2. The Wet Fly Rise: It's characterized by the splashing of the fish as it speeds from the bottom to gulp the emerging fly. This causes its body to break the water surface, and in some cases the fish will come clear out of the water.

Technique: Wet fly fishing is comparatively simple. This fish will probably be in a current, and it is a matter of casting above the rise and letting the fly float past and about 12 inches from the fish's nose. During a sporadic rise, cast across the current, let the fly drift downstream and at the end of its swing, twitch the rod tip a couple of times before retrieving line very slowly. At all times keep a taut line between the rod tip and the fly. When the fish takes, the tug is barely detectable.

3. Nymph Feeding Fish: They are usually stationed in one position from where they will move slightly from side to side to take the nymph as it floats downstream toward and past them. At times the fish will swim a few feet from its station, take the nymph and return.

Technique: Nymph fishing is the most deadly method of all. Locate a smooth-flowing stretch of water about knee-deep, and walk very slowly upstream, looking ahead for feeding fish. For those who have not done this, the fish from behind appears pear-shaped and about the same color as a pear with a dark stripe running from top to bottom. The fish from the side appears as a brownish smudge. But if you look closely, you can detect slight movements.

By walking carefully, it's possible to approach a fish within 20 feet. Cast the nymph a few inches ahead of the fish and to one side of its head. When the nymph lands, keep the rod horizontal and point it directly at the fish. Make sure that there is no loose line between the nymph and the rod tip by continually stripping in line with the free hand.

The fish will move slightly and smoothly to one side to take the nymph, at which time it should be "struck" by tightening the line with the free hand only. Then when the fish pulls back, lift your rod—NOT BEFORE.

It's vital to strike this way at the instant the fish takes the nymph; there will be no sudden jerk, only a slight tug, and you must be on the alert.

4. Lure (Streamer) Fishing: This is employed in rivers where the fish feed on smelt or similar small fish, as in the central North Island districts. It is not used to a great extent in the South Island, except perhaps in the tidal reaches of the west coast streams and the large rivers of the Southland area. In shallow rivers the fish will be seen swimming fast in various directions while chasing the small "fry." The streamer is particularly effective during the whitebait season, September through December in the lower reaches of the rivers. Jack Spratt, Grey Ghost or similar patterns are good choices.

Technique: Streamer fishing is similar to wet fly fishing. It's a matter of casting across the current and letting the streamer swing to your side of the river, where, after a few rod twitches, it is retrieved very slowly against the current. If you are fishing a lake or calm water, cast a long line and retrieve it very slowly with just enough speed to keep the streamer off the bottom. It's particularly effective over a weed bed.

Random Observations: The brown trout is not as easily fooled as the rainbow. The brown's eyesight is extremely sharp, its hearing is acute and it has excellent smelling powers. You should exercise extreme care in your mad rush across the gravel to get to the river. Click some stones together and you will be waving goodbye to the fish. Rush headlong down the fern-covered bank to get within casting distance of the big fish you've seen, and it will either rocket to safety or freeze and laugh at your futile attempts to entice it to take a fly.

The best fishing periods alter slightly from district to district, but as a rule, fish wets from dawn to 9 A.M.; nymphs from 9 A.M. to 1 P.M.; dry flies during the late morning and early afternoon and again at dusk; and fish wet fly or streamers after dark. The heat of the afternoon is for a deserving siesta, whether man or fish. Good luck!—*Tony Busch.*

There are several approaches to fishing the South Island.

1. *Book a lodge that offers guided fishing trips:* Lake Rotoroa Lodge, Cedar Lodge and others provide accommodations, all meals, guides, transportation and, in general, take care of all the details.

2. *Hire the services of an independent guide:* He provides transport (car, jetboat, light plane or helicopter) and accompanies you during your entire stay. He designs an itinerary based on your angling preferences, amount of time, fishing skill and other variables. Small inns are used for accommodations, and he may move from one location to another if necessary. There are experienced independent guides at every important fishing center, such as Gore, Dunedin, Te Anau, Nelson, etc.

3. *''Do-It-Yourself'' fishing:* You rent a car, acquire maps and stay at inns or motels close to the streams you intend to fish. The advantage of ''building'' your own trip lies mostly in the fact that it is cheaper than hiring a guide. If you decide on this, be sure to acquire Tony Busch's *A Trout Fishing Guide to South Island* (about $25) from Sportgoods Ltd., Nelson. He is exceptionally knowledgeable and exuberant and has helped hundreds of visiting anglers. His guide book provides com-

Tony Busch's 8 1/2-pound brown trout. He is particularly skillful at stalking wary trout at close ranges.

plete details, maps and basic information on many of the South Island's favorite streams. Here's a sample of just one fishing spot out of 29 given for the Motueka River near Nelson:

"HAYCOCK'S BUSH—1 km—Without any doubt, the best fly fishing area on the river. Over a mile long and 200 yards wide, this two-feet-deep (average) flowing pool offers excellent fishing while walking upstream on either side. Pull off the left beyond a mail box just inside the bush. (His easy-to-follow map is keyed to the text)."

The first two options, booking a resort or an independent guide, obviously will be more productive for the first-time visitor to New Zealand.

The outdoor travel agencies (including PanAngling Travel Service) can not only provide valuable information but can handle all booking details. The angler who is serious about fishing in New Zealand would do well to read Rex Forrester's *Trout Fishing in New Zealand* distributed by Madrona Publishers, Inc. in Seattle, Washington. It's a fine book written by one of New Zealand's most knowledgeable anglers.

SOUTH ISLAND FISHING CAMPS

LAKE ROTOROA LODGE: This elegant fishing lodge is nestled on the north shore of beautiful Lake Rotoroa, only 60 yards from the Gowan River. Its strategic location provides easy access to a number of excellent streams, including the Buller river. There are 26 trout rivers within 45 minutes' drive of the lodge, so if one river is fishing poor, no problem; there are many others.

The lodge also offers helicopter fishing into remote wilderness trout rivers where trout of over 10 pounds have been taken. Accommodations and meals cost about $85 (U.S.) and guides approximately $105 per person per day on a double occupancy basis. Lake Rotoroa Lodge is about 60 miles from Nelson.

DRY FLY SAFARIS LTD.: Located near Queenstown, on Lake Wanaka, this brand-new lodge is only a 10-minute drive from the famous Clutha River. Its season is from mid-November until mid-March, and rainbows and browns are offered. A variety of rivers and streams are easily reached from this comfortable lodge by four-wheel drive, jet boats or light planes. Earle BuBar, who has flown for Alaskan camps during his off-season, charges $1,695 inclusive for a Saturday-to-Saturday week. Capacity is six anglers, though owner Earle prefers to limit it to four persons for optimum service.

CEDAR LODGE: Dick Fraser's fishing resort is accessible from Queenstown only by light plane; so the nearby rivers have received proportionally less pressure. Each day he flies clients to various rivers, but when weather is poor, the Makarora River, only a few hundred yards away from the lodge, and others, can be reached by 4-WD vehicles.

LAKE BRUNNER LODGE: This is one of New Zealand's oldest fishing lodges (previously known as Mitchell's resort). It's located on the west coast, about a 2 1/2-hour drive from Christchurch (or 45 minutes from Hokitika). Among the better rivers in Westland are the Arnold River, a tributary of the Grey, and La Fontaine. There is excellent dry fly fishing opportunity in a number of nearby waters. The lodge consists of three deluxe suites and six smaller suites. Accommodations (without meals) run approximately $60 and guides $60 (U.S.) per person, per day, based on double occupancy.

TACKLE

Basically two types of outfits are needed to fish both the North and South Islands:

Heavy Fly Outfit: This consists of an 8 1/2- to 9 1/2-foot fly rod that takes a No. 9 or 10 weight-forward sinking line or fast sinking shooting heads, nine-foot leaders tapered to six pounds and a smoothly operating reel equipped with about 100 yards of 20-pound Micron backing. This outfit is used at places like the Tongariro River, where long casts are required, similar to steelhead fishing. Heavier outfits are also gaining popularity on some of the larger rivers in the South Island, such as the Clutha, and are sometimes used to fish the mouths of rivers under very windy conditions (or whenever casts of over 60 feet are needed).

Medium Fly Outfit: An eight-foot graphite calibrated to take a No. 6 or 7 weight-forward (floating and sinking) fly line is widely used on smaller streams for nymphing and dry fly fishing. Leaders up to 12 feet in length tapered to 4X and medium-sized reel spooled with 50 yards of 20-pound Micron complete the outfit. This outfit would be used for casts of 30 to 60 feet in length.

Flies: You will need an assortment of streamers, nymphs and dries. It's best to obtain your subsurface flies in New Zealand because of the localized patterns. Productive streamer patterns include Parsons' Glory, Red Setter, Mallard, Taupo Tiger and Mrs. Simpson. For nymph fishing, you will need Hare's Ear,

It was a wet, but great, day...tired, hungry, satisfied anglers trudge back. Soon the "heli" will remove them from paradise.

Twilight Beauty, Greenwell and Halfback. For dry fly fishing, the Royal Wulff, Adams, Red-tipped Governor, Goofus Bug and Blue Dun. Note: Fly-tying materials must be fumigated prior to entry in New Zealand and a certified letter must be made available. Right now, there is no restriction on commercially-tied flies, but these regulations could change.

Polaroid glasses are essential (along with a wide-brimmed hat). Some New Zealanders wade smaller streams in shorts and wading shoes, but the visiting sportsman is advised to take felt-soled waders.

NEW ZEALAND, THE COUNTRY

New Zealand is approximately 1,000 miles long. Two-thirds of New Zealand's three million population live on the North Island. The land was originally settled by the Maoris, a highly-gifted Polynesian people, and later by Europeans, mostly English. Today, Europeans comprise 85 percent of the total population, and approximately 90 percent of the Maoris live on the North Island. Sheep raising is the dominant industry; New Zealand is the world's second largest exporter of wool. Both islands offer a plethora of tourist attractions, and New Zealand is one of the most important South Pacific tour destinations, playing host to 550,000 visitors each year.

Most international flights funnel into Auckland (pop. 850,000), which is 6,500 miles from Los Angeles or 12 hours of flying time, "losing a day" crossing the International Date Line, but gaining it on the return trip. Many visitors prefer to breakup the trip with short visits to Hawaii, Tahiti or Fiji.

Air New Zealand and Mount Cook Airlines offer frequent, efficient domestic service to all important cities.

Hotels and Restaurants: New hotels are popping up frequently each year as New Zealand keeps up pace with the increasing tourist traffic. Outside of Auckland, hotels of over 100 rooms are rare and considered "giants." New Zealand's elegant Regent Auckland, opened in 1985, is the largest (and most expensive) with over 300 luxury rooms. Most motels and hotels offer 20 to 60 rooms.

New restaurants, offering international cuisine, are slowly increasing in numbers. With 65 million sheep residing in New Zealand, lamb is the most important entree, but beef and seafood are also heavily featured on menus.

Documentation and Currency: North American tourists need a valid passport for visits up to 30 days. The passport must be valid for at least six months after scheduled departure.

As of March 1986, $1.86 NZ equaled $1 U.S., but the exchange rate fluctuates. *Important:* The "plastic card" phenomenon hasn't quite caught on in New Zealand although there are a number of business establishments in larger cities that accept credit cards. It's recommended that traveller's checks are brought for the anticipated expenses.

AND FINALLY... With hundreds of rivers, streams and lakes available on the North and South Islands, the fly fishing potential in New Zealand is immense. Many waters have been explored, and these "steady-Eddies" would qualify for any fly rodder's Hall of Fame, but there are also other waters, not as famous, that often produce above-average results.

One should not expect to catch many fish on most of the classic fly fishing rivers. As Rex Forrester emphasizes: "Look for quality fishing, not quantity."

I've had the privilege of fishing dozens of countries throughout the world. Unequivocally, I can say that the people of New Zealand are among the most courteous, helpful and concerned that I've met.

Christmas Island

The Pacific's Newly-Developed Bonefish Paradise

Hordes of bonefish invade these pristine flats ready to munch on a well-presented Crazy Charlie pattern; don't look for expert guides to point out the fish for you; but even bonefish novices have little trouble in picking out the gray ghosts of the flats.

Bernie Scalin about to land an average-sized Christmas Island bonefish.

Chapter 15

CHRISTMAS ISLAND

BONEFISH IN THE PACIFIC? To my mind, the bonefish is an Atlantic or Caribbean resident, and when found elsewhere, this fish seems out of place. I was aware that big bonefish periodically pop up in Hawaii, but that's a deep-water proposition, and the bonefish was invented to be taken on the flats. Thin-water bonefishing is among the most exciting, and most demanding, facets of angling; in deep-water, it's a very "ho hum" sport. Years ago, I did some deep-water fishing for bones at Mozambique, but after a short stint, I decided to chase other fish instead.

So when the news broke that there was some bonefishing in the Pacific, at a place called Christmas Island, I suspected one of three things: it was deep-water fishing; it would produce a number of small fish; or, if there were any flats, they would be limited.

But logic and truth aren't always in agreement. During the next couple of years, we received reports that Christmas Island not only offered bonefish, but that it harbored large quantities of them, and the flats were quite extensive. At first, most of the bones reported were smallish, but as the flats were explored more thoroughly, bigger fish began to pop up with regularity.

So it was imperative that someone from PanAngling should visit Christmas Island. Paul Melchior won the flip of the coin by a narrow margin (72 to 28 out of 100 flips). The following is his report:

"These bones gobble up Crazy Charlie patterns...don't leave home without them!" advises Tim Clark.

"Bonefishing at Christmas was so good that at times you felt invincible... but there were slow periods, too."—Paul Melchior.

MELCHIOR'S REPORT

Christmas Island, located 1,200 miles directly south of Hawaii, is one of the largest coral atolls in the world.

It's part of the Gilbert Island chain, and its most distinguishable characteristic is that it's crescent-shaped. Within the crescent, and along some of the outside edges, are extensive networks of bonefish flats.

The bonefish are numerous. Our party encountered at least some bonefish on every flat we explored, and some flats offered a virtually endless stream of fish. Most of the bones we sighted were in small groups (two to four, sometimes up to 10, seldom more). The large fish were almost always loners, which is true of most places.

The main lagoon, formed inside the crescent, is really an intricate latticework of interconnected smaller lagoons. Each of these "ponds" has a narrow flat that runs around the outer perimeter. Most flats are 15- to 40-feet wide, sloping gently to a sharp dropoff into blue water. The bones zigzag along the shelf, moving into the shallows at times or hugging the outside edge next to the dropoff, close to the protection of the deeper water.

In some areas, near the village of Poland, for example, the flats are huge, running for miles, with deep channels intersecting along the way. In other areas, the flats are smaller, and one can wade across them in a few minutes. Many of the most productive flats are formed where two lagoons come together or where a large lagoon empties into the crescent, pouring water over vast coral shelves that at low tide are as dry and flat as a highway, but at high tide are alive with bonefish.

About 85 percent of the flats are hard-bottomed, and wading is very easy. Some flats have pieces of loose coral on them, and this can be a bit rough if improper footwear is used. In areas where the bottoms are truly soft, wading is still possible, though difficult, and one must proceed cautiously. After a day or two, anglers can easily evaluate the flats and avoid situations that may be uncomfortable for them.

Fishing at Christmas Island has been touted as some of the finest in the world, and there were times when we had no argument with that claim. But during our week, bonefishing was inconsistent—sometimes frustratingly slow, and at other times, so good you felt invincible.

The slower days came at the beginning of our trip. Strong winds and cloud cover made spotting bones difficult. Initially we found the bones spooky or just plain scornful of our flies. When the tides began to shift, the fish became aggressive. We fooled an occasional bone, but action was not spectacular.

Little Plantation was our salvation. At low tide, this flat is bone dry, and you can see almost a mile of coral so unencumbered we literally drove out to the edge of it to begin fishing. We watched the frigate birds while waiting for the tide to rise. Once it arrived, we had a fast two hours of fishing, for bones were everywhere.

They were unlike the bonefish we had tested previously and behaved as if they had not eaten for days, tailing actively, darting for our flies as soon as they landed and zipping off for the deeper water when hooked. I landed eight bones during that short feeding spree.

The next day we scurried back to the same location. Again the bones were there, only a bit less hot for our flies, as they had been on the flat feeding for some time. Nevertheless, I took another eight before the tide was out. We were regaining our confidence, and it was a dangerous time; another dose of instant success would put already rising egos into orbit. I took another two bones at the edge of the lagoon at lunchtime and explored smaller flats near Little Plantation. The plan was to return later in the afternoon and await the rise of the tide, and more bones.

My expectation, based on the previous afternoon's flurry, was to end the day with at least 20 bones. In fact, I landed 27 and lost another 10 through carelessness. The bones were everywhere, and once the tide began to build, the best strategy was to work your way into it laterally, zigzagging towards the main lagoon until the flat got too soft to wade. You could then work down the flat, side to side, casting to fish already up in very shallow water. Most of the bones were under four pounds and, at times, so plentiful that you would pass up an almost-sure bone for the opportunity for a larger fish. Several times I took three fish on three successive casts, and once four in a row. It was a time to learn, to practice the stalk, to observe the take, to set hook and to experiment. An ideal laboratory. It was also a time to marvel at these wondrous fish: Even a diminutive two-pounder could melt plenty of backing from my reel.

"I cast to 20 big bones, landing one, missing a few others...but, then, that's what bonefishing is all about!"—Paul Melchior.

The fifth day started out like a repeat of the first two, with spooky fish and meager results. But as the tide began to fall, bones again became active, and I took three in quick succession from one flat. Another came a bit later, near Lone Palm. We were to return to Small Plantation that afternoon, again hoping to duplicate our previous success. The tide, however, would not be in for several hours, so we drove to a nearby area in the interval. It was an outside flat where the ocean was on the deeper edge, and the flat was alive with big fish. Like most big bones, they were spooky. I cast to perhaps 20, landing one, missing a few more in the process. Most of the casts at Christmas are to oncoming bonefish, straight-on shots, and with crosswinds to consider, presentations were difficult at times. Wading the outside edges of the flats led to the least spooky fish, but you had to contend with the deeper water, and you not only had to worry about making the right cast but also calculating sink rates for the flies, as the water was sometimes close to mid-thigh depth. I was sorry to reach the top of the flat and be finished with the larger bones, but it was time to return to Little Plantation.

The sun had just about set when we arrived, and while waiting for the tide, we were fighting discouragement. White sand and no sunlight at the lower end made spotting fish almost impossible, and our only chances for over an hour were occasional casts to the rare tailing fish. It was obvious that many less bones were present than previously, and desperation began to envelop us. I retreated up the flat on the hard coral. Bones were coming in but from different directions than the previous day. It was about ankle-deep in some places, and I began to spot and cast to tailing fish. I had to crouch down to spot the tails since the sun had almost disappeared by now. I had to fish by feel as I could not see the fly, but I began to pick up the occasional fish. It was different from my previous experience and far more interesting, since stalking is the ultimate way. I landed eight more bones.

Trevally are another attraction at Christmas. They are similar to jack crevalle: large, aggressive and tough to handle on either conventional or fly gear. Whereas jacks seem to prefer subsurface lures, trevally will smash surface plugs.

Although we saw large trevally, the ones we caught ran three to eight pounds. Most of them were taken on the bonefish flats on small flies. They are exceptionally strong fish, and even a five-pounder can take 100 yards in a flash.

ACCOMMODATIONS: While the Captain Cook hotel will never earn four stars in any guide book, it is a charming, fairly comfortable facility.

The main part of the hotel is composed of double-occupancy rooms, each with private bathroom, electricity and either overhead fans or air conditioning. In addition, a number of thatched roof, duplex bungalows are situated in back of the lodge. These units have private bathrooms and electricity.

The dining room and lounge areas are attached to the main body of the hotel. The bar is stocked with limited supplies of hard liquor, beer and soda.

Meals were good, but don't expect gourmet quality. Dinners featured both a meat and fish entree and typically included steak, lamb, roast beef, chicken, pork, lobster, fish stews or trevally steaks. Bread is baked daily at the hotel. Breakfasts were identical each day: eggs, toast, bacon, fresh pineapple and cereal. Lunches were made by the anglers themselves from a small table stocked with luncheon meats, fruits and bread.

The Gilbertese are shy and gentle people and made a real effort to please guests at the lodge. Their inexperience at serving well-traveled customers is evident at times, but they give 100-percent effort, and whatever glitches may occur are minor.

After the presentation you "touch up" the fly...there's a pick-up...you set hook...then the bone streaks off for Australia.

Experienced guides, as we know them elsewhere, are not present at Christmas Island. A guide will take you out each day, but for the most part, don't expect him to know the intricacies of fly fishing for bones. They know the areas, and some showed a good understanding of tides, but few spotted fish well. From what I gather, there has been considerable improvement in the guides, but more is necessary.

Christmas Island's location close to the equator means year-round fishing. The winter months, we have been told, tend to be the windiest. We had strong winds, but they did not hamper our fishing, as you could always wade with the wind at our back.

GETTING THERE: You must have a valid passport to visit Christmas Island. Trips run Wednesday to Wednesday only. The Air Tungaru jet charter takes approximately three hours from Honolulu to Christmas Island, leaving early in the morning and thus allowing a half day of fishing upon arrival. On the return, you reach Honolulu in the afternoon with sufficient time to make early evening flights to the mainland. Plan to overnight on Tuesday before the trip to Honolulu. The Holiday Inn near the airport is clean and comfortable and provides courtesy airport transfers upon arrival and departure.

The rate for 1987 is $1,550 per angler per week based on double occupancy. This rate includes the charter to the island, all meals, accommodations, fishing and all transfers between the hotel and fishing grounds.

The suggested tackle is fairly basic. Fly rods of 8 1/2 to 9 1/2 feet calibrated to take a No. 8 weight-forward floating line are most suitable here. Any smooth fly reel that accommodates the fly line, plus about 200 yards of 20-pound Micron, can be used here. Leaders ought to be about nine feet, tapered down to eight-pound tippets. If the bones seem spooky, lengthen your leader to 12 or even 14 feet [see "Bahamas" chapter for Winston Moore's leader formula]. Fly patterns? Without a doubt, the Crazy Charlie pattern is by far the most effective in white or light brown tied on No. 4 and 6 hooks. You may want to include a heavier (No. 10) rod for exceptionally windy days or for when you need a little longer cast. This rod can also be used for trevally, though some experts that concentrate on this powerful fish recommend a 12 weight. Lefty's Deceiver streamers and popping bugs tied on a 3/0 hook are very effective for trevally.

It is particularly important to take along good comfortable footwear for wading, as there is plenty of coral. Some anglers prefer to use canvas wading shoes, cotton socks and gravel guards. Our party used the Japanese tabis, which are obtainable from a number of catalog houses or in Honolulu. We found them comfortable and very satisfactory. Scuba boots with heavy soles are also recommended.

Bernie Scalin carefully holds a bone in the water for a few seconds before allowing it to scoot off for deeper waters.

Christmas Island is an interesting and productive bonefishing haven. The fish are numerous, and opportunities for fast action, and an occasional trophy, are abundant. If an angler is willing to make his own strategic decisions about the fishing, select his own flies and, to a certain extent, even decide where to fish, it can be an exceptional bonefish opportunity.—*Paul Melchior.*

What about big bonefish at Christmas Island? Mike Fitzgerald, of Frontiers, has devoted a considerable amount of time and effort to make this sport fishery what it is today. He provides the following testimonials on outstanding catches made at Christmas Island during 1986:

"Although I only took bonefish up to seven pounds, I hooked several between 10 and 15 pounds that I could not control. This was the finest bonefishing I've ever done—catching 126 for the week..." G. B. Barnard—April 2, 1986.

"Absolutely the best bonefishing I've experienced. Best day—32 bones and eight cut-offs. Lots of six- to eight-pounders. Christie and I each had a shot apiece at fish 16 to 20 pounds ..." Mev Van Doren— February 4, 1986. (His best fish was a 32-incher.)

"Our biggest fish was 29 inches, but the fishing, people and experience were superb. I landed between 125 and 150 bonefish, 15 trevally and queenfish on a fly. Christmas Island is all it's cracked up to be... David A. Schulier—April 29, 1986.

"Best fish were 27 to 28 inches. Many bonefish; ideal wading ...wind not a major problem. I caught 158 bonefish on flies; the best day was 48 fish and the slowest full day was 10 fish. I saw and caught more small fish than I expected, based on previous information. Lots of three- to five-pound fish, and steady action on tailing singles..." Joe Doggett—May 27, 1986.

AND FINALLY... Yes, there are bonefish in the Pacific. Fishing at Christmas Island is a relatively new discovery, but it has made tremendous strides in the past few seasons toward becoming one of the world's best places to hunt and stalk the bonefish. It appears that some improvement can be made in the quality of guiding, and this is particularly important as far as the novice bonefisherman is concerned. But with each passing season, the guiding staff is improving. The locals are learning more and more from the many expert fly fishermen. Rick Ruoff, the knowledgeable Florida Keys' guide, spent the 1985 winter season teaching local guides the intricacies of bonefishing.

But there is also the personal satisfaction of being on the flats alone, spotting and stalking a bone, making the presentation and hooking, landing and releasing the fish. And doing it all by yourself!

Iceland

The Angler's Playground for Atlantic Salmon

The Atlantic salmon—the most noble of all species—has intrigued man since the days of the Romans. This nomadic species is born in freshwater streams, migrates hundreds of miles in the ocean, but uncannily returns to the stream of its origin to spawn. Iceland has a number of excellent salmon waters, and anglers from many parts of the world are willing to stand in line to pay over $4,000 a week for a chance at Salmo salar.

With some tricky footwork, Stu Apte conquered this Kjos salmon that gulped a muddler.

Chapter 16

ICELAND

THERE WAS A TIME, many years ago, when I concluded that the Atlantic salmon didn't exist. I was convinced that this fish was conjured up by some masochistic fishermen who insisted on chasing a ghost species, and the more they pursued it the greater their obsession. Of course, I had seen photos of fish purported to be Atlantic salmon and read a number of articles on this species. Lee Wulff even devoted an entire volume to Atlantics.

Those who perpetuated the myth were a clever lot. First, the fish was given a poetic Latin name: *Salmo salar.* Very catchy, indeed. Easy to remember, too. Then they developed an almost Homeric epic concerning the life history of this species. In fact, it's not much different than the trials and tribulations of Ulysses, if you follow Greek mythology.

Consider this. The fish is born in a fresh-water stream and spends its adolescence there. When it approaches the equivalent maturity of a sophomoric teenager and is, therefore, equipped with a know-it-all attitude, it ventures downstream into a great big ocean where the dangers of bigger fish, seals, nets and oil spills loom constantly. The ocean is very different than his fresh-water birthplace in that it tastes salty, almost bitter. The little fish do not merely cavort and frolic in the ocean near the safety of their home stream; instead they swim hundreds of miles to a very special place. Why anyone would want to swim that far is beyond me. Is the food that much better off Greenland? But let's not knit-pick; these script writers are exceptionally imaginative. Somehow, the salmon are able to withstand the dangers of the long journey and, in fact, they

"Yes, Virginia, there is an Atlantic salmon!" But it took several trips to convince the author.

grow big and fat and are quite content. You would think that once they found Utopia they would remain there. But no.

Now the salmon's sexual urge becomes so strong that they compulsively swim all the way back to the waters of their origin, and that may be more than a thousand miles. Think for a moment of how strong that sexual drive must be. We humans are considered a horny lot, but I have never met anyone willing to walk fifty miles, let alone swim a thousand, to "shake hands" with even the fairest of all maidens. Remarkably, a salmon doesn't even know who his partner will be, or if there will be one at all. But the plot thickens. Now get this. After swimming across a vast ocean the salmon don't simply settle on just any fresh-water stream in their urge to merge. Stubbornly, they insist on going back to the same river where they were born, and there are no street signs or landmarks to guide them. You would think that after swimming all that distance, the fish would have lost so much weight and energy that they wouldn't be in any condition to muster enough energy to consummate a relationship.

According to the myth, even if our hero stumbles upon his birth place, he doesn't immediately look for his lady love. Not just yet. He remains in the freshwater currents for some time, which must further drain his precious energy. And according to some mythologists, he doesn't even bother to eat. Then when conditions are exactly right, our persistent little character must ascend great waterfalls, often by leaping time after time, maybe ten feet high, until finally he overcomes this and other obstacles. Okay, let's buy all this for the moment.

Now he discovers his true love, fends off other males that may be just as horny and just as pugnacious as he is, and establishes a boudoir. At last the mating ritual takes place. Pheww! Was it worth it?

Although one must think that he would be totally exhausted after this ordeal, there's more. Instead of living his remaining years in this peaceful setting, occasionally reflecting on the stupidity of his youth, he eventually drifts downstream and swims back to his feeding grounds—a thousand miles or more away—and repeats this process all over again. Maybe several times.

The Pacific salmon species, the Atlantic's first cousins, follow practically the same ritual, but mate only once, and then probably realizing their folly, they have no recourse but to commit suicide on the spot! There is more to the Atlantic salmon's adventures, of course, but this odyssey hopefully serves to explain my initial doubts concerning the existence of the species. In an effort to research this myth, like those who attempted to find "Big Foot" or the Loch Ness monster, I mapped out a personal campaign to prove or disprove, once and for all, the existence of the Atlantic salmon. So I fished many of those famous salmon rivers. This took years, for among the obstacles that beset salmon fishermen is the expense (I forgot to tell you: it costs plenty to track down salmon ghosts). I went to Ireland, and I went to Norway and to Spain and Canada, too. Not a salmon. True, I saw what appeared to be salmon rolling in pools, and I watched them leap over waterfalls, and once, after ten hours of diligent casting, I thought I observed a salmon come not once but twice to the fly. Of course, he didn't take. I dismissed these visions, lovely as they were, as a mirage or a result of my brain playing its usual little tricks.

I didn't give up for, as I told you, anglers who pursue Salmo salar are a masochistic lot. I continued to fish for them, and this would have been an innocent if not rational pastime, I suppose, if I looked for greener pastures, but in many cases I fished the same rivers repeatedly.

SUCCESS AT LAST!

Then I caught a salmon. Honest. And a couple more on another stream. Yes, Virginia there is an Atlantic salmon. I never caught many salmon, and although I did actually touch them, in later days I would wonder if I really had caught them. Or had it been my imagination? So on one trip, I photographed a salmon as personal proof. When I viewed the developed film, the images were not there. Surely, it couldn't be my photographic skills! Or was it those nasty X-ray machines at airports that sometimes eradicate images?

Therefore, years later in Iceland, when Stu Apte and I stood on that high ledge overlooking the big Laxa i Kjos pool, watch-

Rip Cunningham took time away from his editorial tasks at *Salt Water Sportsman* to nail this (and many other) Hitara salmon.

ing hundreds—no, thousands—of Atlantic salmon milling slowly about, I still had my doubts. It wasn't until Stu and I landed many salmon that I finally came to the only rational conclusion: Atlantic salmon actually exist. At least in Iceland.

On that river, we spent 3 1/2 days fishing, and I believe that I landed close to 30 salmon, and Stu well over 40. The best was a 15-3/4-pounder that fell for a Blue Charm pattern. The most memorable fish was not the big one; instead, it was a 12-pounder that Stu hooked after persistently casting a dry fly more than 100 times to a rolling fish (dispelling the theory, popular at the time, that Icelandic fish didn't hit dry flies). The salmon zigged downstream first, and than zagged all the way across, and Stu, who in my opinion knows how to control a fish with a fly rod better than any mortal I've fished with, used all the tricks he had learned in fighting and subduing many tarpon well over 100 pounds. These tactics were to no avail, and precious few yards of backing remained on his whirling spool. He had no recourse but to follow, no, run, after that fish downstream. He, too, zigged and zagged down the river, maybe not as fast as the salmon, but certainly as nifty as an NFL halfback, stepping on slippery helmet-size boulders, avoiding the faster current. He did this for a distance of 200 or 300 yards. Jon Jonsson, one of the leaseholders of the river, and I were totally amazed, not only because he was able to tail that salmon with one fast grab just as the fish was about to tumble over some rapids, but that Stu had, in fact, not fallen into the river during the chase. We cheered and we clapped for we both knew that we had witnessed one of the most surefooted anglers of all time. Now Stu was retracing his steps across the river—pleased with himself I'm sure—only now he was meticulously planting his feet around the slippery boulders. Methodically. And slowly. Of course he fell in. It was right in the middle of the river on a cold day, I remember, and he was soaking wet, and inhibited by the gallons of water that entered his boots. He cussed a little, and then cursed a lot more for he had a decision to make: should he go back to the lodge, about fifteen minutes away, and change his clothes and boots? Since in Iceland you fish only certain hours, Stu made the only decision that any rational angler could make. Cold and soggy, he shook himself like a wet Labrador retriever, stayed in the river, and only when he hooked and landed another salmon did he actually stop shivering.

Is Iceland, then, the place to go for someone who wants to prove to himself, as I did, that salmon do exist? Absolutely. There are 101 salmon rivers in Iceland, of which at least 25 have substantial runs. Probably half of these would be classified as "blue ribbon" waters because they often yield at least 1,000 salmon during a season.

Now a river that produces well over a thousand salmon may not, at first, appear a sufficient incentive to send a prospective fisherman scurrying off to Iceland, especially if he knows that some rivers, like New Brunswick's Miramichi, produce 20,000 salmon or more during some seasons. So an explanation is in order. First, most of the Icelandic streams are relatively small and not very long, offering anywhere from five to 25 miles of fishable water. Second, very few Icelandic rivers permit more than 10 "rods" (lingo for "fishermen") at a time; thus, an angler may have as much as a couple of miles of pool after pool to himself. On some public stretches of the Miramichi you are never lacking for companionship; there might be a dozen or more anglers working the same pool. It becomes obvious then that, to a certain point, the more anglers fishing a river, the heavier the harvest. So we're concerned with quality, not quantity, when we discuss Iceland's salmon waters.

LAXA i KJOS–Up Close and Personal

Let's take a close look at Laxa i Kjos, a typical "blue ribbon" salmon river that's located a scant two-hour drive from Reykjavik (Iceland's capital city). A maximum of ten rods are booked per week, and anglers are accommodated in a comfortable lodge consisting of private rooms, showers, sauna, dining room and kitchen facilities. The works.

Laxa i Kjos varies considerably throughout its course in terms of width, ease in wading and fishing, depth and topography. Close to the mouth of the river a huge waterfall creates a pool about the size of a football field, and hundreds of salmon may congregate here, especially in July. Even though a fish ladder was built to aid salmon in negotiating these falls, many Atlantics nonetheless concentrate here, below this obstruction, waiting for higher waters to ease their upstream ordeal. Above these falls the river flows gently and there are a number of small pools which are relatively easy to fish. As one progresses upstream the river becomes swifter, making it somewhat difficult to fish and wade and thus more challenging. Laxa i Kjos and Bugda (a feeder stream) offer approximately 90 pools of holding waters. Some of the pools are magnificent jewels, easy to read, easy to fish, while others are hardly distinguishable from the river itself.

A river is divided into beats or sections, and basically each angler has a beat to himself for a specific fishing period. An angler is not assigned to a particular beat for the entire week, for it would be a case of feast or famine depending on the pool. Instead fishermen rotate from beat to beat several times a day, so that during the week each will have tasted some of the honey but will also have swallowed an occasional bitter pill, one that isn't sugar-coated. You can stand on a knoll, for example, and see hundreds and hundreds of silvery Atlantics itching to attack a Night Hawk or a Black Doctor pattern. On the other hand, you could stand on another hill and no matter how hard you scrutinize the pool with Polaroids, you may not even see a shadow that bears the slightest resemblance to a salmon's silhouette. The various salmon runs move up a river progressively during the season; thus, the lower third of the river may be good one week, but the following week the middle stretch of the river might hold more fish. So the rotation system is the only fair way to assign beats.

By government regulation, Icelandic streams cannot be fished more than 12 hours a day (and no more than 90 days a season). Most lodges provide for a morning session (usually 7 A.M. to 1 P.M.), a break for lunch and some rest, and a resumption of fishing in the afternoon until the late evening (4 P.M. to 10 P.M.). Remember, Iceland is in "Midnight Sun" country so there is plenty of daylight during summer.

The trouble with the 12-hour fishing day is that it's a little long for most of us. Even at a two-presentations-per-minute pace, that's an arm-wrenching 1,440 casts per day if there were no downtime. At $4,000+ per week, the angler is reluctant to sit at bankside periodically to observe the flow of the river current, no matter how restful or philosophical it may seem. Some anglers share a rod with a friend, which saves casting stamina and reduces the weekly cost per individual by about 40 percent. This allows each person six hours of precious fishing time each day, which many feel is just a little short, but is not as tiresome or expensive as the 12-hour gig. Decisions. Decisions. Decisions.

THE NUMBERS GAME

How large are the salmon? In 1976, Laxa i Kjos produced 2,376 salmon, of which 2,352 were weighed and accurately recorded. Approximately 89 percent of the catch weighed under 10 pounds. The breakdown of salmon of over ten pounds was as follows:

Weight of salmon (pounds)	10	11	12	13	14	15	16	17	18
No. of salmon	96	40	56	21	24	10	4	2	2

The average fish taken in 1976 was 6.3 pounds, but this has steadily increased through selective stocking programs and in 1984 the average Kjos salmon weighed almost eight pounds. Clearly, relatively light tackle can be used here in order to maximize sport.

What's the average number of salmon taken per fisherman per day (rod/day) throughout the 90-day season? Naturally, a lot of salmon are lost during the process of the fight, and often a salmon gains its freedom just as it was about to be landed. But in terms of fish actually landed, here's an accurate picture of Laxa i Kjos season by season:

Year	Total Salmon for Season	Average Salmon per Angler/Day	Year	Total Salmon for Season	Average Salmon per Angler/Day
1972	2,156	2.54	1979	1,633	1.85
1973	2,082	2.32	1980	1,162	1.30
1974	1,463	1.62	1981	1,550	2.20
1975	2,185	2.61	1982	1,159	1.37
1976	2,376	2.73	1983	1,995	2.36
1977	1,940	2.21	1984	1,734	2.05
1978	1,784	2.02			

From the above figures, one easily ascertains that Laxa i Kjos was on a downswing from 1979 until 1983. Actually Kjos fared out rather well in comparison to most Icelandic rivers where catches dropped even more dramatically. Don't think that river owners weren't worried! A ten-rod river may gross over $500,000 a year.

What caused the downtrend of the early '80s? Some years produce poor fishing because of unfavorable weather conditions: temperatures may be too hot or too cold, or waters too high or too low. But many visiting anglers and some Icelandic fishermen are pointing the finger to the Faroe Islands and the increased commercial fishing activity. The islands are north of Iceland, and it has been discovered that the Icelandic salmon migrate to this area rather than to Greenland (as is the case of many North American salmon). Whether the downtrend was caused by cyclic conditions or the Faroese commercial fishing is debatable, and we will return to the Faroese controversy later.

BEST TIME?

While the number of fish per angler/day provides a basis for comparison and ascertaining the productivity of a salmon stream, bear in mind that these averages are for the entire 90-day season and take into account the good and poor periods. As an example, 1,561 salmon out of a season's total of 2,376 were landed during the 43-day period from July 7 to August 18, 1976, at Laxa i Kjos. This averages out to a remarkable 3.63 salmon per angler/day. However, the first 27 days of the season produced only 318 salmon, an unimpressive average of only 1.17 salmon per angler/day. Clearly, if one wishes to fish this

Stu Apte insisted that this salmon would fall to a dry fly. After many casts, he succeeded. Later, Stu took an unscheduled bath.

river at its most potent period, he selects the last three weeks of July and the first two weeks of August. While there are variances from year to year, this five-week period basically applies not only for Laxa i Kjos, but also for probably 90 percent of the Icelandic rivers.

Man has always been conscious of the moon and its effect on fishing. Although there is a definite correlation between moon phases and the quality of fishing for some species in some areas, this may not occur in Iceland. For example, three weeks produced salmon catches of 301, 356 and 341 (which translated to a remarkable average of 4.75 salmon per angler/day). The anglers enjoyed superb fishing during a new moon, first quarter and full moon. Some Icelandic guides still insist that a full moon may bring in a fresh run of salmon, but fishing records don't always substantiate this theory.

The criteria for quality fishing primarily involve water levels and water temperatures. When the water level is normal or high, salmon invariably move upstream and are more evenly disbursed throughout the length of the river. Furthermore, when salmon first move into a pool they are much more active, and fishing is nearly always better. Conversely, in low water conditions salmon may remain in the same pools for days; they tend to become lethargic and fishing invariably is slow. Water temperature is equally important. If it registers below mid-40s or higher than 60 degrees, fishing is generally poor.

The ideal conditions, then, would be: water levels somewhat on the high side; temperatures in the 50s; a slight wind to ruffle the surface; sky partly cloudy or overcast; and waters slightly off-colored. Ideal conditions are seldom encountered during a week, so the angler must resort to his bag of tricks, which hopefully is bulging.

OTHER RIVERS, OTHER PLACES

While the description and analysis of the Laxa i Kjos are typical of many blue ribbon salmon rivers, let's look at a few other choice waters:

GRIMSA RIVER: This delightful "10-rod" salmon river (about three hours from Reykjavik) features a modern lodge designed by architect Ernest Schwiebert, a superb salmon fisherman.

The Grimsa flows through the picturesque Borgarfjordur district. The upper river flows gently through meadowlands, but downstream it assumes a more dramatic character with intermittent waterfalls and rapids. The season commences in mid-June and terminates in mid-September. The Grimsa salmon arrive off the coast of Borgarfjordur in early June and swim up the Hvita river a short distance before entering the Grimsa. By the end of June, they are leaping the falls with continuity, and by early July they are well distributed throughout the course of the river. Bright salmon continue to arrive from the sea well into August.

For the most part the Grimsa provides consistent fishing, with action ranging from good to excellent to occasionally spectacular. In the late 1970s, for example, anglers consistently landed over 200 salmon per week during choice periods. While most Grimsa (and Icelandic) salmon range from six to eight pounds, salmon of over 20 pounds are sometimes caught. In

Iceland's landscape: brooding, somewhat mysterious, stark, treeless, pristine waters and unpolluted air. "You can see forever!"

1984, for example, Gardner L. Grant landed a 25-pound salmon which was topped later that season by Nathaniel Reed's 28-pounder.

In the early eighties, Grimsa's productivity dropped considerably in terms of numbers. Happily, 1983 was a good year, and following a so-so 1984, 1985 was an excellent season. "Despite unusual weather conditions and dropping water levels, the Grimsa salmon runs in 1985 were the best we have seen in many years and our five weeks produced 617 salmon in 280 rod-days for an average of over 2.2 salmon per rod per day," Gardner explains.

The Grimsa is a catch-and-release stream, but sufficient take-home fillets or smoked salmon are furnished to guests. One guide is provided for every two anglers. The weekly rate is $5,500, but if a rod is shared the cost totals $6,750 (or $3,375 each).

MIDFJARDARA: In 1970 this river produced less than 700 salmon. Then through careful river planning and fish management, the Midfjardara became the "darling of Icelandic waters," when for three consecutive years starting with 1977, anglers landed well over 2,000 salmon annually. A most remarkable achievement! Since 1980, however, catches have slumped by roughly 50 percent. Reports Bob Buckmaster: "Our nine rods took a total of 114 salmon, which was a little more than 50 percent compared to the previous year for the same week. What was also disconcerting was the fact that the average salmon weighed between five and six pounds and there were probably no more than ten fish caught over 10 pounds (the largest being an 18-pounder). When I was there the previous year, the average salmon was 11 to 12 pounds, and perhaps 30 percent of them weighed over 15 pounds..."

But the Midfjardara had a good season in 1985, with an expected catch of 1,200 salmon. The feeling is definitely optimistic. Writes Gardner: "Siggi Fjeldsted and Bob Kahn... landed 20 salmon in two days...so the Midfjardara is back, and we expect a better year in 1986."

The Midfjardara River is formed by three salmon rivers only 15 miles from its estuary in the Midfjord. Both the Austura (East River) and the Vestura (West River) are lake-fed, crystal-clear streams with many excellent pools. The central stream, the Nupsa, is a spate river which carries salmon over some 15 miles of its length. The Midfjardara River System provides about 80 pools and runs of varied character. There are 36 miles of productive water readily accessible by car and another 11 miles that can be reached by four-wheel drive vehicles or on foot.

Many experienced anglers believe the Midfjardara to be among the most beautiful and exciting salmon rivers in Iceland. The East River Canyon has no counterpart in Iceland in rugged beauty and it produces a unique, tough and strong breed of salmon, in perfect harmony to the canyon's brawling falls and rapids which these fish must ascend.

An analysis of the fishing records since 1973 shows that the peak weeks are those that fall between July 7 and the middle of August. Salmon average over ten pounds, larger than on most Icelandic rivers.

The Midfjardara has an excellent fishing lodge with a new wing completed only a few years ago. There is a sauna, ten spacious double rooms, each with private bathroom, and ample space in the lounge and dining room. Meals of outstanding quality are served at the lodge before and after each of the two daily fishing sessions.

The weekly rate is $5,500 per person for a full rod or $3,375 on a rod-sharing basis.

LAXA i ADALDAL: This large river in the northern part of Iceland, near Husavik, is the one salmon stream that is distinctly different from most Icelandic rivers in that the river is considerably wider and the average salmon is larger. In 1980, as an example, the average fish weighed 12.4 pounds, and in 1984 it was 11.2. In the mid-seventies, 75 percent of the landed species were over 10 pounds, and 40 percent of these fish were over 15 pounds. Unquestionably, this is the river for big Icelandic salmon; on the flip side, one doesn't get as much action in terms of numbers as on the other rivers. Mike Fitzgerald, of Frontiers, who knows the Adaldal on a very intimate basis, puts it best: "Reasonable expectation in a 'normal' year is about one to two fish per rod per day. Average weight over the past decade varies between 12 and 14 pounds. The best week

"You cast to your left, they jump to your right. You cast to your right, they jump to your left. Good grief!" Frustrating, but fun.

on the Laxa recently was in 1980 when Eddie Robson's party averaged three fish per day during the second week of July. The best week in 1984 yielded 40 fish to seven rods, with as many hooked and lost. The best week in the last decade was the first week of August 1974, when 123 fish were landed by seven rods. A 'poor' week might be 15 to 20 salmon but this is unusual... the largest salmon in the past decade was 36 pounds in 1974.

"The Laxa is a river where the quality of fish and quality of the fishing must be viewed as more important than the sheer number of fish killed. This is the river for you if you'd rather catch one wild, slashing 18-pounder, fishing a floating line, than three or four grilse."

Returning from his 1982 trip, Dr. Arne Youngberg was enthusiastic: "I arrived there on August 7 and the weather was sunny and in the 70s. Our ghillie (guide) said the fishing was worse than in the previous two years. What a way to start a trip. The day after we got there a north wind was blowing, there was rain and snow on the mountains. The temperature dipped to 40 degrees in the valley, but the change of weather picked up the fishing. Three rods in five days landed 20 salmon that averaged 12 pounds; the three largest were 22, 18 and 17 pounds. For us it was excellent fishing, after a poor start, and again this points up that weather controls much of fishing success..."

The Adaldal Lodge, Veidiheimilid Arnesi, accommodates seven rods with superb comfort and provides a competent guiding staff. The weekly rate during prime time is $4,600 per full rod or $2,925 per person sharing.

LAXA a ASUM: The most potent Icelandic salmon river is Laxa a Asum, which allows only two rods. In an eight-year period more than 10,000 salmon were landed, which averages out to 1,250 fish per season or a whopping seven salmon per rod per day. Bear in mind that these numbers are for the full 90-day season which includes some poor weeks at the beginning and at the end. The seven fish per rod/day average is about three times higher than most blue ribbon waters. Clearly this appears to be the place to go, but the chances of getting a reservation are close to nil despite the $800 to $900 daily tab which does not include accommodations, meals, etc. One American angler, who had the privilege (and finances) to fish the Asum for a couple of days remarked: "At first I though I was in heaven, but after a dozen landed salmon I felt that the challenge, which is a very significant part of Atlantic salmon fishing, simply wasn't there. I'm glad I did it once, however..."

LANGA RIVER: The Langa is located in Borgarfjordur on the southwest coast of Iceland, which is about a two-hour drive from Reykjavik. This river is about 25 miles long and the ten rods allowed are fished on three beats. There's a dam on the Langa so the water level can be controlled throughout the season. The average Langa salmon is 5.6 pounds. The most productive season was in 1978 when 2,405 salmon where landed, whereas its worst year was in 1984 when the total catch dropped to 610 fish. However, the Langa rebounded very well in 1985, which yielded 1,182 salmon during the 90-day period (852 of these were caught in Beat No. 1).

Anglers are accommodated at a riverside camp that offers six twin rooms, dining room and kitchen. Rates are on a sliding scale ranging from $350 to $650 per day, depending on the season.

NORDURA RIVER: The Nordura is considered one of Iceland's most beautiful streams and certainly is one of the most productive. During the early '80s, when so many of Iceland's salmon rivers yielded poor results, the Nordura delivered well over 1,000 salmon per season (except for 1984). In 1985 a respectable 1,120 salmon were landed by the 16 rods allowed. The average salmon in '84 weighed 7.2 pounds. It's not as easy to wade as some of the other streams in the southwest, but most anglers who are in fair physical shape should have little trouble. The lodge showed some wear when I fished from it years ago, but I understand that it has been completely renovated. The daily rate is about $630 per day for a full rod, accommodations, meals and two anglers sharing a guide.

THE FAROESE CONTROVERSY

The accompanying chart lists the number of salmon taken by rod and reel since 1969, throughout Iceland.

No. of Rod-caught Salmon in Iceland Since 1969

1969–21,724	'75–45,882	'81–27,777
'70–33,583	'76–39,249	'82–24,634
'71–40,623	'77–41,302	'83–29,956
'72–45,351	'78–52,679	'84–23,737
'73–43,667	'79–43,955	
'74–34,107	'80–30,007	

You will note that starting in 1980 there was a significant drop in catches. In 1975, seven rivers yielded 2,000 or more salmon each. In 1978 two rivers (Adaldal and Thverra) each produced over 3,000 salmon! But since 1981 there wasn't a single river that came close to producing 2,000 salmon. What caused this?

The strong suspicion, as indicated earlier in this chapter, is that the increased commercial fishing by the Faroese may have caused this drop in salmon catches. The escalation in commercial fishing started in the late seventies, and during 1981, 1,025 metric tons of salmon were long lined. This comes to roughly 2 1/4 million pounds of salmon. Since the average weight is about 10 pounds, according to records, approximately 225,000 salmon were taken by the commercial fishermen.

In 1982 the quota was reduced to 750 metric tons, and a further cutback was scheduled for 1983 to 650 metric tons. This still means that approximately 125,000 salmon will not return to their native streams. Although the evidence seems to indicate strongly that the Faroese commercial fishing may be responsible for the downtrend of salmon sport fishing in Iceland, William S. Brewster, in an objective article, "Are the Faroese Ruining Salmon Fishing?" (*The Atlantic Salmon Journal*, September 1982), cautions that more facts are required. He is on the management committee of the Atlantic Salmon Federation and, in March 1982, he and others visited the Faroe Islands. They reported that the Faroese were understanding and sympathetic to the problem and may be willing to cooperate.

If the Faroese are directly responsible for Iceland's reduced salmon fishing, then cutting back their quotas should ultimately produce a positive effect on sport fishing, and it appears that it has.

Some Icelandic salmon experts point to the increased commercial fishing of the capelin for the reduction of salmon fishing. The capelin is a sardine-sized fish that is a prime food source for the salmon at sea. The Icelandic commercial fleets took approximately 900,000 metric tons of capelin in 1979, which was processed into fish meal and exported to Africa. However, in 1982 Iceland's Minister of Fisheries halted all capelin fishing, and the stocks of this important salmon food have been replenished.

Sport fishing for salmon is one of Iceland's most important economic resources, so it's understandable that the Icelanders are doing everything possible to improve it. Fish ladders and even pools have been constructed on many rivers, but the most significant advances are in the stocking programs and the extensive research studies conducted on a continuing basis.

Most Icelandic salmon are small—under ten pounds. But once in a while a big salmon will inhale your fly and then... Watch out!

Earlier I cited the remarkable transformation of Midfjardara from a mediocre salmon river (less than 700 fish per year) into a "blue ribbon" stream with a yield of over 2,500 salmon in 1977. But the numbers game is only one criterion for determining fishing quality; the average size of salmon is also important. Through proper fish management and selective breeding some rivers indicate an increase of almost 25 percent in about seven years.

So the future of Icelandic salmon fishing is optimistic; if it is not shining brightly, it is at least sparkling with hope.

PSYCHING UP

I mentioned previously that if one were to make two casts per minute, one could conceivably make 1,440 casts per day or roughly 10,000 a week. Assuming an angler lands two fish per day (14 salmon per week) and loses an equal number, he has cast 714 times per landed fish or 357 casts per hooked fish. That's on a good week! This is hardly fast paced fishing. (Then again, no one said that Atlantic salmon fishing was easy.) But if landing numerous fish is one's ultimate goal, the angler who ventures on an Icelandic stream would do well to come armed not only with the correct tackle but also with the right attitude.

Few anglers can fish with total intensity for an entire week, thinking out each cast, making every presentation as carefully as possible, drifting and retrieving a fly seductively in productive water, and, of course, picking up on every take or rise. These skills are especially important when fishing is slow. For example, 1980 was a particularly poor year even on such celebrated rivers as the Midfjardara. While many anglers were crying the blues, Ron Weber (of Normark tackle fame) landed 40 salmon during his week on Midfjardara. "It was one of the most fantastic fishing accomplishments I have ever witnessed. Ron takes his fishing very seriously, and he is one of the most skilled salmon anglers that I have ever observed," according to Joe Hubert, who has watched many anglers in action because he spends at least a month each year fishing Iceland's better waters. "It's easy to become discouraged if, upon arrival to a river, the guide informs you that fishing has been poor. On the other hand, I'm sure that Ron regarded this as a challenge. He is skilled, yes, but he also understands that you don't catch salmon from the porch of a lodge. He knows that fishing hard and intelligently can often overcome poor fishing conditions."

Similarly, a number of years ago, Sy Rosenthal encountered particularly poor fishing on Laxa i Kjos. Toward the end of the week, most anglers were so discouraged that they didn't fish. Sy fished with intensity, and on one day he landed seven fine salmon, including several on dry flies. Admittedly, sometimes fishing may be so slow that no matter what an angler does, or how hard he fishes, he may still come out of the stream without any action, but the old cliche, "you gotta have your bait in the water to catch 'em," cannot be denied.

SALMON TACKLE

If it's true that it takes over 350 casts to hook a salmon, it becomes imperative that one has the right tackle, but it's just as important that his gear must be in perfect shape during the entire fishing trip. Baseball great, Ted Williams, one of the most fanatic and skillful salmon fishermen of all times, fastidiously checks his leader and especially the tippet every 40 or 50 casts! "You're kidding yourself if you think that after making a hundred casts your leader is as good as it was on the first cast," Ted claims, and he particularly inspects his tackle when approaching a good pool where big salmon may be holding.

While Iceland is treeless, so you don't have worry about sinking a fly on a branch, there are stones, rocks, boulders and high banks. If your back cast drops a little and flicks the fly against a rock, there is a good chance that the hook will be broken. It happens all the time: an angler misses two or three salmon in a row and, can't understand why until he finally checks his fly and notices that the hook point is broken off. Inspect your fly often, especially if a wind may have blown your back cast against a high bank or boulder.

Knots between backing and line (as well as on leaders) must also be checked, and if a hooked salmon has run through a rock-strewn course, make sure that your backing is not chafed. Above all, sharpen your hooks periodically; it usually means the difference between hooking a salmon solidly or losing him.

FLY RODS

The all-round fly rod for Iceland would be an 8 1/2- or 9-footer that takes a No. 8 fly line. However, the visiting angler is well advised to include a lighter rod such a No. 6 for those calm days on smaller pools and a heavier No. 10 for very windy conditions. Because of their lightness, graphite rods are preferable to glass. The weight difference may seem insignificant but remember, you could make a maximum of 10,000 presentations during a week. Given a half-ounce difference between graphite and glass rods, and assuming that an angler makes two false casts per presentation, this theoretically amounts to pushing an additional 900 pounds during the week. Who needs it?

FLY REELS

The criteria for a salmon fly reel are: (1) enough capacity to comfortably accommodate your fly line plus a minimum of 150 yards of 20-pound Dacron backing; (2) a very smooth drag; and, (3) availability of extra spools. (Tuck a loaded extra spool in your jacket. If something happens to the fly line or backing, it's an easy matter of changing spools quickly.)

FLY LINES AND LEADERS

Either double taper or weight-forward floating lines can be used on Icelandic streams, and the preference is for the weight-

Nowhere else can a man better reflect on life than when he is alone on a stream. But, warns the author, pay attention to your fishing!

forward types. Sometimes one needs a sink-tip line but only occasionally a sinking line. The veteran angler takes along all three—floating, sink-tip, and sinking—with him. And extras of each.

Leaders can taper from .023 down to 10-pound tippets. Nine footers are usually adequate, but of course one carries along some tippet material to lengthen or lighten the leader if conditions warrant (bright sun, clear, low waters).

FLY PATTERNS

Both double- and single-hook flies are used in Iceland. The doubles are recommended for heavier or deeper waters as they sink faster and ride better. Singles are better for low, clear waters since you want the fly to enter the water as unobtrusively as possible. The opinion is divided as to which type has better hooking qualities.

The most popular hook size in Iceland is No. 6, but there is often a need for smaller flies (No. 8 and 10), and in deeper waters hooks as large as No. 2 may be used.

Here are the ten most popular patterns for Icelandic salmon:

Green Highlander	Silver Rat
Hairy Mary	Sheep Series
Blue Charm	Night Hawk
Black Doctor	Crossfield
Thunder and Lighting	Sweep

Additionally, tube flies (black or black and yellow) have been effective although many anglers prefer not to use them. Although at one time most guides believed that dry flies were ineffective, if not a total waste of time, a number of anglers have had good success at times using dry fly patterns such as the White Wulff, Bombers and the Irresistible. There are several fly stores in Reykjavik, and some of the lodges carry small supplies, but by all means bring some patterns in various sizes with you.

There is a new fly called The Sheep Series, developed by Joseph Hubert, that is delivering sensational catches not only in Iceland, but in Norway as well. It has produced outstanding catches when other patterns have failed miserably.

On many streams one can get by with hip boots, but it's best to take along waders, and they should be felt-soled.

Tackle Disinfection: The government of Iceland, fearful that a salmon disease known as U.D.N., or "swirling disease," could possibly spread to its waters from other countries via tackle, boots or other equipment, insists that all gear must be disinfected. To meet these requirements all tackle, including flies, lines, etc., must be immersed in a 4 percent solution of formaldehyde for at least ten minutes. Most veterinarians can do this easily and can provide the necessary certificate or letter indicating that the gear has been treated. It's best that all tackle is sealed in plastic bags and that several copies of the certificate are taken along. If tackle is brand new disinfection is not needed, but a sales slip indicating that it was recently purchased is required. If these procedures are not followed in advance, the gear will be treated at Keflavik Airport, which, among other things, is time-consuming.

WEATHER

Iceland's weather is highly unstable even during the summer season. It can be hot one day, chilly the next, bright or overcast, dry or wet. The thermometer can quickly plummet 20 or 30 degrees (July and August temperatures average 57 degrees). Obviously, warm clothes must be taken along (insulated underwear, heavy sweaters, wool shirts and certainly a rain jacket with hood). On the other hand, Icelandic winters on the west coast are relatively mild and New York, for example, experiences colder weather.

ICELAND, THE COUNTRY

Iceland is almost 40,000 square miles and is inhabited by 225,000 people. Since more than a third of its population lives in Reykjavik, this island is among the most sparsely populated countries in the world.

The moment of truth! The salmon is now tired, exhausted. Mark Sosin's pulse quickens as he is about to tail this salmon.

A first-time visitor to Iceland is initially surprised by the absence of ice, and if he were then to visit Greenland, he would be shocked that this island is not very green at all and is, in fact, quite icy. Whoever was responsible for naming these islands must have been totally confused.

Another shocker is that there are no trees in Iceland. But don't get the idea that it's a barren wasteland. It's a land of mountains and fjords, winding rivers and waterfalls, sculptured lava and sprouting geysers, extensive green valleys and high plateaus, and on a clear day one can see forever, for even Reykjavik is a smokeless city. Its buildings and homes are heated by natural hot springs. Iceland's land, air and waters are virtually free of pollution.

Where to stay in Reykjavik: Keflavik is Iceland's international airport and is located about 32 miles from Reykjavik. Anglers spend at least one night in Reykjavik, and fortunately there are a number of excellent hotels available that include Esja, Loftleider and Saga at the top of the list. Smaller and less expensive are the Borg and the Holt.

Where to dine in Reykjavik: The Naust is the best-known restaurant and features a nautical motif. The Arnarholl is centrally located and specializes in seafood and lamb dishes. The Saga Grill House and Loftleider emphasize smorgasbord. Iceland's cuisine is a blend of Scandinavian and Continental with meals on the expensive side. Note: A tie and jacket are recommended for dining in Reykjavik.

What to Buy: Icelandic sweaters are probably the most popular gift items followed by sheepskin rugs, ceramic vases and silverwork.

Enter Requirements: A valid passport is all that's required from U.S. citizens. One bottle of liquor and one bottle of wine may be brought into the country duty-free. (Additional alcoholic supplies may be purchased from licensed government liquor shops).

Currency: The Icelandic currency is known as the Krona. At press time there are 31 Icelandic krona to the dollar. It is not necessary to exchange currency in advance.

GUIDE TO FLY PATTERN SELECTION

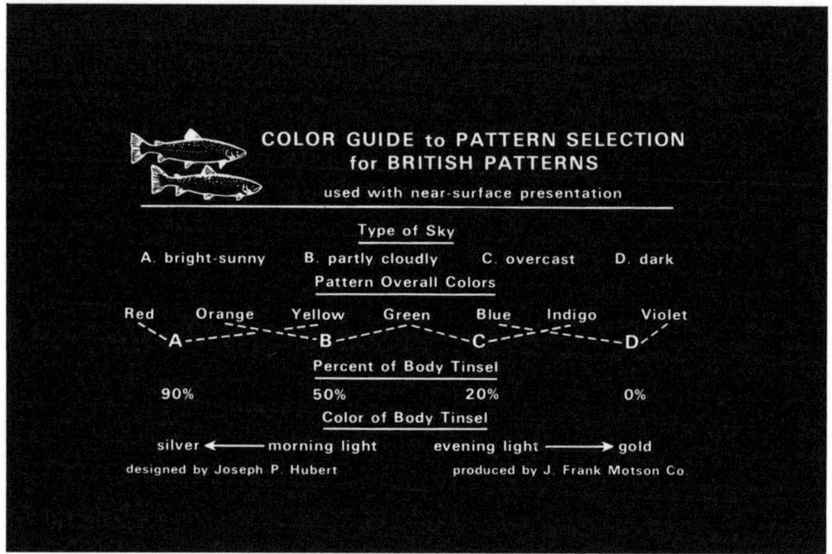

We're sure that Joe Hubert has fished Iceland as much as any visiting angler in recent times. He is totally dedicated to the unending study of the Atlantic salmon and is the author of *Salmon... Salmon* —a limited edition (100 copies), which at $2,000 may be the most expensive fishing book ever produced.

Joe has invested countless hours in researching the effectiveness of various colors of British fly patterns in relation to available day light or "type of sky" and is convinced that the above chart works 80 percent of the time.

AND FINALLY... Here are the reasons why an angler should consider fishing Iceland (and some of the disadvantages, too):

The advantages of Icelandic salmon fishing include:

- Superb river management. Iceland is constantly engaged in progressive research programs and stream improvement.

- Most rivers are easy to fish. There are no trees to hamper back casts. Most waters are relatively easy to wade.

- Icelandic salmon can be taken on small flies (No. 6). Many European waters require the use of huge flies (4/0 and sometimes larger). The use of small flies means that an angler can use relatively light single-handed fly rods, as opposed to 14-foot double-handed heavy fly rods sometimes used elsewhere.

▪ The waters are divided into beats and river-owners wisely limit the number of rods, giving everyone privacy and choice waters.

▪ Iceland is very appealing. There is virtually no pollution. English is frequently spoken and Icelanders are very friendly.

The disadvantages of Icelandic salmon fishing include:

▪ Rivers are extremely expensive. Count on paying $3,000 to over $5,500 per week (plus airfare, and other incidentals).

▪ It's difficult to obtain reservations on most of the better rivers even if one books well in advance.

▪ There is concern about the drop of fishing results in the early '80s, but 1985 and 1986 rebounded nicely.

Norway

Land of Giant Salmon, Land of Angling Tradition

The Alta River—often rewarding, sometimes frustrating—continues to reign as Europe's greatest river for giant Atlantic salmon, and about the Gaula... a charming but temperamental river. Norway's salmon fishing has been damaged, because of drift-netting, but this will apparently be halted. Look for Norway to bounce back!

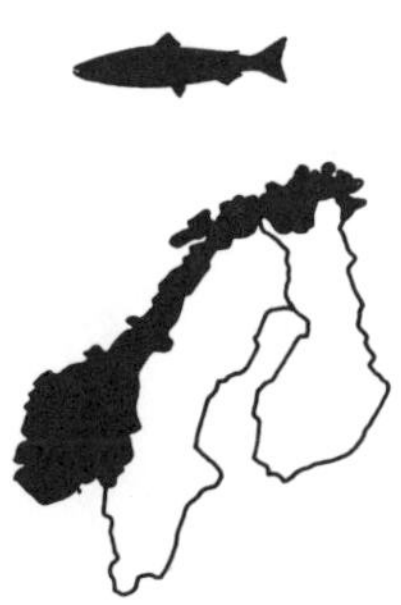

Master angler/writer Lefty Kreh landed this magnificent Atlantic salmon from Norway's Alta.

Chapter 17

NORWAY

ACTUALLY there was no way I could afford to fish Norway's Alta River. I was developing the fishing division for another travel agency, and, at the time, I was barely eeking out a living. The Alta was one of the most expensive fishing trips offered in those days: $3,500 per person, plus air transportation, hotel, tips and other expenses. We were talking $5,000! I heard about the Alta from Charles Ritz, who had painted glowing images of big Atlantic salmon, giant salmon that would rise frequently to the fly. He described the beauty and the potential of the Alta as only Charlie could.

So when the Higgins brothers—Bardon, Bob and Ray—booked a trip to the Alta and asked me to go along, I was more than tempted. The demand for Alta reservations far exceeded the number of rods allocated for each beat, so there was no opportunity to ask for the "ol' travel agent's discount."

But I found out that for a mere $1,000, I could stay at the Alta as a nonfishing companion. I grabbed the opportunity. Although I wouldn't be allowed to fish, just seeing the Alta, being there, would be a privilege. That's the kind of a brainwashing job Monsieur Ritz did on me.

On the first night, just before the Higgins' fishing time was to begin, we all wandered to a pool where we watched Mead Johnson finish up his week. Mead hooked a salmon, fought it brilliantly, captured it, released it. It was a 25-pounder.

I could feel the excitement build within me. It's great to watch another angler land a fish—no doubt about it—but it's greater if you are doing the reeling, the fighting, the releasing.

A successful capture! Norway's rivers yield more 'adult' salmon than grilse.

On the flight to Norway, I had been reading Hemingway's stuff about living life to its fullest, no matter what the cost. I convinced the powers of the Alta Lodge to sell me one day's fishing. After all, it was only an additional $500! How could I resist?

No place in the world is more steeped in tradition than the Alta. The English aristocracy began to fish it in the late 1800s, and established all the ground rules which, to date, are followed. Religiously.

One of the weird aspects of the Alta that the English discovered is that salmon "feed" better at night. So you sleep during the day, and you fish at night. Breakfast is served at 6 P.M., lunch at midnight and supper at about 5 or 6 A.M. Talk about confusing your biological clock. Thankfully, the midnight sun furnishes sufficient light for all the angling essentials. You may not be able to read the classified ads at midnight (who would want to), but there is plenty of light to change flies and cast to the right spots.

Fishing is from long river boats, never by wading, with two ghillies (guides) at the oars, fore and aft. The Alta is a swift, sometimes angry river; hence, two oarsmen are required to hold the boat at a pool so that the "sport," who is standing in the center, can cover the water.

We learned that fishing on the Alta had been poor, and that some of the previous anglers even left at midweek, as they weren't going to waste their time. For them, there would be other years. I waited half a lifetime for the opportunity to fish the famous Alta, only to discover I had picked a lousy year. Good grief!

The "unfortunate" episode of that night is that I landed one grilse and an adult salmon that weighed 18 pounds. It was unfortunate because I became hooked on the Alta salmon fishing. Naturally, I was going to fish the next night. And the night after that. And the entire week. Hang the cost! Live life to its fullest!

The Higgins fared much better that first night. They each caught a salmon in the low twenties, and Ray hooked but lost a particularly big fish. Fishing may have been considered lousy, but this was our first taste of the Alta; no one in our group complained.

Even if fishing is poor, Norway's breathtaking, scenic backdrop and pristine waters are worth the high price of admission.

I must tell you about those midnight lunches. First of all, we each had our own beats so that we were separated. Second, our Norwegian guides spoke no English, so any communication was done with Ole Mosessen, the camp manager, either prior to or after the fishing night.

Every midnight lunch was the same. Two hotdogs, a can of sardines and one apple. At exactly midnight, the guides would row to a shorelunch spot, prepare a fire and, hand you a couple of sticks for the weenie roast. Having fished in Canada dozens of times, I'm a shorelunch person. I look forward to them. But not on the Alta.

Visualize this: You are sitting on a rock, holding a stick with a hotdog over the campfire. There is a ghillie on each side of you, jabbering in Norwegian. Invariably, one ghillie tells what apparently is a helluva funny Norwegian joke. The other guide breaks out in a crescendo of guffaws and laughter. Both are shaking uproariously, their bellies wiggling, their eyes tearing from laughter, and there you are, poker-faced, sitting with the wiener on a stick. Laughter is quite contagious, so you laugh, and they laugh harder until they realize you couldn't possibly understand the joke, so they stop laughing and look at you strangely. Serious conversation resumes for a while, but minutes later, the second ghillie thinks of a joke, and the whole episode repeats itself. The hour stretches out to an eternity.

One night, it was my turn to fish home beat—right close to the lodge. At midnight, wishing to avoid the shorelunch ritual, I suggested that the guides drop me off at the lodge. I was visualizing laxs, sliced ham, homemade bread and tons of other goodies available at the camp. But no. They couldn't do this. Something about the Duke of Roxborough. For decades, the Duke's family had subleased beats on the Alta and established the ground rules for this river.

The Duke. His name came up each day, every night. The Duke this, the Duke that. He had set the pace, the rules, the guidelines.

After our third night of fishing, we came to the conclusion that two beats were extremely good, and two were apparently void of fish. To our logical minds, we could share the two good beats. Surely there was plenty of water! Furthermore, the two anglers sharing a beat could have lunch together each midnight.

We suggested this to Ole, the manager. No way, he said. The Duke would not approve. Hey, the Duke wouldn't have to know about this; he wasn't on the Alta. We finally convinced Ole to broach the subject to the guides. You wouldn't believe it. Suddenly, eight guides were talking at once. They were furious. As a matter of fact, they threatened to strike and not guide us for the rest of the week.

Only through persistent apologies, via Ole, did the guides finally agree to take us fishing. So for the remainder of our week, we did it their way, the way it was done for decades. And

Everett Kircher (left) and Bardon Higgins admire Everett's huge salmon that tore out of a pool and soared down the rapids.

we had our little individual midnight lunches, with the weenie sticks, our sardines, and our apples for dessert.

I suspected that my two guides thought that it was my idea. For the rest of the trip, they kept the boat a considerable distance from the holding waters while they rowed in placid waters. This required vigorous double haul casts, and pumping a No. 4/0 Green Highlander great distances caused tremendous pain across my arms and back. But at those prices, you forget about the aches. You cast one more time.

It was my turn to fish "Broadway Pool." It was aptly named Broadway Pool by some New Yorkers because this is the only good place where the townspeople can watch the Americans and English fish. Apparently, there's not much happening in the village of Alta because it seems as if dozens, perhaps hundreds, of people came to this observation spot. When my boat turned the bend, we were greeted with some car honking, applause and cheers. The Higgins brothers, who had already experienced "Broadway," told me that good manners dictate that you take off your hat and bow to the audience before beginning to fish these prolific waters.

So I did just that. I couldn't tell from the guides' expression whether the bowing was SOP or whether it was a Higgins put-on. Every time I cast, I would hear the buzz buzz of the Norwegians. With my arms and back still in great pain, there was much teeth-gritting with each cast, but there is also sufficient ham in me, and somehow I unfolded some good, long and very lucky casts. I heard a few oohs and some ahhs from the grandstand.

I hooked a good salmon that tore up and down the pool. There was cheering from the gallery and some critical comments, too. Now my arms felt as though they had been punctured with a dozen novocaine shots; there was almost no feeling. But you reel, parry, fight the fish and finally, a 26-pound Atlantic salmon was landed. Cheers from the audience. Then they got in their cars and left. I felt good about this episode; my arms didn't.

We fished another pool where I tied into a very big salmon—even the ghillies seemed to get excited about this one—but the hook tore loose. Up ahead I noticed a small object, almost metallic, splashing periodically. At first I thought it was a bird or a small fish but concluded it was neither. I was curious. I pointed it out to the ghillies. They observed the same splash, spoke hurriedly to each other, then in unison, they rowed furiously in that direction.

When we finally arrived there, we surprised a young man winding some heavy monofilament around a can. The silver object I had noticed was a fishing spoon. When he spotted us, he hurriedly wound the last few feet of line and ran through the woods. The ghillies apparently cussed him out and threatened his life. You didn't need to understand Norwegian to figure that out!

The man was poaching. He had not noticed our boat downstream and was flinging out the lure with the hope of hooking an Atlantic salmon. Even in those days, a salmon could bring $30 or more.

What was peculiar about the whole thing was that the man from a distance appeared to be black. At camp, Ole explained that some poachers apply lampblack or charcoal on their faces and hands and wear dark clothes so that they can't be spotted easily. It's hard to poach on the Alta because of the rugged terrain and the great distances from the roads, but there are a few places where it can be done. The Norwegians guard heavily against poaching, even using patrols and dogs to discourage these "get-rich-quick" schemers.

For the most part, the Alta has been kind to anglers. Sure, this river can be stingy at times, giving up very few fish during a week of poor weather conditions, but usually it's a very generous river—much more than many other salmon waters.

Salmon fishing tends to be cyclic, but there were a few years when even the most fervent Alta anglers thought that the river was doomed. So far, however, it has always rebounded and 1982 was a vintage year.

Lefty Kreh, one of the world's top all-round fishing experts, fished the Alta for the first time in 1982. Here's what *The PanAngler* reported:

"Our party of seven landed 1,867 pounds of salmon in a week—just short of a ton! Average weight of the fish was very close to 25 pounds. Several fish nearly broke the 40-pound mark, and one night one angler caught eight salmon! Obviously, the Alta is among the greatest salmon waters of the world, true, but it is also one of the most beautiful rivers."—*Lefty Kreh.*

Dividing the weight of the catch by the estimated average weight, it appears that the party landed approximately 70 salmon during the week. This wouldn't be a bad number (averaging 10 per person), even if the fish were grilse, or small salmon. When one considers that most of the fish were in the 20-pound class, he begins to understand how spectacular these results were!

On many Canadian salmon waters, there is one salmon for every 20 grilse. On the Alta, the ratio is reversed and an Alta grilse is seldom caught. The main reason why the Alta fish average 20 pounds is that they spend three or more winters at sea (as opposed to one winter for grilse) before returning to the river, and it is in the ocean, where there's an abundance of food, that the salmon add weight quickly.

There are some disadvantages to the Alta. While the extremely high rate (probably upwards of $6,000 today) may be a deterrent for most of us, the cost is really meaningless because the waters are booked so far in advance, and the demand is so tremendous, that a salmon angler has virtually no chance of getting a beat on prime time, which is the month of July.

If there is a fishing disadvantage, it might be that the Alta salmon have a penchant for large flies, 2/0 to 5/0. At least this was our experience. This means using longer, heavier (including two-handed) rods and heavier lines.

"I fished the Alta a couple of times and enjoyed every minute of it, but frankly I'm too old to cast the heavy fly rods, so I prefer to fish the smaller salmon of Iceland using light, almost trout tackle," one angler explains and his point is well taken. He added: "The big Norwegian salmon do not jump often. I caught eight or nine salmon and none cleared the water. To me, salmon fishing is hooking the fish and then watching it jump clean out of the water. But this may be 'sour grapes' to some extent because I'm not able to fish the Alta. And you can't refute the thrill of seeing 20 pounds of fresh silver at the end of the leader, even if it doesn't jump."

There's always been talk of dams for hydroelectric power, but at last word we understand that the Alta is still fishing well. (It's very difficult getting information from the people who control the fishing rights of the Alta.)

The Alta continues to be productive, but the same can't be said for dozens of other Norwegian rivers that have felt the onslaught of drift netting by the Norwegians themselves. The Aroy, one of Norway's famous rivers, produced only two dozen salmon in 1985. The Laerdal, Driva and so many other "storied" rivers have had poor fishing, because there is little or no chance for the salmon to avoid the drift nets and enter the rivers. Happily, in 1986 legislation was passed that will greatly reduce and, hopefully, eliminate drift netting. The results of this action will improve salmon fishing each year, and by 1990 many of the Norwegian rivers will produce tremendous fishing.

There's at least one bright spot in the dim future of the Norwegian salmon fishing. The Gaula River continues to produce fairly good salmon fishing, albeit more quality than quantity.

The Malangfoss pool—the scene of thousands of angling battles with giant Atlantic salmon—is no longer productive.

During the last few years, fishing was relatively poor in comparison to the early '80s. Nonetheless, the Gaula must be ranked among Norway's better rivers.

I haven't fished the Gaula, but the well-traveled Nathaniel Reed has and was kind enough to share his notes from the 1984 trip. Here is his report:

REED'S GAULA DIARY

I organized a party to fish the Gaula July 15-21 with Ted Dalenson and Johan Abelson, via Thomas and Thomas. Our party consisted of Mr. and Mrs. Richard Leach, Mr. and Mrs. Samuel Davis, Jr., Mr. and Mrs. Amos Eno, Jr., Adrian Reed (my son) and myself.

Ted and Johan are two young (late 20s) Swedes who are keen and expert fishermen. Their families have leased various pools on the Gaula for many years. Ted and Johan also operate a salmon fishing school, principally for young nordic anglers. In addition, they offer five to 10 rods to visiting anglers—an extraordinary opportunity to fish one of the most productive salmon rivers in the world.

The fishing starts on June 1 and ends on August 31. The Gaula is in flood in May and June from snow melt in its vast watershed. The salmon enter in late May. The guides figure the kelt death as 90 percent due to ice conditions. Early-season salmon cannot run a major waterfall until late June, which makes several downstream pools particularly effective by either casting or harling (a form of trolling) from boats. The June run is noted for very large salmon with an astonishing average weight in the mid-20s. As soon as river conditions permit, this June salmon run can negotiate the falls and heads upstream. These salmon are followed by successive runs in July and August. (There are late runs in September that are not fished.)

The average weight of incoming salmon declines somewhat, but the river remains evenly stocked, from grilse to very large freshrun fish, all of which supplement the older, earlier runners.

THE WATERS: The Gaula is certainly a beautiful salmon river and has a number of excellent pools and runs.

Froset, the home pool, is one of the most majestic salmon pools in the world. It probably covers 10 acres and is formed by the main river swirling against a rock bank and meeting the River Sokna. The Sokna has a fine run of salmon up to 30 pounds. The combination of these two rivers forms a great complicated pool. While we were in camp, the pool fished poorly, giving up but one 22-pound salmon.

The pool normally accounts for 50 percent of the salmon caught on the entire beat. It is an expensive rental for the Swedes and is a very important part of any fishing week.

Although we saw salmon rolling in the pool, and there were always salmon waiting to go up the Sokna, for whatever reasons, we failed to raise fish. I personally believe that the lip, one of the best long slick holding areas I have ever fished, has filled in. If ice will again dig it out, the Froset should regain its prominence.

Sverre is the island pool that starts with a series of potholes then streams out into a superb run, 300 to 400 yards long.

Road Pool is a 200-yard stream of water, every foot a perfect salmon run.

Satte, or the farm pool, was my favorite beat; 300 yards long with a good, easy flow of water. Salmon could hold in every foot of it. Casting to the opposite green bank produced superb drifts. Every cast scared you out of your boots.

Bridge Pool is a beautiful curving run, easily waded and fished. Standing on the bridge, our guides saw a salmon that they estimated to weigh between 45 and 55 pounds.

Gravel Pit is a very strong stream that flows into a very deep long hole. If the salmon are lying in the stream, they will take a fly. If they are lying in the slow deep water, they are very hard to move. This type of pool will be very familiar to Grand Cascapedia fishermen, as it resembles many of her pools.

Top Pool is a good short run that is easily fished and held fish every day.

The Swedes also control a large stretch of the Budal, a tributary of the Gaula. I do not recommend fishing the Budal unless you are in perfect physical condition. The river lies at the bottom of a sheer steep slope that drops probably 400 feet straight down. Although a copy of a North Carolina mountain river, it supports a run of very large salmon noted for their pale, almost ghostly-white coloration. There is a mounted 49 1/2-pound salmon at the hotel that was killed in this small rocky stream. The Budal is in a rain forest and, while stunningly beautiful, the climb down and then up could kill you.

The Gaula River fishes about 50 miles of water, surrendering 4,000 to 6,000 salmon annually. The river dropped three feet during our week and can go up five feet from a heavy rain. The pools are approximately 30 miles from the sea.

FISHING RESULTS

Sunday, July 15, 1984: After a drive through a lovely green valley countryside, we off-loaded at the Soren. Following a short briefing from Ted, we ate dinner, met our guides and commenced fishing at 7:00 P.M.

I fished the lower right beat of the Froset, a truly great 400-yard stretch. Salmon and fresh sea trout broke water. Changed to a 16-foot double-handed Sage due to a high, brushy bank behind me. Consistently cast 100 to 120 feet of line; fly landed like a feather. No double hauling, no false casts. Must reconsider my position on double-handed rods.

The heaviest concentration of parr I have seen in years fed in the back currents. (The river has one of the best reproduction cycles I have ever seen.)

I fished hard, raised two salmon that were running but kept on moving.

Ray Higgins beat this hefty Alta salmon with a Green Highlander fly. "Alta salmon fishing is addictive; I've been back several times."

Monday, July 16: We started fishing at 7:15 A.M. at the Gravel Pit. As I started, the owner-farmer fished the "hole" with a 10-inch spoon. Infuriating.

Moved to the Bridge Pool. Killed a 14-pound bright cock on a No. 2 Green Highlander. He had been hooked previously and had a torn nose. Lost another fish about the same size.

The river was dropping and clearing in the evening. Had one good pull at 10:15 P.M., but it was all too quiet an evening. Dick Leach lost a fine 25-pound salmon after a bitter battle. Too bad. It was to be his birthday fish. That was the only salmon raised during the evening. Amos moved to a double-handed rod and within an hour, he was casting beautifully.

Tuesday, July 17: Started at 7:30 A.M. Fished Sverre, a great pool! At 8:15 A.M., I rose and lost a fine salmon that took off far across the strong current.

Cool, misty light rain. At 9:00 A.M. killed an 18-pound hen on a Green Highlander No. 4. At 10:15 A.M. I killed an eight-pound cock on the same fly. A number of salmon are running—maybe they will settle.

At noon I looked for Adrian. Found him fighting a 14-pound bright cock on Road Pool. He hand-tailed it. Well done, Adrian!

Fished at Froset at 7:30 P.M. I had one good strong pull at the head of pool. In spite of a large school of mid-teen-weight salmon that jumped and ran the pool, I couldn't budge them. Sam Davis killed two small salmon.

Wednesday, July 18: Fished Froset. Very quiet. Went down the Valley of the Budal. Saw several of the pale ghosts, but I am too old and fragile for that experience.

Amos lost a big salmon—over 30 pounds, to a broken leader.

Back at 7:30 P.M. Big run moving through—19 salmon killed on spoons in one downstream public pool. 14 salmon killed in a famous settling pool in the middle of our beat. Ted has this pool leased for 1985.

Fished hard until 12:30 P.M.—not a touch.

Thursday, July 19: Light rain and 10 percent cooler. Fished from 7:30 A.M. to noon. Not a move. Lost another very large salmon in the Gravel Pit on a tube covered with Christmas tinsel.

I joined Dick Leach in the evening as my knee was acting up.

Dick handled the 14-foot Sage elegantly. Lost a fine salmon at the bank that could easily have been netted.

12:20 A.M.—While at the hut having a nightcap—heard a shout from Froset. Amos, in the dusky summer Norwegian night, fought and killed a fine bright 22-pound fish, which won the trip pool. We all head home bleary-eyed but overjoyed over Amos' first salmon.

Friday, July 20: Warm sunshine! I killed an eight- and an 18-pound brace from Bridge Pool—just a fine morning for me. I starred for a Swedish TV crew doing a salmon special. Amos killed a 15-pounder. So ended my week. Adrian and I continued on to Iceland to fish the Grimsa. The rest of the party fished the Driva for a day without success. They reported, though, that the drive, the Norwegian family that hosted them, the meals and the Driva River added up to a superb experience.

REED'S RANDOM OBSERVATIONS

GUIDES: There is a guide assigned to each angler. The men were young, all Swedes except for one Finn. They are expert fishermen, world-class casters, fly tiers and absolute gentlemen.

They are the best instructors I have ever been with. Even the most expert salmon fishermen can learn from these guides, who fish 18 hours a day. They included every personality, joined us at meals and we were one large, merry family.

My guide, Michael, will always be remembered for his favorite admonition: "One more meter of line please!" When you are out 80 feet, that is asking a lot.

NORWEGIAN CUSTOMS: Be prepared for a totally different set of conditions. The farmers earn far more money from their river leases than they do from farming. For over a hundred years, angling clubs, individuals, even the government, have rented water (apart from the private beats we fished). The public beats might have 20 anglers fishing a single pool. The angling clubs often have 10 fishermen in a single pool. Anything goes in the public waters! Plugs, spoons, worms—whatever. The average fisherman could land a marlin on the gear used here.

On the public waters, salmon are pounded night and day. Many anglers sleep in tents and huts on the river banks, fishing 18 to 20 hours per day. They come from all over Scandinavia. Fishing for salmon is a three-month celebration—almost a manhood issue.

One of Norway's unique experiences is that the farmers who rent the private pools retain the right to fish any time. It is one thing to be followed down a pool by a farmer exquisitely casting a 16-foot double-handed fly rod with style and precision. It is quite a shock, though, to have a farmer head into "your" pool with a large spoon or devon. There is *no* poaching. The river is patrolled 24 hours per day.

TECHNIQUE: The Gaula salmon take with a very long, slow move. The guides want no sudden strikes. With the smaller flies, they wanted a 10-inch loop of line (held by your forefinger against the rod) dropped on the take. At a minimum, they wanted the rod tip pulled into the water!

The greased line technique, slow fishing and the "hitch" are all effective, depending on water speed and depth.

TACKLE: At a minimum, you need a nine- to 10 1/2-foot single-handed rod with a fighting butt. My two favorite weapons were a 10 1/2-foot Sage Graphite II and a 9 1/2-foot Thomas Gaspe. Both rods take a 10 line. The guides want a minimum cast of 60 feet. If you can't cast 60 feet effortlessly, you are in trouble. I recommend to all novices or weak casters that they use one of the double-handed 14-foot Sages

The author's first Alta salmon. "I had planned to fish one day—that's all I could afford in those days—but then..."

that the camp offers, as even a beginner will cast 75 to 90 feet the first day. My opinion of double-handed rods soared on this trip.

I used both a sink-tip and floating line daily, sometimes exchanging rods halfway down a pool. Other anglers prefer intermediate lines. You ought to have two complete outfits with extra lines.

I think a Bogdan is incomparable for a big fish reel, but any substantial reel with a good drag and a minimum of 150 yards of 30-pound Dacron is a must.

The salmon are not leader-shy, so eight feet of 12- or 15-pound test seems adequate.

Flies? The river favors green hairwing patterns; the Green Highlander is the top fly. Fly sizes range from twos to eights. They like slim doubles and Druary trebles. The guides like to "shock" staler fish with enormous gaudy tube flies.

WADING: The cobbles are a nice, uniform size. No slime or weed. The water is clear and suprisingly warm (low 60s). Although I fell and cracked my kneecap, the river (during our stay) was wadeable, and you could cross it in many places. The river resembles the Upper Cascapedia or Matapedia.

CLOTHING: The weather is cool, in the mid-60s, and often misty. I wore poly Farmer Johns, James Scott neoprene waders, a cotton turtleneck and a lightweight Shetland every day. You will need a rain jacket with you at all times.

THE HOTEL: The Soren Inn is 90 minutes from the Trondheim airport. From the hotel, the hut ("fishing headquarters") is eight minutes away. Most of your pools are within twenty minutes' drive. Each guide has a car.

We were comfortable, although the rooms are small. They each have a bathroom with shower and cleanliness was excellent.

MEALS: A simple European breakfast, a fantastic buffet at 1:00 P.M., an early sitdown dinner at 6:00 P.M. We enjoyed luncheon best and, at times, chaffed at the slowness of dinner.

FISHING PERIODS: We were up at 5:30 A.M. fished from 6:30 A.M. to 12:30 P.M., slept until 6:00 P.M., and then fished again from 7:00 P.M. to midnight. It was too much. Exhaustion began to set in. The guides were prepared to fish 16 to 18 hours daily.

CRITICISMS: There were no landing nets. We lost a minimum of five salmon due to this oversight. Nets will be carried next year.

We were a minimum of two pools short in 1984 because they counted on the Froset pool, which was poor. They agree that they must add water, and plan to lease additional pools.

RATES: A week's stay at the Gaula is $2,300 per week. Transportation to Trondheim, Norway, personal expenses and tips are, of course, additional.

WIVES: My wife organized a train ride from Oslo to Bergen, then touring. There is also a coastal packet steamer from Bergen to Trondheim. Non-fishing wives are advised that there are many side trips, but it is simple farm country. Please don't expect Paris.

CONCLUSION: Don't go if you "expect" to kill 50 salmon per week. You may kill 50 salmon—you may not. Go with the strong likelihood that you will hook a big salmon, and if the runs come and the salmon settle, you may have superb fishing. We had a wonderful time and I expect to return.—*Nathaniel Reed.*

AND FINALLY... As mentioned, Norwegian fishing has declined considerably, primarily because of the drift netting. One source claims that there are 750 drift nets (as well as unlicensed commercial fishing). He estimates that the combined netting is enough to cover two-thirds of Norway's coast. Obviously, Atlantic salmon have little or no chance to survive unless the drift netting is sharply reduced or eliminated.

The Norwegians have come to understand the importance of their Atlantic salmon fishery, and laws have been passed to reduce drift netting. So Norway's salmon fishing will recover, but look for exorbitant rates once fishing is on the upswing.

Other Places, Other Waters

New, Potent Fishing Places Emerge

Paraguay's new hot spots for dorado; a touch of northern Australia's fishing on Bathurst for barramundi, queenfish, and other exotics; Yugoslavia's Gacka River—Europe's bargain trout fishing; Chile's new fly-out (a la Alaska) fishing resort; British Columbia—where steelhead trout can be fooled with a dry fly.

Pete Barrett, fishing editor of *Field & Stream,* "stuffs" 12 3/4 pounds of Canadian (B.C.) rainbow into a "small" net.

Chapter 18

OTHER PLACES

THE FLY FISHERMAN'S world is certainly not confined to the places or countries covered extensively in the previous chapters. Here are a number of destinations, most of them "new," that certainly deserve the angler's attention.

PARAGUAY

The dorado, according to some well-traveled anglers, may be the world's best freshwater fighting species. It brawls until its last ounce of energy is expended; its spectacular leaps for freedom easily surpass the Atlantic salmon's; it crushes flimsy plastic plugs to bits with one crunch of its powerful jaws. The dorado is a pugnacious character, and I have observed them fighting each other with total disregard for the Queensberry Rules. Most dorado will weigh 10 to 20 pounds, but because of their strength and stamina, and because they are found in strong river currents, they give an angler the impression that he is battling a considerably larger fish.

The dorado is not widely known because its distribution is limited to a few places in South America. Water and weather conditions must be exactly right for a successful trip. Ned Payne, a top cinematographer, has made numerous trips to several South American rivers in an effort to make a dorado film, but in each case water conditions were unfavorable. "I will continue to go to South America as long as I'm physically able to do so...making a great dorado film is an obsession."

Judging from what I've been hearing lately Ned should try Paraguay. I became intrigued by Paraguay's dorado fishing

Earl Stanek's magnificent steelhead taken from British Columbia.

potential after a very short visit to this country in the early '70s. I was limited to only a day of fishing, and although I didn't have any strikes, I watched another angler land a frisky 25-pound dorado. Because of the lack of time, I fished the Paraguay River not far from Asuncion. However, ensuing clients who fished other places in Paraguay enjoyed good to excellent results.

Recently I've been in contact with Jorge Xifra, a young, energetic, successful businessman and a passionate, skilled angler who would like to put his country on the angler's map. He has explored every piece of water that hints of good dorado fishing and has come up with a number of great fishing places.

"The selected area is based on weather and water conditions and on-the-spot fishing reports that we are able to obtain. Most of the time, we get good results," Jorge explains. "We can fish dorado year-round by moving to different locations during the season. If the Parana River is not suitable for fishing, there are a number of options for normal to great dorado fishing.

"When the waters are in flood, dorado generally change their usual feeding position on the rivers; however, the fishing is not as good as when the water level is very low and clear. Surubi ("tiger catfish"), pacu and pirayagua (a species of payara) are also encountered."

Here are some of Jorge's special dorado places and his comments:

VALLEMI-APA RIVER—UPPER PARAGUAY RIVER: Year-round dorado fishing is available here. Two local airlines offer morning and afternoon flights (flying time—1 1/2 hours). Hotel accommodations in Vallemi are good and include air-conditioned rooms. This is jungle fishing, as the Apa River is the northernmost border of Paraguay and Brazil, and temperatures are well over 100 degrees in the summertime. Fishing is fabulous. In my 25 years of dorado fishing, I have never seen anything like this area. You said once that six fish on fly gear in a day could be considered excellent fishing? What about hook-ups with 20 to 30 big dorado?

The fishing at Cachoerinas ("little falls" or "cascades"), on the Apa River, is often superb; there are times when nearly every cast can result in a strike. Usually the line or leader is bro-

The dorado—possibly the most spectacular freshwater leaping fish—is found in numerous Paraguayan waters.

ken by other fish rubbing against it. So it is hard to say what may be the average daily catch in Cachoerinas, since you are playing fish after fish, and the average catch depends on the tackle used and the angler's fish-fighting skills. Action can be continuous under favorable water conditions.

The Apa River is a jungle river. The trip from Vallemi to the falls requires at least a two-hour boat ride. Alligators, wild boar, small deer and many other kinds of wildlife are spotted during the upstream ride to Cachoerinas.

Disadvantages: It's very warm during the summer (November through March), with temperatures soaring in the 100s; however, it is bearable if it is cloudy, as the fishing is via wading. The other disadvantage is that fishing is too easy. The river is overloaded with fish. It is possible to see hundreds and hundreds of orange fins working the rapids. These fins belong to dorado! There are five cascades with six pools along two miles of river, and most of the dorado are found in these pools.

APA RIVER—At Lambonet: If one is fishing this region, one day should be devoted to the Lambonet area of the Paraguay River, where outstanding fishing can be expected. Dorado of 25 pounds or larger are available here. Last year I caught a 49 1/2-pounder. This area is a 1/2-hour boat ride from Vallemi, and the trip can be combined with trips to the Cachoerinas area in the Apa River (described above). Usually a four-day fishing trip to Vallemi is sufficient. There are plenty of fishing waters.

Disadvantages: Communication with the rest of the world is poor, but the National Telephone Company will soon add a microwave system. Bad weather grounds everybody; there is no practical way—except by plane—to travel between Vallemi and Asuncion. So anglers coming from U.S. should allow a two-day cushion in Asuncion for their return trip home.

PARANA RIVER, AYOLAS (Apipe Area and Coratei area): The dorado fishing in the Parana River can be excellent from the Apipe rapids on downstream. Ayolas and its famous places near Coratei probably provide the best fishing on the Parana River. Adequate accommodations with air conditioning are available at Ayolas, but, if it is not too warm, there is also a fish camp by the river. Ayolas is located 200 miles (paved road) south of Asuncion. Coratei is 10 miles by dirt road from Ayolas; 4-WD vehicles are used in case of rain.

PARANA RIVER (Pto. Stroessner City/Foz du Iguazu): Excellent dorado fishing can be combined with night life, including casinos. You can visit the Iguazu Falls and Itaipu Dam (world's largest). Fly fishing in the tributaries is generally good. Excellent accommodations. Fishing season is August to March, which is the same as Ayolas. Peak season is September through November.

There are several other rivers, including Tebicuary, Manduvira and Jejui, where there is dorado fishing year-round; however, accommodations are not as good as in Ayolas, Vallemi or Iguazu.

About our payara: It seems to be a subspecies or different from those caught in Colombia. We call this fish pirayagua in Paraguay, but in Argentina it is known as the chafalote.

Paraguay welcomes tourists and is a very stable, and totally safe, country. Social or political unrest has been nonexistent during the last 30 years, and this is the only South American country that has never had a terrorist action of any kind.

I personally guide all the fishing trips. By using two boats, I can handle up to four anglers at the Apa River.—*Jorge Xifra.*

Tackle: Fly rodders should bring No. 10 to 12 fly rods, coupled with sturdy, smaller saltwater-type reels like Fin Nors, Pates and Seamasters. Lighter-weight rods can be used, but anglers spend longer periods of time fighting fish. All reels should carry at least 200-yards of 20-pound Dacron backing.

A good supply of fly lines, ranging from extra-fast-sinking to floating, should be included. Leaders should be tapered to 12- to 16-pound test tippets.

Flies tied on saltwater hooks on 3/0 to 5/0 are best. Mylar bodies and wings in a range of colors are preferred. Jorge notes that on the Apa, a fly seldom survives more than a fish or two, so take plenty of flies with you.

Shock leaders are required. Wire (27- to 45-pound single strand, coffee-colored) is preferred. Backup tackle must be brought, as there is virtually no fly gear available in Paraguay.

Miscellany: Long-sleeved shirts, long, lightweight trousers, wide-brimmed hat and polarized sunglasses are "musts." Sunscreen (No. 15) is also highly recommended.

Any tropical location has insects, including mosquitos, although Jorge claims they aren't a major problem. Bring 95 percent Deet repellents (Muskol, Ben's 100 and Repel). Headnets and Shoo-Bug jackets are recommended for those who are especially sensitive to insects.

You will need a valid U.S. passport. In addition, you should procure a visa to enter both Paraguay and Brazil.

Rate: Most of Jorge's trips are customized, so rates are variable. However, a five-day fishing trip, including domestic transportation, costs approximately $1,300 per person, based on double occupancy.

Keith Gardner, editor of *Fishing World*, explored a remote Atlantic salmon river in Greenland. His results were mediocre, but it's always fun to try new places.

AUSTRALIA

Fishermen are always looking for new angling frontiers, and a couple of years ago, *The PanAngler* thought that it had uncovered a very promising area: the Bathurst/Melville Islands in the Northern Territory of Australia.

Reports of fantastic fishing for the powerful barramundi (snooklike species), queenfish, trevally and other exotics interested fishermen. The surrounding waters of these islands, controlled by the aboriginals, had hardly been explored by sportsmen, and the potential was immense.

The first American parties were less than satisfied, however. The primary complaints centered on a very poor camp (canvas), lack of sanitary measures, unsatisfactory boating equipment and insufficient fishing information. Camp conditions improved in future safaris, but not to the satisfaction of most visiting anglers, despite fast fishing.

But this is changing rapidly. Ian Atkinson, an ardent sportsman and successful businessman, became involved in the operation and objectively scrutinized each facet of the camp. He immediately set out to make improvements.

Heading his priority list was the construction of a permanent lodge that would incorporate comfort and modern sanitation. Private rooms, air conditioning, indoor plumbing, large patio, lounge, bar and even a swimming pool are now offered. Atkinson has upgraded the boating equipment and is training guides and crews. The quality of meals and service has been vastly improved.

"It's not an overnight process, I assure you," Ian explains, "but we've made excellent progress and I'm sure that future parties to Bathurst will find comfort, better organization and tremendous improvements in all areas of our operation. We're not worried about the fishing because it is there, and we've learned a lot about it. Our barramundi fishing can be spectacular, and this applies to other varieties as well.

"We try to match the variety of fishing with the desires of the fishermen," Atkinson continues. "Light tackle. Fly fishing. Big fish. Whatever. We're convinced that we can offer the best barra fishing in Australia. And there's plenty of wildlife that will thrill the visiting angler."

Colin Roberts, a very knowledgeable angler, helped to promote the fishing at Bathurst. Here are his descriptions of some of the interesting species encountered at Bathurst:

"The barramundi is a magnificent fish. It has the power to smash lures to bits. Before casting to a barramundi, it is necessary to change to stronger trebles. Barra also love flies, especially the 'Lefty's Deceivers' pattern and fly fishermen have been quite successful.

"Barramundi, when hooked, jump repeatedly with their gills flaring in their attempt to throw the lure or fly. The saltwater barra fight much harder than freshwater barra. They also grow larger. I have taken out American skippers, and they just can't get over the jumping and fighting ability of the barra.

"Mangrove jack are very similar to the cubera snapper. They are toothy, strong fighters. They do not grow very big, however, averaging three to four pounds.

"Threadfin salmon are a great fish. They, too, jump, also fight hard and run great distances. They average from three to 12 pounds, but can grow up to 60 pounds.

"I don't think the trevally family needs much of an introduction. They are the 'dirtiest,' meanest fighters, pound for pound in the sea!

"The queenfish is one of my favorites. Found in inshore waters from rocky headlands to sandbars they generally weigh 14 to 24 pounds. If you think barra leap, wait until you see the queenie. They are absolutely masters at acrobatics. They go crazy over poppers.

"Tanguigue (narrow-barred mackerel) are speedsters. They average 30 to 35 pounds and we commonly catch them up to 65 pounds. Only two weeks ago, I nailed a pair of 44-pounders off one pinnacle only a quarter mile from shore.

"There are some huge barracuda just waiting to be caught. They are taken in all sizes from 20 to 80 pounds," claims Colin.

The 1987 rate per person (double occupancy basis) is approximately $1,400 U.S. (depending on the U.S. vs Australian dollar exchange). This includes the return airfare from Darwin, all meals, seven nights' accommodations, professional guides, fishing tackle and even the hotel room in Darwin.

And that's not all. Ian Atkinson's organization is offering other fishing tours in Australia. Of particular interest to the trout fisherman is the Monaro/Snowy Mountain region in New South Wales. There's a mixture of lake, river and stream fishing for brown trout. Under the guidance of master angler John Sautelle, novice fly fishermen and experts can learn the basics as well as new techniques. The cost is $100 (U.S.) per day, based on double occupancy, and it includes instruction and guiding service, all equipment, lodgings and meals.

Or if you would like a shot at sailfishing, you can fish out of Townsville in Northern Queensland. Five days of fishing, seven nights' accommodations and meals cost $1,500 per person (U.S.). The best time for sailfishing is from mid-May to August, and, in addition to light regulation tackle, fly fishing for sails has been successful. Write to PanAngling Travel Service, 180 N. Michigan Avenue, Chicago, IL 60601, for detailed information.

CHILE

In the "old days," Chile received a considerable amount of play in the outdoor press and was a very important fishing destination. Big-game angling writers Kip Farrington, "Uncle Lou" Marron and others publicized the giant broadbill swordfish that were available at Iquique. In the mid-fifties, the swank Rainbow Fly Fishing Club was the place to go if one wanted trout. Roderick L. Haig Brown devoted most of his *Fisherman's Winter* book to Chile's lake district. Adrian Dufflocq continued to promote his Cumilahue Club for trout, but little else was emanating from Chile during the past few years.

Until late 1986. Enter Puyuhuapi Lodge (pronounced "poo-you-WOP-ee"). It's a brand new fishing lodge that has been constructed on a Pacific Ocean inlet in Chile's Patagonia region. Its strategic location will take advantage of not only resident browns and rainbows but also the sea-run versions that can scale up to 15 pounds. Furthermore, there is talk of brook trout and even landlocked salmon.

Here are some of the fishing appetizers gleaned from the lodge's brochures: "Trout, four to five pounds, are frequently caught...Cisnes River offers superb stream fishing, both rainbows and browns...Trophy rainbows up to 15 pounds and browns up to 20 pounds have been taken from the Carrera Lake region...In Rio Cacique, 20 minutes by air from the lodge, rainbows average five to six pounds, but up to 14 pounds..." And on and on. Happily, Puyuhuapi Lodge is encouraging catch-and-release fishing.

One of the tremendous advantages offered by Puyuhuapi Lodge is that it has a Cessna 206 float plane as well as jet boats that can whisk its guests swiftly and efficiently to any number of rivers or lakes. Fishermen can be dropped off at one lake, drift down a river via rubber rafts, and be picked up at another lake and returned to the lodge that night for a deluxe dinner.

Mark Sosin, outdoor writer, landed this fine trout from Chilean waters. Chile, like Argentina, offers a "reverse" trout season.

Wild rainbow trout is one good reason anglers will travel to distant spots such as Chile. Trout are not native to South America.

This is a tremendous advantage because it opens up an area of up to 150 mile-radius from the lodge, although most of the better waters are within 30 miles.

This type of fishing (fly-outs) has been practiced with great success in Alaska and Canada but perhaps never in South America.

In the past, we have heard of the great potential of this area, but it was basically unavailable without the services of a float plane.

What is also remarkable is that the owners and operators have not only opened up a superb fishing area, they are also providing great comfort along the way.

The lodge is located in the picturesque Puyuhuapi region. Guest rooms are modern and include private bath. Maid and laundry service are provided. Meals are sumptuous with famous Chilean wines. Box lunches are offered or, if preferred, the guide will prepare a famous "asado" (barbecue).

The owners and operators (the Leasures and Curreys) have had a vast amount of outfitting experience that stretches from Alaska to the South Pacific to the U.S.

The lodge offers set dates of arrival and departure, but there is flexibility. Most trips are weekly, departing from Miami on a Saturday and returning the following Sunday. This allows about six days of fishing. The price per person is $3,495, which includes the round-trip airfare from Miami to Santiago (Chile) to Balmaceda on scheduled airlines. It also includes the hotel accommodations in Santiago, and Miami, daily fly-out fishing (weather permitting), guides, meals (including wines), laundry service and just about everything except gratuities, liquor and personal purchases. Lodge capacity is limited to eight anglers. The season is from November through early April.

YUGOSLAVIA

My trip to Yugoslavia in the late '60s produced mixed results. After the first two days of fishing, Bob Kukulski and I thought we discovered a salmonid utopia. We caught five different species of fish that were unrecognizable to us. One had the shape, colorations and markings of a brown trout, but its mouth resembled a bonefish. "Ahh, you caught a mekousna," our interpreter told us. We didn't argue.

We caught another species that was even more puzzling. It was a big fish, close to 18 pounds, the shape and color of a lake trout but equipped with the fiercest set of pin teeth we'd ever seen this side of a muskie. "Maybe a trout got together with a northern pike and did some 'off-track choo-chooing,'" quipped Bob. The fish was called a Zubatec. "Long live the Zubatec," we toasted that night. (There's a lot of toasting in Yugoslavia, we noted.)

We caught another small salmonid that resembled the mekousna—its name escaped me the minute after our interpreter said it. This species, we were told, lives in underground rivers most of the year and feeds entirely by sensing vibrations.

It loses most of its sight, and when, at times, it comes out into the "real world of daylight," it still feeds by honing in on vibrations. Myth or fact?

We caught several different species that the interpreter called char, but their resemblance to the char we've seen in our hemisphere was very slight.

At the Buna River, next to a picturesque little outdoor restaurant, we caught brown trout. The action was fast-paced during a sedge (caddis) hatch.

However, during the next couple of days, we did poorly. At one beautiful area, we saw some large swirls, but our streamers were perfectly safe. We even switched to spinning rods and Mepps lures, but to no avail.

We tried several other trout streams with results ranging from poor to fair. We were headquartered in picturesque Mostar, half of which is modern, and half of which maintains the strong Turkish influence stemming back to the 400-year period when Turks ruled Yugoslavia and much of southern Europe.

The Yugoslavs insisted that we do some sightseeing of nearby areas. We saw Tito's hunting lodge, a modern wine factory, an underground rock-and-roll club for youths, minarets—the works. Interesting, yes, but it certainly reduced our fishing time.

One day we were taken to an old castle-like building. In the center of one large room was a casket. We were told that the remains in the casket belonged to a Turk who had met with a particularly painful death. At night, the ghost of the Turk would come out of the casket, a la Dracula, and walk around, sometimes accompanied by harpsichord music, before finally settling back in the casket.

Of course Bob and I laughed when we heard this. But the man who related the story was serious.

"Perhaps you would like to spend the night in the room. You may see the ghost. He will not hurt you," the man with the Peter Lorre smile told us. We opted for our luxurious rooms at the Bristol Hotel.

We were often frustrated during this trip because it was necessary to obtain local fishing licenses for different rivers and these were issued by locals. To fish one river we had to wait several hours before the farmer who issued the licenses returned from the fields.

But that was two decades ago. Yugoslavia has streamlined its fishing trips considerably. This country has always played host to European anglers, but it never caught on with North Americans.

Today, an angler who is interested in fishing Yugoslavia should concentrate on the Gacka River region, near Zagreb, which is better organized for visiting anglers.

This delightful trout fishing river was brought to my attention by George Mendoza, the writer-poet, who has been fortu-

Yugoslavia's scenery is rugged, captivating: "He who drinks the waters of the Neretva River will remain thirsty until he returns."

nate to fish many of the world's prized trout waters. I contacted Vinko Bartolac of the Hotel Gacka for further details:

Best Time: There are two excellent periods. April 15 to June 15 and September 1 to 30. June 5 to 15 is probably the optimum time.

Trout Info: An average "good" brown is 20 inches. The best last year was 24 inches. The size limit is a hefty 17 1/2 inches for brown trout and 12 inches for rainbows. The river's population consists of 70 percent rainbows and 30 percent browns. There are a few grayling in the Gacka and the size limit is about 12 inches.

Best Hours: During most days the period from 10 A.M. to 1 P.M. and from 5 P.M. to 8 P.M. are most productive . Fishing is permitted from 6 A.M. to 8 P.M. (except in August and September when angling after 7:00 P.M. is disallowed). Fishing is always illegal after dark.

Ghillies: A ghillie or guide is not needed on these waters. However, if one is required, Milan Stefanac is highly recommended. His rate is $40.00 per day. He offers counsel, shows the angler the proper technique and indicates the best places.

Other Info: While spinning was allowed until 1981, it is no longer a legal fishing method; fly fishing only is permitted on the Gacka. Dry flies, wets, nymphs and terrestials in small sizes are most effective. Long, fine leaders and delicate presentations are essential. An experienced angler should do well on the Gacka.

Location: The Hotel Gacka, located at the Plitvice National Park, serves as headquarters to the international angling fraternity. Zagreb is the largest city near the Gacka.

Rates: In these days of inflation, the Gacka may very well represent the best bargain on earth for quality trout fishing. A weekly package, including board, meals, fishing permit and taxes, costs $450, based on double occupancy. Add $60 for a single supplement.

And finally, here is a description of the Gacka from France's celebrated fishing publication, *La Peche et Les Poissons:*

"There are excellent waters for trout in France and elsewhere. We know many of them, but we have never yet discovered one as rich in fish as is Gacka in Yugoslavia. International specialists that have visited it consider this river one of the best in the world for its exceptional richness in fine large trout. All essential conditions unite to make Gacka what it is: completely clean water, no pollution of any kind, and very rich aquatic vegetation with many larvae and nymphs, an important constant source of food enabling trout to grow rapidly, sometimes as much as one kilogram a year. Trout of half a kilo are 'babies,' those of one kilo are small...only those of a kilo and a half and over are considered to be real fish."

BRITISH COLUMBIA

Stu Apte had a magazine assignment to compare the Atlantic salmon and steelhead. We went to Iceland's Laxa i Kjos for the salmon portion of the article where we enjoyed spectacular results, and then we flew to British Columbia's Dean River. I assured him it was a "sure thing," because every client we had booked to this river had excellent fishing.

When we arrived at the old Rimarko outpost camp, the manager told us that the steelhead had not come in; they were stacked out in the ocean. A few fish had ascended the river, but not many.

The weather was very warm. Bright sun, blue skies. The water was low. We fished as hard as any two people could, and after the second day, we were grim. Simply, there weren't any fish in the river, or certainly not many. If it weren't for the cooperative humpback salmon, we would have been skunked.

It was depressing, and then one morning Stu said: "You know, we're spoiled. Here we are in one of the most beautiful settings in the world, and we haven't done much but complain about our bad luck. We don't know how fortunate we are to just be here." And he was right.

We didn't even hook a steelhead on the Dean, although we later fished at Rimarko's main lodge for a day and landed quite a few rainbows on flies. So Stu had to confine his article to Atlantic salmon fishing.

After we left, a heavy downpour cooled the weather and raised the water level. Later we found out that a friend of Stu's fished the Dean and enjoyed enormous success.

For many years, the Dean River was considered one of the premier steelhead rivers of B.C. Its steelhead were not as large as those taken from the Kispiox, but anglers could fish the Dean during the summer months because of its early run, whereas most other B.C. waters are fished in the fall.

Unfortunately, with road construction, lumbering and increased traffic, the quality of fishing on the Dean has diminished. It still produces good fishing, but not of the same quality that made this stream famous in the '60s and early '70s.

RIVER WEST TOURS: However, other rivers and outfitters shine somewhat brightly on the steelheader's horizon. Collin Schadrech's River West Tours is one good example. While he

Dr. Rod Neubert's tremendous steelhead from the Dean River. "I don't know what it weighed...it was released...but over 25 pounds!"

fishes several waters in the area, he has probably put his beloved Bulkley River on the steelheader's map.

Collin has received some good press in the outdoor magazines because—to quote one of his clients—"He put the fun back into steelhead fishing."

This angler was referring to Collin's persistency in using dry fly techniques for steelhead. In many rivers, fast-sinking lines, long casts and large weighted flies are paramount to steelhead success.

"We found that sometimes the steelhead would hit a wet fly right on the surface before it had a chance to sink. Why not fish for steelhead on top?" Collin wondered. And he did just that.

"In 1978 the great fly experiment began, and by the end of the season, the prototype of the 'Bulkley Mouse' was born. The following two seasons we fished the Bulkley River almost exclusively on top with unprecedented results. By 1980, we found we could bring steelhead to the surface from any depth of water throughout the entire fall," Collin writes. "In our three-month season last fall (1985), our guests hooked (not landed) 1,431 steelhead on dry flies."

While the Mouse and dry fly fishing has been tried elsewhere, Collin says that only sporadic success has been achieved, except on the Bulkley.

"You have to be a good caster," Collin warns. "If you can cast 40 to 70 feet of line in moderate winds without dropping your back cast, you are in the game. I suggest nine- to 10-foot fly rods for No. 6 to 8 lines. Your reels should hold 150 yards of 20-pound Dacron."

To host steelhead addicts, Collin has two main lodges as well as river outpost camps. His guests can conveniently cover 76 miles of prime Bulkley water.

The season starts in mid-August and runs through October. The 1986 rate for six days of fishing and seven nights of accommodations is $1,600. Guests fly to Smithers, B.C., via Vancouver. River West Tours meets clients at the airport and transfers them to camp by car (25 minutes).

So it's all quite convenient.

NORTH PACIFIC SPRINGS: One day, Serge Mazerand decided to chuck his lucrative cologne business and build

North Pacific Springs (NPS)—a luxurious floating lodge. It's located approximately 160 miles north of Vancouver, British Columbia. Why a floating lodge? Versatility. It can be moved to where the action is best, so long boat rides aren't needed.

"It's taken us a long time to put this dream lodge together," says Serge Mazerand, "the comfort and convenience are only part of its attraction. Our best selling tool is our fishing!" Serge hired Peter Machek, easily one of B. C.'s most talented guides who is particularly knowledgeable on steelhead. Guests can fish for king salmon, silvers, pinks, chums, trout and steelhead. The season is from mid-April to mid-October. Trout fishing is on secluded lakes, whereas steelhead fishing is available via short fly-outs to a number of B. C. rivers.

"The rivers we fish from our floating lodge are nearly always in good condition, because they are short and do not silt up much," explains Serge. "All options are available to our guests, from steelhead to trout to salmon fishing."

Rates: The Mini-Week package should be popular—it starts on a Monday and terminates on a Friday. The $1,510 (U.S. funds) tab includes accommodations, meals, tackle, guiding service and the float plane flight between Vancouver and the lodge. The full week package costs $2,150.

AND FINALLY... There are many other fishing places for the fly rodder. Tasmania is certainly a superb place for big brown trout; Venezuela will become one of the most popular fishing places in the next few years for billfish, tarpon, snook and jungle fishing for peacock bass; Bolivia has some fine dorado fishing that hasn't been properly nurtured; Brazil also will make a pitch for the sportfishing business; and, as this is being written, through the efforts of Trout Unlimited, it appears that anglers may soon be heading to Russia to investigate its sportfishing potential.

There's a world of fly fishing opportunities. They are there for us to cherish but also *to protect* so that future generations of anglers may also enjoy the challenges, the thrills, the excitement of taking fish on a fly rod. Just like we do.

Enjoy!

© Chas B Mitchell 1980

Index

© Chas. B. Mitchell · 1980